Asia's New Crisis:

Renewal Through Total Ethical Management

Asia's New Crisis:

Renewal Through Total Ethical Management

John Wiley & Sons (Asia) Pte Ltd

Other Wiley Editorial Offices

John Wiley & Sons, Inc., 605 Third Avenue, New York, NY 10158-0012, USA
John Wiley & Sons Ltd, Baffins Lane, Chichester, West Sussex PO19 1UD, England
John Wiley & Sons (Canada) Ltd, 22 Worcester Road, Rexdale, Ontario M9W 1L1,
Canada
John Wiley & Sons Australia Ltd, 33 Park Road (PO Box 1226), Milton, Queensland
4046, Australia
Wiley-VCH, Pappelallee 3, 69469 Weinheim, Germany

Library of Congress Cataloging-in-Publication Data:

ML ISBN 0-470-82129-9

Typeset in 10.5/13 point, Times by Linographic Services Pte Ltd
Printed in Singapore by Saik Wah Press Ltd
10 9 8 7 6 5 4 3 2 1

CONTENTS

Foreword *by Klaus Schwab*   ix

Prefaces by
* Mahathir bin Mohamad   xi
* Corazon Aquino

Contributors   xiv

PART 1: ASIA'S ETHICAL CRISIS   1
1. Why Ethics? *Frank-Jürgen Richter & Pamela C.M. Mar*   3
2. The Big Picture *Lou Marinoff*   16

PART 2: FOUNDATIONS   41
3. Confucianism *Wang Gungwu*   51
4. Buddhism *Pipat Yodprudtikan & Phra Saneh Dhammavaro*   63
5. Hinduism *Sundeep Waslekar*   83
6. Islam *Farish A. Noor*   96

PART 3: APPLICATIONS   119
7. Regional Relations *Rini Soewandi*   127
8. Labor *Lim Boon Heng*   145
9. Leadership *Jaime Augusto Zobel de Ayala II*   160
10. Management *Karuna Shinsho*   174
11. Media *Hu Shuli*   181
12. Public Relations *Shelly Lazarus & Matthew Anderson*   190

PART 4: TRANSFORMATIONS   201
13. Social Development *James Wolfensohn*   209
14. Mutual Trust *Motohisa Furukawa*   221
15. Societal Governance *Christine Loh*   233
16. Global Citizenship *Uwe R Doerken & Alyson Warhurst*   248
17. Public Accountability *Samuel A. DiPiazza Jr.*   270
18. Corporate Governance *Chang Sun*   292
19. Industrial Renewal *Duk Hoon Lee*   306

PART 5: TOTAL ETHICAL MANAGEMENT   323
20. The Global View *Rolf Eckrodt*   325
21. A Model for Asia *Frank-Jürgen Richter & Pamela C.M. Mar*   334

Index   339

FOREWORD

Klaus Schwab
Executive Chairman & Founder, World Economic Forum

I cannot recall a time when the issue of trust was so much at the forefront of global discussion as now — trust in business, trust in private and public institutions, and trust in politics and international relations. But trust, particularly in the business sphere, does not operate in a vacuum. It must be created, nurtured and sustained; it must be based on solid ethical foundations. Without these foundations, public confidence and public trust will continue to crumble. The challenge, then, is to build a transparent code of ethics that underpins business and gives rise to public confidence in the way that business is conducted.

At a time when our ability to achieve social, technological and global progress is unequalled in history, we must overcome the hurdle of uncertainty and mistrust if we are to harness the positive benefits of globalization. We must work to build a system of commonly held values on which business can operate. Without it the opportunity to help those in most need, to improve the state of the world, will be compromised, and this need is as pressing in Asia as it is for the rest of the world. Indeed, in many ways the problems are more acute in Asia, a continent of huge contrasts:

- Incredibly rich, developed countries, next to those which are poor and needy.
- Well-governed financial markets, known for their strict corporate governance, amidst volatile capital markets.
- Governments which lead Transparency International indexes of honesty, alongside those which fall far short of common standards.

- Societies known for their technological advancement and ability to innovate, against some of the most widespread abuses of intellectual-property rights.
- Companies known for their high ethical standards, and those which are corrupt, polluting, and abusing the rights of their populations.

In the late 1990s, corruption, cronyism and poor governance were blamed — rightly or wrongly — for the collapse that led to the Asian financial crisis. The legacy of that crisis is still with us and many Asian economies are still dogged by the question of ethics — or, rather, the lack of them. This collapse in trust and the subsequent need to rebuild a system of ethics to underpin the recovering economy was the issue at the origin of this book. The answers, after all, will come from within Asia and from Asia's interaction with the global community. *Asia's New Crisis: Renewal Through Total Ethical Management* is not a simple blueprint for achieving better corporate governance but it is at the center of a debate from which a new system of ethics can emerge — the ethical foundations required to rebuild and nurture the trust necessary for all our futures.

This book is the result of collaboration between key leaders from business, government and civil society. We hope that it will help outline the way forward, not just for Asia but for the rest of the world, too. Some of the World Economic Forum's members and friends took part in this project and, among those, I would like to thank two in particular. Malaysian Prime Minister Mahathir bin Mohamad and former President of the Philippines, Corazon Aquino, agreed early on to contribute to the book. Both individuals should be commended for their willingness to be heard — in an uncertain environment — on an issue that is by nature controversial. I thank them for their confidence.

PREFACE

Dr Mahathir bin Mohamad
Prime Minister of Malaysia

We live in a world today where there is little or no trust. World governance is not good and ethical standards are low. In fact we have made a mess of the world. Two millennia of experience and mountains of knowledge have not made us more capable than the Stone-Age people at managing our affairs.

Now, we add fear. We live in fear, every one of us. We fear the terrorists and their alleged supporters, in the same way that the terrorists fear us. We fear flying, we fear traveling to certain countries, we fear night-clubs, we fear letters, parcels and cargo containers, we fear white powder, shoes, Muslims, pen-knives, and even metal cutlery. They — the other side — fear sanctions, starvation, lack of opportunities, shortage of medicines. They fear military invasion and being bombed, captured and detained.

The world has become small, some say like a village. But we have not made much progress in the management of our world — our village — despite its diminished size. Just as in the Stone Age, when the man with the biggest club ruled, in our modern, sophisticated global village, power rules. The applied ethical standard of our globalized world is one in which a country's killing power dominates.

It was not supposed to be like this. When the Cold War ended, we thought that we would see peace and prosperity. After all, those who believed in peace and universal justice won; "the Evil Empire" had been overthrown. But the loss of the Evil Empire created a hole in the balance of justice, fair play and global powers. When there was communism, capitalists curbed their greed and avarice. They showed a friendly face.

Now there is no other side and this friendly face of capitalism is no longer needed. Now capitalists can do what they like without restraint, and what they like is simple self-enrichment. They want to make more money for themselves.

In a free world there must be competition. Out of this competition, the strongest and most efficient will win. If you are small, weak and inefficient, it is best that you go. In athletics, this may work, as there are different classes of competitors. However, in competition between countries and corporations, there are no categorizations or classifications, and no handicaps are given. Thus, the biggest and the most efficient are allowed to dominate and take all. This new ethics of competition inspires financial and corporate mergers, and virtually ensures that tiny banks and businesses in poor countries do not stand a chance. The small and the poor are swept aside, and big is beautiful.

Unfortunately, there are no guarantees that the big will not cheat, fall or go bankrupt. Indeed, we should take note of Enron, Global Crossing, Arthur Andersen, and United Airlines, to name a recent few. Are these exceptions or the rule?

Today, the disparity between the rich countries and the poor countries is greater than ever. The richest have a per-capita annual income of more than of US$30,000, the poorest US$300. Of the world's six billion people, one billion are malnourished, under-educated and without a roof over their heads. Many scrounge for food, clothing and materials for their shelter. Despite the world's political transition into the post-Cold War era, their fate has not improved. The misfortunes of the weak are their problems.

The exploitation by the greedy, the double standards of developed nations, hypocrisy over human rights, disregard for human suffering, the oppression of the weak by the strong — all these have been aggravated by the ending of the Cold War and the victory of the righteous and rich. Some say that September 11th was an attempt by the poor and disenfranchised to hit back in the only way they can.

Now, groping for the enemy, the strong hit out in every direction. No part of the world is excepted, no one is free. We now live in fear. Even the rich are not as prosperous any more, while the poor are actually poorer. We can safely conclude that we have done a poor job of managing our Global Village. We have not built trust, nor created good global governance.

So how do we create trust and good governance in the new era?

This is fundamentally a question of our ethics. We must build trust through proper ethics and compromise. We must be good people who live up to high ethical standards. Good governance will come if we simply curb the greedy and realize that markets cannot be self-regulating. Governments are not yet anachronistic. They have a crucial role to play in good governance, ensuring ethical behavior and promoting compromise.

The world is big enough and rich enough for everyone. A win-win solution is possible. I sincerely hope that this work, and the work of Asians and the World Economic Forum, can be small steps towards overcoming poverty — in all its forms — in the world today. Together we must build a better world through better ethics, more trust and real governance.

This Preface is based on remarks made at the Annual Meeting of the World Economic Forum, Davos, Switzerland, 28 January, 2003.

PREFACE

Corazon Aquino
Former President of the Philippines

Understanding the intricacies of ethical practices in Asia has never been easy. Whereas trust is implicit in the Asian handshake that still seals significant business deals today, the unique "Asian way" has also given rise to much crony capitalism and opacity. Indeed, ever since the East Asian financial crisis in 1997, the ethics and standards of conduct in the region have been the subject of criticism and debate. While some of the criticism has certainly been deserved, much of it just points to a lack of fundamental understanding of how ethical standards for business are set in the region and how these developed differently from the West, given the diversity of cultural, social and historical circumstances each country has faced.

It is a simple fact of life that nothing of enduring value can be built or stand for long on a base of misconduct, whether in politics or business. This is clearly shown in the common fate of large corporations embroiled in recent governance scandals, as well as in the eventual downfall of reputedly invincible Asian dictatorships. It is a belief instilled by faith and borne out by experience that what takes longer to build on a foundation of ethical conduct lasts. Even political risk to business is best addressed that way. The enemies of free enterprise do distinguish between free traders and freebooters. There is a difference between mistake and malice that is recognized even in political upheavals. You simply cannot go wrong doing right.

Global trends show that conceptions of right and wrong are basically universal. Manners and customs may differ, but bedrock ethical rules are the same. Stealing is wrong anywhere. So is fraud and leaving the public holding the bag, with the government paying for one's mistakes. Crime cannot be raised as a standard of conduct, even in a country that is not your own. Whatever the promise of easy success, it will catch up with you. The golden rule first articulated in Asia still holds sway around the world, and it is not "He who has the gold rules" but rather "Treat others as you would be treated." At the very least, commonly shared expectations of business performance demand a globally accepted standard of conduct by which to judge success and failure.

This book is an attempt to point out the ethical component of doing business in Asia and fills the need to give it a common expression. While focused on the region, it can easily be applicable anywhere in today's globalized landscape. Business is a powerful force for change in the world and a great deal needs to be changed in the world, not least mass poverty. For that reason business should know how to conduct itself so as to foster the conditions for long-term success: the harmony that comes from fair dealing, the stability a decent standard of living spreads, and the dignity that is every person's birthright and whose denial is the first sign of trouble. At the end of the day, the basic concept of decency should rule one's actions, be it in governing a country or in running a business.

The purpose of this book is not to suggest that the standards of ethics in Asia are superior to those of the West. Nor does it attempt to render judgment, play one off against the other or point at each other's shortcomings in mutual recrimination. Rather, the aim here is merely to present a balanced and comprehensive perspective on the foundations and practice of ethics, corporate governance and social responsibility in Asia today and, in so doing, promote a greater understanding of the corporate values prevalent across the region.

CONTRIBUTORS

Lou Marinoff earned his Doctorate in Philosophy of Science at University College London. After holding research fellowships at University College and the Hebrew University of Jerusalem, he became a Lecturer in Philosophy at the University of British Columbia, and was also Moderator of the Canadian Business and Professional Ethics Network at UBC's Center for Applied Ethics. He is currently an Associate Professor of Philosophy at The City College of New York, and founding President of the American Philosophical Practitioners Association. He is the author of an international bestseller, *Plato Not Prozac*, HarperCollins, NY, 1999, aimed at a popular audience and published in twenty-one languages. His textbook, *Philosophical Practice*, Academic Press, NY, 2001, provides a more technical "insider's view" of the profession. His latest popular book, *The Big Questions*, is published in English by Bloomsbury, New York and London, 2003, and in many other languages.

Wang Gungwu is Director of the East Asian Institute at the National University of Singapore and Distinguished Senior Fellow at the Institute of Southeast Asian Studies, Singapore, and emeritus professor of The Australian National University. He was born in Surabaya, Indonesia, and brought up in Ipoh, Malaysia. His research on and academic contribution to the history of the Chinese Diaspora is seminal works in the field. His Publications include *The Chineseness of China*, 1991 and *The Chinese Way: China's Position in International Relations*, 1995.

Pipat Yodprudtikan is chief executive officer of ThaiName.com Ltd., Thailand. He has more than 15 years of experiences in software industry and information technology. He worked as an experienced engineer in information technology management area for several domestic and international enterprises. Before founding ThaiName.com, he was a senior technology consultant at Accenture. Pipat holds a bachelor's degree in electrical engineering from Kasetsart University and a master's science degree in management information system from Chalalongkorn University. He was an author of *Starting business on Internet* and has published hundred of articles related to Internet and eCommerce. He regularly participates in social and community development project by utilising his experiences in IT. He also spent his spare time in Buddhism Studies.

Phra Saneh Dhammavaro is director of Academic Affairs office at Mahachulalongkornrajavidyalaya University, Chiang Mai Campus. He is lecturer in Faculty of Buddhism at Mahachulalongkornrajavidyalaya University, Chiang Mai Campus. Phra Saneh has B.A. in Religion from Mahachulalongkornrajavidyalaya University, Chiang Mai Campus; M.A. in Philosophy from University of Mysore, India; M.Phil. in Philosophy from Bangalore University, India; and Ph.D. in Pali & Buddhism from Dr.Babasaheb Ambedkar Maradavada University, Aurangabad, India.

Sundeep Waslekar is the founder of International Centre for Peace Initiatives and president of Strategic Foresight Group, Mumbai. He is one of the pioneers of track two diplomacy as well as scenario planning practice in South Asia. He has authored three books on governance and several research reports on future strategic environment. His latest publications include *Shifting Sands: Instability in Undefined Asia* and *Cost of Conflict between India-Pakistan: Water Wars*.

Dr Farish A Noor is a Malaysian political scientist and human rights activist currently based at the Centre for Modern Orient Studies (ZMO), Berlin. He has taught at the Centre for Inter-Civilisational Dialogue and the Department of Science and Philosophy at the University of Malaya (UM) and the Institute for Islamic Studies Freie Universitat of Berlin. He is presently an affiliated fellow with the Institute for Malaysian and International Studies (IKMAS), National University of Malaysia (UKM) and associate fellow with the Bureau of Nation-Building and National Security at the Institute for Strategic and International Studies (ISIS), Malaysia. He has just completed his book on the historical development of the Pan-Malaysian Islamic Party (PAS) and is currently studying the socio-cultural and political impact of transnational religious movements in Malaysia. His recent publications include, *The Other Malaysia: Writings on Malaysia's Subaltern Histories*, Silverfish, Kuala Lumpur, 2003, and *New Voices of Islam*, ISIM, Leiden, 2002.

Rini Soewandi is Indonesia's Minister of Trade and Industry. She is a graduate of Wellesley College Faculty of Economics. A former private sector executive she was formerly with the US Finance Department, Citibank, and as President with Astra International, an Indonesian automotive manufacturer. In 1998, she joined the Indonesian Banking Restructuring Agency (IBRA) as Deputy Chairman.

Lim Boon Heng is Secretary General of the National Trades Union Congress, Singapore and Minister, Prime Minister's Office, Government of Singapore. He is a longtime member of Parliament of Singapore, and formerly served as Deputy Speaker, Chairman of National Productivity Board and National Productivity Council, and Senior Minister of State for Trade and Industry. He holds an Honors degree in Naval Architecture.

Jaime Augusto Zobel de Ayala II is President and CEO of Ayala Corporation, the oldest business house and the largest and most widely diversified conglomerate in the Philippines. As President and CEO, Zobel is responsible for the overall management of Ayala Corporation and its subsidiaries and affiliates in real estate and hotels, financial services, insurance, telecommunications, food, electronics and information technology, automotive and infrastructure. He is also the President of the Ayala group's social development arm, Ayala Foundation, Inc., Zobel was born in Manila and educated in Harvard University Where he earned his Bachelor of Arts, cum laude, in Economics and Master in Business Administration degrees. Zobel assumed the presidency of Ayala Corporation on January 1, 1995.

Joichi Ito is the founder and CEO of Neoteny (www.neoteny.com), venture capital firm focused on personal communications and enabling technologies. He has created numerous Internet companies including PSINet Japan, Digital Garage and Infoseek Japan. In 1997 *Time* Magazine ranked him as a member of the CyberElite. In the year 2000, he was ranked among the "50 Stars of Asia" by *BusinessWeek* and commended by the Japanese Ministry of Posts and Telecommunications for supporting the advancement of IT.

Oki Matsumoto is President and CEO of Monex, Inc., Tokyo. He graduated from the Faculty of Law of Tokyo University in 1987 and entered the Fixed Income Section of Salomon Brothers Asia Limited. He left in 1990 to join the Fixed Income Division of Goldman Sachs (Japan) Ltd. In 1994, Matsumoto became a general partner, the youngest in the company's history. In April 1999, he co-established the online securities company, Monex, Inc. with Sony and serves as President and CEO. The company went public in August 2000.

Karuna Shinsho is a freelance journalist based in Tokyo. She was CNN's acting Tokyo bureau chief and worked for *CNN International* in Hong Kong. Prior to that, she was as *NHK Television* in Japan, where she anchored the programs "Japan Weekly", "Today's Japan Weekly" and "Japanscope".

Hu Shuli is one of China's leading journalists, and has trailblazed China's financial and business news sector through *Caijing* magazine as Managing Editor since 2000. She has formerly worked as a journalist at the *Worker's Daily* and *China Business Times* in China. She was trained in Journalism at the People's University of China and has undertaken numerous honorary fellowships, including ones at the World Press Institute and Stanford University. She has won numerous accolades for her work in China's media field, and most recently was awarded the World Press Review's 2003 Editor of the Year award, especially for the reporting on SARS.

Shelly Lazarus is Chairman and Chief Executive Officer of Ogilvy & Mather Worldwide. Lazarus has spent the past 30 years at Ogilvy working with blue-chip clients such as American Express, Ford, IBM and Unilever. Ogilvy CEO since 1996, Lazarus also serves on the boards of a number of business, philanthropic and academic boards including General Electric, New York Presbyterian Hospital, and The September 11th Fund. She is a former Chairman and current Special Representative to the Smith College Board of Trustees, and has also served as Chairman of the Board of Directors of The American Association of Advertising Agencies (AAAA). She has been frequently honored by her peers, most recently with Columbia Business School's Distinguished Leader in Business Award.

Matthew Anderson is Chief Executive, Asia Pacific & EAME of Ogilvy Public Relations Worldwide. He has spent the past 13 years at Ogilvy in the US, Europe and Asia Pacific. In Asia, Anderson counsels a number of senior executives on branding and corporate social responsibility matters. He works particularly closely with STAR Group/News Corp., Nokia, UPS and Warburg Pincus. Under Anderson's leadership, PR Week has twice named Ogilvy PR "Asia Pacific Network of the Year."

James Wolfensohn is the President of the World Bank. He served as an officer in the Royal Australian Air Force and was a member of the 1956 Australian Olympic Fencing Team. He became president of the World Bank Group on June 1, 1995 and is its ninth president since 1946. Prior to joining the Bank, Wolfensohn was an international investment banker with a parallel involvement in development projects and the global environment. He has held a series of senior positions in finance. He was Executive Partner of Salomon Brothers in New York and head of its investment banking department. He was Executive Deputy Chairman and Managing Director of Schroders Ltd. in London, President of J. Henry Schroders Banking Corporation, in New York, and Managing Director, Darling & Co. of Australia.

Motohisa Furukawa was first elected to the House of Representatives in October 1996. At 30 years of age, he was the youngest person to have ever been elected to the House of Representatives. Furukawa is perhaps best known as one of a new breed of young politicians who vows to change the landscape of Japanese politics by breaking down traditional party factions and forging a more policy-oriented approach to politics. Furukawa received a B.A. in law from the University of Tokyo and participated in the Ministry of Finance Exchange Program at the School of International and Public Affairs at Columbia University. He is also a Japanese Delegate for the United States-Japan Leadership Program, a program of the United States-Japan Foundation.

Christine Loh is the CEO of the Hong Kong-based non-profit public-policy think-tank, Civic Exchange. She is a lawyer by training but spent 15 years of professional life in business, once heading the Asian regional office of the commodities trading arm of Salomon Inc in the 1980s and early 1990s. She then spent nine years in politics, serving in the Hong Kong Legislative Council. She now speaks and writes frequently on issues related to politics, political economy, corporate social responsibility and sustainable development.

Uwe R. Doerken is Chief Executive Officer of DHL, the worldwide express and logistics provider. Uwe Doerken started his career in banking in 1979. After completing an MBA at St. Gallen's University in Switzerland he joined McKinsey in Amsterdam in 1986. In 1991 he joined Deutsche Post to build the International Business Division and was appointed as a Management Board Member in 1999. In 2001 he was appointed Chairman and Chief Executive of DHL Worldwide Express. In 2003, subsequent to the merger of DHL, Danzas and Deutsche Post Euro Express, Uwe Doerken became joint Chief Executive Officer with specific responsibilities for DHL's Express business outside Europe and Global responsibility for DHL's Logisitics and Global Customer Solutions.

Alyson Warhurst is Professor of Strategy and International Development at Warwick Business School (UK) where she directs the Corporate Citizenship Unit and the Mining and Energy Research Network, which she established in 1991. Professor Warhurst has been contributing to the area of Corporate Citizenship for 25 years and was one of the youngest women in the UK to be appointed to a Chair in a leading University in 1996. Professor Warhurst has an established academic reputation in research at the public policy/corporate strategy interface, and has lectured and published several books and numerous articles.

Samuel A. DiPiazza Jr has been CEO of PricewaterhouseCoopers since 2001. He most recently served as Senior Partner and Chairman of the U.S. firm with executive responsibility for U.S. operations, and as a member of the Global Leadership Team. DiPiazza received a dual degree in Accounting/Economics from the University of Alabama and an MS in Tax Accounting from the University of Houston. DiPiazza is currently serving a three-year term as a Financial Accounting Foundation Trustee and is also a member of the Frankfurt-based Mergers & Acquisitions Group.

Chang Sun is Managing Director of Warburg Pincus, Hong Kong. He was an executive director in the investment banking division of Goldman Sachs (Asia) LLC before joining Warburg Pincus in 1995. He received a B.A. from the Beijing Foreign Languages University, an M.A. from the Joseph Lauder Institute of International Management at the University of Pennsylvania and an M.B.A. from The Wharton School of Business at the University of Pennsylvania. He is a director of Asia Info, Eagle Brand, Hong Leong Asia and MediaNation.

Duk Hoon Lee is the Chairman & CEO of Woori Bank, Korea. He started his career as a researcher at Korea Development Institute, a state-run think tank, from 1981. In 1989, he was appointed the Advisory Council to the Minister of Finance & Economy for the Development of Financial Industry, Banking Sector. In 1997, he became a member of the Council for the Development of Financial Industry and in 1998, he was promoted to Team Head at the Korea Development Institute and appointed the vice president of the CBK-Hanil Bank merger committee. He was appointed the president of the Daehan Investment Trust Company in 2000. He joined Woori Bank in 2001 as the Chairman & CEO. He received a B.A. in Mathematics from Sogang University, Korea, an M.A. in Economics from Wayne State University, Michigan and a Ph.D. in Economics from Purdue University, Indiana.

Rolf Eckrodt is President & Chief Executive Officer of Mitsubishi Motors Corporation. Throughout his 37 years in the automotive business, Rolf Eckrodt has built an impressive reputation as a corporate leader in Germany as well as overseas. Before joining Mitsubishi Motors Corporation as Executive Vice President and COO for Car Operations in January 2001 and later as Chief Executive Officer, Eckrodt was in charge of two major turnaround successes. The first was President of Mercedes-Benz do Brasil, a major producer of trucks and buses, which he turned around from massive losses to profits between 1992 and 1996. Then in 1998, after becoming President and Chief Executive Officer of Adtranz – the Railsystem Unit of DaimlerChrysler Group, he managed that firm's major restructuring and return to profitability.

PART

1

Asia's Ethical Crisis

1

WHY ETHICS?

Frank-Jürgen Richter & Pamela C.M. Mar

 The Asian financial crisis and the attendant dethroning of "Asian values" set Asian business ethically adrift. Indeed, the crisis created an ethical void, marked by the inability of Asia's elites to inspire and propose a new ethical grounding for the region. The void has become more pronounced as some of the elites which provided leadership — or at least prosperity — in the past have been discredited, through scandal, shame or simply lack of vision. This is not just an Asian phenomenon, but rather a global malaise. Never before in public life has trust in leaders and elites been so much questioned as it has been at the beginning of the 21st century.[1] In Asia, this is felt intensely in some quarters, and refers to leaders from politics, business and other sectors of society.

Asian philosophy could have in no way predicted this state of affairs. If anything, Asia's philosophical and religious underpinnings comprise a rich and fruitful grounding for social harmony, community prosperity and the development of commerce as a positive driver of national development. This book thus asserts that, in order for Asia to regain its ethical groundings, we must examine the past, select what is appropriate for the present and, with this as a base, transform our beliefs for future and current challenges. While ethics may be derived from seemingly abstract fields of religion and philosophy, it sprouts and finds applications across society. This is even more the case in our advanced industrial age, with deeply

---

[1] The 2003 Annual Meeting of the World Economic Forum, for instance, focused on the issue of "Building Trust". See www.weforum.org

3

drawn connections between nations, societies, social classes and social sectors. We are ALL economic actors. Thus, imagining the field of business ethics necessarily touches the seemingly disparate fields of economy, social development, public trust and the media, and regional relations.

This book proposes TOTAL ETHICAL MANAGEMENT (TEM) as a way for Asians across society — in business, politics, the media and civil society — to envision, manage and transform their organizations for positive, sustainable and respectable change. While it is ambitious to enjoin those in positions of power to change their ways without the appearance of urgency and, moreover, without a guaranteed return, we assert that Asia's ethical void is its most drastic, and that without a new ethical grounding, the consequences of continuing the ethical drift will be grave. The consequences will be quantifiable in economy and business, but will also appear in unpredictable forms — from migration and social or labor unrest to social cynicism, among many others. Ethics touches all aspects of society; and as long as corrupt or unethical business practice remains an open sore, it will inhibit long-term sustainable development and economic prosperity.

Are we claiming that a resurgence of ethics in society is the answer to Asia's economic slump and political upheavals? Of course, peace and recovery will take much more than a mere acknowledgement of ethics; but certainly ethics is a fundamental first step.

The void

Since the Asian financial crisis, the region has experienced what can be regarded as a high level of unease, uncertainty and, in many cases, scandal and a stripping away of what were once regarded as "sacred" pillars (or people) of society. Though there have been no outright wars, public tension is at an all-time high. No country, no class or social actor, no power center, has been spared. A complete listing would fill many more volumes, but a few highlights will suffice to show a common thread that leads back to an ethical void.

Japan's malaise is often referred to as an economic problem — or a political one that reverberates across the economy through stasis — but, in reality, its roots are much deeper. Motohisa Furukawa, a Member of the Japanese Parliament, calls it a breakdown in society's "chain of trust." But it can also be seen as a breakdown of ethics in a system in which success was rooted deeply in ethics. We thus see a crumbling of trust between employers and employees — in which the employee is no longer guaranteed lifetime employment, but also in which work is no longer the central purpose in people's lives. Likewise, trust between companies and society has also broken down, not only due to corporate collapses and bankruptcies, but also to scandals in which very public companies have been exposed as abusers or abrogaters of ethics in operation.[2] Lastly, there is frequent talk of people losing faith in the government. Having believed once too many times that a new government or new minister would be the key to implementing change to a system that is widely regarded as discredited and insufficient for the huge tasks before it, the people are now tired. The degree to which government has been unable, repeatedly, to build a new basis for Japan's 21st century has created more than a few disbelievers. It has also spawned grassroots movements for change,[3] which, irrespective of their roots, almost always touch on the need to recapture a strong ethical base in society.

In South Korea, labor issues have always been a hot issue. In recent years, however, the disputes have spread to other areas of society and have, in consequence, become much more prominent. The pace of corporate and political scandals since the Asian crisis has remained brisk, touching even those who had been revered or regarded as kingmakers.[4] The South Korean public has also been disillusioned with governments as harbingers of change many times since the Asian crisis. It is a familiar story (and not only in South Korea): an idolized ruler comes to power riding the wings of change, promising to overturn the corrupt ways of the past and install new ethical standards within government and beyond. In most cases — and whether he comes from business, politics or the third sector — the ruler is brought down or ends his term under a cloud of ethical questions. The recent election of Roh Moo-hyun has come about on a wave of support from young people tired of the ways of the past. This time, there is real hope that President Roh will transform the Presidency, enabling it to rise above the shackles of the past. He has a labor background himself and knows about the seduction of power.

---

[2] For example, the widespread food poisoning from Snow Brand Milk Products in 2000 and the same group's false labeling of meat products, uncovered in 2002; the falsification of nuclear safety documents in power plants operated by the Tokyo Electric Power Company.

[3] For example, "Blueprint for Japan", a project of the World Economic Forum's New Asian Leaders, see www.weforum.org/pdf/NAL-executive-summary.pdf. See http://joi.ito.com/archives/2002/08/29/blueprint_for_japan_2020.html,

[4] For example, the conviction of the son of Kim Daejung in 2001; the conviction of Anthony Chey of SK Corporation for bribery and embezzlement; the August 2003 suicide of Chung Mong-Hun of Hyundai Asan Group, who had been under pressure arising from the "cash for summit" scandal involving North Korea.

Although it is clear that he needs great powers of persuasion, he has the ability to convert his citizens' cynicism into an ethically-grounded belief and willingness to personally sacrifice for the good of the country.

Once a country deeply rooted in ideology, with clear social lines, roles and power structures, China's development has brought greater prosperity and social openness but has broken down the pillars which previously defined the nation. "Opening up" has meant that Communist (and even Marxist) ideology has been swept away and replaced with the notion that "to get rich is glorious," in which often the best examples of capitalism at work are closest to the Party and the powerful. The family structures, once built solidly on Confucian principles of respect for elders, honesty and righteousness, find their contemporary incarnations in the growth of retirement homes for neglected old people, the disintegration of village life through poverty and migration, and the almost routine disavowal of honesty and commitment in the quest for fortune. Education, which used to provide the ethical basis for action, is today merely a required credential and a route to wealth — and thus it is no surprise that China is awash in purveyors of fake degrees and diplomas. The Party, which has until recently been tasked with providing a role model for social action, today struggles with the weight of corruption and the abuse of power. The new heroes of Chinese society are not selfless cadres but, rather, rich private entrepreneurs, regardless of the source of their wealth. Unfortunately, those who are looking to the business sector to provide an ideology to fill the void will be disappointed. In state-owned enterprises, the uncovering of graft, the widespread abuse of power, and scandal has become a routine part of the reform process.[5] Likewise the private sector's tactics often prove to be no more based in ethics than the public sector. Perhaps the only compensation is that they do not present themselves as ethical actors but, rather, acknowledge the pursuit of wealth as the main driver of their success. Although they are widely seen as sometimes skirting the law, their downfalls are more likely to be politically rather than commercially linked.[6]

---

[5] For example, the downfall of Wang Xuebing, former Chairman of China Construction Bank, for abuses of power when he was at the Bank of China based in Beijing and New York; the Guangxia Yinchuan stock scandal involving the falsification of accounts.

[6] For example, Yang Bin, the Chairman of Euro-Asia Holdings, was indicted on charges of commercial crime, but is largely regarded as a political victim because of his unapproved plan to become the head of a North Korean special economic zone; the downfall of Yang Rong, of Brilliance Automotive holdings; the early 2003 scandals surrounding Zhou Zhengyi and Shanghai land transfers.

Most recently, there has been, from the outside, renewed hope for a wave of change marked by a new transparency and the instilling of a new public ethic under President Hu Jintao and Premier Wen Jiabao. The low-key nature of both leaders and their disdain for the gaudy self-aggrandizement of past eras, combined with the openness following China's admission of the SARS crisis in Spring 2003, seem to herald a different era. It is still too early to determine what these trends mean for China's ethical void. What is certain is that as long as the void persists, development in China will continue to be subject to the adverse impacts of scandal, uncertainty and a lack of clear operating principles.

Hong Kong, once a booming gateway to China and a global purveyor of financial services, is suffering its own crisis. Although it is possible to regard Hong Kong's crisis as purely economic, the mass public protest on July 1, 2003, in which nearly 10% of the population took part, in addition to several smaller incidents, seem to imply a greater significance. Crisis can be most easily measured in economic terms, as the downturn affects increasing numbers of those who call Hong Kong their home.[7] What indicates something more widespread is the public crisis of confidence, a disbelief in not only the current leadership and government, but also in the opposition's ability to provide viable alternatives and Hong Kong's lack of a thriving civil society to provide new ideas. Ruminating on Hong Kong's decline and/or advocating suggestions to restore growth are repeated themes in the media, which further underscores the public search for answers.

While the answers lie across the fields of economy, business and governance, without the implementation of ethics across society Hong Kong's malaise will continue. In a sense, Hong Kong's most serious crisis is not one of economy, for it remains a rich, hugely capable city full of potential. Rather, the more serious malaise lies in the gradual erosion of a public sense of community, which derives from a common feeling of what it means to be a "Hong Kong person" and what values are held in common. As long as this fundamental question remains, Hong Kong will continue to drift.

While Singapore has what Hong Kong does not — a deeply imbued sense of identity and what it means to be Singaporean — it has not managed to escape from ethical questioning.[8] Notwithstanding this,

---

[7] Unemployment in 2003 hit 7.6%, the highest in the past decade. In June 2003, 22% of mortgages in Hong Kong were considered to have "negative equity," where the value of the mortgage exceeds the value of the property concerned.

[8] Singapore's companies have occasionally experienced questioning of post-dated accounting admissions.

Singapore does stand out in Asia as hosting one of the cleanest governments and operating structures worldwide, and continues to win accolades on this account. The picture for the rest of Southeast Asia is much less palatable and, in a world which considers investments around regional hubs or supply chains, Singapore suffers from the dalliances of its neighbors. Unfinished skyscrapers across Southeast Asia document an era gone wrong, and the reputations of many of the designers of Asia's boom lie in the dust. Southeast Asia is grappling with social ills such as drugs and illicit sex, environmental degradation, ethnic tensions, and regional security threats. What counts against it most, however, is the rampant practice of corruption, nepotism and patronage. Some observers in Asia have argued that corruption can, at times, be beneficial to development — the "oiling-the-wheels-of-commerce" argument. Nepotism and using government power to enrich oneself is almost seen as acceptable in some Southeast Asian countries. The Global Competitiveness Report, published annually by the World Economic Forum, shows that, from an 80-country ranking, Indonesia, the Philippines and Vietnam are amongst the worst performers when it comes to corruption's impact on growth.[9] Their respective rankings against a range of economic measures are shown below.

Types of irregular payments	Rankings		
	Vietnam	Philippines	Indonesia
Fxports and imports	69	77	79
Public utilities	66	69	74
Tax collection	67	76	77
Public contracts	59	71	79

The recent withdrawal of some investment funds from several Asian countries (for instance, by Calpers, one of the largest pension funds) is a case in point, as lack of appropriate regulation of corporate governance was foremost among the reasons given for the decision to withdraw. The cohesive social arrangements in Southeast Asian societies have permitted

---

[9] Peter K. Cornelius, Klaus Schwab, Michel E. Porter, *Global Competitiveness Report 2002-2003*, Oxford University Press, New York and Oxford, 2003. The Global Competitivenss Report is widely recognized as the world's leading cross-country comparison of data and information relating to economic competitiveness and growth.

detrimental excesses that masquerade as goodwill gestures. Opportunities for substantial economic growth and increase of individual income have given tremendous authority to gatekeepers who turn out to be rent-seekers. These are elites with the ability to either ease or obstruct access to markets, business partners and governments.

A common characteristic that distinguishes Southeast Asian economies from most Western societies is the weakly developed legal system, its subordination to state elites, and the relatively unimportant role of formal contracts and agreements. In particular, the Western separation of legal institutions from the formal apparatus of the state and the considerable autonomy enjoyed by the legal profession are not so evident in Southeast Asia. This has meant that the political executive has not been constrained by the rule of law to the same extent in these societies and litigation is rarely used as a means of gaining redress. It has also resulted in there being little reliance on legal institutions for developing and policing agreements and trust relations. Judicial authorities lack the ability to arbitrate in disputes between parties or to rule on complaints against government officials. Hence, corruption is barely avoidable: bribes ease business-government transactions. A climate of corruption and insider dealing is pervasive.

For example, the Philippines, Indonesia and Thailand have experienced multiple cases of unethical behavior, even since the system of corruption was highlighted in the Asian financial crisis. The crisis should have made clear the need to punish and outlaw corrupt ways. What has resulted instead is a legalization of corruption through loopholes, or the co-opting of those in power. Indonesia's Bank Bali's payment of a US$80-million fee to government officials to collect a supposed government-guaranteed debt worth US$116 million, for example, is testimony that the culture of patronage is still alive in Southeast Asia. Impeachment proceedings against the executive in all three countries help to unearth ethical failings, although in most instances the guilty parties escape unharmed.

Even after the infamous Marcos era, the public in the Philippines has been subject to high degrees of corruption and rent-seeking. The former president Joseph Estrada, for instance, was brought down by corruption and personal dalliances. Manipulation and insider trading continue to discredit the stock market. In Thailand, the constant struggle of creditors to gain proper access to corporate and personal assets in corporate embezzlement cases, and the lack of public authority over government officials who routinely abuse their power for personal gain, provide a steady stream of examples of ethics gone awry.

What about Asian values?

Asia was not always awash in disillusionment with its elites. In the early ages, business existed within society and grew up with strong roots in philosophy and social theory. Under Confucianism, the merchant class was a clear social actor, who made profits for the community, and whose respect stemmed from the community benefiting from his largess. This developed into the modern-day concept of "lifetime employment," in which the employee gave loyalty to a company in return for a guarantee of employment for life. In South and Southeast Asia where Hinduism and Buddhism have taken root, the ideas of karma, right treatment of others, produced rewards in subsequent lives. As we shall show later in the book, this resonates in the concept of corporate citizenship, in which a company will spread social benefit in order to be appreciated in the future. Despite the heterogeneous nature of Asian religions and their national, cultural or ethnic variances, there are a number of common threads which are significant for modern day economic activity. These are outlined in Part 2, Foundations, which traces how principles which are largely geared towards individual action may be translated or applicable to the organized business entity.

It may be surprising that few of these resembled the lauded "Asian values" that were widely praised during the so-called Asian economic miracle. This ill-fated attempt by outsiders and Asians alike to derive a regional values system from a superficial and almost coincidental free-flowing of money across Southeast Asia, credited Asia's success to "values" such as a strong work ethic; a belief in education; a willingness of employees to sacrifice or maintain a positive mental attitude; entrepreneurship, creativity and problem solving; and high levels of savings.

Today, the notion of Asian values is all but discredited, with the Asian economic miracle exposed as a scam. Indeed, the attempt to formulate a value system for Asia has largely fallen by the wayside, in a manner typical of trends and fashion. What little truth there was in the original claims has also been discarded. We do not propose to undertake a re-examination of the Asian economic miracle in search of a truer version of Asian values but, rather, to rebuild the values on a more solid footing that is able to withstand economic cycles and a world that today is far more complex than that of the early and mid 1990s. There were elements of the Asian-values argument which may have held credence, but those need to be rigorously tested against what we know of Asia's own religious and philosophical foundations.

The Asian crisis and the widespread fallout from years of conducting "business in bad faith" or business in the absence of ethics,[10] should have left clear instructions on the need to return to a firmly grounded system of ethics. Unfortunately, instead of a return to roots, countries focused largely on the seemingly more urgent tasks of getting their accounts and economies in order, if only to satisfy international financial commitments. Some have even managed to effect economic turnarounds without confronting questions of ethics; certainly the continuing evidence of corruption at the highest and lowest levels seems to indicate this. However, as long as the ethical question remains unanswered, Asia's growth and development will continue to be impeded by uncertainty (not least concerning who the next crackdown will expose), a lack of trust and, potentially, social unrest.

Demands of the complex economy

The urgency of filling the ethical void is amplified in a world that is tending rapidly towards integration and inter-connectivity in all spheres. No sector, no country and no company can escape this trend — globalization, technology and access to information are the guarantors. Thus, we see governments adopting more active approaches to business and countries reaching out more proactively, whether for trade or to address regional tensions. This is true not only on their own borders, but also far away. Much of this "outreach" can be seen as opportunistic or, at least, mutually advantageous.

In addition, today's companies are becoming more deeply integrated, if not by shareholding, then by interest, regular consultation, and constant communications at all levels of the company, with other organizations, social groups, governments, and experts or commentators. In the larger companies, in particular, the CEO has become just as much public persona and statesman as someone concerned only with managing a company. CEOs are held to the highest ethical standards, at least publicly, and the recent round of corporate blood-letting in the USA only testifies to the fact that the CEO must be ethically impeccable in addition to being a visionary and manager.

Where does Asia fit into this picture? In some instances, it's off the screen or barely flickering. While Asia's governments have begun to

---

[10] We mean here an encompassing term of business, as conducted by the corporate sector as well as government, social organizations and others who acted solely for selfish gain.

reach out, Asians as a whole remain reluctant to confront common affairs, preferring not to meddle in the widely defined field of "internal" matters. However, the silence is especially deafening when one examines Asian companies. While Western-based multinationals have actively developed sophisticated programs of social engagement, albeit often in a self-interested or defensive manner, Asian companies have been laggards in this regard. Not only do they view business as being largely divorced from the social milieu, they often do so in flagrant violation of public trust of social well-being. Pollution is just the tip of the iceberg and other cases are amply highlighted above.

The primary relationship: Business and government

Some Asian businesses have begun to implement the "social contract" through deeper or reformed relations with government. Progress is uneven and depends largely on a given economy's level of development. Thus, in Asia's developing economies, business may be either entirely linked to or de-linked from politics, as businesses have been unsure of how to deal with "outside" actors. Thus, economies are almost entirely owned and run by the state, or dominated by a private sector that keeps close relations with the government or other actors only on an opportunistic basis where there must be concrete and direct benefits for the business. As examples of the former, one has Vietnam or, perhaps, China 20 years ago, where a true business sector did not exist. Eventually, as the private sector develops, they will have to determine their modus operandi vis-a-vis other parties in society, and will likely first start with the government. In the latter category, there is Indonesia, in which close relations between government and business was usually a sign of corruption. In such cases, the business sector often does not know how to deal with other parties and thus chooses total subservience, relinquishing any independence or control.

In Asia's middle-income economies, the business community is moving more towards the development of the private economy, where the company is a fiefdom inside but increasingly subject to social norms and codes on the outside. In these cases, there is a mixed amount of government involvement in the business, sometimes veering towards favoritism and orchestration of business activity in the most important fields, while adopting a hands-off approach in other areas.

In Asia's developed economies, the relationship between business and government has usually matured and stabilized. Thus, in Singapore, government is a majority shareholder in companies across the economy, but generally observes a hands-off approach for operations, except in a few identifiable areas such as those around the "national interest" or in the selection of the CEO and chairman. By contrast, in Hong Kong, a few former public utilities or services are government-owned, but the majority of the largest companies are majority-owned by private concerns or families. The "arms-length" relationship between business and government is framed by standardized and transparent consultative bodies in which business participates in the task of policy-making or advising. Many Hong Kong companies have also developed a strong sense of social responsibility and regularly engage in the community through charitable or other third-party organizations.[11] Companies want to be seen as positively embedded within the community, which is a sign of ethics in practice. There are also signs of a deeper integration of social responsibility in the finance sector, which is significant given the latter's huge role in Hong Kong's economy.[12]

The real question for Hong Kong remains whether or not, amidst these signs of ethics in practice, it can move beyond isolated activities towards a deeper connection with ethics. We do not propose that all companies in Hong Kong should adopt a core code of ethics, but that eventually the majority of Hong Kong's companies, especially small and medium-sized enterprises (SMEs) which comprise the great majority, should do so. While Hong Kong has a few good corporate actors, there are still many instances — in both government and business — where the ethical bar is placed very low. In addition, despite all the good acts of business, public respect is still accorded to members of society based on wealth, regardless of ethical comportment.

One of the factors holding Asia back in achieving a more rooted sense of ethics in business and public life is the relative absence of a civil society, at least in comparison to the US, Latin America or Europe. In

---

[11] For example, the MTR Corporation has established itself as a leader in corporate social responsibility. Leading members of the Hang Seng Index (for the largest listed companies) such as HSBC, Hutchison Whampoa, Cheung Kong, and Wharf regularly support the Community Chest, local hospitals and other social organizations.

[12] For example, ASRIA (Association for Sustainable and Responsible Investment in Asia) has steadily increased its following and has links with major finance companies in Hong Kong. Civic Exchange, a local think tank, has done several projects on social responsibility with CLSA Emerging Markets.

those regions there are deep traditions of religious groups, independent labor unions, political groups, think tanks, social organizations, community and grassroots movements, and the like. In Asia, some countries have one or two of these elements — in South Korea labor unions are strong, the Philippines has strong grassroots movements and Thailand has poor-people's social organizations — but there is rarely the rich variety that makes for a thriving civil society. The consequences of this are serious, for it means that countries in Asia are deprived of a true marketplace of ideas, which is instrumental in enabling and facilitating the private sector's achievement of TEM. Civil society provides independent and "market-tested" pressure, ideas and frameworks for business to realize ethical management.

Building towards a civil society

Today, Asia's civil society movement is just beginning. On one side are Asian branches of Western non-government organizations, such as small indigenous groups which have, in many cases, grown out of a single person's determination and belief. While the former are important to providing pressure and nodes for a civil society network, Asia urgently needs its own organizations which do not bear the stigma of "imposed ideas" and which cultivate programs and ideas catering specifically to local conditions. The start of entrepreneurial organizations within civil society is a good sign; the key is to ensure that these organizations grow and are able to sustain themselves based on their ideas and programs alone, and even in the absence of the "activists." This step, along with continuing integration and outreach beyond the immediate civil society network, will deepen their sophistication and ability to provide society and the business community with tools for ethical management.

The actualization of TEM will come from within the corporate sector as well as from independent organizations and government. With this book, we hope to provide a vision for building TEM and a basis for beginning to implement it. Thus, we examine Asia's philosophical and religious foundations through four major schools of thought against the development of business in the region (Part 2, Foundations). Secondly, we look at ethical applications across society; that is, what ethics has meant and will continue to mean in various aspects of economic and public life (Part 3, Applications). Then, we extend these beginnings to consider the transformations which will need to be enacted by the business community in order to adapt and practice TEM holistically and authentically (Part 4,

Transtormations). The book closes with a tentative model of Total Ethical Management (Part 5, Total Ethical Management). We have endeavored in each case to present contributions which articulate clearly the developed thought of leaders in their respective fields. As a further guide to the reader and practitioner, we present some sections with an introduction that provides added coherence, insight and material for consideration.

TEM in Asia is in its very early stages. This book thus intends to provoke thinking as a work in progress and serve as a guide for practitioners across the activity spectrum. Asia urgently needs to fill its ethical void. We hope that will be a start.

2

THE BIG PICTURE:
What is Business Ethics?
What are its Prospects in Asia?

Lou Marinoff

Associate Professor of Philosophy at The City College of New York

Introduction

Business ethics is both an ancient and a modern subject. It bears increasing relevance to the optimal functioning of the global village, and thus to the overall improvement of the state of the world. Business ethics addresses one central question, and many sub-questions that flow from it. The central question is: How can business be both profitable and good? Some important sub-questions are: Which ethical norms conduce both to profitability and to goodness? How do we best transmit and practice such norms? How should we deal with those who violate them? How can governmental regulation be juxtaposed with *laissez-faire* economics? How can integrity and accountability (among other virtues) survive in hardened economic climates? Can we evolve an inclusive set of "best practices" for business that provides sufficient scope for the multiculturalism and diversity of the global village? What is the role of business in creating social value? What theories of social and political justice inform our notions of "goodness," and thus pre-condition our evaluations and assessments of "good" business practice? These, among other important questions, must be addressed in order to stimulate constructive thought in enterprises, to further meaningful dialogue between producers and consumers, and to achieve significant results in the overall cause of human progress.

I would be remiss not to add a personal note. When Carl Jung wrote his brilliant foreword to the Wilhelm translation of that venerable work of Chinese philosophy the *I Ching*, he began by acknowledging his relative ignorance of China itself.[1] However, Jung's lack of familiarity with China "on the ground" did not prevent him from grasping and introducing the essentials of the *I Ching*'s universally applicable philosophy and psychology of change. Similarly, I must confess to a relative lack of familiarity with Asia itself. Although I travel in Asia with increasing frequency, and interact with Asians all over the world, like Jung I neither speak an Asian tongue nor inhabit an Asian country. However, I have studied, taught and practiced Asian philosophies for more than 30 years, mostly as an inhabitant of North America, Europe and the Middle East. On that basis, I can certainly offer a philosophical perspective on the ongoing evolution and fusion of business ethics with Asian thought.

Plurality of ancient sources

The codification of ethical practices began in the ancient world, and was an indispensable artifact of permanent human settlements — that is, of civilization. For example, the ancient Code of Hammurabi[2] stipulated that if a builder made a house that later collapsed and killed members of the family inhabiting it, the builder's corresponding family members would be put to death accordingly. While such primitive retributive justice is long-since passé in the modern world, one can still appreciate its intent: to provide a strong disincentive to shoddy building practices. Even today, one needs countervailing measures, albeit less draconian ones, to combat the temptation among building contractors to increase their profits by employing sub-standard materials or workmanship.

A more celebrated and venerated model of professional ethics is the Oath of Hippocrates, which is still taken ceremonially by physicians (although some of its precepts, such as those proscribing surgery, are long-since outdated). The main ethical idea, not stated explicitly by Hippocrates but implied throughout, is "First, do no harm."[3] This doctrine of non-maleficence has become enshrined in virtually every contemporary code of professional ethics, from health-care to engineering. The same notion has been widely extended to modern consumer-protection

---

[1] See C.G. Jung, Foreword, *The I Ching or Book of Changes*, the Richard Wilhelm translation, rendered into English by Cary Baynes, Princeton University Press, Princeton, 1950.

[2] Hammurabi was King of Babylonia in the 18th century B.C.E.

[3] Hippocrates was born between 470–460 B.C.E. "Into whatever houses I enter, I will go into them for the benefit of the sick, and will abstain from every voluntary act of mischief and corruption; and, further, from the seduction of females or males, of freemen and slaves." The tenet "First do no harm," "Primum non nocere," has been attributed to the Roman physician Galen.

legislation, from restrictions on advertising tobacco products to consumer-controlled testing of children's toys.

The most general doctrine of non-harm, or *ahimsa*, was articulated and promulgated by ancient Indian philosophical schools, notably Jains and Buddhists. The theory and practice of non-harm toward sentient beings was never intended solely for religious ascetics, although it gradually acquired this special connotation. *Ahimsa*'s broader intention is to respect life and to value conscious beings as a way of maximizing and realizing one's own human potential, both temporally and spiritually. Thus one should avoid earning one's secular livelihood through harmful activities or practices. Harming others also harms oneself. It is both possible and desirable to engage in profitable business transactions without inflicting harm on others.

Similar notions are expressed in ancient Chinese philosophy. The metaphysics of Taoism, which informed both Lao Tzu and Confucius, may appear somewhat abstruse at first blush — for example, "Tao is ever inactive, and yet there is nothing that it does not do."[4] However, consistent with and perhaps formative of the undeniably pragmatic reputation of Asian thought, the Tao embodies a very practical set of precepts for governing one's affairs — whether personal, social, economic or political — via a minimization of strife and a maximization of fulfillment. Thus Taoism applies manifestly to the governance and harmonization of business dealings too.[5] By contrast, while neo-Darwinian "survival of the fittest"[6] remains a prevalent notion in highly competitive commercial arenas, it is nonetheless a crude and ultimately misguided prescription for human affairs, especially compared with the Tao's sophistication and efficacy in promoting "survival of the sagacious."

From this brief but wide-ranging overview, it should be clear that deep and diverse philosophical traditions from the ancient world contain the seeds of contemporary business ethics.

---

[4] Lao Tzu, *Tao Tê Ching*, trans. Ch'u Ta-Kao, Allen & Unwin Ltd., London, 1959, chapter 37.

[5] "Albeit one governs the country by rectitude, and carries on wars by stratagems. Yet one must rule the empire by meddling with no business." Ibid, chapter 57.

[6] This is one of the most pervasive misconceptions of Darwinism. Herbert Spencer, not Charles Darwin, coined this tautological phrase. In fact, we behold only the "survival of the survivors."

The ABC of virtue ethics

Before addressing current issues, it is useful to characterize three main schools of ancient thought that bear much relevance to modern business ethics. These are the Aristotelian, the Buddhist and the Confucian: literally, the ABC of virtue ethics.

If we agree that harm is bad, and thus that harming people is intrinsically and fundamentally wrong, a perennial question of philosophy still needs to be asked: What is good? For if we simply equate goodness with non-harm, we can establish a list of behaviors to be avoided in business (and more generally in life) — such as lying, cheating, stealing, and so on — without addressing the complementary affirmative question: What should be done?

In his most ambitious and enduring work, *The Republic*, Plato delivers a theory of justice that ultimately raises this very question, "What is good?" Although Plato could not provide a definitive answer,[7] his student Aristotle later did. For Aristotle, goodness is not something we define intellectually; rather, something we attain through the practice of virtues. Aristotle understood virtue as a mean, lying between vices at either extreme.[8] For example, courage is a virtue, and is also a mean between the extremes of cowardice and recklessness. Applied to business, fear of taking any risks at all is a form of cowardice, and a vice. Similarly, fearlessness in undertaking all risks is a form of rashness, and a vice at the other extreme. Extremes are usually bad for business. The virtuous and profitable mean lies in taking prudent or calculated risks, which accords with Aristotle's theory, and whose estimation is a task for risk-assessors and risk-managers in today's marketplace.

This doctrine was independently and earlier asserted by Buddha, in his definitive conception of the Middle Way.[9] Whether one is pursuing personal or corporate growth, the optimal route lies neither in asceticism,

---

[7] Plato, *The Republic of Plato*, trans. Francis Cornford, Oxford University Press, London, 1941, chapter 23.

[8] Aristotle, *Nicomachean Ethics*, ed. Louise Ropes Loomis, Walter J. Black Inc., Roslyn, NY, 1943, book 2.

[9] For example, see Buddha's *Sermon at Benares,* in which he describes the two extremes to be avoided: "That conjoined with the passions and luxury: low, vulgar, common, ignoble and useless; and that conjoined with self-torture: painful, ignoble and useless. Avoiding these two extremes, the Tathagata [i.e. Buddha] has gained the enlightenment of the Middle Path." E.A. Burtt, ed., *The Compassionate Teachings of the Buddha*, Penguin Books USA, NY, 1955, pp. 29–32.

nor in over-indulgence. Applied to the issue of public trust in large corporations, so severely eroded of late, it is clear that the leaders of prominent organizations should practice neither excessive denial nor excessive greed. While a leader's stature, and that of the organization he or she serves, is bound to be reinforced by expected trappings of office, ostentation or corruption are likewise bound to have the reverse effect, and will diminish the moral stature of the leader and organization alike. Greed was a primary ingredient in Asia's recent financial crisis, in the collapse of Argentina's economy, and in the Enron-Andersen scandal. Taking a moderate amount of profit is virtuous, because it also enhances one's capacity to create opportunity and to stimulate more widespread generation of wealth. But manipulating a currency, looting a treasury or falsifying an audit to satisfy a gluttonous appetite for money lead inevitably to suffering — for oneself, and for many others.

Buddhism teaches that people who perpetrate such non-violent harms are conflicted within, and must confront and defeat their own "demons" — that is, deleterious mind-states — if they would do more good than harm in the world. In contrast to Augustine's theology,[10] Buddhism does not assert that people are born corrupted. We actively choose the principles by which we govern our affairs and lives, or by inaction passively accept the principles already in place. Either way, we are both free to choose and responsible for our choices. Those who perpetrate harms have made poor choices.

Terrorists, like other criminals who plan and perpetrate violent murders, are even more conflicted. Fanatics usually suffer from severe psychic toxins such as deep-seated hatreds or intolerances, often politically programmed and culturally reinforced from cradle to grave, by a zeitgeist of imposed delusion that prohibits competing perspectives and obviates all possibility for human fulfillment. No equivalent of a "Marshall plan" for the Middle East will stand a chance of de-fanaticizing the next generation unless it embodies profound educational reform. And Asians take note: Indonesian schoolchildren (among many others) are now being taught that the doomed airplanes on 9-11 were hijacked by Americans and Israelis, to give the West a pretext to invade "peace-loving" Islamic nations. Poisoning young minds in this fashion will lead only to further suffering, not to its alleviation. Secular Buddhist philosophy, for example as expressed in the principled educational humanism of Daisaku Ikeda, offers the best prospects for de-fanaticizing

---

[10] Augustine's theory of "original sin" is found in his *City of God*.

intolerant populations and emancipating humanity via the possibility of constructive choice.[11]

Similarly, Confucius attempted to persuade the warlords of his day that government by virtue was superior to government by coercion.[12] Needless to say, Confucius was far ahead of his time. His enduring influence on Asian cultures is remarkable, and outweighs even that of Aristotle in the West. However, Confucian ethics are often attenuated at the level of the family or community, whereas they were meant to extend to the civil service, to other branches of government, and to political leadership as well. By extension, Confucius's conception of virtue ethics also applies manifestly to the business world. For example, when asked about leadership, Confucius said: "Get as much as possible done first by your subordinates. Pardon small offences. Promote men of superior capacity."[13] In today's parlance, he is clearly advocating delegation of authority, avoidance of micromanagement, and promotion based on merit (as opposed to favoritism or affirmative action, and so on) — all essential ingredients for a wholesome enterprise.

This rounds out a brief survey of some ancient roots of modern applied ethics. I would like to make one final point before focusing on the contemporary era. Philosophy as a whole consists of several well-defined main areas with associated sub-specialties, some of which merge seamlessly at the edges. One main area is called axiology, meaning "philosophy of values." It bifurcates into two very large fields: ethics and aesthetics. Canonical ethics treat theories of good and bad (meta-ethics), notions of right and wrong (morality), systems of justice and injustice (legality), and moral claims of providential religions (theodicy). Outside Confucianism and Taoism, there are few credible philosophical treatments of political ethics. Machiavelli attempted a guide to the ethics of leadership, but Bertrand Russell called it a "handbook for gangsters."[14] The absence of political ethics, however, places even greater demands on business ethics, as we shall see.

---

[11] See, for example, *Choose Life: A Dialogue, Arnold Toynbee and Daisaku Ikeda*, Oxford, Oxford University Press, 1976; and George Miller (ed.), *Peace, Value and Wisdom: The Educational Philosophy of Daisaku Ikeda*, Amsterdam, Rodopi, 2002.

[12] "He who rules by moral force (*tê*) is like the pole star, which remains in its place while all the lesser stars do homage to it." *The Analects of Confucius*, trans. Arthur Waley, George Allen & Unwin Ltd., London, 1938, book 2, verse 1.

[13] *The Analects of Confucius*, book 8 verse 2.

[14] Niccolò Machiavelli, *The Prince*, trans. W. Marriott, J.M. Dent & Sons Ltd., London, 1958.

The domain of aesthetics is the philosophy of the arts, where "art" is most broadly and generously construed. Classically, statecraft itself is categorized as an art-form — as the highest art of all, by Aristotle. Politics embodies many ancient and venerable sub-arts, including leadership, oratory, rhetoric, dialectic, legislation, as well as modern communication arts like TV personification, and that perennial art lately known as "spin-doctoring." Aside from the political, one finds an abundance of artistic endeavors under heads such as the creative, the performing, the culinary, the medical, the mathematical and so forth. Even in these most plastic and synergistic of domains, some apparent laws hold sway. One law suggests that the more refined the art-form, the greater the technique and insight required to aspire to true artistry in the given idiom.

I mention these two main branches of axiology — ethics and aesthetics — for an important reason. It is philosophically conceivable that human life itself is an art-form, whose creative aspects and potential for individual flourishing are liberated, constrained, or else corrupted in very large measure by the ethical system by which the individual chooses to be governed. The implications for business are clear enough. When we come to speak of applied ethics and applied aesthetics, this linkage reasserts itself. A given professional, corporate, administrative or political culture will itself either flourish or flounder (and will encourage its constituents to do the same) in similar accordance with the quality of the ethics and artistic values by which it chooses to be governed.

Finally, it must be emphasized that I am presupposing a degree of choice in these matters. It is agreed by most philosophers (a rare enough occurrence) that if there is no capacity for choice, there is likewise no capacity for morality. Thus one has to choose to be good or evil, choose to do right or wrong, choose to serve justice or injustice. While both genetic and environmental factors undoubtedly influence temperament, behavior and preference, humans appear intermittently if not incessantly capable of making wiser or more foolish choices in the governance of their affairs. This presumption of choice is at least as vital for ethics as for any other endeavor. And even though the intricacy of business ethics rivals the complexity of everything else these days, it remains true of axiology (as of science) that the simplest of principles is often the most elegant, and universally applicable.

Applied ethics:
A growth industry in its own right

Business ethics is part of the field of applied ethics, which has become a significant growth industry in the academy during the past three decades. The higher education of a growing number of aspiring professionals is not considered adequate unless they have been exposed to at least one course of applied ethics, designed to address the current ethical issues and latent moral demands of their respective professions. Accounting ethics, biomedical ethics, business ethics, computer ethics, engineering ethics, environmental ethics, journalism ethics, leadership ethics, legal ethics, and management ethics are taught by philosophers in a growing number of colleges and universities, many of which have established centers, institutes or chairs for further research in applied ethical domains.

The applied ethics industry entails many activities, including developing curricula; doing scholarly research; writing textbooks; elaborating case studies; framing key issues that inform media debate, public policy, regulation and legislation; building, implementing and interpreting codes of ethics for the professions; and undertaking proactive consulting work for professions, corporations and governments.

There are two main reasons for the rapid growth of the applied ethics industry during the past few decades. The first is the perennial necessity for ethics education. Moral reasoning is not innate; rather, it must be learned. The demands of doing business in the global village mandate an appreciation of comparative religious ethics as well as secular philosophical ethics. Such knowledge is most readily assimilated in the course of formal studies. Plato famously hung the following sign over the entrance to his Academy (the prototype for our contemporary universities): "Let none ignorant of geometry enter here." Plato maintained that mathematics was the surest tutor of reason, owing to its inherent logicality and instrumental exactitude. He therefore supposed that students ought to study Euclidean geometry (the *sine qua non* of applied deductive reasoning) for 10 years before undertaking ethics and politics, which are far less exact but much more palpable in quotidian affairs. There is no greater litmus test of the quality of an organization, culture or civilization than the ethics it teaches (or fails to teach) to its stakeholders. Plato knew this well, but too many contemporary Western university administrations have forgotten it entirely. They nowadays promulgate *ex cathedra* edicts and absurd ideologies, but too often fail to prepare their charges for the realities of the world. Without ethics education, university graduates are bound to be morally stunted and ideologically unbalanced, and therefore ill-prepared to become responsible inhabitants of the global village.

The second reason for ethics education, and particularly applied ethics, is the inevitable moral lag between the leading edges of science, technology and business and the trailing edges of consumption, regulation and legislation. Novel and evolving technologies enable the opening of new markets and the realization of hitherto unimaginable goals, but also compel a vital normative question: *Should* we implement a given technology, merely because we *can* do so? Some examples: We can perform neo-natal tissue implants. Should we? We can clone animals. Should we? We can genetically modify foodstuffs. Should we? We can painlessly euthanize terminally ill patients. Should we? We can harvest and sell body parts for transplantation. Should we? We can freely distribute intellectual property on the World Wide Web. Should we? We can monitor our employees' computer keystrokes, and surreptitiously read their e-mail. Should we? We can employ non-unionized labor in developing countries, keeping wages and benefits to a minimum. Should we? And so forth. Every new technology invariably raises moral questions. Such questions cannot in general be answered with anything like the precision of solutions to mathematical equations, yet they urgently need to be addressed in the interests of individual guidance, workplace functionality, organizational coherence, and with a view toward multi-stakeholder consensus.

Moral quandaries do not admit of unique solutions. There are in principle several dozen different ways, derived from as many competing ethical systems, in which a question of the form "Should we do *X*?" can be answered. I have elsewhere illustrated some varieties of moral choice available to laypersons, and have applied them to cases from my philosophical counseling and consulting practice.[15] I note in passing that in most situations, whether personal, corporate or governmental, there are indeed some systems of ethics that work better than others. When searching for an optimal ethical framework in a given context, it is usually necessary to juxtapose at least four factors: background ethos (i.e. inherited cultural norms that exhibit longevity); recent moral trends (i.e. current consensus that nonetheless shifts periodically); regnant moral authority or authorities (i.e. source or sources of ultimate sanctioning power, singular in theocracy or dictatorship, plural in democracy, null in

---

[15] See Lou Marinoff, *Plato Not Prozac: Applying Philosophy to Everyday Problems*, HarperCollins, NY, 1999 (published in 21 languages). See also idem, *The Big Questions: How Philosophy Can Change Your Life*, Bloomsbury, New York and London, 2003.

anarchy); and unique characteristics of the client (for example, a strong need to be governed versus a preference to become more self-governing, and so on). By ascertaining the positions of each of these four factors through dialogue with the client, one then quadrangulates a philosophical disposition that the client could most naturally assume, and from which an ethical prescription can usually be inferred.

Take an example from a business context: phase one clinical trials of drugs. Such trials require stringent experimental guidelines, because good science will help cure more disease in the long run than will bad science. Thus some candidates must be placed in a control group, and will receive a placebo instead of the drug — even though the drug might help them. This is undeniably cruel to the desperate individual who wants only a decent chance to fight his disease, and may also appear impartial when even wealth and privilege do not guarantee access to all things at all times. But it is also undeniable that good pharmaceutical science has produced formulations that have saved many millions of lives. When undeniable cruelty to a few persons in the present is justified by undeniable beneficence to a multitude in the future, we classify the principle ethically as a species of utilitarianism, invented by Bentham and Mill but best-summarized by Joseph Priestly as "The greatest good for the greatest number."[16]

Take another example: the constellation of raging international legal battles over the issue of intellectual-property rights. For instance, consider the case of sharing music files over the Internet, and an American court's decision which led to the shutting down of Napster.[17] That decision having been reversed on appeal, consumers can now resume downloading music for free instead of buying it. This means in turn that recording artists will have to work harder or more effectively to retain their market share. The legal question concerns a judgment that soft copy — unlike hard copy — is not strictly copyrightable. The philosophical question pertains to the very nature of private property itself, and the way in which storage or transmission of electronic data via public media de-privatizes then re-privatizes ownership. The evolution of human civilization and globalization depend squarely on the notion of private property, among other things, yet the ontological status of IP (intellectual property) is quite unprecedented, and not at all the same as that of material goods. Neither

---

[16] See Jeremy Bentham, *Deontology*, William Tait, Edinburgh, 1834; John Stuart Mill, *Utilitarianism*, (1861) Bobbs-Merrill Educational Publishing, Indianapolis, 1957; Joseph Priestly, *An Essay on the First Principles of Government*, J. Johnson, London, 1771.

[17] See http://news.findlaw.com/legalnews/lit/napster/

ancient conceptions of goods and chattels (such as those espoused in the Bible) nor even modern ones that justify capitalism (such as Locke's theory of property) apply well to IP. Thus different ethical norms must be evolved to deal rightly and justly with the sale, possession and ownership of IP. This epitomizes the moral lag created by new technologies. Ironically, Proudhon's contentious and politically naïve aphorism "Property is theft,"[18] may be most applicable to IP. From Francis Drake to Bill Gates, definitions of and perspectives on "piracy" and "monopoly" continue to evolve.

As a whole, Asia has earned an unsavory reputation, in the West, for being near the forefront of disregard for intellectual-property rights. While this is partly attributable to legendary Asian corruption (a topic we will take up later in this essay), it is important to note that staunch opponents of certain forms of IP have likewise emerged in the West. For example, there is mounting opposition from consumer groups and global-justice advocates to agreements such as Trade-Related Aspects of Intellectual Property Rights (TRIPS), and the "Information Feudalism" stemming therefrom.[19] Again one appeals to a virtuous Middle Way, such that IP is protected within reason. At one undesirable extreme lies Proudhon's anarchy, where all IP is routinely "Shanghai'ed," at the other lies TRIPS's systemic disenfranchisement of would-be consumers in the developing world by ostended developers, with the complicity of governments.

Take a third example: white collar (and pink collar) crime in the corporate world. The overall costs of such "internal" crime are many billions of dollars per annum, yet employees often fail to cognize their actions as criminal. If one employee of a large corporation takes home a ream of paper, no-one will miss it. Moreover, as increasingly large numbers of people take work home from the office, it seems defensible to take home work-related materials too. However, if every employee of a large corporation took home a ream of paper in a given week, the paper supply would be depleted and the replacement costs would surely be significant. Kant provides a secular ethical principle that forestalls this kind of behavior. Known as the categorical imperative, Kant's rule is this: "Act only on that maxim such that you can will it to be a universal law."[20] No employee can will it to be a universal law that all employees take

---

[18] Pierre-Joseph Proudhon, *Qu'est-ce que la propriété?*, Lacroix, Paris, 1873.

[19] See Peter Drahos with John Braithwaite, *Information Feudalism*, London: Earthscan Publications, 2002. TRIPS: Trade Related Aspects of Intellectual Property Rights.

[20] Immanuel Kant, *Foundations of the Metaphysics of Morals*, trans. Lewis White Beck, Bobbs-Merrill, Indianapolis, 1969.

home whatever office supplies they don't wish to buy for themselves, for the simple reason that there would be no supplies remaining in the office if everyone did so. If there were no supplies in the office, no-one could work at all. Since the maxim is unworkable universally, it is proscribed individually. The categorical imperative does convince a vast majority of people to behave honestly, because it turns out that most people can indeed will honesty to be a universal law.

But this invariably leaves a residue of "free-riders" on the system; that is, a minority that profits dishonestly from the honesty of a majority.[21] The decision-theoretic model that describes such behavior, and which necessitates the evolution of strategies for preventing it, is *The Tragedy of the Commons*, which is also a kind of N-Person Prisoner's Dilemma.[22] Like any species of crime, free-riding can never be completely eradicated, but can always be minimized wherever sound social theories intersect with best social practices.[23]

From these brief illustrations, it should be clear that a rich matrix of philosophical thought underlies and informs many dilemmas in and of the marketplace. Next, we briefly assess the ethical relationship between national sovereign politics and multinational business interests.

The role of government in globalization and business ethics

In the West, two momentous decouplings enabled the genesis of globalization: the separation of church from state, and the separation of state from business. Wherever politics remains a branch of theology, human knowledge and progress are stultified by intolerance and dogma. And wherever business remains a branch of politics, human opportunity is marginalized by colonialism, imperialism or despotism — or paralyzed

---

[21] Philip Pettit, "Free Riding and Foul Dealing," *Journal of Philosophy* 83 (1986): 361–79. See also Lou Marinoff, "The Tragedy of the Coffeehouse: Costly Riding, and How to Avert It," *Journal of Conflict Resolution* 43 (1999): 434–50.

[22] Garrett Hardin, "The Tragedy of the Commons," *Science* 162 (1968): 1243–48.

[23] Lou Marinoff, "The Geometry of Defection: Cascading Mimicry and Contract-Resistant Structures," in Cheryl Hughes and James Wong, eds., *Social Philosophy Today, Volume 17: Communication, Conflict, and Reconciliation*, Charlottesville: Philosophy Documentation Center, 2003, 69–90.

by centrally planned economy. Priests cannot and should not run governments; politicians cannot and should not run corporations. Nonetheless, in the absence of stable governments and progressive political systems, economic potential cannot be fully developed either. Thus there is a necessity for sovereign governments to work with — and at times to step in and regulate — business interests as well as professional practices. I will illustrate this necessity with brief case studies, but first I wish to illuminate the central ethical issue at hand, an overarching one which justifies political intervention in business; namely, commerce's lack of intrinsic moral content.

Religious and political systems do not lack intrinsic moral content. On the contrary, they are often over-endowed with moral rules. Every world religion has identifiable moral precepts enshrined or elaborated in its scripture, which it transmits to its adherents and to which it holds them accountable. Most people want and need moral guidance in life, and organized religions tend to err only on the side of providing too much of it. Similarly, every democratic political system also has identifiable moral precepts, enshrined in its constitution if not spelled out in its bill of rights, which in practice translate into civic virtues. The separation of church and state allows for the retention of private religious morality, but allows too the public unfettering of science, technology and commerce — which come hand-in-glove with individual rights and liberties, and the creation of social and cultural value. This is primarily why Western civilization became and remained ascendant, from the times of the Reformation and Industrial Revolution, through to the end of the Cold War. But for reasons I will touch on, the balance of economic power, along with what Kishore Mahbubani calls the "hinge of history," may now be shifting decisively toward Asia.[24]

Business, however, conspicuously lacks intrinsic moral content. Money is neither good nor evil in itself; rather, it is a morally neutral instrument. While possessing money enhances one's capacity to do good or evil, the quantitative measure of a person's net worth makes no qualitative pronouncement about that person's moral character. While any given business venture may be commercially justifiable on the merits of its profitability, no moral evaluation can be made until one ascertains the ethical standing of the goods or services on offer, and the qualitative effect (for better or worse) of their infusion in the marketplace. While one can gauge the moral intent of religions by their most ubiquitous homilies

---

[24] Kishore Mahbubani, *Can Asians Think?*, Times Books International, Singapore & Kuala Lumpur, 1999.

(for example, "The Golden Rule"), or the moral intent of political systems by their most universal values (for example, "life, liberty and the pursuit of happiness"), the commonest maxim applied to business is surely *Caveat emptor*: Let the buyer beware. The defensive alarms rung by this disclaimer stand in stark contrast to those of religious and political maxims. Religions seek the souls of their adherents, but (if non-fanatical) return to them some measure of solace or other spiritual comfort. Politicians seek the votes of their constituents, but (if democratic) offer them promises of temporal benefits in return. But producers of goods or services seek the monies of their consumers, and what they offer in exchange is subject to the most moral variance of all. The freest markets generate the greatest opportunity and wealth, but also allow the most unscrupulous opportunists to capitalize on human inclination toward vice and capacity for suffering. "Caveat emptor" offers Job's comfort to victims of unscrupulous commercial predators.

Sovereign governments can and should provide checks and balances against immoral opportunism, provided they are not too preoccupied engaging in it themselves. Regrettably, the history of every great empire — and empires are often mighty civilizing forces, and good for business too — is riddled with horrors of government-sponsored or government-sanctioned crimes against humanity, that were nonetheless immensely profitable business ventures. The late British Empire, for example, among whose laudable global legacies are the English language, the British Commonwealth of nations, parliamentary democracy and a model civil service (rivaling the Chinese Mandarinate), nonetheless derived enormous but immoral profits from the Opium Wars in China, and the Triangular Trade in African slaves. The East India Company and the plantations of the New World were state-run and state-sanctioned enterprises respectively, which brought untold human suffering to millions. It is the responsibility of enlightened governments to protect their citizens against political, commercial and criminal predators, and not to join or encourage them.[25] Of course and on balance, many Imperialists did far less good and much more ill than the British in their day.

But Asia as a whole did not evolve along Western lines, where separation of Church from State became a prerequisite for progress. Thus one plausible root of deep-seated corruption in Asia is its historic lack of

---

[25] In John Stuart Mill's words: "To prevent the weaker members of the community from being preyed on by innumerable vultures, it was needful that there should be an animal of prey stronger than the rest, commissioned to keep them down." *On Liberty*, Longmans, Green & Co., London, 1903.

religious morality imposed by political culture. Corruption, when idiosyncratically exposed, remains scandalous in the West, owing largely to residues of Puritan mores enshrined in the Protestant work-ethic.[26] By contrast, corruption is an accepted fact of life in much of Asia, and so too becomes an implicit premise of business.[27]

According to John Stuart Mill, in a free and open society the sole justification for governmental interference or constraint placed upon citizens is to prevent them from doing harm to one another.[28] Mill's "harm principle" provides the common ethical foundation for civil and criminal laws, as well as the bases of regulating professional and commercial activities. Some examples of American lack of regulation are instructive. In the 19th century, boilers on Mississippi steamboats were unregulated. Hundreds of them exploded, and the boats burned or sank — injuring, killing or drowning thousands of people. Eventually, government stepped in and regulated the construction and operation of such boilers. While this increased the expense of operating steamboats, the casualties virtually ceased. Another example: In late 20th-century Oregon, body-piercing parlors profited from the rise in popularity of self-mutilation among the young. Like much else in America, these enterprises were unregulated by default. However, lack of proper hygiene and non-standardized piercing techniques resulted in alarming increases in hepatitis and other diseases. So the state government stepped in and regulated the industry, thus reducing infection (and contagion) among consumers of piercing services to acceptable baseline levels.

Larger and much more profitable industries prove correspondingly more resistant to regulation. The tobacco industry (regulated in Western advertising only after millions of deaths by cancer) is one glaring example; the auto industry (regulated in safety issues thanks mostly to Ralph Nader) is another. Wherever governments are lax, corrupt, apathetic or fatalistic, there the commercial predator finds fertile ground for profiteering on human suffering. Nestlé's unconscionable sales of Similac in Africa, Union Carbide's disaster in Bhopal, the Chernobyl meltdown in the former USSR, and the destruction of the earth's ozone layer by aerosols are all examples of how lack of governmental regulation —

---

[26] See, for example, Max Weber, *The Protestant Ethic and the Spirit of Capitalism*, New York, Scribner's Press, 1958, 47–78.

[27] For example, see Zamira Eshanova, "Central Asia: Corruption, a Common Feature of Daily Routine," 17 July 2002, http://www.muslimuzbekistan.com/eng/ennews/2002/07/ennews22072002_8.html

[28] Mill, *On Liberty*.

whether locally, nationally or internationally — can abet catastrophes or long-term harms for the sake of "business as usual".

Naturally, regulation does not guarantee non-harm. Our world is imperfect in every way, and no process is 100% efficient. Prescription drugs, for example, are carefully regulated in the developed world, yet Thalidomide and Fen Phen (to name but two) slipped through the regulatory meshes and caused lifelong deformity or premature death to consumers. But governments have a duty to regulate potentially harmful business enterprises, as well as the prerogative of strategically integrating globalization into local economies.[29]

Ethics and education

Ethical theory and moral practice must be learned, and continuing education is a hallmark of today's knowledge economy. Organizational cultures committed to lifelong learning are those which stand the best chance of thriving in the complex and shifting nexus of the global village. In particular, corporate cultures that pay appropriate attention to the ethical dimension of human interaction reap the largest dividends in organizational harmony and productivity. Virtuous organizations are more functional — and not less profitable — than vicious ones. Thus an increasing number of professional associations, corporations and governments are hiring philosophical consultants to help them proactively manage and resolve moral dilemmas and kindred conflicts in the workplace, and to help formulate ethical and allied policy issues in the organization. The engagement of philosophical practitioners — as motivators to individual employees, facilitators to teams, counselors to management, and advisors to directors and officers — is increasingly necessary in the wake of the 30-year (and ongoing) deconstruction of higher education in America and Europe.

There are only three places remaining in the world in which centrally planned neo-Marxist economies still pretend to thrive. Needless to say, their administrations promote human suffering and prevent human flourishing primarily because of their die-hard anti-realist commitments to unworkable ideologies instead of best practices. While despotism persists throughout the world, the three remaining bastions of collectivist totalitarianism are Cuba, North Korea, and the North American academy.

---

[29] This latter point is well articulated by Mahathir bin Mohamad, "Globalization: Challenges and Impact on Asia", in *Recreating Asia*, eds. Frank Jürgen-Richter and Pamela Mar, John Wiley & Sons Asia, Singapore, 2002, 5–21.

The academy differs from these polities in that its centrally planned economy is one of thought, not goods. Unsound social theories, contempt for truth, intolerance of merit, confusion of right with privilege, and the imposition of insidious quota systems at the expense of substantive content have resulted in the drastic debasement of standards of literacy and numeracy in North American higher education. Neo-Marxist political indoctrination — mostly hatred for the West and its civilization — has replaced education in the humanities. Great books are censored, brilliant thinkers proscribed, freedom of speech and academic inquiry suppressed, and thought itself controlled, by proto-Stalinist and proto-Maoist university administrations. Their "vision" of higher education is the destruction of the mind-politic itself, without which the body politic cannot long endure. Thus America has become Rome in full decline: its military power is unrivalled, but its brain-trust is increasingly intellectually deprived and morally defective.[30] Most of today's college graduates, even of the formerly "finest" institutions, could not pass high-school leaving exams of a century ago.[31] The general state of ignorance is simply appalling, and attention spans as well as basic thinking skills continue to be attenuated by the historically unprecedented meta-paradigmatic shift from a written to a visual tradition.

Graduates of such a system also lack a moral compass. Brainwashed with the doctrine of cultural relativism, which asserts that anyone's beliefs about what is good or true or just are as valid as anyone else's, and mind-controlled by rabid political correctness, which refuses to utter truths that anyone might find "offensive," millions of Americans can no longer evaluate the political or moral difference between George Bush and Saddam Hussein, between a free and open society and a brutal dictatorship. Prior to 9-11, some leading American political and cultural figures (and apologists for its educational catastrophe) publicly defended Arab terrorists as "freedom fighters." After 9-11, only radical Islamic

---

[30] For example, see Allan Bloom, *The Closing of the American Mind*, New York, Simon and Schuster, 1988; James Traub, *City on a Hill: Testing the American Dream at City College*, Boston, Addison-Wesley, 1994; Alan Kors & Harvey Silvergate, *The Shadow University: The Betrayal of Liberty on America's Campuses*, New York, The Free Press, 1998. See also http://www.thefire.org

[31] See, for example, Ed Hirsch, Joseph Kett & James Trefil (eds.), *Dictionary of Cultural Literacy*, Boston, Houghton Mifflin Company, 1993. This book contains basic but vital knowledge that is no longer imparted in America's K-12 school systems, and without which College or University students cannot contextualize higher education. TV, video games and computers have supplanted reading, writing and thinking.

agitators, anti-realist academics and totalitarian administrators continued to blame Arab terrorism on America itself, and dared compare George Bush to Adolf Hitler. I reiterate that this political blindness and moral depravity originate and emanate from some of North America's "leading" universities, whose cultures of conformity censor open discussion and balanced debate.

Similarly, the Enron scandal highlights the dearth of ethical education in some American professions. If business ethics regularly attracts the label "oxymoron" (that is, "contradiction in terms"), which needs time and again to be painstakingly refuted,[32] what label does "accounting ethics" deserve in the wake of Andersen's role in the Enron case? Once again, education lies very near the heart of the matter. Professional practices that are recognized and regulated by legislation (for example, medicine, psychology, law, chartered accountancy) are also governed by stringent codes of ethics as well as rigorous standards of practice. While isolated individuals in every profession exhibit unethical behavior, which invariably brings them into disrepute, the reputations of professions themselves are maintained by the overwhelming preponderance of good over ill done by the vast majority of professionals. Public trust in medicine is not irreversibly eroded by any given case of malpractice, because of the overwhelmingly reputable services that health-care professionals render. Similarly, notwithstanding the well-deserved ill-repute of some unscrupulous lawyers in America's "shark-infested" seas of litigiousness, the legal profession's reputation (like every other) is enhanced by the good works of so many of its practitioners.

In particular, one defining criterion of every profession *except* accounting is the willingness of its practitioners to render a proportion of their services *pro bono publico* — for the public good (that is, free of charge). This is vital, both for helping offset the nugatory effects of individual instances of malpractice, and because professionals enjoy special privileges that carry correlative obligations to "give something back" to society. Why, one might well ask, does every reputable profession *except* accounting consider it a norm to offer *pro bono* services? I submit that accounting students are not properly educated about their professional privileges and correlative responsibilities. This is obviously a systemic failure, which can be remedied systemically without heroic measures. It is a matter of exposing all accounting students to professional ethics, in place of whatever ersatz has been on offer, and of

---

[32] For example, see Sterling Harwood, ed., *Business as Ethical and Business as Usual*, Jones and Bartlett Publishers, Sudbury, MA, 1996, part 1.

demanding that their professional development courses (required of all certified or licensed practitioners) devote sufficient attention to regularly exercising moral faculties. This would not prevent unethical individuals from practicing accounting; but it would enhance the repute of the profession and help restore public trust.

The decline of the West

Contemporary business ethics is based on a model of enlightened self-interest. When the "enlightenment" factor is overpowered by excessive (and therefore ultimately counterproductive) selfishness, or when self-interest and its collateral individual rights are subordinated to anti-realist or collectivist ideologies, we witness a failure of civilized progress, and a weakening of the ability of civilization to stem the perennial tides of barbarism and savagery ever-ready to engulf the human estate. Civilization is a thin veneer over savagery, maintained by a precious few for the sake of a great (and often ungrateful) many. Wherever civilization is allowed to wear away, either by external abrasion or internal neglect, the wear exposes and emboldens the most primitive and least salutary impulses of the human being. By contrast, wherever the best practices of civilized progress are implemented and defended, all forms of human flourishing and commodious society are made possible.

Large-scale philosophical, geopolitical and cultural analyses suggest that Western civilization, following its centuries-long period of ascendancy, is indeed in decline.[33] Although globalization is not (or is no longer) identified as a uniquely American phenomenon, the American penchant for catering to the lowest common denominator of consumer taste is nonetheless spreading world-wide. From McDonald's to reality TV, the bread and circuses of today's Rome are popular and profitable wherever they are permitted. Europeans are also succumbing to this trend. Their educational standards are likewise entering free-fall, playing catch-down with America. At the same time, social democracies like Canada have blazed retrograde trails from nanny statecraft to "velvet totalitarianism."[34] The European Union is politically fractured on the issue

---

[33] Famously, see Oswald Spengler, *The Decline of the West*, trans. Charles Francis Atkinson, A. A. Knopf, NY, 1928–1929, 2 vols. See also Kishore Mahbubani, 1999 (footnote 20).

[34] Phrase coined by John Furedy, "Ice Stations Academe: Is an Iron Curtain of Speech Being Erected in North American Universities?" *Gravitas*, Fall Issue, 18–22, 1994. See also Lou Tafler, *Fair New World*, Backlash Books, Vancouver, 1994.

of Arab terrorism, and some of its leading members are as unwilling to confront their historical responsibility for perpetuating current Middle Eastern conflicts as they are willing to appease the most belligerent of despots.

America has long held the unenviable job of policing the world. America did not start World War One, but ended it. America did not start World War Two either, but ended that too, at an incalculably higher cost. Two of the most pacific and prolific economic powers of the latter 20th century, namely Germany and Japan, resulted from regime change imposed militarily and politically by America.[35] America did not start the Korean War, but ended that as well (hopefully). It did not start the Vietnam War either, but also ended it though not, for a change, on its own terms. Nor did America start the Cold War, but outlasted totalitarianism and preserved freedom for the world, including some forgetful nations. America has also walked political tightropes, propping up dictatorships as the lesser of two evil forms of government, the greater evil being Marxist-Leninist revolutionary communism. Kishore Mahbubani has called America "the most benevolent great power in history," and he is historically correct (if politically incorrect, and more power to him).[36]

Yet America cannot police the world indefinitely. Its military might is supreme, like Rome's at the height of Empire, yet America was sacked by Al Qaeda's barbarians on September 11, 2001 as surely as Rome was sacked by Alaric's barbarians in 410 A.D. While American military power will protect democracy and capitalism to the extent that its citizens, beneficiaries and allies permit, America is also imploding from the deconstruction and decay of its own intellectual culture.

Thus the Enlightenment project, furthered by the likes of Hobbes, Locke and Mill, which helped separate church from state and state from business, which created the Western philosophical foundations for enlightened self-interest, emancipation and globalization, and which America inherited, translated into practice and shared with the free world, is now in dénouement. Enlightenment is being replaced by Endarkenment in America and the West. Hard-won and long-defended individual freedoms have been undermined by craven collectivist ideologies, promulgated from within the universities themselves, and now

[35] It is regrettable that, in the wake of 9-11, many French and Germans have conveniently forgotten the origins and defenders of their liberty and democracy. It took years to de-Nazify Germany and democratize Japan; one should not expect that de-fanaticizing the pan-Islamic world will require only months.
[36] Kishore Mahbubani, 1999, p. 130.

metastasized, like opportunistic political cancers, under the entire foundations of the culture. So-called "group rights" are promoted at the expense of individual entitlements, and the shrillest litanies of "historical disadvantage" have attracted the most unmerited favor. The creators of all that is best and noblest in Western civilization now stand accused of the "crime" of Western civilization itself. Thus the worst nightmares of George Orwell, Aldous Huxley and Ayn Rand[37] are played out daily in North American classrooms, courtrooms and boardrooms. Such a debased polity, bent on celebrating mediocrity, venerating untruth and undermining morality, is so contrary to Tao that it cannot long endure.[38] Arnold Toynbee understood this tendency perfectly, as he charted the demise of 50 civilizations along the sublime gradient of Taoist metaphysics.[39]

The current phase of the West's decline was foreseen most presciently by a handful of Teutonic prophets and artists of genius, including Nietzsche, Wagner, Mann and Spengler. The individual greatness of Germanic scientists, mathematicians, composers, literati and philosophers — so vital to the Enlightenment project — succumbed to the 20th-century totalitarianism of mass-movements spawned by communists and fascists, planting in either case a jackboot — whether left or right — in the face of high culture. The aesthetic decline continued with high art's forlorn hopes consigned in turn to impressionism, surrealism, Dadaism, Bohemianism, hippie counter-culture of the 1960s, and pop-culture thereafter. Thanks to Pax Americana's benign mass-marketing, which replaces jackboots with Nikes, Michelangelo's David nevertheless continued its descent into Warhol's soup-tin; Shakespeare's plays into trash TV; Bach's fugues into gangster-rap.

Yet 20th-century America remained overall the freest place on earth, although afflicted to this day with the legacy of slavery, and prone to intermittent bouts of persecution by assorted witch-hunters, prohibitionists, supremacists, holy rollers, McCarthyites and university administrators. It also remained the richest place on earth, largely because Pax Americana afforded Americans and others global opportunities to market contemporary breads and circuses, from Starbucks to the Superbowl. The American dollar remains the near-universal unit of currency, a symbol of unabashed opportunity and opportunism alike.

---

[37] See Huxley's *Brave New World*; Orwell's *Nineteen Eighty-Four*; Rand's *Atlas Shrugged*.

[38] "What is against Tao will soon come to an end." Lao Tzu, chapter 30.

[39] Arnold Toynbee, *A Study of History*, in 12 volumes, London, Oxford University Press, 1934–61.

The rise of Asia

The Tao compels complementarity: when one thing wanes, another waxes. Thus Asia will not rise because it necessarily deserves to do so. Nor will it rise because Asians will necessarily avoid their own versions of the ghastly, incessant and internecine wars of European Christendom that followed Rome's collapse, and which mostly ceased only through the imposition of the Cold War. Nor will Asians necessarily succeed because Arab terrorism has damaged the West's economy and jarred America's psyche: the American ethos was vulnerable before 9-11, weakened by three decades of escalating decadence, spoiled by three decades of orgiastic consumerism, stultified by three decades of dumbed-down education, and rendered culturally "brain-dead" by three decades of misapplied postmodern French philosophy.

Asia is rising because some place has to rise, and some place has to rise because America is sinking — more slowly than the Titanic to be sure, but probably much faster than Rome. The economic climate of Pax Americana, mostly stable and prosperous for a remarkable half-century, willingly engineered and abetted the evolution of global civilization, whose ablest architect is arguably the World Economic Forum. But as American culture succumbs from within, it gradually passes the torch. But to whom? Europeans are politically irresolute, while the UN is increasingly a relic of the Cold War. The Middle East, Africa and Latin America are (each for different reasons) far from progressively self-governing regions. Asians, however, are awakening to their potential greatness. Asia may become the next long-term custodian of global civilization.

Asia's philosophical traditions are intuitively deeper and metaphysically broader than those of the West, although less logical and analytical as noetic partners of science and technology. Nonetheless, Asian philosophical ethics are potentially much more conducive to individual fulfillment, social harmony, productive industry and political stability even than those of the Enlightenment. While the EU and NAFTA have coalesced into powerful trading blocs, the birthrates and educational standards of their constituents are declining. ASEAN's population alone is larger than either of them, and Asia overall contains enough people to sway and eventually to dominate world markets, provided of course that Asia evolves in constructive political and socio-economic pathways.

Since Asia is not only more populous, but also more culturally diverse than Europe or the Americas, it is worth asking what foundational philosophical system could possibly unify multicultural approaches to business ethics in Asia, or at least could provide a meta-ethical umbrella capacious enough to shelter a vast variety of indigenous (and not necessarily compatible) cultural norms. I believe that a judicious blend of secular Taoist, Confucian and Buddhist ethics would be most palatable and effective for a vast majority of Asians in business. The metaphysics of Tao underlie every human process, and Confucianism (as noted) persists in Asian familial life. Moreover, secular Buddhists ethics are compatible with every religious morality extant — even though religions are not always compatible with one another, and are too often incompatible with secularism.

I offer two compelling reasons why Asia shows promise as a guardian of global civilization. First, Asia itself has been home to several great civilizations, from ancient to modern times. Civilization is not therefore a foreign concept to Asians who, by extension, appear comfortable with the added factor of globality. Many Asians have mastered Western languages, cultures and customs; few Westerners have mastered Asian ones. Second, and more immediately, Asians of note from many countries are manifesting — with consummate Jungian synchronicity — a supremely vital virtue of any civilization: public scrutiny, leading to public remedy, of its most conspicuous defects.

Only thus, by open and balanced debate, can a nation entire achieve near-consensus on the proper way to rectify political and other large-scale errors. Unabashed and exuberant self-examination allowed the greatness of Western empires past to flower: Greece, Rome, Britain, America. Each of these constantly confronted, philosophically and publicly, its worst defects, and thereby each gradually improved its human estate. Now that Asians are becoming free and responsible enough to confront Asia's worst defect, arguably corruption, they can strive for consensus on the proper ways to rectify it. Nations that prohibit self-examination face much higher risks that their defects will worsen. Only the worst governments on earth, and the formerly best ones now in decline, refuse to confront and remedy their own failings, and seek instead to blame others for them.

Contemporary Asian philosophy faces two big challenges. First, it must provide an antidote to Islamic as well as other religious fanaticisms, which combine intolerance with proselytization, and which (along with communism and despotism) count among the greatest obstacles to modernization, globalization and the fulfillment of human potential. A protracted clash between Islamic and Judaeo-Christian civilizations is not a fruitful paradigm. Secular Buddhism may be able to debellate both overzealous factions. Second, Asian philosophy must provide a remedy to the endemic corruption of Asia, which plagues its political and economic development, and which will impede Asians from assuming lasting leadership roles in world commerce if it continues unabated.

It is clear from Transparency International's indices of perception that Asian corruption is deeply-entrenched.[40] Only city-states like Singapore and Hong Kong have managed to reduce it to tolerable levels, owing primarily to benevolent political will imposed on manageably small polities, reminiscent of Hellenic civilization. On larger geopolitical scales, however, the vicious circle of corruption is harder to break. The three main socio-economic causes of Asian corruption — low salaries, lack of better opportunities, and absence of law enforcement — produce effects that circumvent its cures.[41] Corrupt political elites partnering with unscrupulous investors can only inculcate the least desirable business behaviors in a polity. If Japan's political economy can defeat deflation, and if China's experiment with modernization succeeds, then Asian corruption will metamorphose in the process, and across the entire region.

One must remain in awe of the sheer potential energy of Asia, and of the willingness, vigor and courage of so many of its visionaries to confront and surmount even the most stubborn obstacles to progress. Thus, for example, do Islamic moderates like Karim Raslan denounce Arabian Islamic fanaticism, and champion the compatibility of Islam and modernity in Asia?[42] And thus, in a different sphere, does Zhu Rongji's unprecedented transformation of China's economy illustrate the advantages of economic sagacity over political ideology?[43]

While Asians are incorporating the best of Western democracy, science, technology, arts and philosophy into their political and socio-economic cultures, they should also invest more seriously in studying and applying comparative business ethics. Ultimately, it is for Asians to determine how indigenous Asian philosophies can best be utilized to enhance the virtues of corporate culture. But in my experience as a philosophical counselor and consultant, having served individual and organizational clients world-wide, Asians are at once the most practical

---

[40] See http://www.transparency.org/pressreleases_archive/2002/2002.08.28.cpi.en.html

[41] For example, see Jon Quah, "Comparing Anti-corruption Measures in Asian Counties: Lessons to be Learnt," *Asian Review of Public Administration*, 11, 1999, 71–86.

[42] Karim Raslan, "A Southeast Asian Plea for Moderation," in *Recreating Asia*, 2003.

[43] See, for example, Lawrence Brahm, "Zhu Rongji's 'Managed Marketization' of the Chinese Economy," in *China: Enabling a New Era of Changes,* eds. Pamela Mar & Frank-Jürgen Richter, John Wiley & Sons Asia, Singapore, 2003, 71–83 *et passim.*

and philosophical beings I have yet encountered. Americans can be as practical but are not on the whole as philosophical; Europeans can be as philosophical but are not on the whole as practical. Many Americans regard philosophy — even applied philosophy — as requiring intellectual effort, and therefore as something to be avoided. Many Europeans regard philosophy — even applied philosophy — as an intellectual luxury, and therefore as something mostly unaffordable. By contrast, many Asians regard philosophy — and especially applied philosophy — as supremely useful, something without which no human being can even begin to become a fulfilled individual, dutiful family member and constructive contributor to society. If the quality of one's life depends ultimately on the principles by which one lives, and the ideas which one most values, then Asian philosophy offers enriched prospects for viable business ethics in the global village.

Such prospects in Asia remain highest where governments are least corrupt, investors most scrupulous and educators most vigilant. Like packaged foodstuffs, governments should have "best before" dates, and should be democratically replaced before they expire. Investors in developing nations should study enough history to avoid re-enacting the dehumanizations of the Industrial Revolution, and thus to avoid fueling collectivism's perennial challenge to civilized progress. And educators must offer equal opportunities without compromising standards, and without socially engineering arbitrary outcomes based on wishful thinking or myopic visions of justice.

Ethical prospects and moral results are inevitably separated by a gap, which can be bridged by philosophical practice. If no bridge is built, then the gap between potential ethics and actual morality can widen into a chasm, which eventually becomes unbridgeable and swallows the potential itself, no matter how great. Philosophical practice would help Asians create a more invigorating intellectual climate, in which their rich indigenous wisdom traditions would be reconnected to their daily business affairs. This in turn would generate value as well as profit, so ensuring that the foundations of emergent Asian civilization, and its potential custody of global civilization, remain qualitatively robust, and not merely quantitatively compelling.

PART
2

Foundations

INTRODUCTION

Trying to understand the role of religion in public life and business in Asia is like trying to solve a puzzle that lacks clear boundaries or rules. "Religion" actually encompasses at least four major schools — Confucianism, Buddhism, Islam and Hinduism — in addition to countless sects, sub-sects and modern-day adaptations. There may be few distinctions between everyday practices of the "real" religions versus the merely popular. Moreover, religions in Asia have grown up over the centuries and sprouted across national boundaries, becoming socially embedded in multiple ways depending on the nation. That is, Islam in Malaysia bears very different traits from the same religion in Indonesia or the Philippines. Christianity in Korea is vastly different from the Christianity in the Philippines. Lastly, Asia harbors a multitude of different ways of practicing religion — at the personal and societal levels — which may relate neither to edict nor popular law.

The heterogeneity of Asian religions and social adaptations has had fundamental consequences for the way that religion has shaped business in Asia. While there are a few identifiable cases of religion directly shaping business, most modern-day adaptations of religion are barely perceptible. Falling into the first category may be businesses with ties to religion — such as the Trappist Dairy in Hong Kong, or shops or tour businesses operating out of Buddhist temples in Thailand. In the second category is "everything else", from the entrepreneur who brings his beliefs directly into building his business, through his social responsibility, to the leader who views visits to temple or church as a regular part of working life, to be undertaken by self and employees. One can even refer to daily exercises or prayers performed by some labor forces in an effort to cultivate a healthy attitude towards work and soul.

Given the many applications of religion in society today and the impracticality of gathering anecdotal evidence of the above, how can we trace the religion's imprints on business today? Certainly it must start with a review of religious foundations which touch economic life and the merchant class. One must examine how these noticeable traces have evolved into contemporary business practices, and how they may continue to be transformed and to transform, with new social or global developments. Religion gives us roots and an ethical grounding — which will inevitably leave marks on economy, or sustenance as one of humankind's primary activities.

This section is thus meant to provide our enquiry into ethics with an understanding of the foundations, both for the past and future. We thus examine — led by Asia's foremost experts in these areas.

Confucianism

The origins of Confucianism lie in the collection of sayings known as the Analects, attributed to Confucius (551-479 AD), a Chinese philosopher, and in ancient commentaries such as that of his disciple Mencius (372-289 AD). Confucianism is a system of ethical perceptions for the management of society. It is based on the practice of *jen* (sympathy) and human-heartedness, as shown in one's relations with others and demonstrated through adherence to *li*, a combination of etiquette and ritual, as a principle of cosmic order. It was Confucius's belief that if everybody lived up to his duties according to his position in society, the right political and economic order would prevail.

Buddhism

Based on the teachings of the historical Buddha, Siddharta Gautama (563-483 BC), Buddhism flourished first in India, later in Thailand and China, and finally in Korea and Japan. Buddha renounced the pleasures and materialism of this world to search for the truth. Through this quest he developed his basic principles for living. For him, suffering and release from suffering were the major concerns. Buddha saw the clinging to existence as the reason behind suffering. Such clinging to existence referred to the conditions of the empirical eternity namely, body, feeling, perception, will and reason. The transpersonal growth of the individual culminated in nirvana (salvation), which was possible through a thorough understanding of the profound metaphysics of Buddhist teachings inherent in the Noble Truths.

Hinduism

The nomenclature of Hinduism is used to designate the traditional religious structure of the Indian people. It is the most ancient of the world's living religions and, as such, it is a blend of ancient legends, beliefs and customs which has itself been adapted and blended with numerous creeds and practices. Common to all Hindus is the teaching of the law of *dharma*, a comprehensive term used to refer to that which determines our true essence or righteousness. *Dharma* is the basis of human morality and ethics, the lawful order of the universe and the foundation of all religion. For the individual, *dharma* is inseparable from *karma*, since *dharma* can be realized by the individual only to the extent permitted by that individual's *karmic* situation. *Karma*, simply put, can be understood as the chain of cause and effect in the world of morality.

Islam

Islam was founded by the Prophet Mohammed (570-632 AD) on the Arabian Peninsula. Even though today's Saudi Arabia and the main parts of the Middle East are geographically part of Asia, we do not consider Islam as a genuine Asian religion as we only focus in this book on Asia east of the Arab world and Iran. The fact that we included Islam as a major pillar of Asian thought is because Asia hosts the majority of Muslims in our world today — in India, Indonesia, Malaysia, Pakistan and Bangladesh. The Koran is considered the main canon for the social and spiritual life of Muslims. The five pillars of Islam are bearing witness, daily prayer, fasting, charity and pilgrimage to Mecca.

Of course, there are other important schools of thought, such as Shintoism or Zen that are indigenous to Japan, Taoism in China, and Jainism and Sikhism in India. Even Christianity has played a significant role, mainly in some former Western colonies.[1] However, in each of these

---

[1] The Philippines, with its long historic link with the Catholic Iberian world, for instance, may appear today more like a South American country than a member of ASEAN (Association of Southeast Asian Nations). France left many churches and French missionaries many followers of Christianity in Vietnam.

instances, these religions sprouted for the most part in isolation and did not spread widely. More importantly, their historical influence pales in comparison to that of the four main religions named above.

We accept a priori that religion in Asia — because of its characteristics as a value system, closely crossing over into philosophy — may strongly influence business and its conduct. This may be equally in the West. Studying the relationship between religion and economic behavioral patterns, the sociologist Max Weber, for example, suggested a connection between the rise of capitalism in the West and the Protestant ethic.[2] From this observation, Weber suggested that a person tends to unconsciously translate values from his religious beliefs into inspirations for his economic behavior. In this way, religion spreads into other aspects of life. Because Asia is heterogeneous in both religion and business practices, and yet has been the subject of attempts to generalize its values or the "Asian way of doing business," it is tempting to explore the fundamentals of business ethics for Asia. This is especially relevant in an area that quickly tends towards regional integration, where in 10 or 50 years time, those businesses which survive will be Asian businesses rather than Thai, Malaysian, Singaporean or other national businesses.

Tracing the impacts of religion on Asian business is particularly challenging for four reasons. The first stems from the fact that Asia is a continent of contrasts — in philosophies, religions, ethnic groups and cultural practices, economic systems and business styles. Even Western culture and symbols are adapted in highly diverse ways by different countries. For these reasons, among others, Asia has been "slower" than Europe or even Latin America in reaching unity or agreement on a variety of issues. One may even contend that Asia's divergences on cultural, political, religious and other perspectives are more severe than those which exist in other parts of the world.

The second challenge stems from the fact that the majority of Asia's nation-states are not driven by one dominant religion or philosophy alone. Several religions co-exist, in most cases harmoniously. For instance, in Japan, there are people who believe in Shintoism, different forms of

---

[2] According to Weber, Protestants believe in their individual efforts, trying to master their environment in the way they deem right while nourishing a strong work ethic. See Max Weber, *The Protestant ethic and the spirit of capitalism*, Los Angeles, Calif., Roxbury Pub. Co., 1996. In the face of this, the world is viewed as a material to be fashioned ethically according to a widely respected norm. This view is held to be responsible for the rise of Anglo-Saxon capitalism — as most entrepreneurs and businessmen in North America and the UK are Protestants by belief.

Buddhism and even Christianity, which is striking given that Japan's population can be seen as highly homogeneous. The average Japanese citizen tends to choose Shintoism for the rituals of birth, Christianity for weddings, and Buddhism for funerals. Thus, Japanese have taken ideas from abroad, absorbed them and mixed them with indigenous traditions and adapted them for their own purposes. Thus, Shintoism has been able to survive, despite the many challenges from other religions and beliefs, including "Western thinking" with the Meiji Restoration of 1868 and again after 1945.

Similarly, religion in China is a potpourri of several families of belief, including ancestor worship, Buddhism, Taoism, Confucianism and the ideology of Communism. This mixture created at least three common salient features: a belief system founded on the assumption that gods and ghosts not only exist but possess influence over human affairs; the mapping of a non-human realm mirroring the hierarchy and practical conditions of traditional social life and the subscription that fate and luck are the key determinants of life; and that luck can be manipulated. These three beliefs guide both spiritual and practical life through practices such as fortune-telling, "sweeping the grave" and feng shui. The overlap of religions and seemingly spurious beliefs can be illustrated nicely by the fusion of Buddhist temples and Shinto's shrines in Japan, as well as Confucian and Buddhist temples in China. In short, Asians tend to graft the new onto their old stems, without discarding the old.

The third challenge in studying religion in Asian business is that religion and philosophy in Asia are part of the same family, and often indistinguishable from each other. Confucianism, strictly speaking, is not a religion. It is a school of thought that affirms the real world and the unity of man with the universe; it is not oriented toward a transcendent extrinsic view of the world. While Buddhism, Hinduism, and Islam may be religions in the proper sense, they may all at various points tend more towards philosophy in addressing issues of epistemology and existentialism.

The final difficulty lies in the occasional misinterpretation of the link between Asian religions and economic behavior, starting with Weber himself who stated that the Confucian work ethic tended to exhort people to accept or adjust to their environment. Practitioners of Confucianism are not seen as actualized for material success, as Confucianism does not advocate individualism, which is the single major driving force for the success of Protestantism and the underlying rationale of the Anglo-Saxon economic world. Weber was, of course, proven wrong: the Confucian societies of Korea, Japan, Taiwan, Singapore, Hong Kong and China have been widely acknowledged to be the most successful economies in the years after 1945 — at least until the Asian crisis of 1997. The Confucian emphasis on consensus and obedience to authority and the propensity to save have been identified as some of the major drivers behind East Asia's past and current success. The Confucian ideal of the self as the center of relationships led to a new kind of entrepreneurial spirit and managerial style.[3] Weber may be excused for his misjudgment — Asia was a backward continent mostly engaged in agriculture when Weber expounded his theory. However, his case may teach us that universal theories meant to explain and steer economic processes across time and cultures are likely to mislead.

Study of the past is most useful when it yields clues on the present and future and, for that reason, we try to identify the principles which will guide future evolutions. The fundamental question for us, therefore, is: Based on current incarnations of religious belief, how will business continue to be shaped?

These four chapters thus present visions for the continued evolution of religion in modern business. These can form a backbone for our analysis. However, having acknowledged that they seldom exist in pure fashion, we must adapt our analysis to its non-canonical and highly heterogeneous existence today. The highly syncretic approach to worship in Asia is bound by the utilitarian, opportunistic and adaptive logic of religious practice on the one hand, and by the multi-ethnic and multi-religious nature of Asian societies on the other. Notwithstanding the multiple worlds of Asian ethics, we need some features as a basis for ethical behavior in Asian business:

- **Money and business exist for the social good.** The creation of wealth is seen as good, as long as it is used to support social or community enrichment. Likewise, business should always seek an existence firmly embedded within society and the pursuit of common prosperity.
- **Transactions have to be sustainable.** However, business always has to be conducted with due respect to the prevailing corporate environment. Unethical behavior has to be avoided. The ethical imperative to do the right thing is incorporated in all corporate transactions, leading to a strengthened sustainability of business.

---

[3] See Tu Weiming, *Confucianism in a Historical Perspective*, Singapore, Institute of East Asian Philosophies, 1989.

- **Sacrifice or goodwill will yield future benefits.** This is found in the religious principle of Karma, or the performance of good deeds today with the assurance that rewards will eventually come. This position combines an individual's concern for both self-interest and the interest of future generations.
- **Pragmatism outperforms dogmatism.** In contrast to Western models, there are no a priori best practices. The self in relation to the whole is more important than one single set of principles. Perceptions can change over time to adapt to changing environments.
- **Collectivism is favorable to individualism.** Asian religions are largely centered around multiple actors and decision-makers. This fits in well with the collectivist or team-based actions required in today's business world. It also reminds business of the force of globalization — that a company is never an isolated actor. Thus it lays a grounding for alliances, networks and partnerships.
- **Tolerance allows multiple growth.** As Asian religions are non-exclusive with regard to the free choice of faith, Asian business ethics should allow, and even promote, the existence of different or even competing opinions, concepts and transactions.
- **Performance over proselytizing.** Asian religions have devoted practitioners but generally steer away from evangelizing or the forceful conversion of non-believers. In contrast to Western missionaries, Asian believers would shy away from attempting to convert others, unless the appeal is first made by the other.

Thus it is clear that Asian religions harbor a wealth of positive implications for business grounded in strong ethics. Notwithstanding the many examples of malfeasance outlined in the first chapter (Why Ethics?), we believe that a return to religious principles — if not necessarily outright religious practice — holds much promise for those who seek renewal.

3

CONFUCIANISM
The uses of Dynastic Ideology:
Confucianism in Contemporary Business

Wang Gungwu

Director of the East Asian Institute, National University of Singapore

Scholars of the Confucian classics like the *Book of Change*, the *Book of Songs*, the *Book of History*, and the basic Four Books by Confucius and his disciples, would not be surprised to see the fresh interest in Confucian values in a modernized global world. The generations of literati down to the present who studied the writings that Confucius and his followers left behind believed that the concerns of these works were universal. The writings transmitted knowledge, and ultimately wisdom, that was distilled from the centuries of practical experience and observation inherited by humans in the course of reaching out for civilization. At the core of what Confucius considered to be universal were the moral foundations that enabled people to build a good society for this world. Qualities that were central for this purpose included the following: to be educated and thus to act humanely and righteously, to observe all the rites and duties of a family in a civilized society, to cultivate the trust of others through having a sense of shame or what today we would call conscience, and to be diligent in using the intelligence we have. Most of these ideas could have been directly useful to members of the merchant class. Underlying all these qualities was the idea of being true to oneself in this world. This was normally manifested in being filial, fraternal, respectful and loyal, qualities that are extendable from one's own family to the community, from domestic affairs to business and political activities, and ultimately to the whole social order embodied in the person of the ruler. It was not the intention of these Confucians that

this knowledge would later be identified as belonging to one region of the world and governing only the lives of the majority of the peoples living in China and its immediate East Asian neighbors.

The starting point, whether man (and the Confucian focus was on man) was born good or bad, was his capacity to learn and prepare himself to serve his family and community. This was mastered in stages, beginning with the discipline needed for self-improvement, most tangibly seen in behavior towards parents and elders and in the willingness to study the ethical values essential for social harmony and practical living. It was recognized that relatively few people could achieve enough self-improvement to provide the leadership that the larger polity would need. It was, therefore, all the more important that those who did were given the heavy responsibility to develop and protect the edifices of the civilized human condition. In the preparation for this larger duty, however, there was no place for the merchants who had their own specific roles to play. Far less was demanded of them. For them, there was no identifiable set of *business* ethics. There was only ethics and merchants would have to perform ethically like everyone else. The Confucians were not concerned that this lack of a respectable social position, and the strong constraints on the moral behavior of these merchants, eventually restricted their contribution to the commercial and industrial development of the East Asian world.

The "business" of Confucianism

Let me briefly review what the business of Confucianism was meant to be. Between Confucius and his disciples (5th–4th centuries BC) and the final emergence of the state ideology of Confucianism (end of the 2nd century BC) were several centuries of disorder and desperate wars. These were brought to an end by the unification of the Qin empire in 220 BC and the victory of the Legalists, one of the groups that despised all that Confucius stood for. The Confucians managed to survive the dangerous centuries. By stressing the values of benign governance through the employment of men of learning, the Confucians ultimately made themselves more valuable to the imperial court than those who stood for other schools of thought. By the middle of the Han dynasty, they were invited to provide the empire with an ideology for the long haul. Beginning with the reign of Han Wudi (141–87 BC), good governance became the business of Confucianism. From then on, the success of this ideology depended on the Confucian mandarins being able to balance the ethical criteria they considered vital with the compromises that were necessary for strong and stable governments to function. However reluctantly, this included increasingly harsh laws of punishment and a proliferation of institutions to extract revenues from all sectors of the population for the comfort and security of the realm. And, not surprisingly, these Confucians tightened controls over the rich merchants whom they regarded as not having any primary productive value to the state. On the contrary, successful businessmen had the independent wealth to play political roles and this the Confucians saw as disruptive to their responsibilities and a danger to the realm. Thus, matching their emphasis on harmony in an agrarian economy and paying critical attention to the interests of the peasant majority, the Confucian mandarins regulated merchant activities with great care.

For the purpose of this essay, the Confucian idea of profit is of particular interest. The idea was double-edged. On the one hand, Confucius's disciple, Mencius, made it abundantly clear that it was immoral of rulers to concentrate on profits for their respective states. His advice had stressed that the ruler (or the government) should not think of profiting himself or of engaging in activities in competition with his own people. At the same time, the advice also conveyed the idea that profit was something immoral, something that rulers and their mandarins should not seek but should leave to lesser people; that is, those willing to be merchants. On the other hand, such merchants were socially useful because their risk-taking trading activities could supply the people's different needs. What was needed was to have these activities controlled so that excessive profits through such activities as cheating, manipulating supply and demand to bring about higher prices, and corrupting public officials, were largely prevented. By insisting that ethical behavior in the marketplace be governed by the same ethical principles that applied to homes, families and all social and political relationships, the merchant classes were thereby severely constrained.

The consequences of this approach went beyond the areas of commerce. All society felt the heavy hand of the moral strictures that governed everybody's lives. Ethical principles that were backed by the Legalist foundations of administrative powers soon became absolute in themselves. The Confucians, whose qualifications led them to claim a monopoly of moral wisdom, were thus able to gather great power into their hands. This power affected relationships ranging from the patriarch in the family and clan to the heads of community organizations, and ultimately to the Son of Heaven and all the central and local officials and magistrates that he had appointed. And, by allowing the ethics of men who considered themselves to be morally superior to govern the laws of the land, the whole system of rule became authoritarian. Eventually, arbitrary power was increasingly concentrated in the hands of those who cared little for trade and indeed chose to know only that part of the economy that guaranteed revenues for the ruling house. Fortunately for these Confucians, none of the enemies of their moralistic ideology knew any better about wealth-making. For some 2,000 years, the mandarins were clever enough to adapt their revenue-raising methods to changing economic conditions as the population grew and lands were cleared and new wealth was produced. They never found it necessary to acknowledge that merchants contributed anything to the long-term welfare of a strong and stable empire. Fortunately, the rest of the population admired successful merchants, especially if their wealth made them philanthropic and thus respectable.

Consequently, merchants tended to adopt Confucian ideas about ethical behavior and practice in order to gain the favor of mandarins and even in order to survive in their trade. Over time, they managed that set of ethics well by mastering the rhetoric and the performance that were needed to gain themselves some respectability among public officials. And, in some cases, it can be shown, as among the Huizhou (or Xin'an) and Shanxi merchants in the 15th century, that their successful members managed to achieve high social status and won a degree of mandarin respect. Despite such exceptions, it became increasingly clear, especially after the fall of the Tang dynasty in the 10th century, that the aim of Confucians was ultimately to Confucianize the practitioners of business. This was their duty even if it was done at the expense of the economic development of the society as a whole. This is the reason why modern Chinese reformers, revolutionaries and social science scholars have judged Confucianism to have been an obstacle to progress and modernization. It has also led to the common view in the West, confirmed by the writings of Max Weber,[1] that Confucianism failed to encourage the kinds of innovation and competition among the merchant and artisan classes that made the industrial revolution possible in the West. This view has been further supported by the researches of Joseph Needham that explained why Confucian mandarins also did not encourage the advances in science and technology that supported that revolution.[2]

---

[1] Francis Fukuyama. *Trust: The Social Virtues and the Creation of Prosperity.* New York, Free Press, 1995 Thomas Menkhoff and Solvay Gerke. Eds. *Chinese Entrepreneurship and Asian Business Networks.* London, RoutledgeCurzon, 2002.

[2] Joseph Needham. *Science and Civilisation in China.* Vols. 1 and 2. Cambridge, Cambridge University Press, 1954.

Rejection

It is intriguing, therefore, to link Confucianism to business ethics today. This is especially so because Confucianism, as a body of thought that did not recognize such a thing as *business* ethics, has been replaced by modern ideologies such as capitalism, communism and socialism for nearly a century. As for the idea of business ethics, this refers to the struggle to establish an independent system of values that could somehow rise above the pressures of aggressive capitalism. How can we speak of these two in the same breath? On the one hand, where modern ethical systems are still supported by highly visible formal religions, the philosophy that embodies Confucian ethics is now virtually invisible. No state admits to endorsing Confucian schools or claims to follow Confucian teachings. There is no church and there are no priests. The mandarins and elite literati who were immersed in its classics for centuries are all gone. The surviving self-consciously practicing Confucians and their organizations are almost irrelevant in contemporary affairs. Although often described as Confucian, the Singapore government really owes it success to a colonial state that gives primacy to laws that protect property and trade and is distinct from the fact that its largely Chinese population accept as normal the underpinnings of Confucian values for their families and social relationships.

Business ethics, including the lack of it, on the other hand, is a subject that has become increasingly important and catches the headlines almost every day. Indeed, unethical behavior has become a matter of great concern among those who have come to believe in the importance of business and to depend on global market forces for their successes. But, despite the frequent calls for businessmen everywhere to embrace modern ethical ideas and practices, many in Asia are skeptical that the two words "business" and "ethics" can comfortably co-exist. In recent years, this skepticism has been fueled by the fact that the Enron debacle exposed corrupt business and accounting practices in the United States. That exposure has, at the same time, muffled criticisms of the cronyism and lack of transparency that led to the Asian financial crisis of 1997. Given the current uncertainty as to how ethics might regain its rightful place in business, it is appropriate to take another look at older ethical systems to see if there are any lessons to be learnt there.

Here is where Confucianism occupies a curiously ambivalent position. During the past century, it has been subject to much reappraisal in East Asia, especially among the Chinese. Its position today represents one that has been reached after much painful agonizing by the Chinese about how this tradition can still serve the present. The attacks on it had begun during the crucial decade after the May Fourth Movement of 1919. Within a few years, there was a revolt of the young against the shackles of an ancient "feudal" philosophy. This was stimulated by the injection of Western philosophical and social science writings translated from their Japanese versions. They reached the reading public largely through newspapers and magazines in which fierce and exciting debates encouraged all those ready for rebellion to reject everything to do with the "imperial" state and the Manchu Qing dynasty. The most prominent of the rejects was the ideology which had been used to support the political system in one form or another for some 2,000 years.

The young were the most articulate in denouncing the uselessness of these outdated values that did not help China defend itself against the powerful West. These rebels did not always agree as to why Confucianism was no longer useful. Many reasons for rejection were proffered. The three that attracted the most support represented the views of the disillusioned literati, the frustrated businessmen and the radically minded who sought a total change in direction. In each case, the opponents focused on the role that Confucian mandarins had played in the political system. The mandarins were now held to have been responsible for a "failed state" — both the imperial system that had just been dismantled and the warlord regimes that could not win support either within and without. We know the result of their opposition. They set out to replace Confucianism by importing value systems from the West that could help China survive the efforts to break it up and thereafter help to make China safe and prosperous again. One large group chose the direct route of nationalism as the means to build a new powerful nation-state. The other large group resorted to the new communist internationalism that would unite all oppressed peoples against an exploitative imperialism dominated by Western powers and an aggressive Japan. As it turned out, neither can claim to have been responsible for the economic successes of Chinese entrepreneurs that have led the world to talk of "the rise of China" today.

The frustrated businessmen within China during the past century, who had their own reasons for rejecting Confucianism, found themselves left out of the efforts to modernize China. Their need for a value system that would enable them to compete with the capitalists embedded in the Treaty Ports all over China was not satisfied. Their choices were limited if they wanted to be on the winning side. They could choose to support the nationalists, but these politicians tended to see businessmen as people who were likely to place profit before country and therefore had to be closely controlled or at least frequently squeezed for political funding in order to demonstrate their patriotism. The opposing communists were even more unsympathetic. Their ideologues were inclined to treat all businessmen as potential capitalists who would, if given a chance, be all too ready to exploit the laboring classes who leaned towards the communist party. There was for a while a third choice, but this was open only to the few businessmen who worked for, or with, foreign firms which enjoyed extraterritorial rights in and around the Treaty Ports. These so-called compradores and their local partners could do well for a while, but they knew that they would have to prepare for a nationalistic backlash one day.

Thus, although deeply committed to ethical behavior at all levels of state and society, Confucianism had become, by the end of the 1920s, irrelevant in so far as it played no publicly acknowledged part in nation-building, nor in the idealistic visions of international socialism, least of all in the shaping of modern business ethics. As a result, for the next five decades, the image of Confucianism among at least two generations of young Chinese was increasingly negative, either as something dead and gone or something they wanted to see the end of. But, despite all that, there continued to be books, articles and debates that indicated that the ancient "imperial" ideology was not easily dismissed. What is most interesting was the fact that, during the 10 years of the Cultural Revolution, from 1966 to 1976, Mao Zedong and his radical young supporters found it necessary to direct their destructive urges against all residual Confucian elements in Chinese society. By that time, there were no businessmen in China for the Maoists to attack, so no links with the question of business ethics were associated with these destructive attacks. But these attacks suggest that the roots of Confucian values were still deep and even the most revolutionary efforts could not ensure the total uprooting of the values from the thoughts and practices of most Chinese.

The attacks remind us of a paradox in the modern story of Confucianism. At the level of state ideology, it was killed off, and all efforts to revive it, or replace it with something similar, seem to have been doomed to failure. For example, the republican state, whether nationalist or communist, modeled itself on France, the United States and then the Soviet Union, and that model did not have anything to do with Confucianism. It became inconceivable for Confucianism to survive in the state system. But this was not necessarily true at other levels of society, notably outside the cities where agrarian families remained stubbornly loyal to select bits of popular Confucianism. In addition, there is evidence that Confucian values have survived in a variety of East Asian communities, especially in Korea, Taiwan and even Hong Kong, even though not necessarily among young modern professionals trained in

Western ways. Among the Chinese themselves, however, the difference was most marked between the people on the mainland during the Maoist regime and those Chinese who were living outside.

Inside Communist China, those who could still live in the more private world of the family, whether in village communities or relocated in towns and cities, could still hope to hang on to many Confucian values in defining the place of parents and children, households and neighbors, and even their respective roles as good citizens or comrades. As business transactions were limited, there is little evidence that ethical concerns depended in any way on Confucian moral precepts. Among Chinese outside the mainland, however, the responses at each level were better recorded and it is obvious that they were much more varied. For example, despite the advent of the nuclear family which led to diminishing extended-family arrangements, traditional social and cultural habits, and kinship, locality and trade organizations that sustain them, have been kept alive. The nexus between family and business in every country (including those where the Chinese are minorities) appears to have found fresh strength by adapting itself to local customs and modern laws and to an increasingly more intrusive modern nation-state. Thus, wherever the family business remained a dominant vehicle for economic activity, family values continued to be important. In most cases, traditional practices prevailed, although increasingly protected by legal systems that favored property ownership and business trustworthiness. That the traditional practices worked reasonably well when modified in this way may be seen in the continued prevalence of the family firm that is still run in well-established ways.

The survival of certain aspects of Confucian ethics under very unfavorable conditions warns us to be careful about what we mean by Confucianism today. How can it be so openly discarded by so many of the "best and brightest" Chinese for the past hundred years and yet be a factor in social life and economic activity today? Why do people still think that this set of values has retained a meaningful place in Chinese (and Korean, and possibly also Japanese and Vietnamese) social and business life? I am not convinced that the reason lies in the totality of Confucianism as a philosophy. More important are two factors. The first is the basic universalism in the core ideas of Confucius about family and the social order — not the exaggerated accretions in later commentaries, but those expressed in the *Confucian Analects*. The second is the way Confucianism was constructed for political ends, and then pared down and re-shaped over the centuries in the face of deadly challenges from foreign conquests or imported new ideas. This enabled its core values to be gradually adapted to deal with social change. In the context of business ethics, the universalism affirms that business should take into account the natural bonds of family and kinship and build the edifice of trust around that understanding of basic human relations. When that was understood and the family-based business structure became viable, it was easier to reconcile business with the goals of the state. Business gained official respect not only because many more mandarins were drawn into business activities and the state depended more on them for revenues. This happened also because, after the 15th century, many more merchants became literate in the classics and mastered the language so that they could integrate Confucian ethical concerns with their business practices. In this way, Confucian doctrines embodied in the state system could be utilized to support business needs. The strictures in earlier versions of Confucianism against the rise of merchant classes were steadily diluted as merchants gained credibility as people who cared for the value system as a whole.

In short, Chinese businessmen developed their own traditions about the relevance of Confucian ethics in their transactions and relationships during the past five centuries. Through empirical means, they selected the concepts they found useful and integrated them into the corpus of business handbooks. These orthodox demands to be humane, righteous, correct, intelligent and trustworthy did not need much philosophical elaboration. Like the aphorisms of Samuel Smiles, they formed the basis of business bonding both within and outside the kinship groups from which the businesses were built. And, insofar as these were shown to contribute to a prosperous and responsible merchant class, they in turn modified Confucian strictures about them.

How important then are Confucian ethical values for businessmen today? Why should businessmen look to Confucianism when there are fully developed legal systems now? Do businessmen succeed because of their Confucian ways or despite them? Even if businessmen claim that Confucian ethical values are important to them, is that only true of them individually for their self-cultivation, or do they believe that their success depends on more businessmen behaving in correct Confucian ways?

Recombination and survival

From the above, it is clear that there are different kinds of Confucianism. Of these, Confucianism as a dynastic ideology is gone forever. If it were to recover a place in the corridors of power, it would have to adapt to the rhetoric of republics, to new standards of freedom, to the calls for democracy, equality and human rights. I would not underestimate the plastic nature of the ideology. It had adapted many times before. It had accepted the need for some of the savage penal codes of Legalism; it had tamed but not dismissed the millennial and egalitarian ideals of the peasantry; it had been reinterpreted to accommodate not only the compassion of the Buddhist faith but also the subtleties of Buddhist metaphysics; it could also adapt to the different cultural needs of the Korean, Japanese and Vietnamese peoples; and, to cap it all, it survived the discriminatory "barbarian" controls of the Khitan, Jurchen, Mongol and Manchu conquerors and went on to demonstrate to them all that Confucianism was essential to their rule in China. Who is to say that it will not adapt again?

But if it does, what would survive from its original formulations and what would be the main new ingredients? Clearly, Confucius's emphasis on the educability of man is likely the most appropriate and resilient value for the new knowledge economy. It needs one modification; to extend "man" to include women, and that has already been widely accepted. There is now nothing un-Confucian about the growing number of women following modern professions and taking technical and engineering degrees. Another is the idea of self-discipline that may be tied to the willingness to take on hard work and responsibility, on the one hand, and saving and investment, on the other. The first has readily been modernized for office and factory routines and procedures, and the second plays an economic role that may be compared with the great virtues of the Protestant ethic in Europe.[3]

No less important is the quality of trust that goes together with honesty and reliability. It may not be the kind of trust that Francis Fukuyama associates with large industrial and capitalist enterprises, but it is still the cornerstone of family businesses that remain the backbone of most small and medium enterprises today.[4] As long as there is the perception that this kind of trust leads to the dependence on kinship structures and encourages nepotism and cronyism, it is uncertain how its Confucian version will serve the larger corporations. But it is instructive to observe how the Japanese had translated filial piety and loyalty from family to feudal lords and then to modern corporations. That had never been regarded as un-Confucian and there is no reason to believe that

---

[3] R.H. Tawney. *Religion and the Rise of Capitalism: a historical study*. London, John Murray, 1926.

[4] Max Weber. *The Religion of China: Confucianism and Taoism*. Translated and edited by Hans H. Gerth, with an introduction by C.K. Yang. New York, Macmillan, 1964.

others in East Asia will not learn from that experience. The challenges of the global market economy, however, may not allow this kind of loyalty to continue for long, but we should note that loyalties have been transferable when accompanied by suitable rewards that are both measurable and predictable. If that leads to new ethical formulations, I expect it will be found that there is nothing un-Confucian in that either.

Two aspects of the reality today are *not* found in the Confucian classics; the rule of law and the wealth-enhanced status of the merchant classes. Confucianism as ideology had embraced a large body of administrative laws as the path to political and social order for the dynastic state. We know that, although more tardily and reluctantly, Confucian mandarins did adopt laws that were needed for economic order and development. Whether that willingness to adapt will eventually lead to something deeper like the rule of law at all levels of society is still not clear, but I expect that pragmatism will decide on this issue when it becomes necessary. As for the status of merchants, this is likely to be very different from the past. For example, the position of the merchant as trans-border entrepreneur, and as industrialist, financier and activist in local and international political affairs, is contrary to the Confucian order. Any recombination of Confucian ideas and institutions will have to take into account the power of the business classes in the service of the modern state. Again, it is useful to examine the role of modern business in Japan, Korea, Taiwan and Hong Kong where interpenetrations of politics and business have not required the explicit rejection of Confucian values. Should this condition continue to evolve, and Confucian ethics remains relevant to the social and economic relations among the business classes, it may have considerable influence on how business and political power in the People's Republic of China today may be reconciled.

It is notable how the government in Beijing has become extra sensitive to the problems created by corruption. They proclaimed a series of new measures against the businessmen and the officials involved. This show of determination could lead China in two different directions; either towards a new judicial structure aimed at ending unethical practices before which no one was exempt, or back to the older mandarin-like control of the merchant classes. Whatever emerges after these changes, the result may not be recognizable as the Confucianism found in the history books, but it will demonstrate once again that any rigid description of an unchanging China cannot be sustained. Confucianism has been massively adaptable because the core of its ethical values is small and can be universally applicable. But possibly the most important underlying factor is the fact that Confucius offered a this-worldly approach to state and society and that, up till now, this attitude is the best suited to the post-Enlightenment secularism that the West has bequeathed to our globalized age.

There is no reliable data to say how many enterprises today depend on Confucian values for their success. Individual businessmen, mostly from various parts of East Asia, may claim that the strictures of hard work, discipline and saving for investment have helped them start their businesses, and that, in educating future generations in the complexities of modern business, we must include basic values like trustworthiness and sincerity in all dealings. But far more important, and increasingly so, is the ability to compete and to do so speedily and accurately. And, clearly, those who are now best equipped to compete aggressively owe nothing to Confucianism. We know that there is nothing to prevent businessmen who have followed useful bits of Confucian values to adapt to new technologies, including methods of management and innovation. It may be that businessmen will find that accommodating new attitudes towards high-tech competition would itself be nothing un-Confucian.

This leads me to conclude that Confucianism still has its uses for those who carry its traditions in some form; that is, for those Chinese, Koreans, Japanese and Vietnamese who admit to living by some Confucian values in their daily lives. For the businessmen among them, the relevance of these values to their work, especially when interpreted freely and couched in modern language, is probably unconscious and self-evident. On the other hand, I do not see Confucianism being transmitted hereafter as a body of thought, even as a secular religion of some sort, to people outside of East Asia, to those who have not been immersed in its long and complex history. But I do expect the core values that I have described above to survive as a recombined set of principles among those people who have directly experienced its benefits. As long as East Asian leaders in politics, business and the professions find the principles useful in their respective communities and are convinced that they do not stand in the way of meeting the challenges of globalization, these values will find new strength and relevance. Should these recombined values prove effective in assisting the rest of the world to meet new crises, other societies and economies may find them rational and enriching. In time, that would give the ideas of Confucius a chance to regain the universalism that Confucians have always claimed.

4

BUDDHISM
Saving Business through Enlightened Ethics

Pipat Yodprudtikan
Chief Executive Officer, ThaiName.com Ltd., Thailand
and
Phra Saneh Dhammavaro
Director, Academic Affairs Office

Today's society has evolved by embracing the ideals of capitalism, ideals which recognize materialistic development as the real development of mankind. This materialistic society is founded on almost-unlimited technological development which often has the capacity to decrease our natural resources, harm the environment and threaten ecological equilibrium. While the rich countries consolidate their wealth, the poor countries become more indebted and the gap continues to widen.

The challenge facing our generation is: "Do we need to continue our obsession with material wealth?" Ironically, we all believe that the well-being of society is determined by something we call "the quality of life," but we still measure this by the quantity of material possessions. Do we really comprehend the meaning of "the quality of life"?

In looking for a solution to today's problems, it is easy to despair. There is, however, a ray of hope. Our world is now full of conflict and disharmony — between individuals and society, and between people of different races, nations, ideologies and religions. When we look at these problems from the Buddhist perspective, we can certainly say that all problems are universal and are of human origin. People are responsible for these problems and they themselves can find the solution. The unique aspect of Buddhism for the modern age consists in the fact that it embodies a world-view and a philosophy of life that centers around ethico-religious values. The whole body of the Buddha's teaching is practicable. It paves the way to cultivate peace and happiness for all who sincerely follow. Understanding the basic Buddhist principles from a socio-ethical perspective will prove highly rewarding in this regard.

The basic teaching

After attaining enlightenment, the Buddha concentrated on preaching his doctrine mainly for the moral uplifting of mankind through the cultivation of virtues such as friendliness and charity, wisdom and compassion, renunciation and meditation, and non-violence and loving-kindness. He taught the people and showed the way of purity, peace and happiness, here and hereafter. We call his teachings "*Dhamma*."

The term *Dhamma* is variously translated as doctrine, truth, law, norm, duty and nature. The *Dhamma* is held as the essence of Buddhism and is regarded as being more important than the Buddha. He himself regarded the *Dhamma* (doctrine) and *Vinaya* (discipline) as most important and placed them as the guiding principles for his followers.

For 45 years the Buddha wandered and taught his numerous doctrines to people. He taught different doctrines to different kinds of people according to their situation, tendency and potential. His main and most essential doctrines are The Four Noble Truths and The Noble Eightfold Path.

The four noble truths

The Buddha begins his first Noble Truth with the primary indisputable fact that suffering (*Dukkha*) is associated with all stages and conditions of life. In other words, all things are transitory, are void of any essential reality, and are the subject of suffering. The Buddha explains the term "suffering" in the following words:

> "Now this, O Monks, is the Noble Truth concerning suffering. Birth is attended with pain, decay is painful, disease is painful, and death is painful. Union with the unpleasant, and any craving that is unsatisfied, that too is painful. In brief, the five aggregates which spring from attachment are painful."[1]

Dukkha, therefore, incorporates imperfection, the pain of impermanence, disharmony, discomfort, irritation and the awareness of incompleteness and mental suffering, birth, decay, disease, death, union

---

[1] *Sacred Books of the East.* XI, p.148.

with unpleasant things, separation from the beloved and unsatisfied desire. Also, our attachment to the whole five elements of our body is a cause of suffering. In brief, suffering arises when human beings are ignorant about the different natural phenomena connected with life.

In his exposition of the second truth, the Buddha examines and explains how suffering (*Samudaya*) arises through various causes and conditions, including He:

> "… craving which gives rise to rebirth, which is accompanied by delight and lust, now taking pleasure in this and now in that, namely; craving for sensual pleasures, craving for recurring existence and craving for annihilation."[2]

The Buddha has shown that the main cause of suffering is desire or craving (*Tanha*); that is, the craving for pleasant experiences, the craving for material things, the craving for eternal life and the craving for eternal death. Such cravings are not related only to sensual pleasure, wealth and power, but also to ideas, views, concepts and beliefs. Craving arises out of ignorance; that is, failing to understand the reality of experience and life or not taking things as they really are. Under the delusion of self and un-realization of *Anatta* (non-self) a person clings to things which are impermanent, changeable and perishable. The failure to satisfy desire through these things causes disappointment and suffering. This Noble Truth deals with the examination and explanation of the origin of life's problems.

After expounding on the origin of suffering, the Buddha teaches how suffering can be ended. Cessation of suffering refers to a state of being when a person has gotten rid of the defilements of desire (*Raga*), ill-will (*Dosha*), delusion (*Moha*) and ignorance (*Avidya*) completely and permanently through the acquisition of true knowledge. Only such a person will finally attain *Nibbana*.

Human craving causes a renewal of existence in the cycle of rebirth which, in turn, leads to continuous suffering. The way to extinguish this suffering is to destroy the craving for existence. The Buddha explains it thus:

> "It is the destruction, in which no passion remains, of this very thirst; the laying aside of, the getting rid of, the being free from the harboring no longer of this thirst."[3]

---

[2]   Ibid.
[3]   Ibid., p.149.

The path leading to the cessation of suffering is called "the Middle Path" (*Magga*). It is very comprehensive, what might be called an "integrated therapy." It is designed to cure the disease through eliminating the causes, through treatment that applies not only to the body but also to the mind. The Middle Path is also called the "Noble Eightfold Path."

The Noble Eightfold Path

Right Understanding: This simply means acquiring the knowledge of the Four Noble Truths. In other words, it is the understanding of oneself as one really is.

Right Thought: Right Understanding leads to clear thought; that is, thinking without desire, anger or wilful harm. In other words, it is thinking removed from covetousness, wrath and foolishness.[4] It is the thought to abandon sensual pleasure, selfishness, hatred and ill-will. It is also the thought to abstain from doing harm to any living being.

Right Speech: Right Speech means timely, truthful, and useful speech. It also deals with abstaining from telling lies, from slander, from backing-biting, from insult, from harsh words and all malicious speech which might harm others. In its positive sense, it means to speak kindly and with tenderness to others, and to be modest in referring to oneself.

Right Action: This means good, moral and honorable conduct — refraining from killing any living being, from stealing and from sexual misconduct. In its complete sense, it means to perform only actions which do not cause pain and suffering to oneself and others.

Right Livelihood: This path expounds that one should earn one's living by peaceful and honest means, by abstaining from bad occupations or trades which cause suffering for others. Thus, it is forbidden to trade in arms, in human beings and in flesh through, for example, breeding animals for slaughter or manufacturing/selling intoxicating drinks and poison.[5]

Right Effort: This is the intentional action taken towards achieving a moral life and consists of (i) the endeavor to discard evil that has already arisen, (ii) the endeavor to prevent evil arising, (iii) the endeavor to develop un-arisen good, and (iv) the endeavor to promote the good which has already arisen.[6] In short, it is the effort to abstain from and destroy evil, and the effort to cultivate and develop goodness and maintain it.

---

[4] Kogen Mizuno, *The Beginning of Buddhism*, trans, by Richard L Gage, Tokyo, Kosel Publicating; 1983, p. 55.

[5] Narada Maha Thera, *The Buddha and His Teachings*, Singapore, Singapore Buddhist Meditation Centre, 1973, p.184.

[6] Ibid.

Right Mindfulness: This is the stage of eliminating the unsteady and fleeting mind, concentrating on deep meditation and contemplation of ourselves. There are four applications of right mindfulness. The application of mindfulness is to contemplate body, feeling, mind, and the *Dhammas*.[7] Right mindfulness of these four objects leads to eradication of misconceptions with regard to desirability and the so-called permanence of happiness and the immortal soul.[8]

Right Concentration: Right effort and right mindfulness lead to right concentration or single-mindedness. A concentrated mind acts as a powerful aid to see things as they truly are by means of penetrative insights.[9] It is the stage of freeing oneself from feelings of happiness and unhappiness.[10]

Thus, the Middle Path reveals itself as a gradual perfecting of the mind to the highest wisdom and insight of the true facts of life. It can also be classified into three stages; namely, *Sila* (ethical conduct, which includes steps 3, 4, and 5), *Samadhi* (mental development, which consists of steps 6, 7, and 8) and *Panya* (wisdom or insight into the real nature of things; that is, steps 1, and 2).

The characteristics of Buddhist ethics

Buddhism can be said to be an embodiment of social welfare, social harmony, and social peace. In other words, Buddhism refers to a code and a way of living. This means there are no marked differences between Buddhist theory and Buddhist ethics. What we call Buddhist teachings (*Dhamma*) and precepts (*Vinaya*) are mainly intended as methods for educating and training members of a Buddhist community. These doctrines and disciplines are a set of general guidelines which help individuals, as well as society, travel the path of happiness, and also enable the individual to attain the final goal — *Nibbana*. In this sense, the virtue of Buddhism is rooted in its ethics, of self-responsibility, self-training, self-determination and moral judgment.

Buddhist ethics begin with the individual's conduct and expand to society as a whole. It is up to each individual to strive towards moral

---

[7] See Ledi Sayadow, *The Noble Eightfold Path*, Kandy, Buddhist Publication Society, 1985, pp.56-58.

[8] Narada Maha Thera, Op. Cit., p.184.

[9] Ibid.

[10] Harbans Singh and Lalmani Joshi, *An Introduction to Indian Religion*, Delhi, Kailash Colony Market, 1973, p.133.

improvement and self-purification. In other words, everyone is responsible for their own actions — good and bad, past, present or future. There is no other power, whether human or divine, which can make a person good or bad. Thus, each individual can mould his own destiny only through what Buddhist ethics call "self-responsibility."

Generally, the emphasis in Buddhist ethics is on motivating people to be good in their mental, physical and verbal actions, on controlling their thoughts, actions and speech so as not to harm any living being. Observance of such virtue plays a great role in improving individual and human society as a whole.

Essentially the whole body of Buddhist ethics is dealt with and summarized in three simple principles: keeping away from all evil deeds; cultivating good habits/deeds, and purifying the mind.[11] This is the advice given by the Buddha. Each individual, however, is free to think and use reason to decide what is right or wrong. By reasonable thought, by abstaining from evil, by following a moral code, by developing and purifying his mind, he will be able to live a more prosperous life here and now, both materially and spiritually.

Autonomy

One of the most distinguishing features of the Buddhist ethics is the concept of the autonomy of our "will." According to Buddhist ethical principles, each individual has to strive for salvation through his own power. Each in his own path has to struggle for moral improvement and spiritual enlightenment, the attainment of which entirely depends on his own effort. No one else, human or divine, is able to do this for him.

In the course of his teaching, the Buddha made reference to three erroneous ideas about the happiness and misery of this life:

> "There are, O monks, some people who maintain and believe that all the pleasures, or pain, or indifference to pleasure and pain, that this person feels, are results of his acts in previous births. There are some people who maintain and believe that these are all results of creation by the lord of the universe. And there are some who think that all these have neither reason nor cause."[12]

Here, the first group believed their actions had been decided by a previous life and thus no moral improvement was possible. The second

---

[11] Dhammapada, Verse 183.
[12] Anguttara Nikaya, I, p.173.

group believed that the happiness and misery of their present life was the outcome of divine interference and so they were not to be blamed for their offence. The third group believed there was no cause or reason for their present condition and everything happened by chance. The Buddha refuted such ideas by presenting the doctrine of "causation" or the doctrine of "deed" or *Karma*.

According to the Buddhist doctrine of *Karma*, our present birth is the result of the accumulated *Karma* performed in our previous existences and our present different dispositions are also determined by our previous *Karmas*. Though this makes the Buddhist doctrine of *Karma* seem fatalistic in character, it is not completely so because an individual can mould his own fate in the next birth through his actions, the will being free. There is no one to interfere with the individual's fate, and destiny continues to happen regularly as the individual ordains it, without any digression, through the law of causation. In other words, we have the key to our fate in our hands throughout our repeated births. Improvement or degeneration, ascent to heaven or descent to hell, happiness or misery are all the results of our own deeds. Buddhism emphasizes the freedom of the will. Autonomy is a prominent characteristic of this religion.[13]

The doctrine of *Karma* is nothing but "intention," which includes volition, will, choice, and decision or the energy which leads to action. Intention is what instigates and directs all human actions. It is the agent or prompting force in all human creation and destruction. Therefore, it is the actual essence of *Karma*.[14] As the Buddha says,

> "Monks, intention, I say, is *Karma*; having willed, we create *Karma*, through body, speech, and mind.[15] ...Whoever is the owner of a *Karma* will also be the heir of their *Karma*; the *Karma* is their womb from which they are born; their *Karma* is their friend, their refuge. Whatever *Karma* they perform, good or bad, thereof theirs will be the heirs."[16]

Neither being nor external force can handle the operation of the effects of *Karma*, *Karma* itself will yield the results as a neutral operation of the law of cause and effect. Good begets good, bad begets bad.

---

[13] S.Tachibana, *The Ethics of Buddhism,* New Delhi: Cosmo Publications, 1986, p.92.

[14] Bhikkhu P.A.Payutto, *Good-Evil and Beyond: Kamma in the Buddha's Teaching*, Bangkok: Buddhadhamma Foundation, 1993, p.6.

[15] Anguttara Nikaya, III, p.415.

[16] Nyanatiloka, Buddhist Dictionary, Taiwan, The Corporate Body of the Buddha Educational Foundation, 1987, P.77.

Pleasure and pain are the results of good and bad *Karmas* committed either in the present life or in a previous life. Buddhist ethics function as a process of cause and effect.

Practicability

Practicability is another characteristic of Buddhist ethics. Buddhism holds that there should be no distinction between ethical theory and moral practice. The theory is regarded as imperfect without practice. The former always presupposes the existence of the latter.[17] There is no meaning if there is theory without practice. Buddhist ethics teach individuals how to behave towards others, the main objective being to help people live harmoniously, happily and peacefully in society, and ultimately, to attain perfect freedom, or enlightenment by rooting out ignorance, which is the root cause of suffering.

According to Buddhism, there are many kinds of knowledge and truth. Some of them are not useful, having no concern with solving the problems of life. The Buddha did not teach such truths and was not interested in finding out about them. He concentrated on teaching only those truths which would be of practical benefit.[18] In *Patthapada Sutta* of *Digha Nikaya*, the Buddha declined to answer metaphysical questions such as, "Is the Universe finite or infinite? Does it have a beginning?" He did so because "such problems are not conductive to the purpose, and to the *Dhamma*. Such questions do not lead to disenchantment, to dispassion, to cessation, to higher knowledge, to enlightenment, and to *Nibbana*."[19] The only purpose of the Buddha's teaching is to bring about the extinction of suffering. The Buddha was convinced of the impossibility of purification except through practice.

Universality

Another characteristic of Buddhist teaching is its universality. *Buddha-Dhamma* is the natural truth, applicable to all mankind without distinction and discrimination. One of the Buddhist precepts (*Sila*), for instance, is to

---

[17] Vyanjana, *Theravada Buddhist Ethics*, Calcutta: Punthi Pustak, 1992, p.57
[18] Bhikkhu P.A.Payutto, *Towards Sustainable Science: A Buddhist Look at Trends in Scientific Development*, Bangkok: Buddhadhamma Foundation, 1993, p.65.
[19] Maurice Walshe (tr.), *Thus Have I Heard*, London: Wisdom Publication, 1987, p.164.

abstain from killing. This precept is universal because it is not restricted to a particular person or group, but can be practiced and applied by human beings of any faith, race, language, caste or nation. Kamala Jain observes, "Every religion or social system has accepted (*Sila*) as the basic code of conduct for all individuals, in relation either to his own self, or to the society of which he is a part. Whosoever neglects these basic principles, which are both social as well as spiritual, is considered pernicious to himself or to society; he is a sinner or a criminal."[20]

It is noteworthy that Buddhist ethics are accompanied by an adherence to the doctrine of *Karma* — action (which conceives of the individual as the inheritor of his deeds and the sole maker of his future destiny) — which underlines the potential perfectibility of the individual and therefore the need for individual exertion for its attainment. Buddhism does not rely on any conventional authority, and refuses to deal with any traditional morality, it itself being free of all religious dogmas, class distinctions or convictions.[21]

The principle of loving-kindness (*Metta*) also shows that a desire to kill or the act of killing is improper as it involves violence. It is a universal and timeless truth that all living beings are entitled to happiness and do not like to live with hatred, suffering or misery.

Freedom of acceptance

There is no compulsion or threat to follow the Buddha's disciplines and doctrines. He merely pointed out the consequences of actions, both good and bad, in such a way that everyone would be able to investigate, consider, analyze and prove in the light of their own experience. Hence, following the *Dhamma* is an individual decision. In this sense, the Buddhist precepts and disciplines are not commandments.

The system of Buddhist ethics is "a study of the consequences in every phenomenon, a reaping of some previous sowing"[22] and is as powerful as the domain of physics. Though there are neither rewards nor punishments in the future world, there is the law of cause and effect. The Buddha himself says that he only shows the way to achieve happiness, freedom and salvation. But whether they choose to follow such a way is

---

[20] Kamala Jain, *The Concept of Pancasila in Indian Thought*, Varanasi: Parshvanath Vidhyashram Research Institution, 1983, p.240.

[21] G.S.P.Mishra, *Development of Buddhist Ethics*, New Delhi: Munishiram Manoharlal Publishers Pvt. Ltd., p.54.

[22] P.Lakshmi Narasu, *The Essence of Buddhism*, New Delhi: Asian Educational Services, 1993, p.62.

up to each individual. He always teaches individuals to remain masters of themselves through self-reliance and not to surrender their dignity or free will. His guidelines in this regard are revealed in *Kalama Sutta*:

> "Do not accept anything based upon mere reports, tradition, or hearsay,
> Nor upon the authority of religious texts,
> Nor upon the logic and inference,
> Nor upon reason,
> Nor upon some theory,
> Nor upon one's own speculative opinions,
> Nor upon another's seeming ability,
> Nor upon the consideration – these are our teachers."[23]

The religion of the Buddha is a come-and-see religion,[24] and not a come-and-believe one. The Buddha once asked one of his disciples, Sariputa, "Do you believe what I have been explaining to you?" Sariputa answered, "Yes, I see that it is so." The Buddha asked him, "Are you saying that just out of faith in me?" Sariputa answered, "No, I answered in agreement not because of faith in the blessed one, but because I clearly see for myself that this is the case."[25]

According to Buddhism, people are advised and encouraged to believe and accept anything only after careful observation and analysis, and only if they are certain that the method agrees with reason and is conducive to the good of all. Buddhism allows people to use their own judgment; no one is asked to embrace Buddhism without first having an understanding of its teachings.

Non-violence

Non-violence may be said to be another important characteristic of Buddhist ethics. Buddhism encourages caution in action, word and thought so as not to harm any creature. Buddhist ethics are directed towards achieving harmless behavior.

Inner purity

In Buddhist ethics, more importance is accorded to the purity of inner life. The emphasis is on internal practice rather than on external exercise. The

---

[23] Anguttara Nikaya, I, P.173.
[24] Mishra, Op. Cit., p.73.
[25] Samyutta Nikaya, V, p.220.

mind must be purified from ignorance and craving. Greed, hatred and delusion must be rooted out if perfect peace and real happiness are to be enjoyed. Controlling the mind to purify the inner life by eliminating unwholesome roots, and living together happily and harmoniously in mutual respect and understanding is the basis of Buddhism's social ethic.

Freedom from suffering

The ethics of Buddhism find practical expression in the various doctrines, and its disciplines are nothing but general guidelines pointing the way to an inner freedom from all defilements, suffering and ignorance. Attaining freedom (*Vimuthi*) is the keynote of Buddhist practice.

The place of Buddhist social ethics

The spiritual principles of religion must be translated into social values, ideals and interests. Buddhist ethics are not concerned with the next life but with this life and the suffering of human beings. The main teaching of the Buddha is to solve the problems of human life and to make society better. The Buddha, indeed, intended to establish a new society in the midst of a host of various socio-religio-philosophical tendencies in his time. His teaching is deeply concerned with improving the conditions of human life —material welfare as well as spiritual development and inner freedom.

It is, therefore, a wrong view to hold that Buddhism is only concerned with personal salvation. Some have thought that *Theravada* Buddhism, the spiritual life, lacks doctrines dealing with social affairs and urges the individual to retire from social involvement, to become a recluse in a monastery, uninterested in doing something of benefit to the rest of society.[26] Such a misconception results from an improper learning and understanding of the teachings of the Buddha.

In both the life of the Buddha and in the *Buddha-Dhamma* there is no idea of escaping from the problems of human existence. On the contrary, his teachings require people to free themselves from the illusion of self-ignorance, from defilements, and to cleanse their hearts and lead a life of righteousness. When the Buddha started his religious missionary activities by sending the first group of 60 *Arahants* (holy ones), their purpose was to uplift individual conduct and to develop their spiritual value, which

---

[26] Siddhi B. Indr, *The Social Philosophy of Buddhism*, Bangkok: Mahamakut Buddhist University Press, 1973, P.11.

leads to improvements in social well-being and social happiness as a whole. He instructed them as follows:

> "Go ye now, O Monks, and wander, for the gain of many, for the welfare of the many, out of compassion for the world, for the good for the gain, for the welfare of Gods and men."[27]

When we carefully consider the entire doctrine of the Buddha, we understand that it is absolutely involved with our present world. The essence of his teachings indicates only what is to be done and what is not to be done here and now. He emphasizes the suffering (*Dukkha*) of mankind; how to erase such suffering and to achieve peace and happiness. He places humanity at the core of his teachings. This idea of proper living is held as the place and significance of Buddhist social ethics.

The basic tenet of social ethics is concerned with mankind as a whole. The socio-ethical ideas are born out of the intention to establish peace and happiness in society. That is why Buddha first laid down five fundamental moral principles (*Panca Sila*) for lay Buddhists to follow: (i) abstinence from killing any living being, (ii) abstinence from taking what has not been given, (iii) abstinence from adultery, (iv) abstinence from speaking falsehood, (v) abstinence from taking intoxicating drinks.[28]

A well-developed society: Good member of society

Each member of society has a responsibility to establish, maintain and develop social well-being. A well-developed society, according to Buddhist ideals, is one of peace, harmony and welfare. Such virtues must begin from individual conduct. Buddhists believe that society is an agglomeration of individuals whose characters, good or bad, determine the character of society. Buddhism favors permeation, infiltration, and evolution of a good society through good people.[29]

Buddhism is a religion founded for the development of human beings, by a human being. If society is to survive and grow strong in our present world, it is imperative for us to work towards reinforcing the social structure with the desirable qualities preached by the Buddha. This will be truly possible only through developing both our inner and outer qualities; that is, moral and spiritual development is necessary.

---

[27] *Sacred Books of the East*. XIII, P.112.
[28] Anguttara Nikaya, III, P.151.
[29] Winston L. King, *In the Hope of Nibbana*, USA: The Open Court Publishing Company, 1964, P.241.

Individuals must be trained to have good thoughts, speech and actions. They need to be guided how to earn a living in relation to others. The Buddha gave the guidelines for bringing the fundamental development of human society through ethical practice. There are four kinds of development, into which inner and outer developments are integrated. These are:

Physical Development (Kaya Bhavana): This involves the development of the body as well as the material world. This development enables people to obtain the basic needs of life — food, clothing, shelter, health care, and a healthy natural environment.

Social Development (Sila Bhavana): This involves the development of good relationships with other individuals, with the community and with the social environment. It can be realized by observing at least five precepts (*Panca Sila*) and by following the Buddha's principles of social justice.

Mental Development (Citta Bhavana): This involves the development of such internal qualities as love, compassion, sympathy, joy, equanimity, mindfulness, concentration, mental strength, and perfect mental health. The practice of meditation enables the development of these mental qualities and helps purify the mind of all defilements, as well as emotional and mental illness.

Intellectual Development (Panna Bhavana): This involves the development of the intellect through knowledge and wisdom. This includes a high capacity for perceiving and learning, independent thinking and judgment and for seeing all things as they really are. Intellectual development is achieved through the practice of insight meditation.[30]

Physical development and social development are necessary for the achievement of outer peace; that is, peaceful coexistence with other human beings and the natural environment. Mental development and intellectual development are necessary for the realization of inner peace, or peace of mind. The four aspects of development have to go together to achieve balance in life. To emphasize one at the expense of the other may cause a person to slip into one of two extreme positions. A person who is obsessed with physical and social development, neglecting mental and intellectual development, may fall into the extreme of sensual indulgence (*Kamasukhallikanuyoga*), whereas a person who is obsessed with mental and intellectual development at the expense of physical and social development may fall into the extreme of self-mortification (*Attakilamathanuyoga*). The middle way consists of the balanced development of these four aspects of life.

---

[30] Anguttara Nikaya, III, P.106.

Our society seems to be on the brink of collapse on account of man's greed, covetousness, hatred, immorality and delusion. People of different groups, blocs, nations, races, castes, ideologies, and even religious faiths are in conflict with and killing each other, expending vast resources and energy on producing deadly new weapons to destroy each other.

Everyone seems to be thinking only of immediate gains in wealth and power, ignoring the far-reaching *Karma* effects of their actions on themselves, on others and on the natural environment. These are the root causes of our progressive disintegration and continue to infect our lives with fear, distrust, misunderstanding and strife, and to breed insecurity.

We need to rekindle self-awareness. If the individual in the society expresses concern for the long-term results of his actions and modifies his behavior in accordance with sound socio-ethical principles, there will be a drastic transformation in the current situation.

No one would dare to do things that harm others if they realized that their present actions will create bad *Karma* and suffering for themselves in the future. If such awareness could be brought about on a large scale, we could certainly say that morality in society was being revived and a new society could be born in a healthy environment.

Good conduct evolved out of a proper understanding of human nature and man's role in society is the core of social ethics. Many great thinkers, philosophers and religious leaders have established codes of socio-ethical principles and the Buddha is one of the most prominent of these. His code was qualitatively different from earlier codes of conduct. In the Buddha's scheme of things, there is no role for a god, an unseen or supernatural power, to influence the individual's *Kamma* or destiny.

According to the Buddha's socio-ethical principles, all things originate from and reflect the individual. When the individual attains perfection, society is spontaneously transformed. The Buddha did not exhort every individual to attain *Nibbana*. In the Buddha's scheme of things, every individual could travel the path of *Nibbana* at his own pace and according to his own will and strength of determination.

Buddhist ethics emphasize individual conduct. If the individual is good, automatically society will also be good. The development of the individual and the betterment of society are the objectives of Buddhism. Whatever the teachings of the Buddha are, they are practicable to one and all universally.

Since the Buddha's teaching is natural law, not commanded or supernatural law, there is no idea of force in its practice and belief. Buddhism believes that man is free to choose to believe and practice according to his own preference. However, it is suggested that, for a peaceful and happy life, he should choose to practice only what is going to bring benefit to himself and others. Whatever is harmful or leads to ruin for self and others should be avoided.

Purification of individual conduct and the development of spiritual values is the yardstick by which to measure an individual's status and quality. There is no classification of people on the basis of birth, caste, creed or profession in the teaching of the Buddha. These things lead to social injustice and inequality. Men are born equal in nature — high or low, noble or ignoble, good or bad depends on each one's moral conduct and spiritual purification.

In order to make this idea a concrete feature, the Buddha therefore established a new society of monks to which people from all walks of life regardless of their background and gender were wholeheartedly admitted. Its members have preserved and carried forward through centuries the message of the Buddha for every new generation to follow. Buddhist monks (*Sangha*) have been preserving the Buddha's *Dhamma* for the last 25 centuries. Monasticism is vital for the personal training in Buddha *Dhamma*, in lived-out truth.

It is important to note that, historically, in all fields of Buddhist society men and women were equal. The Buddha founded a community of woman monks with equality that still prevails in our present era. According to Buddhist history, there were many nuns (*Bhikkhuni Sangha*) who attained the Buddhist ideal: the state of *Arahant* or *Nibbana*.

For the welfare and happiness of society, and particularly for the affairs of ordinary people, the Buddha indicates the necessity for a balanced development of both the moral and the material aspects of life. However, he placed greater emphasis on moral development, because only moral people can establish and maintain real peace and happiness.

Buddhist ethics in a business environment

Business or "busy-ness" seems somehow at odds with the Buddhist goal of peace. The main characteristic of business is to make material wealth, usually unending. The current business environment is too much influenced by capitalism, with the effect that people think only of themselves and of how to make maximum profit without concern for their social responsibilities.

But the quest to "maximize profits" usually comes at a cost to others. Often, it is the government which has to take responsibility for repairing the environmental, social and cultural damage inflicted by irresponsible businesses. To do so, it spends its citizens' taxes. Today's business needs a framework to prevent such damage.

An example of how this can be done can be seen in Thailand in the "sufficiency business" initiative[31], which derives from the philosophy of the sufficiency economy addressed by H.M. King Bhumibol Adulyadej. In this environment, business will balance human capital, physical capital, social capital, and environment capital in its organization. The nine guidelines[32] for business to achieve this are:

1. Use appropriate technology (optimum technology with minimum cost).
2. Use every material saviest and worthiest.
3. Avoid using technology to replace people where it's not necessary (except where this will cause damage to products).
4. Obtain production capacity which is manageable and controllable.
5. Don't be greedy or focus only on short-term benefits.
6. Be honest; avoid taking unfair advantage of customers, suppliers and employees.
7. Spread risk by having a variety of products and/or flexibility to adjust production.
8. Reduce risk by utilizing in-house or in-community capital; avoid creating unmanageable debts.
9. Produce goods and services which serve the local market first, then the regional market and then world market.

"Sufficiency Economy"

"Sufficiency Economy" is a philosophy bestowed by His Majesty the King to his subjects through royal remarks on many occasions over the past three decades. The philosophy provides guidance on appropriate conduct covering numerous aspects of life. After the economic crisis in 1997, His Majesty reiterated and expanded on the "Sufficiency Economy" in remarks made in December 1997 and 1998. The philosophy points the way for recovery that will lead to a more resilient and sustainable economy, better able to meet the challenges arising from globalization and other changes.

---

[31] ThaiPat Society, ThaiPat Background (Sep, 1999), http://www.thaipat.com
[32] Edited by Prof. Dr. Apichai Puntasen, author of *Buddhist Economics*.

"Sufficiency Economy" is a philosophy that stresses the middle path as the overriding principle for appropriate conduct by the populace at all levels. This applies to conduct at the level of the individual, families and communities, as well as to the choice of a balanced development strategy for the nation so as to modernize in line with the forces of globalization while shielding against inevitable shocks and excesses that arise. "Sufficiency" means moderation and due consideration in all modes of conduct, as well as the need for sufficient protection from internal and external shocks. To achieve this, the application of knowledge with prudence is essential. In particular, great care is needed in the utilization of untested theories and methodologies for planning and implementation. At the same time, it is essential to strengthen the moral fiber of the nation, so that everyone, particularly public officials, theorists and businessmen, adheres first and foremost to the principles of honesty and integrity. In addition, a balanced approach combining patience, perseverance, diligence, wisdom and prudence is indispensable to cope appropriately with critical challenges arising from extensive and rapid socioeconomic, environmental, and cultural changes occurring as a result of globalization.[33]

Under this program, businesses are classified according to their willingness and readiness to participate as follows:

Level 1: Monetary Contribution — This is the entry level for any organization that is willing to adapt itself to the concept. The business donates a certain amount of its profits to charities or other social organizations that support the community.

Level 2: Resource (working hours) Contribution — This is the intermediate level, where employees devote a certain number of working hours to participate in community service along with other businesses at this level. They also perform a mentoring role for businesses in Level 1 to help prepare other organizations to move to the next level.

---

[33] *The Chaipattana Foundation Journal*, "Sufficiency Economy: Direction of the Ninth National Economic and Social Development in Pursuit of His Majesty's Philosophy", Dec, 2000, http://www.chaipat.or.th/journal/dec00/eng/e_economy.html

Level 3: Mind Contribution — This is the highest level, in which the business owner, executives and staff practice ways of thinking, planning, strategizing for their business in accordance with the nine guidelines so that their business operates automatically in accordance with the sufficiency business concept.

In line with this, the structure of the business accounting system has also been developed so that it can be understood by the public. The new structure is an extension of the old dual-aspect accounting system invented by a 15th-century Franciscan monk, Lucas Pacioli, which concentrates only on what happens within the business entity. The new system, namely the four-aspect accounting system, also takes external factors. Table 1 illustrates the differences between the two systems.

Table 1: Differences between the dual-aspect and four-aspect accounting systems

Dual-aspect	Four-aspect
1. Focuses on self interest	1. Focuses on balanced interest
2. Internal entity concern	2. Internal/External entity concern
3. Benefits shareholders	3. Benefits stakeholders

The first portion of the four-aspect system is the traditional accounting system relating to current business. It consists of income statement and profit/loss statement, which concern only activities inside the entity. The second portion of the four-aspect system also accommodates the activities of outside entities, reflecting the social, community and environmental effects on the stakeholders as a whole.

Table 2: Sample of income statement items in the second portion of the four-aspect system

Revenue	Expenditure
– Net profit (domestic portion)	– Social cost
– Employment value	– Environment cost
– R&D value	– Culture cost
– IP value	
– HRD value	

Sufficiency business is based on Buddhist principles of self-reliance (*Attattha*), self-satisfaction (*Santosa*), moderation (*Mattannuta*) and the middle path (*Majjhima patipada*). These are the principles of Buddhist economics. The Buddha encouraged the individual to balance both moral and material values. In the same way, a business should also balance its capital to create both internal and external values. Individuals within such an organization can look after their material development while, at the same time, developing moral values by participating in activities that make a contribution to society.

Conclusion

It is good to remember that the Buddha walked into a world which was in total chaos. There was no binding force to bring all different people under one faith and make them strive for a good purpose in life. In the absence of such a binding force, people lived like animals, causing each other a lot of suffering and pain. While the rich and the powerful had wealth or power to help them get whatever they wanted, the poor and the downtrodden had no way of making a decent living. Moved by their misery and suffering, the Buddha developed his socio-ethical principles, convinced that a healthy society could be one which evolved out of a moral order. The essence of Buddhist socio-ethical principles is to help people become aware of their own ignorance regarding their birth and the very nature of their existence. These principles also enable them to determine their own future and destiny and help them understand that these principles are natural laws and objectively verifiable truths. Violating such ethics creates severe problems — individual, social or global — and these are caused by man himself. But they can also be solved from within man himself. Training humanity is only the way to solve those problems. The Buddha laid down three ways of training — moral (*Sila*), mental (*Samathi*), and spiritual or wisdom (*Panna*). The systematic approach to this three-pronged training is aimed at individual and social well-being, spiritual excellence and mental freedom. When the individual achieves moral and mental excellence, the society also progresses. So instead of thinking about changing and improving society, Buddhism aims at improving individuals, which automatically leads to social change and social progress.

This paves the way to social peace and happiness, with every member of society living together in mutual trust and understanding, working to be free from the defilements of greed, selfish desire, anger and hatred. This is a society where individuals cultivate the feelings of loving-kindness (*Metta*), compassion (*Karuna*), sympathetic joy (*Mudita*), and equanimity (*Upekkha*) within themselves and towards all living creatures.

By following these three patterns of training, people will live happily without selfish desire and hatred. Everyone is imbued with the feeling of responsibility for the welfare of themselves and others on the basis of good will, compassionate love, sympathetic joy and equanimity.

On the basis of the ethical concepts in Buddhism discussed above, it can be concluded that an individual has to be a righteous and virtuous person. Achieving such virtues, the individual has to attain self-control, self-confidence, self-discipline, self-examination and self-salvation. Society is the aggregate of the individuals who live within it. The society which comprises such virtuous individuals will emerge to be a modern society of mutual respect and mutual understanding, of peace and happy co-existence.

5

HINDUISM
Remaking India: Values, Society and Business

Sundeep Waslekar

Founder of the International Centre for Peace Initiatives and
President of the Strategic Foresight Group, Mumbai

Why question the functioning of India's value framework at this stage? Policy change is fine. In any case, it takes place from time to time. Structural transformation is okay. It creates some disturbance, but it is inevitable. Values are the deeply held beliefs of people. To question them, or their practice, is to assume that something needs to be changed at a very basic level.

At first glance, India is performing well. The GDP growth rate has improved to 6% since the 1990s — discounting a year here or there. Poverty has declined to 26% of the population. Our granaries are full with 58 million tonnes of surplus food grains. Our democracy enables a poor woman from a backward caste to head the country's largest provincial administration. In some sectors, the country seems poised to lead the world. India is confident of finding a permanent place in the UN Security Council, if and when the highest body in the world is reconstituted. We meet the software needs of 185 of the Fortune 500 companies. Our authors and beauties win international titles. We have one of the most diverse media in the world, with Bollywood as famous as Hollywood, and *The Times of India* with the largest circulation on earth. A few companies have succeeded in the global marketplace and more will follow. There are difficulties but management reforms in government and business will address them. If something more serious is required, we can always review current policies.

The elite often reacts to concern for India's crisis of values with derision. Prime Minister Indira Gandhi used to say that corruption was a global phenomenon. Today's nationalists cite examples from American to Russian businesses to prove the point. President George Bush's willingness to pour US$100 billion of taxpayers' funds into the Iraq war is seen by many as an open scam. In South Korea, the president sanctions secret loans to Hyundai to invest in the North. In Mozambique, Carlos Cardoso is killed for investigating bank fraud. In Ukraine, Georgy Gongadze is decapitated and burnt for exposing the misdeeds of the government. In Colombia, narcotics networks dictate terms. There is a global crisis of values, and global institutions will address them. Why worry about India?

The issue is not that, beyond the first glance, India's global performance is dismal in these days of globalization. It's not just that the country is in the bottom one-third of most international indicators — human development index, per-capita income ranking, growth competitiveness scale and corruption perception index. It's not just that it attracts only US$2–3 billion of foreign exchange, as compared to US$50–60 billion in neighboring China. It's not just that our companies have not created any global brands. It's not just that our sportsmen do not win gold medals in the Olympics. The issue is not merely that we do not succeed in a competitive global economy.

The issue is that India as a nation has failed to actualize itself. It has the potential but it is not being realized. In 1750, the country accounted for 24.5% of the global manufacturing output. At present it is 1%. Clearly a decline has taken place. Until independence in 1947, Indians in India won Nobel prizes in literature and physics. Now, Indians living abroad, or expatriates living here, do so. Those who can afford to emigrate reject the country by obtaining a green card. Others reject it by launching separatist agitations in Jammu and Kashmir, the Northeast, and elsewhere.

The issue is does India really want to focus on realizing its potential? Bernard Shaw once wrote: "You see things; and you say 'Why?' But I dream of things that never were; and I say 'Why not?'" To raise the question "Why not?" underpins faith in India's future. A mere policy review cannot answer this question. Structural changes are inadequate. A much deeper probe is required.

Sustainability

It is in the spirit of Shaw's "why not" that an inquiry into India's value framework is essential. In fact, it is urgent. For first glances are often deceptive. What appears is often not there and what does not appear is there. The truth is many-a-time hidden in layers of realities. Those who wish to preserve the status quo miss the view beyond the first glance. But it is in their self-interest to be aware, so that they can sustain themselves in the long run.

India's famous classic *Panchtantra* tells the story of two village friends, Shakti and Bhola. Shakti is a smart businessman. Bhola is a simpleton. Shakti asks Bhola to join him in the city to earn riches. On their way back, he persuades Bhola to deposit their wealth in a chasm in the forest. As Bhola falls asleep, Shakti collects the treasures. Shakti then lives in opulence, while Bhola continues to lead a simple life.

Years pass, Bhola begins to ponder whether he too can improve his lot, and suddenly remembers the hidden treasures. He asks Shakti to join him on a visit to the forest. Together they dig in the chasm and find it empty. Shakti, the smart one, accuses Bhola of stealing the wealth. They decide to go the village headman for justice. The headman returns to the chasm with Shakti, Bhola and a large number of witnesses. Since there is no evidence of the crime, they ask the Forest God, as per the village tradition, to name the culprit. A voice from a nearby tree pronounces Bhola to be the guilty man. Shakti is relieved.

Feeling frustrated and dejected, Bhola decides to kill himself. He collects some dry leaves and arranges them around the tree, which had just convicted him. Smiling, Shakti watches as Bhola sets the tree on fire with a view to leaping into it. Suddenly there are screams from the tree. Shakti's father, who is hiding inside the hollow trunk of the tree pretending to be the Forest God, is engulfed with fire. The villagers realize the machinations of Shakti's family. They banish him from the village immediately and confiscate all his property.

In the age of *Panchtantra*, Shakti could enjoy his riches for several years. In those days, the rich and mighty could maintain their hold on the society because of ignorance and a rigid social structure. Today's information revolution has raised the awareness of the weak and the poor. The debate on regulated or free market is over. The debate on captured or fair market is just about to start. Those who capture markets can gloat over the capture of the state and judiciary as well, but not for long. In the days prior to the information revolution, regulation of markets lasted for half a century. The capture of markets is bound to be much more short-lived. Internationally, terrorists and anti-globalization activists have already upped the ante. Within the country, too, rising violent conflicts sound a warning.

It was possible to deregulate the market with new economic policies. But to prevent the capture of the market, the state, the judiciary and all other institutions, it is necessary to dismantle the prevailing mental framework.

While researching for a recent report of the Strategic Foresight Group, *Rethinking India's Future (1)*, we discovered that the India that we believe is one, is actually divided sharply into three economies. The Business Class economy, consisting of the people who form the market for consumer durables, cars, mobile phones, and credit cards, comprises only five million households or 2% of the country's one billion population. The Bike economy, comprising another 15% of the population, consists of people on the periphery of the market, with the purchasing power of its constituents limited to television sets, telephones and housing with basic amenities. The remaining 83% of Indians belong to Bullock Cart economy, which is outside the market.

The 2% elite cannot sustain themselves forever, surrounded by 98% periphery. It is not a question of inequity. Almost every Western country has 2% or 5% or 10% of wealthy citizens. They constitute the periphery, whereas the heartland is made up of a large middle class. Those who control the market are not allowed to capture the state, the judiciary, the press and all other institutions of the society. To have 2% elites is normal; to have them at the core rather than the periphery of the nation, is not sustainable.

The issue of sustainability has not found a place in the Indian public debate. Globally, too, sustainability is still defined mainly in ecological terms. Until the 1960s, growth was never questioned. In the last 40 years, the West has understood the limits to growth. It has initiated a project to balance relations between human beings and the environment. It is yet to realize the need to balance relations amongst human beings, despite the World Trade Centre, Seattle, Florence and Prague. India, too, misses the point, despite Assam, Gujarat and Kashmir.

There is no doubt that the fabric of humanity is being torn apart by forces of greed. Terrorist groups, and their state sponsors, personalize this force. But there is another side of the story — grievances. For economists in planning commissions and corporate headquarters, economics is business. For India's poor masses, economics is life. Poverty, for the poor, is measured not in terms of statistical indicators, which may provide evidence of improvement. Poverty is measured in terms of their ability to meet socially defined expenditure. Poor people feel poor not only when they consume less than 2,500 calories a day. They also do so when they see a minister's daughter hosting a lavish wedding, not because of her own accomplishments, but because of her father's control over the public treasury. Poverty is then seen as a result of absence of power. Those who are born in power-endowed families, tend to be rich. Those with less power-endowment, tend to be poor, however competent they may be. Investment reforms are introduced so that colas and perfumes can be availed of easily by the endowed segments of the society. Land reforms are aborted half way, so that those who are really competent may not eventually overtake those who are merely born in the right families.

A friend of mine who is a good runner, always used to complete the famous New York marathon. She believes that once you cross half the distance, it is most important that there are other people with you. It's only then, you will be able to reach the destination. If you go ahead alone, it is quite lonely in the front. You think you are winning the race, but you are not able to complete it. It is, of course, different in the Olympics. You are not alone; the crowd is one with you with its cheers. In the marathon of life, you sustain if you can carry others with you; not if you leave them behind.

In *Rethinking India's Future*, we have surveyed violent conflicts in India. Foreign sponsored terrorism and greed for extortion plays a role in protracting them, especially the conflicts in border regions. But the root cause of all strife was found to be the exploitation of farmers and the neglect of agriculture, leading to unemployment and a sense of deprivation in the rural economy. Added to this is the closed political space, arising from its monopolist control by dynasties, landlords and small urban elite. The frustration caused by closed economic space and closed political space pushes the energy of youth to violence. As the fire spreads, the elite cannot escape.

India's conflicts are still limited to a few parts of the country. There is a lesson to be learnt from neighboring Afghanistan, Pakistan and Nepal. Monopolist control of agriculture, the creation of classes of a privileged few in cities through expansion of the state sector, and the capture of political institutions by a few has generated a demand for violence. In Afghanistan, warlords of today and Taliban of yesterday woo the dejected youth, as Al Qaeda will do again tomorrow. In Pakistan, clerics use latent frustration to create battalions of religious extremists. In Nepal, the Maoists produce ideological extremists. Different names. Different forms. But the same underlying dynamics. India need not look too far to understand the implications of the neglect of the periphery for the sustainability of the core.

Indian values, and global ones

The foundation of Indian thought, dating back 4,000 years, considers sustainability most important. The central theme in all ancient scriptures is Dharma. This term is derived from the Sanskrit letter *dhr*, which means "to uphold." Dharma embodies those principles which sustain an entity, whether it be an individual, society or the state. These are the principles of right action. But what is right action? The first verse of *Isha Upanishad* has an answer.

> *Om Isha Vasyamid: sarv yatkinch jagatyan jagat*
> *Taen tyaken bhujitha ma grudhah kasyaswidhnam*
> (All that is there in the universe is pervaded by God; act with detachment; enjoy yours but do not covet what is not yours.)

Thus, Dharma is a law of right action, which is an action undertaken to perform the duty allowing you to enjoy what is yours, but not to aspire for what is not yours. *Isha Upanishad* only authorizes fruits from such actions, which do not violate the supreme moral order. Thus, corruption and exploitation are contrary to the law of Dharma. The control of market or political space to exclude the participation of the weak also violates Dharma. The law of the jungle, where mere might succeeds, is the antithesis of the law of Dharma.

The scriptures which profess Dharma — the *Vedas, Upanishads, Ramayan, Mahabharata* (including the *Gita), Manusmriti* — are known as Hindu doctrines. In fact, 4,000 years ago, when they were conceptualized, there was no Hinduism. Indeed, there was no religion there at all. Moreover, the faiths that followed, Buddhism, Jainism, Zoroastrianism, Islam, Christianity, Sikhism, all endorse ethical principles constituting the concept of Dharma. They just use different terms to explain it.

Buddhism proposes the eight-fold path of right view, right thought, right speech, right action, right livelihood, right effort, right mindfulness and right contemplation. Jainism is based on the trinity of right belief, right knowledge and right conduct. Zoroastrianism calls it the law of *Asha*, incorporating the maxim of good thoughts, good words and good deeds. Sikhism emphasizes that a person should be *khalsa*, embodying ethics, compassion and dignified character.

It is not merely Indian religions which share Hinduism's advocacy of Dharma or an ethical code. Other religions, whether they originate in India or not, are in unison on the necessity for ethics in human conduct.

For instance, the holy Qur'an says in Sura IV (verses 122–124):

> "But those who believe
> And do righteous deeds
> We shall soon admit them
> To the garden beneath which rivers flow
> To dwell therein forever!"

Confucius's teachings echo the same spirit:

> "The moral law is the one from whose operation we cannot for one instant in our existence escape. Wherefore it is that the moral man watches diligently over his secret thoughts. When passions have not awakened, that is our true self. When passions such as joy, anger, grief awaken and each and all attain due measure and degree, that is the moral order."

Besides the concept of ethical conduct, Hindu, Buddhist, Jain, Sikh, Islamic and Christian doctrines share consensus on the importance of justice. They profess tolerance, brotherhood, compassion, and oppose oppression and slavery.

The wisdom drawn from the ancient religious scriptures is in harmony with current international thinking. In the 1990s, the World Bank, the UNDP, the Inter-American Development Bank and the OECD led a debate on the concept of good governance and a just society. Their agenda was very much in congruence with the concept of Dharma, or ethical conduct, and justice. The multilateral institutions suggested measures for making ethics a reality in the modern world, through accountability, transparency, fairness and the rule of law. More recently, the corporate sector has joined the bandwagon. George Soros began the trend, in an article in *The Atlantic Monthly* in February 1997, when he condemned social Darwinism in global capitalism. Now business ethics are no longer private business. They are subjected to codes of conduct, training programs, new reporting methods and media coverage.

The harmony between Indian wisdom and global norms arises because of the universality of values. This is real globalization. Forget trade. Forget investments. Forget the Internet. Trade, investments and the Internet integrate only 2% of Indians in the international economy. The globalization of values connects the Indian masses to the whole world. If India wants to succeed in the global marketplace, it needs global values — as much as techniques of trade, investment and communications — which are also reflected in the original tenets of Indian thought.

Crisis of values

Whenever the core Indian values of right action and justice triumphed at home, India achieved success in the global space. From 500 BC to 700 AD, the first period for which detailed records are available, evidence shows the existence of an ethical and just society. During this period, monarchy did not follow the principle of dynastic succession. Each claimant to the throne was required to possess certain virtues and be free of certain vices. Justice was supreme and above the ruler. Since entitlement to rule depended on ethical principles, exercise of power was also generally just, virtuous and fair. During this period, India experienced renaissance. It gave birth to great scientific discoveries and literary masterpieces. It had a thriving economy. It was the world leader in almost all fields of human endeavor.

After the seventh century, as the rulers slowly departed from the ethical code, India gradually lost its independence to foreign invaders. For the next 1,000 – 1,200 years, ethics took a backseat as the Indian mind was seized with the issues of control and freedom. With freedom in 1947, Indian society had an opportunity to rediscover its roots. Instead, it tried to seek economic growth, without a strong foundation of values. Therefore, degeneration, which began with the invasion of Mohammad of Gazni in 1001, still continues.

And pray, what is the character of today's society? An advertisement issued in February 2003, *Indian Express*, a leading daily, pronounced:

> "Our lives are a scam. Corruption is our constitution. We abide by it. Every move is a motive. Every breath, a bribe. Indeed, truth is a file attracting dust in some dingy office. Everything has a price. We barter our conscience, conscientiously. Corruption is like the appendix in our body. It's very much there. You just don't feel it."

Corruption *per se* exists everywhere. So does injustice. The issue is not just about the scams that have come to public light. For there are many more that may have escaped scrutiny. It's not just the US$5.5 billion in bribery that Transparency International discovered in a sample survey in late 2002; for there are many sectors which the survey excluded. It's not just about the 26 million cases pending in higher courts; for there are many more in lower courts. It's not just about more than 10,000 companies being prosecuted as per the Ministry of Company Affairs; for there are several cases which may never reach the formal judicial process. It's not just that a quarter of a million companies are reported to have defaulted, out of the total of 6,00,000-odd companies in the country; for all those who have not defaulted cannot claim they have observed all the other laws fully. It's not just the US$200 billion of black economy, equivalent of 40–60% of the GDP; for the future of the nation depends on its gross social fabric which is not included in GDP.

There are two issues: profits and acceptance. Violation of ethics and justice proves to be profitable, at least in the short run. A hard-working farmer barely earns Rs.1000 (US$20) per month. An adulterator of food items in Mumbai or New Delhi makes at least 100 times as much. If the farmer does not sell his produce through government monopolies, he is punished. If an adulterator is arrested by the police, the higher authority releases him. In theory, values are a matter of philosophy. In practice, values are a matter of economics. The character of a nation is judged by the values that are profitable in it. As human beings by nature try to gain, they prefer values which enable them to earn profits. India has run into ethical deficit because it is not profitable in today's India to follow ethics and justice.

A breach of ethics destroys the level playing field; it works against honest people, since their competitors can win by unfair means. Moreover, those who amass wealth by crooked means tend to display it. As they host bigger and bigger parties, in more and more expensive designer clothes, at larger and larger houses, with smaller and smaller mobile phones in their pockets, the teenager from the slum next door feels restless. Since he cannot inherit an industry, he sets up an extortion racket. He discovers that he can command even greater fame, inspiring many others to follow. In this culture, every boy wants to be a don and every girl a beauty queen.

The greatest benefit from an unfair and unjust system is derived in the game of democracy. Elections cost money and also provide an excuse to raise funds far more than required for the cost of campaigning. Of course, illegal receipts have to be reciprocated with illegal favors. Never mind the resulting policy distortions and structural anomalies. In the 1970s, the election law was changed, banning corporate contributions to political parties, and paving the way for unofficial bribes to individual politicians — sometimes in cash, sometimes in overseas accounts, and sometimes in properties held in fictitious names. Some call it donations. Some call it speed money. Some call it protection money. Some even call it education money.

Besides graft, the political class profits from the government's direct control over two-thirds of productive capital and organized employment. As the private corporate sector provides only 10% of GDP and 2% of employment, it has limited ability to influence the national value structure. As a result, it simply follows the dominant values, however distorted, in the society. This is especially true of the media — the one segment of business which can, in fact, play a catalytic role in influencing the value system. Alas, it seems to believe that newspapers are commodities, and readers are just consumers, who want nothing more than glamour, scandals and sports.

The more serious issue is acceptance of the unethical. When executives at Arthur Andersen abetted a scam, the firm collapsed. When the managing director of Tata Finance engineered a scam in India, the company survived. Kenneth Lay, chairman of Enron, became *persona non grata* before his investigation. In India, Harshad Mehta was invited to deliver talks and write newspaper columns, even after his conviction. When Staple Inc and de Beers were criticized by consumers, the former stopped sourcing raw material for paper from endangered forests and the latter agreed to purchase diamonds only from outside conflict zones. In India, consumers do not boycott fire-crackers and carpets made with child labor. In the West, stock prices of companies tainted by scams fall. In India, they often go up. In 2002, the All India Bank Employees Union released a list of defaulting companies. A few weeks later, it was found that the shares of many of them were doing fine. When Mona Selin was caught purchasing baby diapers on a government credit card, she lost the leadership of Sweden's Social Democratic Party. In India, an incumbent government leader is rarely guilty. India has run into an ethical deficit not merely because of scandals, but more so because the culprits enjoy respect in the society.

Forty years ago, ethics still mattered. As a child, the most popular story I heard was that of a poor schoolboy who stole a neighbor's gold chain. His mother patted him affectionately, as she could now buy him good clothes and food. The boy went on to steal bigger things. As he graduated from one level of crime to another, he finally attained skill in big time robberies. In one robbery, he also killed his victim. He was arrested and sentenced to death. When he was asked his last wish, he sought to see his mother. He then bit his mother's ear and said: "If you had done this to me the day I stole the gold chain, I would not be dying today." We were taught that the sin of the mother was greater than that of her son.

Even today, those who behave without integrity are few in our large nation of more than a billion. Unfortunately, those who tolerate them and applaud them are many more. That is why India is facing a crisis of values. And as for childhood stories, they are replaced by heroic tales of underworld dons.

The supporters of an unethical way of life defend it on the grounds of pragmatism, even though they may believe in India's core values. The Indian mind is seized with a conflict between the ideal and the practical. What is ideal is not considered practical and vice versa. India's future depends upon its ability to establish a unity of the ideal and the practical.

Ethical contract

The essence of almost all Indian wisdoms is that the ideal should be made practical. *Ramayana, Mahabharata* and *Panchatantra* in Hinduism and *Jatak Katha* in Buddhism tell stories of how princes, as well as ordinary people, lived principled lives — indeed these scriptures argue that an active life in pursuit of ideals is essential. The site of the *Gita,* one of the key foundations of Indian thought, is a battlefield. It is not a monastery. The very first word in the very first chapter of this great epic describes the site as *Dharmakshetra*, the battleground of a moral struggle. The heart of a person is *Dharmakshetra*, where the war between good and evil takes place all the time. Similarly, the world or society is *Dharmakshetra*, where there is a permanent conflict between good and evil. In this conflict, neutrality or passivity is not acceptable. According to the *Gita*, one must act. Instead of wishing that there were no imperfection, it is necessary to address distortions caused by friction between positive and negative energy. One must act to establish the reign of good over evil. Thus, the *Gita* advocates the practical for the sake of the ideal.

> *"Na karmanyam anarambhan*
> *Naiskarmyam puruso'snute*
> *Na ca samnyasanad eva*
> *Sidhim samadhigacchati"*
> (Not by abstention from duty does a man attain freedom from action; not by mere renunciation does he attain to his perfection.)

The *Vedas* have exactly the same message embodied in the tenet of the Dharma, or right action. The union of righteousness and action implies the unity of the ideal and the practical. It is only when such a union is achieved that society is sustainable.

There are examples at the micro level of individuals, companies, voluntary organizations and government departments that attempt in their own way to operate ethical and just institutions. But most of them have a local impact. They have not yet been able to create a new credo across the country. Highly successful business companies completely free of scams, non-performing loans and accounting malpractice, and with a strong social responsibility and fair labor record are few and far between. Some of them are in the New Economy. India needs new economics for its agriculture and industry — not just for the New Economy of information technology.

India once negotiated a social contract when it gave up its feudal structure soon after independence. But the feudal mindset has not yet disappeared. The intermediary class, which replaced the feudal interests in Indian politics and business, has also adopted the feudal mental framework and adapted it to its rent-seeking mentality. The intermediaries flourish in a system where trading and control have primacy over creation. Under this system, the state sector grows in a distorted fashion. To establish an India based on core values of right action and justice will require negotiating the underlying ethical contract. This is obviously challenging. It will need initiative from the creative agents of the society. In 1757, and again in1857, princes lost battles to the British. In 1947, the foreign rulers had to leave. In the 1960s, land reforms and abolition of privy purses ended feudalism. The time is now up for rent-seeking civil servants, politicians and businessmen. This is not to say that there is no place for any civil servants or politicians. In fact, those politicians and civil servants who abolish rents, and seek partnership with entrepreneurs and social entrepreneurs, especially from the agrarian economy, can construct the architecture of a new ethical order. A critical mass of change agents needs to play a catalytic role in raising the national consciousness to a higher level.

The transformation of India is inevitable because life is not about the survival of the fittest. Life is about the advancement of each and all. The question is whether we want to see the transformation taking place by violent means — conflict and collapse of the civil society — or whether we want to facilitate a peaceful change.

If we want peace and prosperity instead of discord and decay, it is necessary for the Indian mind to rise above the conflict between the ideal and the practical. We have to reject the prevailing concept of life as a cricket match, fixed through manipulation, or a wrestling tournament, where the winner takes it all. We need to perceive life as a marathon. Of course, this means nothing less than reform of the Indian mind.

If Indians, led by a values-driven critical mass, sincerely and seriously desire a new ethical architecture, it should be possible for them to construct it. There will be difficulties since most things worth doing are declared to be impossible, until they are done. But if people are committed to emancipate themselves, they will be able to do so, just as they were to able to liberate themselves from colonialism only 50 years ago. Someone just needs to make a beginning.

About 30 years ago, I used to live in a small suburb of Mumbai which was notorious for crime and communal conflicts between Hindus and Muslims. Communal violence was a regular feature of our town. One afternoon, in the heat of the riots, a militant Hindu mob wanted to kill our Muslim neighbors. We offered shelter to the latter in our kitchen. As the angry mob learnt that the Muslim family was in our house, they tried to enter. My illiterate grandmother dared the mob to kill her before they could cross the threshold. We were extremely tense. They were puzzled. After some time, one by one they bowed before her and walked away, without harming the Muslim neighbors. That was the end of the riots that evening. And there have been no more riots in my small town ever since, despite the extremely painful rupture between the Hindu and Muslim communities in the last decade. The ethic of the town has changed forever. It has other problems, but the specter of communalism seems to have disappeared.

It's one thing to pacify one town. It's something else to make a breakthrough in an unethical and unjust social architecture. So, what should we do? We can start by emancipating 250 million farmers and agricultural workers from draconian laws. Agricultural market reforms, if complemented by public/private partnerships for capacity building, will empower rural youth. Second, we should lobby our chief ministers to hold district magistrates and department heads accountable for publicly announced development objectives. The chief minister of Andhra Pradesh has tried it and it works. Third, we should demand change in campaign finance laws to introduce heavy penalties on givers and takers of payments in cash. In addition, we should demand an electoral ban on criminals. Fourth, we should form a coalition of clean businessmen, civil society activists and others, to draft standards for the performance of parliamentarians and state legislators. The coalition should then publicize the performance of our representatives, with a view to naming and shaming them. Fifth, we should demand ethical audits of companies. Of course, this will all create friction. But breakthrough, by definition, creates friction.

If we make a beginning with these, or similar, initiatives, it will still be the beginning. There will be greater challenges ahead. Is it possible? When someone insists on the incongruence of the ideal and the practical, I recall that afternoon in my childhood. And when someone asks the question "Why?", I wonder "But why not?"

6

ISLAM
In Search of Islamic Economics: The Malaysian Model

Farish A. Noor
Research fellow, centre for Modern Orient Studies (ZMO), Berlin

Going for the "real thing": The battle for the minds and wallets of Muslims today

Visitors to Muslim countries may soon find that they will not be able to quench their thirst with a sip of Coca-Cola. Instead, they may well be offered the "real thing" — Mecca-Cola — instead.

Contrary to what some people may think, "Mecca-Cola" is not a joke. The new brand of Cola was launched earlier this year in France by a French-Tunisian entrepreneur who saw both the market potential and political necessity to break the near-hegemonic grip of American consumerist culture on the rest of the world. He could not have chosen a better time to launch his new product, what with anti-American sentiments at an all-time high the world over. Armed with the catchy slogan "Don't drink like an idiot, drink with commitment," the Mecca-Cola company was inundated with orders as soon as the red-and-white look-alike bottles hit the shops. Within a week, orders for nearly half a million bottles came from Muslim countries the world over, most of all from Pakistan.

But Mecca-Cola is not the first Muslim initiative to reproduce fast-food products that are, ironically, American-inspired but also aimed at challenging American hegemony at the same time. There has also been

Qibla-Cola in the Arab world, and for those living in Shia communities, Zam-Zam-Cola that was pioneered by the Iranians.[1]

The growing popularity of brands like Mecca-Cola, Qibla-Cola and Zam-Zam-Cola reflects the contradictions of the times we live in. On the one hand they show just how low the status and image of America is the world over, and how people are prepared to alter their consumption patterns in a show of protest against what they see as American arrogance and economic-cultural imperialism. But at the same time it cannot be denied that all of these brands have one thing in common: they reflect precisely the same thing that they reject and they imitate that which they deny. Imitation is said to be the best form of flattery, and if that be the case then what can we conclude from these attempts by Muslim entrepreneurs to counter the challenge of economic globalization and American cultural hegemony?

Here, then, lies the twisted irony of hegemony. For one feature of cultural and political hegemony is that it conquers and subdues in the most sophisticated of ways. As the North African philosopher and founder of modern political sociology Ibn Khaldun argued in his text the *Muqadimmah*, "It is when a people imitate the ways of their conquerors that they are well and truly defeated. This is the true sign of submission."

It is undeniable that we now live in a globalized world that bears the heavy cultural, political and economic imprint of the United States and its consumerist culture. All over the world, anti-globalization and anti-American groups and movements have appeared to challenge and resist growing American dominance. But ironically many of these groups have ended up imitating and reproducing all that is bad in America — down to the junk food that has made that nation of overweight consumer-citizens so famous.

A cursory survey of the state of cultural affairs in the Muslim world today will support the claim that Muslims hate America more than ever before and yet are closer than ever before to becoming Americans themselves. On our campuses we can see young girls wearing the *tudung/ hijab* (headscarf) as a symbol of their Muslim identity and rejection of Western values — except that sometimes these headscarves happen to be made of denim, like the Yankee-style jeans they wear. The contradiction

---

[1] Nor are these initiatives exclusive to the Muslim world. In former East Germany there was the East German equivalent of Coke, called Vita-Cola. Vita-Cola still exists today, and the company even sponsors a football team of its own, Hansa Rostock. Oddly enough, sales of Vita-Cola remain confined to the parts of Germany that were once Communists such as Berlin, for instance.

seems to have been lost somewhere amidst their fuming and ranting against the "Great Satan" that they hate so much.

The fact, however, remains that one cannot simply negate an enemy through simplistic dialectics, for the simple reason that being in an oppositional dialectical relationship with the Other merely confirms one's dependency on that Other in the first place. The present impasse between the West and the Muslim world sums this up, with the leaders of both sides mouthing a bellicose and confrontational rhetoric that sounds more and more similar by the day. But the nations and communities of the developing world must learn that confronting Western (and specifically American) hegemony cannot be done through piecemeal gestures such as imitating Western products and lifestyle. This does nothing to challenge American hegemony. If anything it merely reinforces it and confirms its dominant status. Mecca-Cola may be a challenger to America's Coke, but it remains an imitation.

American economic power and influence today is neither accidental nor preordained: it is the result of unfair and unequal economic practices in a world governed by market forces that are unbridled and beyond the control of anyone. To deal with this problem requires more original thinking than simply imitating American products. It will require a sustained political commitment to changing the fundamental laws and norms of global economics and finance instead. Thus far, the developing world has not been able to do that. So for Muslims to think they have defeated the "Great Satan" by drinking an "Islamic" soft drink every bit as bad as Coke would be a cruel joke on ourselves. American hegemony will not disappear with a gulp.

Our aim here is to explore the phenomenon of Islamic economics and to see how Islamist thinkers have attempted to construct an alternative economic model to counter the challenge of Western capitalist hegemony to date. Our focus will be on one particular country, Malaysia, and our analysis begins in the early 1980s as the country is gripped by the wave of Islamic political resurgence the world over.

Islamization of Economics: The Malaysian model from the 1980s to the present

The Muslim world has witnessed several attempts at constructing an alternative economic system to call its own. From the 1970s onwards, numerous Muslim academics, economists, social scientists and political leaders have experimented with various forms of state-sponsored and government-led Islamization programs.

Following the declaration of Pakistan as an Islamic state in 1979 and the Iranian revolution that came in the same year, in 1983 Sudan had its own Islamic "revolution"[2] led by Colonel Ghafar Muhammad Nimeiri. By then Tunisia, Libya and Egypt were also experimenting with their own forms of state-sponsored Islamization and it comes as no surprise that Malaysia embarked on its own Islamization drive from 1981, with the ascendancy to power of the country's fourth prime minister, Dr. Mahathir Mohamad.

Malaysia's Islamization program was determined by both local and international factors. The global wave of Islamic resurgence meant that Malaysia — as a Muslim-majority country — could not be seen as doing nothing while other Muslim countries were trying to "Islamize" their institutions of governance and economics. Meanwhile the ruling United Malays National Organisation (UMNO) party led by Dr. Mahathir was also forced to deal with the growing strength of the country's main Muslim opposition party, the Pan-Malaysian Islamic Party (PAS), as well as a number of Malay-Muslim Islamist NGOs and social movements like the Malaysian Islamic Youth Movement (ABIM), the Malaysian Islamic Reform Organisation (JIM) and the neo-Sufi alternative social movement *Darul Arqam*.

By the 1980s, PAS's discourse of political Islam had grown to be increasingly radical as a result of exposure to developments abroad and the entry of a new generation of Islamist-activists and *Ulama* who were influenced by the Iranian revolution and the Islamization of Pakistan at the hands of General Zia 'ul Haq.[3] Along with the other Islamist movements in the country PAS called on the government to scuttle the old British-style constitution and create an Islamic state and economy in Malaysia that was based on the *Qur'an* and history of Muslims elsewhere. Linked to this was the Islamists' rejection of the economic model of the Malaysian government on the grounds that it was un-Islamic and contrary to some of the fundamental tenets of Islamic law and ritual. The Islamists

---

[2]   The Islamic revolution in Sudan was launched on 8 September 1983 by Colonel Ghafar Muhammad Nimeiri. The country's constitution was then changed to an Islamic one.

[3]   Elsewhere we have discussed the growing radicalization of the discourse of PAS from the 1980s onwards. See "Blood, Sweat and Jihad: The Radicalisation of the Discourse of the Pan-Malaysian Islamic Party (PAS) from the 1980s to the Present" the *Journal of the Centre for Southeast Asian Studies* (CSEA), Singapore, Vol. 25. no. 2, August 2003.

in Malaysia were then deeply influenced by the ideas of Islamist economists such as the British-based Kurshid Ahmad.[4]

Moved by the anti-Western critiques of Islamist scholars and activists like Ismail Ragi Faruqi, Tahar Jabir al-Alwani and Khurshid Ahmad (who were in turn strongly influenced by an earlier generation of Islamist thinkers like Hassan al-Banna and Abu'l Alaá Maudoodi), this younger generation of Malay-Muslim activists were attracted to the fiery rhetoric of PAS's leaders. They were enthused by PAS's uncompromising ideological stand and its willingness to confront the state and government of Dr. Mahathir on a number of issues such as the New Economic Policy (NEP), the "Look East" Policy and the Islamization policy of the UMNO-led government.

Unlike the governments of many other Muslim countries, the Malaysian government under Dr. Mahathir preferred to beat the Islamists at their own game. It has to be noted that throughout his political career Dr. Mahathir has had a different way of addressing the challenge posed by the Islamist opposition in his own country. He did not favor the confrontational approach of other leaders like Tunisia's Habib Bourguiba[5],

---

[4] The Indian-born British Islamist scholar and economist Khurshid Ahmad was born in Delhi, India, in 1932. He established the Islamic Foundation which was, from the outset, closely linked to the *Jama'at-e Islami* in Pakistan and its network of Islamist organisations. Through the work of the foundation and his teaching activities, Khurshid has managed to gain a huge following among Muslim students studying in the West, and in Britain in particular.

[5] One of Habib Bourguiba's main aims was to modernise Islam and turn it into a modern ideology that was compatible with development and capitalism. Bourguiba claimed that the *Quran* contained many contradictions and that it needed to be re-interpreted in the light of present-day realities. He issued a law which forbade the use of the *hijab* (veil) in public offices. He made French the official language of the political administration of the country, and he replaced the Islamic *Shariah* courts with civil courts instead. Bourguiba's relentless attack and persecution of Islamist activists, organisations and institutions led to him being openly censured by a number of Arab Muslim scholars and *Ulama*, including Sheikh Abdul Aziz ibn Baz (d. 1999), Sheikh Abul Hasan Nadwi (d. 1999) and Sheikh Ali al-Khafeef, the Grand *Mufti* of Egypt. A great believer in economic development and material progress, Bourguiba laid great emphasis on the need to modernize the Tunisian economy at all costs. In 1964 he shocked the conservative sections of Tunisian society when he publicly declared that fasting during the month of Ramadhan was no longer needed as the Muslims of Tunisia were on a *jihad* (struggle) for development in order to keep up with the developed Western world. He publicly defied the *Ulama* by drinking a glass of orange juice during the day, when others were fasting around him.

the spectacular displays of piety by the likes of Nimeiri[6] or the vague conciliatory maneuvers of Indonesia's Soeharto.[7] Dr. Mahathir had a clear idea of which course he wanted Islam to take in the country. If the increasingly radical discourse of PAS was shaped by a form of oppositional dialectics which divided the world between "good Muslims" and "*kafirs*," the Islamist worldview of Dr. Mahathir was one which divided Muslims into "moderate progressives" and "misguided fanatics" instead. As Shanti Nair puts it:

> "Domestically, Islamisation focused on the distinction between a 'moderate' Islam deemed more appropriate in the context of Malaysian society against more radical expressions which were unacceptable to the government. The conflict between 'moderate' and 'extreme', in effect, encompassed intra-Malay rivalry."[8]

UMNO's brand of modernist and moderate Islam was based on a chain of equivalences that equated Islam with all that was positive in its eyes. Islam was equated with modernity, economic development, material progress, rationality and liberalism. (It is interesting to note that other values like democracy and human rights were not part of this chain of equivalences.) In the same way that PAS's oppositional dialectics framed a reversed chain of equivalences as its mirror opposite, UMNO's understanding of Islam was also framed against a negative chain of equivalences which equated PAS's Islam with obscurantism, extremism, fanaticism, intolerance, backwardness and militancy. This was the "wrong" version of Islam to which UMNO's Islam was the answer. The

---

6   Gaafar Muhammad Nimeiri's own Islamization program that was launched in the early 1980s in Sudan involved some spectacular (and, some might argue, counter-productive) displays of religiosity on the part of the leader and his government. In 1983, Nimeiri ordered US$11 million-worth of alcohol be thrown into the Nile, marking the end of alcohol consumption in the country. In the following year his government banned all forms of mixed Western dancing in public. A number of people found guilty of doing so were publicly flogged.

7   In the same year (1983) that Malaysia began its Islamization program in earnest, President Soeharto of Indonesia ordered all Indonesian political movements and organizations to adopt the vague, non-sectarian *Pancasila* principles as their basic foundational philosophy (*asas tunggal*). This was rejected by many Indonesian Islamist movements, but it was accepted by the *Nahdatul Ulama* which was then under the influence of NU moderates who wished to co-operate with the government. The NU made the Pancasila its *asas tunggal*, and declared that Islam was its *aqidah*.

8   Shanti Nair, *Islam in Malaysian Foreign Policy*, Routledge and ISEAS, London, 1997, p. 91.

aim of the state's Islamization policy was to normalize and institutionalize the "right" version of Islam against the "wrong" version promoted by PAS, both in terms of ortho-practic behavior as well as state policy.

To this end, the machinery of the State was directed towards an Islamization program that was meant to eliminate the discrepancies between different sites and sources of Islamic authority while outdoing the claims and promises of PAS and the other Islamist movements, such as ABIM, in the country. (The National Fatwa Council was formed in 1978 to effectively centralize religious power and authority and keep it in the hands of the Federal government.)

In 1981, the UMNO General Assembly issued a resolution to the effect that the Federal and state Islamic councils should enforce and defend the "purity of Islam."[9] By 1982, the Prime Minister's office had more than 100 *Ulama* working under it and the Ministry of Education had some 715 *Ulama* on its payroll.[10] The Fourth Malaysia Plan (1981–1986) also explicitly declared that henceforth Islam would play a major role in the development of the country — albeit on an *inspirational* level.

In 1983, the *Universiti Islam Antarabangsa* (UIA — International Islamic University of Malaysia) was founded. The UIA project was announced after the Prime Minister's visit to the Arab Gulf States. The UIA's initial funding came from Malaysia, Saudi Arabia, Pakistan, Bangladesh, the Maldives, Libya, Turkey and Egypt and the university's first president was the ex-ABIM leader turned UMNO politician, Anwar Ibrahim.

To add substance to the UIA initiative a string of international conferences around the theme of Islamic knowledge and science were held. Between 1983 and 1989, Kuala Lumpur played host to the International Conference on the Islamic Approach towards Technological Development (1983), Islamic Civilisation (1984), Islamic Thought (1984), the International Islamic Symposium (1986), Islamic Economics (1987), Islam and Media (1987), Religious Extremism (1987) and Islam and the Philosophy of Science (1989).[11]

In the same year that the UIA was opened, the Malaysian Islamic Bank (*Bank Islam Malaysia*) was launched by the government (on 1 July 1983).[12] *Bank Islam* became the first bank in the country to offer regular

---

[9]   Shanti Nair, 1997, p. 36.
[10] Shanti Nair, 1997, p. 112.
[11] Shanti Nair, 1997, p. 115.
[12] The plan for the Malaysian Islamic Bank was announced one year earlier, on 6 July 1982.

banking services that were meant to be in accordance with Islamic restrictions and norms related to commerce. It did not charge interest on loans and (on paper at least) avoided the practice of *riba* (interest on lent money). The Islamist economist Abdur Razzaq Lubis condemned the Malaysian Islamic banking project on the grounds that the bank did not and could not represent a radical challenge to the existing global banking system that was rooted in the practice of interest. Lubis argued that the Islamic Bank in Malaysia was doing the same thing and basically collecting interest in a different form. Such nominal changes were for him cosmetic and ineffectual. Despite the fact that the Islamic Bank was condemned as a cosmetic attempt to bolster the government's Islamic credentials by Islamist economists like Abdur Razzaq Lubis, other Islamic economic initiatives followed suit.[13]

Soon after, the Islamic Insurance Company (*Tafakul*) was launched as well as the Hajj Pilgrims Management Fund (*Lembaga Urusan Tabung Haji*, LUTH). By creating the UIA, *Bank Islam, Tafakul* and LUTH it appeared as if UMNO was the only party in the country that could keep its promises to the Malay-Muslim constituency.

By initiating its own Islamization program, the government of Dr. Mahathir had effectively stolen a march from the Islamists of PAS. In time, the labors of the Mahathir administration began to pay off: the UIA project received considerable financial assistance from the governments of numerous Arab states. Cash injections came from countries like Kuwait and Saudi Arabia, though they were aimed more at projects related to Islamic *dakwah* (missionary) activities.[14] Apart from that, Dr. Mahathir himself was gaining recognition for his efforts as a Muslim leader. In 1983 the Malaysian Prime Minister was awarded the "Great Leader" award by none other than President Zia'ul Haq of Pakistan (who had previously anointed Anwar Ibrahim).

Not surprisingly, the Islamists of PAS were quick to react to the policy initiatives of Dr. Mahathir. The then president of PAS, Ustaz Yusof Rawa, argued that the Islamization program proposed by the UMNO-led government was not really designed to lay the foundations of an Islamic

---

[13] See Abdur-Razzaq Lubis, *Tidak Islamnya Bank Islam*, PAID Network, Georgetown, Penang, 1985.

[14] In 1982, Kuwait donated more than RM120 million for projects launched by the *Pusat Islam* (Islamic Centre) under the Prime Minister's department and the *Yayasan Dakwah Islamiah* (Islamic Dakwah Foundation). Later, in 1986, eight loans totalling RM390 million were secured from the Saudi Fund to help with other missionary and welfare projects for Muslims in the country.

state but was, in fact, part of an elaborate scheme to make the country appear more Islamic while remaining firmly entrenched within the global liberal-capitalist economic system. He asked:

"Do these Islamic projects really give us the hope that we will one day escape from this vicious economic cycle and that our country will achieve independence in the truest sense of the word? The answer has to be no. For the independence of our country is being obstructed by the global system that is sustained by the superpowers who have created this vicious cycle in the first place, and this global system cannot be undone by the efforts of a handful of people who pretend to be really committed to Islamisation but who have only offered us Islamisation programmes that are limited in their scope."[15]

The fact that some of these state-sponsored Islamic institutions were themselves deeply enmeshed within the local corporate culture and were directly involved in some decidedly dubious dealings made it all the easier for the Islamists of PAS to dismiss them as being cosmetic in nature.

For the Islamists of PAS no Islamization program could ever hope to succeed without the committed effort to make Islam the religion of State and Islamic law the supreme law of the land. They regarded the Malaysian government's attempts at Islamization as hollow and of little consequence, on the grounds that the inculcation of Islamic values and norms would not be possible unless the State was prepared to enforce these norms through legal means:

'The Islamisation programme in Malaysia simply seeks to inculcate Islamic values without having to implement Islamic law. But to try and instil Islamic values while rejecting the necessity of Islamic law is not only ridiculous, it is in fact a conceit and a plot full of lies. This is because these Islamic values will never be inculcated without the implementation of Islamic law. How could such Islamic values emerge if the source of these values — namely the *Qur'an* and *Sunnah* are rejected? If these Islamic values are not based on Islamic laws then what are they supposed to be based upon? Are these so-called Islamic values really the creation of a coterie of planners and advisers based in

---

[15] Kamaruddin Jaffar, *Memperingati Yusof Rawa*, Pan Malaysian Islamic Party (PAS), 2000, pp. 52–53.

Washington or Tokyo, Moscow or Paris, London or Tel Aviv; or are they the products of glib tongues that do not mean what they say?"[16]

The Malaysian Islamic economic model in the 1980s and 1990s: Growth with contradictions

Notwithstanding the critiques from the Islamist camp, Malaysia witnessed tremendous economic development — albeit with ups and downs — for nearly two decades between the early 1980s to the late 1990s.

During the early-to-mid 1980s, Malaysia, along with the other economies of Asia, suffered from the worldwide recession but was saved in the nick of time thanks to the inflow of Foreign Direct Investment (FDI) particularly from countries like Japan and South Korea. By 1985–1986, economic analysts in and out of Malaysia agreed that the country was about to enter its first recession since Independence. This came about after the country had made its successful transition from a commodity-producing economy to one based on industrial manufacturing. But despite increased public-sector support of local industries and the advances made through providing new infrastructure, Malaysia in the mid '80s was losing its competitive edge thanks to the lower labor and production costs in neighboring countries like Indonesia and Thailand. In the field of agricultural production Malaysia was also losing out to its neighbors. (Thailand competed with Malaysia in the production of natural rubber while Indonesia managed to become the world's main exporter of tropical hardwoods. Indonesia also posed stiff competition in the production of palm oil.)

The situation was made worse by the global downtrend that was taking place elsewhere in the world and in the economies of Malaysia's trading partners in particular. As a result of these combined variables, Malaysian export earnings dropped significantly. By 1985, Malaysia's GDP growth registered a negative 1.1%. The heavily promoted and State-supported electronics and electrical manufacturing sectors were particularly hard hit during the recession that followed. By then it was clear that the level of local research and development (R&D) and technology transfer from Malaysia's trading partners was deplorably low as well.

---

[16] Jaffar, 2000, p. 83.

Malaysia managed to squeeze its way out of the 1985–86 recession by actively courting more FDI, particularly from Japan, South Korea and Taiwan. Attractive investment programs were offered to Japanese, Korean and Taiwanese companies that were treated on favorable terms. Many of these companies were invited to work with Malaysian concerns in pursuing joint projects such as the manufacturing of the first Malaysian car, the Proton Saga. This accommodating approach paid off in the short to medium term, as the Malaysian economy soon showed signs of recovery. The country's GDP growth rate rose from –1.1% in 1985 to 1% in 1986, 5% in 1987 and 9% in 1988. FDI contributions helped the Malaysian manufacturing sector grow by 20% during the second half of the 1980s, effectively taking Malaysia out of the recession and paving the way for the boom years that followed.

It has to be noted that despite the Islamization rhetoric employed by the Malaysian government, and the apparent shift of diplomatic focus closer to the Arab-Muslim world, Malaysia's own economic links with the Muslim world at large were minimal. Malaysia's main trading partners in the 1980s and 1990s remained the United States (which has been Malaysia's main export market for electronic goods in particular) and the East Asian economies of Japan, Korea and Taiwan. Malaysia's biggest Muslim trading partner then was Pakistan, though the volume of bilateral trade between the two countries was no more than 1% of total Malaysian exports. Collectively Malaysian trade with Saudi Arabia, Iran, Egypt, the Emirates and the Gulf States accounted for less than 4% of its total export earnings in the 1980s and 1990s, and this pattern has remained largely unchanged.

Contrary to the rhetoric of Muslim solidarity and unity in the face of globalization, it was not the Muslim countries that Malaysia turned to in times of crisis, but rather the developed economies of the West and East Asia. The Arabs, Iranians and Pakistanis may have supported Malaysia's efforts at Islamization and spoken highly of Malaysia as a "model Muslim state" but, at the end of the day, it was the non-Muslim countries that saved Malaysia's economy when it needed it the most.

Between 1988 to 1990, Malaysia's economy experienced a radical turnaround. During this period growth was kept at an average level of 9.1%. Unemployment also dropped to 6% in 1990 (from 8.3% in 1988). Thanks to a growth in demand for the country's exports the volume of commodity earnings also increased considerably from RM23.93 billion in 1985 to RM28.97 billion in 1990. The Malaysian economy benefited greatly from the influx of cash from America, Japan and Europe between 1993 to 1996. In 1985, the total amount of investment inflow into

Malaysia, Indonesia, the Philippines, Thailand and South Korea from abroad was nearly US$20 billion. After plummeting in 1987, investment began to rise again in 1990 (US$20 billion) and soared to US$35 billion in 1991. By 1995 it was estimated to have risen to US$50 billion and in 1996 had reached a peak of nearly US$70 billion.

But this rapid development was not without its political and economic costs. State management of the economy also meant that the country's economic and financial system was very closely linked to the ruling political party and political elite. Soon, a number of financial and business scandals erupted in public, further weakening the Malaysian government's claim that theirs was a model Islamic economy. The Bumiputera Malaysia Finance (BMF) scandal of 1983–1984 became the first major financial scandal of the Mahathir era. Though many more (such as the Perwaja Steel and Maminco scandal[17]) were to follow soon after, the scale and magnitude of the losses incurred was staggering by local standards then. The Prime Minister was forced to appoint an investigative committee to look into the matter.[18] But as the media probe into the BMF scandal intensified, it soon became clear that senior members of the government and leaders of the UMNO party were also involved. When the findings of the committee were kept secret, PAS and the other opposition parties were quick to point the finger of accusation at UMNO itself.

The Malaysian government's claim that its economic policies were geared to the needs of the ordinary masses was also questioned by

[17] The Maminco scandal involved the Malaysian Mining Company (Maminco) that was set up to serve as the Malaysian government's price-support vehicle in the global tin market. Malaysia was then the major tin producer in the world and the Malaysian government was keen to ensure that there would be a price-support system that would prevent the global price of tin from fluctuating wildly as a result of the activities of commodity speculators. Originally set up to help prop up the price of tin on the global metal exchange, Maminco began to speculate on the price of tin in the world market between 1981 to 1982. But in 1982 the London Metal Exchange changed its standard operating procedures and allowed traders to pay a fine instead of losing their stocks if they were to fail to meet a contractual delivery. This suddenly caused a depreciation of the cost of tin worldwide, and Maminco was landed with a large stock of unwanted tin as a result. Even after the collapse of tin prices, the Malaysian government refused to admit that it was behind the speculation on tin prices. It was only in 1986 that Dr. Mahathir openly admitted (at the 1986 UMNO general assembly) that it was the Malaysian government, operating via Maminco, that was the "secret buyer" of tin stocks in 1981–1982. Teik, 1995, pg. 214.

[18] The specially appointed BMF Investigation Committee was set up by the Prime Minister's command on 11 January 1984.

economic analysts over the years. Shireen Mardziah Hashim[19] points out that poverty had been substantially reduced in many of the target occupations between 1970 to 1990. But her analysis also shows that with the exception of fishermen and estate workers during the 1980s, this was largely accomplished by mobility out of the target occupations rather than by increasing income levels within these occupations. The government's development policies had effectively solved the problem of rural poverty by dismantling the structures of the rural economy and bringing about mass migration from the rural areas to the urban manufacturing centers on the west coast instead. By doing so, it had accomplished two objectives at the same time: it had eliminated the problem of chronic Malay poverty in the rural Malay heartland and it had also effectively destroyed the rural communities that were once the bedrock of PAS's political support.

Edmund Terrence Gomez and Jomo K. Sundaram have also alluded to the close working relationship between the Chinese captains of industry and commerce and the leaders of the UMNO party. By 1995, Malaysia's "Chinese capitalists also found that they either had to establish links with Malay patrons, capitalists or politicians, or fund UMNO to develop their businesses. The new Chinese capitalists who appeared in the 1980s — Vincent Tan Chee Yioun, Danny Tan Chee Sing, Ting Pek Khiing, Robert Tan Hua Choon, T.K. Lim — were seen to be closely associated with leading Malay politicians rather than independent businessmen; there is much unverified speculation that some of these men have even operated as business proxies for certain UMNO leaders, particularly Tan Sri Daim Zainuddin."[20]

By the mid 1990s, Malaysia was poised to take off once again, and a myriad of grand infrastructural projects were announced by the state in its bid to transform Malaysia into a newly industrialized country (NIC). The grand Multimedia Supercorridor (MSC) project was first unveiled in 1997, and the Prime Minister himself took a two-month break in order to tour the world and popularize the idea. The plan was to build the world's first fully-electronic working and living environment within a restricted area that would serve as a test-bed for experimentation. The mammoth development plan included the construction of the nation's new "paper-free" electronic capital, Putrajaya, the new Kuala Lumpur international airport (KLIA) and the new cyber-city, Cyberjaya. While the MSC project

[19] Shireen Mardziah Hashim, *Income Inequality and Poverty in Malaysia,* Rowman and Littlefield Publishers, Oxford, 1998.
[20] Edmund Terrence Gomez and Jomo K. Sundaram, *Malaysia's Political economy: Politics, Patronage and Profits,* Cambridge University Press, Cambridge, 1997, p. 181.

met with official endorsement and support from a number of foreign multinationals like IBM, Netscape and Sony, it also courted controversy thanks to the package of new regulations that the Malaysian government agreed to introduce. In order to win the support of foreign investors, the Malaysian government agreed to a "bill of guarantees" which included: (1) the provision of world-class infrastructural support, (2) unrestricted employment of foreign (non-Malaysian) workers, (3) freedom of ownership by exempting companies within the MSC from domestic ownership regulations, (4) freedom for companies to source capital from external sources, (5) providing regional leadership in the enforcement of cyberlaws and protection laws, (6) ensuring no censorship on the Internet, and (7) providing freedom of movement and extradition of capital. The proposal to set up the MSC as a semi-autonomous "state" with its own separate laws and regulations also caused concern amongst sections of the Malaysian community, who regarded such provisions as an official acceptance of double standards on the part of the government, thus heralding the arrival of the "two-nation" state in Malaysia.[21]

Such "mega-projects", as they came to be called, soon came under the scrutiny of the country's Islamist opposition, who argued that they served little public worth and were more designed to suit the ambitions of Malaysia's political and corporate elite. The leaders of PAS and a number of Islamist economists questioned the wisdom of such projects and demanded the government to demonstrate how "Islamic" they were in form and content. (The government's response was to press ahead with these moves and further intensify its Islamization program by building even more grand mosques, such as the new national mosque in Kuala Lumpur and the grand mosque in Putrajaya, the new capital.)

Such cosmetic measures at Islamization did not, however, save the government from further embarrassment as a result of the political and economic scandals that affected even its ostensibly Islamic economic ventures. In the 1980s the National Hajj Fund — *Lembaga Urusan Tabung Haji* (LUTH), for instance, was involved in the operations of the Malaysian Rare Earth (ARE) company along with the Japanese concern Mitsubishi Chemicals. The company was later accused of dumping radioactive waste in the state of Perak.[22] The Asian Rare Earth (ARE) company was a multinational concern that brought together the Japanese

---

[21] See Farish A. Noor, "Cyber-Paradise: Cyberjaya. Odyssey to Multimedia Super Corridor", in *Impact International*, Vol. 27, No. 7, July 1997.

[22] See Tan Sooi Beng, "The Papan-Bukit Merah Protest", in *Tangled Web*, Carpa, 1988, pp. 28–29.

Mitsubishi Chemicals company and the Malaysian BEH Minerals company. The *Lembaga Urusan Tabung Haji* was also one of the major partners in ARE. The company was first set up to extract rare trace elements from tin tailings. But the factory that was based in the state of Perak was also producing thorium hydroxide, a radioactive waste product. This radioactive waste had to be disposed of and, in the end, dumping sites were found in the state itself — first in the area of Papan and later near Bukit Merah. Local residents and environmental groups protested against this and this led to an international outcry from local and foreign environmental groups.

During the economic and financial crisis of 1997–1998, the Malaysian political establishment was rocked to its foundations with the split within the ruling UMNO party that led to the fall from grace of the Minister of Finance (and Deputy Prime Minister) Dato Seri Anwar Ibrahim. Between 1997–1999, the country was swept by the *reformasi* (reform) movement led by the ousted ex-Deputy PM, who called on the government to come clean about its own economic record and to address the problem of cronyism and corruption in the ruling national coalition. Anwar was soon detained and imprisoned on charges of abuse of power and sexual misconduct (via a trial process that brought into question the independence of the country's judiciary) but the calls for reform were not silenced. Critics of the government pointed out that many of the government's attempts to address the issue of corruption and nepotism were cosmetic at best, and that the numerous investigations conducted by the government have proven to be slow and ineffective.[23]

The economic downturn that followed after 1997–98 led to a state of political crisis in the country where a moment of radical dislocation had set in. It was clear that the two decades of growth that Malaysians had witnessed in the 1980s and 1990s were sustained by an economic arrangement that was riddled with inconsistencies and contradictions, not least the fact that for a so-called Islamic economic system the Malaysian economy was deeply enmeshed in the workings of the global market and that the Malaysian economy was very much exposed to external variable factors beyond its control. Despite assurances that the Malaysian

---

[23] One of the most galling examples was the lack of progress in the investigation carried out into the dealings of Perwaja Steel, the country's main steel producer. Funds were being channelled to mysterious companies abroad and tenders were given out to companies owned by the senior management's friends. When Perwaja finally fell to pieces, the early enquiries into its dealings revealed a catalogue of management errors and cases of blatant abuse of power and authority.

economic system would be tempered by "Islamic values" of moderation and control, it was clear by then that much of the economic activity in Malaysia was sustained by currency and stock price speculation; and that its rapid development was fueled by indiscriminate credit expansion by both local and international banks that were lending money as if it grew on trees. The fact that the Kuala Lumpur Stock Exchange (KLSE) had grown to become the third-largest in Asia ought to have been read as a warning sign by the economic planners that the economy was in danger of overheating. Much of this activity was based on speculation that was fueled by a seemingly-endless flow of easy money from within and from abroad.[24]

The crisis of 1997 brought to light the extent to which the Malaysian economy had become enmeshed within the global economic and financial system that has developed since the end of the Cold War. This was a global system that presided over the transaction of an estimated US$1.5 trillion on a daily basis (a sum greater than the GDP of Germany), and where currency speculation was a daily affair. It was also a system that was kept together and informed by the workings of the international media (mostly owned and based in the West) and which was littered with

[24] The role of the stock market and banking sector in building up the momentum of development in Malaysia and the rest of ASEAN in the '90s is undeniable. By the mid '90s foreign journalists were noting that even street-hawkers and taxi drivers in Kuala Lumpur were buying and selling shares on the market, thanks to the ready availability of loans from the banks. Earlier, the IMF authorities had warned the Malaysian government that it needed to play a firmer role in controlling and managing the country's banking sector in particular. During the consultation session between the IMF and the Malaysian government in 1996, the IMF proposed that there should be "prudential supervision of Malaysia's commercial banks and other financial institutions in facilitating further financial liberalisation." The concern of both the IMF and foreign investors was to ensure that there would be greater transparency and accountability in the management of banking and lending practices in the country. These concerns did not appear to have been heeded though, and by the time of the crisis the level of domestic loans had risen to 160% of GDP, making the country's economy even more vulnerable to currency attacks. However, it has to be pointed out that the big Malaysian banks and financial houses were not the only ones guilty of adding fuel to the already blazing economy: the role played by foreign banks in accelerating the mad rush of the '90s cannot be overlooked either. The IMF estimated that by the end of 1996, the total volume of loans from European, Japanese and American banks amounted to US$318 billion, US$260 billion and US$46 billion respectively. Much of this went into the rapidly developing economies of ASEAN, including Malaysia's.

an array of uncontrollable variables such as public opinion and market sentiment. The crisis showed how vulnerable the Malaysian economy was in the choppy waters of international trade. There were simply too many variables that were entirely beyond the control of the Malaysian authorities. What made things worse was the ineffectiveness of the Malaysian media in trying to address foreign reports and disinformation, and their failure to win public confidence from the Malaysians themselves. What the crisis taught the Malaysians was the lesson that a small developing country like theirs was no match for the combined forces of currency speculators working in tandem with a hostile international media that was bent on destabilizing the economy.

For the Islamist opposition the crisis also demonstrated the point that they had been making all the while: that despite all the talk of the Islamization of Malaysia's economy, the country remained a fundamentally capitalist state that was part of the global capitalist system and thus exposed to its internal weaknesses and contradictions. In 1999, the Islamists finally had their opportunity to put forward their own vision of an alternative economic system when they won control of the two northern states of Kelantan and Trengganu during the elections.

In search of an Islamic economic system to call their own: A critique of the Islamist economic model thus far

During the elections of 1999, the Islamists of PAS managed to gain control of the two northernmost states of the Malay peninsula, Kelantan and Trengganu. As soon as they came to power, PAS claimed that it would expose the economic mismanagement of UMNO and put forward an alternative economic system of its own that was based on the principles of Islam as laid out in the Qur'an and Sunnah of the Prophet.

But in time it appeared as if the alternative Islamic model of PAS was just as superficial and ineffective as that of the ruling establishment they condemned. Among PAS's first efforts was the abolition of the Eastern highway toll, the closing down of "immoral" business premises and practices such as mixed unisex barbers and hairdressing salons; and the shutting down of pubs and gambling establishments without licenses. Later came other measures that were intended to mark Islam's imprint on the states of Kelantan and Trengganu. In Trengganu, the Islamists soon banned mixed tourist trips and closed down mixed swimming pools and beaches. They also insisted that in future all tourists would be guided by guides of the same sex and that immoral establishments, such as cinemas, would be tightly regulated. (It was even reported that in some cinemas the lights were left on as the film was showing, to ensure that couples would not engage in "indecent" activity in the dark.) It appeared as if the Islamists of PAS were themselves degenerating into the caricatures of narrow-minded conservatives that the government-controlled media had accused them of being all along.

This is not to say that the Islamists were entirely bereft of clear ideas and critical thinking. Over the past few years (1999 to 2003) PAS has been at the forefront of exposing the economic dealings and mismanagement of the government in Malaysia. One particular scandal which helped to give the Islamist opposition the added leverage that they sought was the financial crisis within the *Lembaga Tabung Haji* (Hajj Pilgrims Management Fund) which reported a loss of several hundred million ringgit — allegedly due to financial wrong-doing by a number of the body's administrators as well as to poor investments made elsewhere.

Described as the "UMNO government's last frontier of Islamic respectability,"[25] the *Tabung Haji* had always been a major landmark in the new political landscape created by the State's own Islamization program. The financial scandals surrounding *Tabung Haji* only helped to erode the government's standing and Islamist credentials even further, much to the delight of PAS and the Islamist opposition movements. To compound the already messy situation, the open conflict between the two men who had been given the responsibility to run the institution — Dato' Dr. Hamid Othman (Religious advisor to the Prime Minister) and Dato' Abdul Hamid Zainal Abidin (ex-Brigadier General turned Cabinet Minister) — only made things worse. The crisis was only (tentatively) resolved when the Prime Minister stepped in personally and called for an investigation into what had gone wrong in the institution.

In May 2003, the PAS Member of Parliament Husam Musa released the party's audit of the government's financial activities over the past two decades in a book entitled *Dokumen Rasmi: BN Khianati Amanah Rakyat* (Official Documentation: The BN Coalition has Betrayed the Trust of the People).[26] Among other things, the extensive document noted that government-awarded contracts were paid in full to a number of

---

[25] M.G.G. Pillay, *A Jihad of Two Hamids*. Harakah, 16 September 2001, p. 15.
[26] Malaysiakini.com, *26 May 2003*, BPR Patut Jadikan Lapuran Audit Atas Siasatan.

contractors and developers even before the construction programs were finished.

The Islamists have also been hard at work chastising the government for its apparent u-turns and contradictions in policy. Between March and May 2003 the Islamists of PAS attacked the government's Islamic credentials and Islamization program after they revealed that an UMNO Member of Parliament (Tengku Adnan Tengku Mansor) and a subsidiary of the Pahang State Development Corporation (PASDEC) owned shares in a tourist resort that was granted the right to operate gambling slot-machines. This was a major issue as gambling is forbidden for Muslims in Malaysia and the country has only one legalized casino (operating at the Genting Highlands Resort). To make things worse, PAS also pointed out that the National Hajj Fund was also implicated, as it had major shareholdings in PASDEC, thus making it indirectly involved in the operation of the gambling machines in the resort.[27]

Scandals such as these did nothing to salvage the reputation of ostensibly Islamic institutions and the Islamic economic system that the Malaysian government has been trying to build. But having made all these allegations, what has PAS done to develop its own alternative economic model in the country?

Herein lies the problem that many Islamist movements, organizations and parties in the world have singularly failed to address. Enmeshed as they are in a global economic system that is shaped and guided by the logic of capitalism and its maxim of exploitative practices and profit-maximization, Islamist ideologues and economists have yet to address the negative effects of these practices in their own society. PAS in Malaysia is not alone in its failure to address the power-differentials and class structure that are the products of capitalist production. As Syed Vali Reza Nasr has argued in his study of the Islamist *Jama'at-i Islami* party of Pakistan, the same failure to challenge the dominant economic order in the country is seen in the politics of the *Jama'at*, despite its having been around since 1941:

> "Islamic revolution in the *Jama'at's* rhetoric is not the battle-cry of the masses but an elitist crusade aimed at appropriating the state. As a result, the *Jama'at* has adopted a pedantic and literary style and ignored populist themes. *The party even continues to respect the right of private property and has avoided challenging the existing economic structure of Pakistan…* In sort, the *Jama'at*

---

[27] Malaysiakini.com, 22 May 2003, "PAS MP: Umno bigwig second largest shareholder in 'slot machine' resort".

has failed to convert revivalism as an ideology into revivalism as a social movement. It has failed to mobilise the masses for collective action for any sustained period of time under an Islamic banner."[28]

It is this failure to use the discourse of normative Islam strategically and intelligently as a vehicle for social mobilization and economic-political reform that has moved critical Islamist scholars like Chandra Muzaffar to note that:

"(Today) many Islamic movements are seeking to understand the contemporary world through a perspective which has for centuries guided them and motivated them to seek justice and to pursue progress ...The perspective itself is not a problem. The real issue, however, is the way in which a majority of Islamic movements apply (or misapply) principles, values and laws associated with the *Qur'an*, the *Sunnah* and Muslim history to the contemporary world. It is this that raises some doubts about their capacity to address some of the fundamental questions of social change confronting Muslims today."[29]

The failure of many state-sponsored Islamization programs was, as we have seen, due to the fact that many of these grand projects were neither radical nor revolutionary. In the hands of statist-developmentalist elites, the discourse of Islam was merely used as a convenient ideology to justify and rationalize developmental projects that were often costly, counter-productive and of little social value. The state's manipulation of Islam — in the Malaysian case to use it in order to create a Weberian discourse of work, thrift and enterprise — merely led to the intensification of the Islamization race between the state and its Islamist opponents and raised the levels of expectation of the ordinary Muslim masses, but with little transformative effect.

Linked to this has been the apparent failure of Islamist thinkers themselves to adopt the intellectual and ideological tools from the schools of modern social sciences (political economy, political sociology, political science) in order to understand how and why such exploitative and divisive practices come about in the first place, and how concrete

---

[28] Seyyed Vali Reza Nasr, *The Vanguard of the Islamic Revolution: The Jama'at-i Islami of Pakistan*, I. B. Tauris, London, 1994, p. 222.
[29] Chandra Muzaffar, Islamic Movements and Social Change, in *Rights, Religion and Reform: Enhancing Human Dignity Through Spiritual and Moral Transformation*, Routledge Curzon, London, 2002, p. 204.

measures can be taken to regulate the economies of their countries in order to protect ordinary citizen-consumers as well as fledgling local economies. Islamists have also been visibly absent at most international rallies, demonstrations and conferences where the issue of globalization has been seriously discussed, giving the impression that they are uninterested in these developments, despite the fact that practically the entire Muslim world belongs to the developing Third World and that it is the ordinary Muslims of the world who are among the primary victims of the uneven and disruptive effects of globalization.

Can there be a way out of this ideological-political trap? One of the first things that the Islamists would have to do is move away from their own dependency on history and the discourse of Islamic historical authenticity in order to deal with the realities of the present. As Chandra has noted, this tendency to anchor one's political program and aspirations to models of the past has been the factor that has retarded and distorted the form and content of economics and politics in many Muslim countries, producing piecemeal alternative measures that in no way address the fundamental root causes of the problem with capitalism itself:

> "Some segments of the Islamic elite strata in the countries concerned are trapped in a mind-set which inhibits them from approaching the challenge of economic transformation from perspectives that are practical and dynamic. This explains, to some extent, why they often try to implement immediately what is proscribed in the *Quranic* text such as the prohibition of *riba* (interest) without first attempting to ameliorate the underlying problem of exploitation within the prevailing economic structures since one of the most abhorrent aspects of *riba*, as the *Qur'an* itself observes, is its exploitative element. It is precisely this inability to give due emphasis to the principles and values behind prohibitions and prescriptions that there are Muslim countries today which continue to be weighed down by glaring social-economic inequalities — in spite of the elimination of riba and the implementation of *zakat*."[30]

The Islamization programs in countries like Malaysia, Pakistan, Sudan, Iran and elsewhere have, by and large, failed because the Islamists themselves have not been able to understand the realities of globalization itself, and the tremendous power that international capital possesses today. While Muslim thinkers and politicians may be inspired by the past, it

---

[30] Chandra, 2002, p. 206.

should be remembered that we are living in the present where the problems that Muslim societies face are radically different from the challenges that were faced by the early Muslim community. As Chandra puts it:

> "While Muslims will continue to be inspired by the illustrious accomplishments of the past, they will have to reinterpret anew the values of the *Qur'an* in order to construct alternate models to the capitalist democracies they live in today."[31]

What is needed now, more than ever, is a melding of the universal ethical values of Islam with a coherent, systematic and thorough analysis of the failings and contradictions of global capitalism at the same time. This can only come about if and when the conservative *Ulama*, as custodians of Islamic knowledge and learning, learn to work hand in hand with scholars and social scientists from the fields of economics, finance, business, political science and sociology.

Thus far, the efforts to create a school of progressive Islamic thought that can halt the advances of global capital have been, simply put, pathetic and disappointing. As the world's media continues in its unstated campaign to demonize Islam and Muslim concerns, and as we are fed more and more negative images of Muslims as stereotypical terrorists and fanatics (from Osama bin Laden to Mullah Omar and the Taliban), the Muslim world needs a major breakthrough and a success story that provides them and others with a counter-factual example of progressive, dynamic Islam at work. Till then, the dream of an alternative Islamic economic system will remain a pipe-dream for many, and the Islamists will still be searching for an Islamic alternative model to call their own while they sip away at their Mecca-colas, which remain an imitation of "the real thing" and a testimony to the state of mimesis that contemporary Islamist economics has fallen into.

---

[31] Chandra, 2002, p. 25.

PART
3

Applications

INTRODUCTION

Business ethics as a form of conduct stretches over many different areas of economic behavior. It is fair to say that ethics (or the need for ethics) is the basis of all economic reasoning and practice, and the key reason that we advocate Total Ethical Management (TEM). The whole economic value chain observed within a TEM framework will ensure the long-term survival, sustainability and prosperity, in all senses, of the firm. Unethical behavior in a remote place in Indonesia where a multinational company runs a sweatshop, the unethical behavior of a contract supplier, or the unethical behavior of one single employee who enriches himself illegally can cause major corporate crises. Sweatshops, for instance, are commonly found in industries such as clothing, shoes, toys, sporting goods and some electronics, where production relies on modest technology and unskilled labor.[1]

If Asian businesses want to achieve sustainable recovery, they will have to fix ethical deficiencies along most links of their corporate management chains. This is mainly a short-term agenda and can be done immediately. As the value creation of any strategy begins with concrete reasoning and action, we want to answer very practical questions: What should corporations do differently? What imperatives should be

---

[1] In recent years, pressure has been mounting on companies which use sweatshop labor. The sportswear maker Nike, for example, has been the target of constant criticism because of its labor practices in Indonesia. Nike finally raised the minimum age for its workers in Indonesia and other places in Southeast Asia, requiring all factories to comply with US indoor air-quality regulations.

followed? And how does this ultimately lead to an approach of Total Ethical Management?

Higher ethical standards can be applied within the corporation — How do you treat your workers on the production lines? Are you an Equal Opportunity Employer? Do you adhere to the highest quality standards? — and in interactions with the corporate environment — How do you treat your shareholders? Are opaque business practices an option? and so on. Businesses are increasingly realizing that they are not separate from but part of their environments. Business ethics are ultimately a matter of trust and of relationships between individuals and/or companies.

We see the following as areas in which business ethics are to be applied and substantially incorporated:

Labor

High ethical standards in a corporation's relations with its employees are one of the prerequisites of Total Ethical Management. Even though improving work conditions, safeguarding employment and protecting workers in case of illness and after retirement are almost commonplace across the globe today, there are still black holes when it comes to implementation. Labor-employer relations have often been of a very hostile nature as pure Manchester-capitalism calls for the optimization of the finance portfolio of the investor. In order to overcome the traditional divide between labor and capital, unions should be perceived as social partners of the corporations. Moreover, as a prime concern of corporations is to attract and retain talented people, they should consider how to empower their employees. Companies with a reputation for bad ethical standards may have difficulties in creating a culture of high-performance and sustainable growth. Each employee should be given the opportunity both to earn a living and to obtain personal fulfillment. A fulfilled employee is more likely to give outstanding performance.

Leadership

The next step in the ethical value chain is leadership. True leaders adhere to the highest standards of ethical behavior. Leaders demonstrate their integrity on a daily basis and are not afraid to talk about values — they are inspiring models of values-based performance. Such leadership is more likely to result in employees giving the company their loyalty and superior performance. Employees want to feel proud of the company they work for and comfortable with its culture and values.

Management

Ethical principles are often state-of-the-art legal matters. Leaders have to ensure that they acknowledge, store and practice these principles throughout the organization. It is not enough to be a role model of ethical leadership — the implementation and management of business ethics is the next important part in the ethical value chain. This should include recording the values, developing policies and procedures to align behavior with preferred values, and then training all personnel in these policies and procedures.

The media

The media is a critical part of TEM, though in ways that are different from the other applications listed here. At the most basic level, the media serves as a public watchdog to expose cases of unethical behavior in business, politics and other spheres of activity. Indeed, this is how Caijing Magazine and websites such as malaysiakini have grown and extended their influence. There is a market for the public watchdog and, eventually, the rewards come. Beyond this, the media also serves to reinforce the practice of ethics by various actors on a day-to-day basis. By reporting fairly on relevant happenings, the media can inform the public and thus support positive trends. Lastly, the media also sets a very public example of the implementation of ethical precepts. In fact, the media is perhaps the one sector where ethical practice yields quick and identifiable rewards in readers, popularity and influence.

Public relations

Modern public relations has evolved in two stages. The first stage was when companies needed specific services to extend or create a public image, such as through advertising or events. The second stage is roughly seen as "corporate communications" and involves the actual development of this image in more strategic terms, which may include more extensive and meaningful efforts such as partnership, marketing, government relations and the like. Inside companies, public relations or corporate communications officers are their counterparts, the public's main channel for receiving news about the company. For both agents — inside and outside the company — the challenge is to present situations fairly, notwithstanding the company's vested interest, and to always engage the public in a transparent and trustworthy manner. Consumers in some regards expect to be "marketed" to but also trust in the company to uphold the highest ethical principles.

Regional relations

Corporations not only have to interact with their immediate corporate environments, they also have to gauge their position and possible interaction in a macro-economic and regional context. The envisioning of regional groupings, for example, is a task not only for governments and international organizations; corporations have to contribute as well — to bridge the proverbial divide between the different stakeholders in society.

Developing companies, whether in Asia or other regions, exhibit difficulties in achieving the level of ethical behavior required to play an active role in an interconnected and interdependent world. Even though the need for fair labor practices and leadership models may be recognized, many Asian corporations still fail to address the whole ethical value chain. High ethical standards are to be applied in all areas in which corporations conduct their economic activities.

It is interesting to observe that many Asian companies have applied high ethical standards within their local environments but have neglected to apply these ethical standards vis-à-vis stakeholders located outside the community, region or country. Japanese companies, for example, are renowned for caring for their employees, resulting in the typical pattern of lifetime employment.[2] In foreign subsidiaries, however, Japanese companies have been known to apply lower ethical standards. For example, in the late 1980s, a number of Japanese manufacturers provoked clashes with their workforces in Indonesia and Malaysia, where they refused to allow female assembly-line workers to wear traditional Muslim dress, citing safety reasons. A Japanese proverb goes "Leave home and cast away shame."

This is a well-known dichotomy expressed in the Japanese *uchi* (what is inside) and *soto* (what is outside). Different rules apply within the group (uchi) from those applied on the outside (soto). With this, the attitude toward a subject has to be differentiated from the position represented by the outside. The basic model of this behavioral pattern is

---

[2] Lifetime employment and promotion based on seniority are still fairly common in Japan, although this practice is changing towards Anglos Saxon-style promotion practices, especially since the end of the so-called bubble economy (1993) and the outbreak of the Asian financial crisis (1997).

the family (Japanese, *ie*, Chinese, *jia*, Korean, *taek*). In traditional Japanese society, the smallest uchi unit was the family; the next level was the extended family, followed by the village, the prefecture and the nation. Similarly in China, the basic social group is jia, the family, beyond which is *dajia* (big family, ie., the larger social group that includes non-family members). The largest group is called *guojia* (the country, state).

For Asian companies to fully realize the significance of these terms would require them to actively expand their respective circles of stakeholders. Currently, "good business practices" are usually applied in narrow terms to the company's inner circle (for example, its direct and major clients) and in legally required instances (for example, government or stock market filings, investor briefings). Such a short-term, selfish and opportunistic approach will not suffice for the 21st century, and the backlash has already begun in the West. Asia must be quick to adapt and companies which do not heed the signs will suffer the consequences.

To achieve a more rigorous ethical program, companies should extend this narrowly defined concept of stakeholders to include the public, society at large and, indeed, the global community. We are not referring here to advertising campaigns designed to convince the public of an image, but rather to a holistic effort to evaluate operations and plan development along lines of community benefit, in the wider sense. Taking each of the aspects addressed above, the company should seek to first examine its own ethical make-up and then to enact its holistic transformation. This is conceived of as a process of looking in and reaching out, in coordinated action driven by principle. This transformation is discussed in Part 4.

7

REGIONAL RELATIONS
Ethics and the Evolution of Asian Affairs

Rini Soewandi

Minister for Trade and Industry, Indonesia

This chapter aims in part to define those aspects of Asian business that can contribute to the development of ethics in general in the global society. In this context, I would like to point to the Asian value of doing business based on the trust of the individuals concerned. In Asia, irrespective of the size of the company, people count and trust is developed over time. Business and friendship go hand in hand.

Apart from the factor of trust, I will also draw attention to the number of Asian companies that have developed their own codes of ethics without prompting from government. However, the crucial issue facing the international community is whether business ethics are compatible with the untrammeled pursuit of profit. I believe that as long as a company's sole perspective is to generate profit, there may be little room for ethics.

In the Indonesian context, recent increases in labor costs have resulted in decisions taken by a number of companies to relocate, with all the attendant problems this causes. This is not an ethical approach to doing business. Where there is a lack of productivity, the company concerned should invest the time and resources to identify the problem and improve its overall performance.

It is important to embrace a very wide concept in defining business ethics. In particular, companies operating in the private sector, however large or small, should endeavor to contribute to the social and economic welfare of their employees. While the pursuit of profit remains of importance to the private sector, costs associated with developing human resources, enhancing innovative capacities, supporting activities, etc., should be readily accepted, particularly in those companies that form a large part of a country's industrial landscape.

At the same time, it is important for government to secure the confidence of the private sector. In general terms, the rule of law and good governance should be respected and implemented. In the particular case of developing countries, governments should strive to encourage the optimum allocation of resources and encourage a performance-oriented environment. These are often sadly lacking.

Above all, a primary goal for a government is to be able to encourage conditions for economic growth that would allow companies to readily adopt social and welfare obligations in fulfilling and contributing to the wider obligations of society.

In the West, the level of economic development is such that companies are able, and often willing, to contribute to the social and economic welfare of their workforce. They are able to invest in, amongst other factors, increasing productivity and developing human resources. In developing countries, the only means of achieving similar aims is to generate sufficient economic growth to allow companies not only to generate profits, but also to embrace the wider social and welfare goals mentioned.

In addition to being ranked among the developing nations, Indonesia also faced the worst of the Asian crisis, with negative growth rates during the period 1997–1998. At the same time, we have embarked on the establishment of what is the largest democracy in Asia. The new Indonesian government has been committed to rebuilding Indonesia as a functional and democratic nation. Strenuous efforts have been made to restore political stability and implement economic reforms. Our country is now beginning to experience modest development, and overall national strength has also started to gain momentum after years of difficulties since the onset of the financial and political crisis in mid 1997. Last year, the Indonesian economy experienced growth of 3.7%, supported by export revenue of US$57 billion. For the year 2003, growth is estimated to be around 3.5% to 4%. While this growth is positive, it is barely adequate to meet the existing debt burden, let alone the creation of a social and welfare fabric in the country.

To achieve the creation of such a social fabric, market access for developing countries is crucial and while the Doha Declaration was noble in declaring a Round for the benefit of developing countries, subsequent negotiations have fallen well short of this mark. The inability to meet commitments made in trade negotiations may also be considered as an unethical business practice of the highest order.

Introduction

The following contribution addresses ethics in the context of business in Indonesia, regionally and, taking account of the effect of globalization, at the international level. I address the issue of ethics at three levels deliberately because, ultimately, instilling ethics into a society can no longer be achieved without coordinated action at national, regional and international level.

Indeed, the global economy has opened up all of our markets, not only from the standpoint of economics and trade, but it has also imposed its own standards, or at least influenced our social and moral behavior. This in itself poses both opportunities and possible dangers. In the case of Indonesia, promoting ethics in business requires us to identify and focus on what is good in our particular society so that it is not lost. At the same time, we must be open to regional and international influences that also contribute to introducing sound ethical practices worldwide.

There are many ways to define what constitutes business ethics. Recent corporate scandals in the West would suggest that business ethics can only be assured through fair, transparent and honest accounting. As a consequence, as long as accounting standards are upheld and, where necessary, with the effective force of law, this will encourage sound business ethics.

Ethics in business is not merely a question of accounting and legal standards and practices, but covers a much broader perspective. I do not believe that business and social and moral responsibility should be separated. *A sense of business ethics is not born out of effective controls, but should arise naturally out of society, which we create and to which we are bound to contribute.*

Good, ethical business practices in the private sector are not merely a question of honesty in pursing business, but represent the overall approach of a company in taking care of the people it employs. Business ethics requires companies to show responsibility to their personnel, to develop human resources, to generate enthusiasm amongst the workforce, to be fair in setting wage levels, to use a policy of advancement which identifies promising staff on the basis of performance and, in so doing, contributes to a performance-oriented environment.

From the point of view of government, I uphold the importance of strong legal and accounting standards. However, these standards do not in themselves promote business ethics. On the contrary, they are often designed to address the consequences of a lack of business ethics.

Ethics in Indonesian society can best evolve by ensuring the optimum allocation of resources through improved education and social services, and ensuring material prosperity for the population through economic growth. Government has to promote policies which can create the basis for the private sector to implement business ethics along these lines.

As Minister of Industry and Trade for Indonesia, I also have to stress that advancement of these goals, which are largely taken for granted in most Western societies, will only be achieved if developing countries are allowed to fully benefit from the global economy; notably through substantially improved access to the markets of developed countries.

Development of business ethics in Indonesia

During the period of Indonesia's sustained economic growth, the country was considered a model by, amongst others, the World Bank. We certainly achieved very impressive growth rates and were considered to be on the doorstep, if not already a part, of the new Asian Tiger economies.

At that time, there was a growing perception and fear in the West that Asia would soon overrun the economies of the developed countries. It was commonly believed that Asian people worked harder than Westerners and were more loyal to their companies. This was considered to be a potent cocktail for success. Success was also considered to be partly a reflection of the number of family-run businesses, which were able to take quick decisions without the need for lengthy corporate discussions. A number were also able to instill paternalistic instincts in their workforce and this helped instill the business ethic of hard work.

This is not to say that all Westerners believed in the Asian miracle. In this context, I recall Viscount Etienne Davignon of the European Union questioning the miracle in Japan, saying that it reflected, among other factors, an all-too-cozy relationship between the owners of companies and their banks.

After the economic crises, the truth of the Asian miracle emerged cruelly. In Indonesia, the economic miracle very much depended on foreign investment, low labor costs and an abundance of raw materials. Large numbers of family-run businesses had not invested in the future competitiveness of their companies, and all too many were convinced by the banking community to speculate and invest in non-core assets. In addition, the cozy relationships between bank owners and companies were also seen to be responsible for what can be considered to be the equivalent of economic collapse. When the Rupiah plunged, vast sectors of Indonesian industry became technically bankrupt.

A number of observers consider that the economic crisis was brought on by a breakdown of traditional Asian business ethics based on the development of long-term trust. The economic crisis was made significantly worse by a lack of awareness of business ethics, both within the country and from those dealing with Indonesia. Of the former, a number of family-run businesses had focused on securing short-term profit without developing a strategy for the long term. In the outside world, the international banking community was quick to offer loans to Indonesian companies that were encouraged to speculate in non-core assets, notably property. The lethal cocktail of short-term profit and diversion of investment to non-core assets affected a number of Asian companies, not only in Indonesia.

As the Asian crisis unfolded, closer scrutiny of the industrial fabric of Asian society was found wanting. Close co-operation based on trust posed the danger of collusion, corruption and nepotism. As a consequence of such practices, there is an urgent need to reconsider the structure of Indonesian industry and, in particular, the ethics upon which it is based.

Western model of business ethics

At the time, the meltdown of the Asian economies was partly attributed to a lack of accountability and transparency at company level, particularly in family-run businesses. In Indonesia, it took the authorities several months to actually account for the loans raised by the private sector.

As a result, family-run businesses were urged to adopt corporate structures along Western lines. It was considered that the involvement of professionals, combined with responsibility to shareholders through public offerings, would improve transparency and the honesty of business practices. This is not to say that all family-run businesses lacked a corporate approach to business, but many did.

While the Western model of corporate business philosophy is increasingly taking root in Indonesia, recent developments have cast a shadow over the corporate structure as the best means of securing viable business ethics. Among other factors, the excesses of CEOs and the emphasis of many companies in the West on defending and shoring up their share price, seems to divert efforts away from the fundamentals of running a business, and puts on a pedestal the importance of generating profits or reducing losses in periods of recession. As a result, we have seen the collapse of Enron in the United States, and, many years before in Europe, that of the Maxwell empire. Furthermore, a lack of business ethics is also visible in times of recession, with the apparent readiness of companies to downsize employment to maintain the "bottom line" in spite of the social anguish that this entails.

These failures and practices should not overshadow the notable success of a number of companies in the West such as Shell, ICI and Unilever which adopt a comprehensive social policy and are willing to absorb the cost of improving the social and economic welfare of the people they employ and the environment in which they operate.

On balance, I would be very cautious about developing Western-style corporate structures wholeheartedly as the basis for sound Indonesian business ethics. The application of the rule of law, the adoption of fair accounting principles and controls on trade in securities are all valuable attributes and experiences to be gained from the West in safeguarding business ethics. However, I believe Asian social and moral responsibility can be tapped to develop Asian business ethics, which in turn could be promoted internationally.

Asian experience of business ethics

Within Asia there are examples of family-run businesses that have adopted long-standing and very sound business ethics. In Indonesia in general, the cultural environment developed within our society moulds corporate behavior. In particular, emphasis is placed on harmony and the importance attached to religion is often reflected in the tolerance shown by management with respect to the religious holidays of all the major faiths and to the time for individual prayer. There is probably no other country in the world that respects all religions in the manner of Indonesia.

Having worked in the private sector prior to my current appointment, to avoid favoritism I hesitate to cite an example of an Indonesian company. I will therefore refer to other companies in the Asian region. The Siam Cement Group (SCG) in Thailand is a family-owned company established in 1913. While its core business is cement, it has diversified significantly through subsidiaries and joint ventures into activities such as plaster-board, plastic and so on. There are a number of Siam Cement subsidiaries in Indonesia. Siam Cement has adopted a code of ethics based on four cardinal principles:

Adherence to fairness

As laid out in their corporate literature, this involves:

- providing quality products and services at appropriate and fair prices
- providing employees with salaries and benefits comparable to leading employers in the same industry
- striving for business growth and stability leading to good long-term returns for shareholders
- being fair to all parties — customers, suppliers and others.

Belief in the value of the individual

The company acknowledges that its personnel are its most valued asset. Owners and management stress that it is the employees who have contributed to the growth and prosperity of the company. They further highlight the importance of a performance-oriented environment by highlighting the practice of recruiting quality employees, and encouraging them to grow with the company. They also attach importance to treating personnel in such a way that they feel secure in their jobs and are committed to their assignments so that they can be performed with confidence.

Concern for social responsibility

The company stresses that it "operates on the basis of a firm sense of responsibility towards the nation and the society of which they are a part. The Siam Cement Group places national interest above its own economic gains." I also believe that dedication to fulfilling the national interest is crucial.

Dedication to excellence

The company highlights the importance of innovation: there are always better ways of doing things. It is committed to performing better through mobilizing resources to achieve further improvements.

This Group exemplifies the best in good Asian practices. Western business society would do well to follow the example of such a company. While profit remains important to the Group, it is also concerned about the well-being of its personnel and about its reputation in the wider environment.

I understand that the Group has restructured in the face of the Asian crisis. While this has involved limited redundancies, the Group has maintained its principles, which have proven to be able to withstand the worst of the Asian crises and to have emerged strongly.

There are further examples of companies, such as the Tata Group in India, that have also developed their own business practices. The development of human resources is considered to be of particular importance within these groups and they actively contribute to the overall social welfare of the nation.

In the two examples cited, the pursuit of profit alone or the exploitation of cheap labor is not the *leitmotif* of these companies. They have accepted the additional costs associated with participation in strengthening the social fabric of the nation in which they operate. They are therefore good role models for the adoption and the definition of business ethics.

Promoting business ethics in Indonesia

Indonesian industrial development is of recent date and the business ethics that may have existed in the past were voluntary in nature. This is not to say that they did not exist in one form or the other, but they usually depended on the company and individual concerns.

During the years of its "dirigisme" policy towards economic growth, the Government of Indonesia promoted the development of prominent state enterprises to cover the development of, among others, the oil, cement, steel and chemical sectors. In receiving the benefits of virtually captive markets, they were also expected to contribute to the overall social goals of the nation through generating employment, developing human resources, training, health and insurance and assisting in the industrialization of Indonesia. This system worked quite well, though over time it may also have contributed to certain companies being able to dominate the industrial landscape and to the attendant inefficiencies that this may have caused.

Following the Asian crisis, recommendations to broaden the industrial base of the economy have contributed indirectly to providing guidelines for the development of business ethics. In particular, anti-trust laws have been introduced to encourage greater competition on the Indonesian market. At the same time, import tariffs have declined substantially, thereby increasing competition. In addition, efforts are being made to encourage the rule of law. A number of organizations have been established in an attempt to control and eradicate corruption.

I consider these mechanisms to be of importance to Indonesia, though they are insufficient in themselves to encourage business ethics as previously defined. Overall, they are intended to offer a framework within which Indonesian business can function but do not in themselves instill the social responsibility which, I stress, is the key to the development of overall business ethics.

At this juncture, I would like to turn to the role of the Government of Indonesia. The government should, of course, endeavor to promote and implement mechanisms such as competition policy effectively, though I believe that their effectiveness increasingly depends on a global approach to such issues. However, as I have mentioned, the key to developing business ethics is to encourage the private sector to embrace a number of social responsibilities. In this respect, the Indonesian Government can of course contribute to the process in a number of ways.

Encouraging proper allocation of resources

Without interfering in the economy, it is crucial to encourage, to the greatest possible extent, the proper allocation of resources. Our Government must be able to promote and maximize the allocation of resources. Urgent priorities would include education in general; but the development of specific skills, in particular, is needed to render our industrial base competitive in the global economy.

At the private-sector level, there are a number of leverages that can be used, particularly the introduction of fair and transparent rules through competition laws. The process of abolishing all types of exclusive permits and business monopolies that created inefficiency in the Indonesian economy is at an advanced stage. We enacted the Anti-Monopoly and Unfair Business Competition Law in March 1999. This is an instrument of economic law that protects the interests of small enterprises and cooperatives, as well as consumers, which serve as the foundation of the economic activities of the nation. The other main objective is to prohibit vertical restrictions on competition and any deals or contracts allowing for oligopolies, monopsonies, price-fixing cartels, market manipulation and geographical designation of markets between suppliers. The Law embodies "market behavior principles" instead of a market structure. Under the Law, companies that behave in a manner that abuses a dominant position are liable to be investigated.

Within the Government, public-sector salaries need to be improved. Individuals and their families should be able to rely on their salaries to maintain a reasonable standard of living. While we strive for ethical standards, we have to provide the basis for their development within society.

Encouraging a performance-oriented environment

It is crucial for our country to encourage the development of performance-oriented environments throughout our society. There should be a system to identify those elements in our society that are among the most capable, in both the public and private sectors alike.

Social safety net

The encouragement of ethical standards also requires the development of a social safety net so that there is basic health care and education for everybody.

Quality of life

Quality of life is important. In particular, programs and projects should be oriented to improving traffic congestion in major cities, particularly in Jakarta, and environmental controls need to be developed further.

Private sector

The private sector in Indonesia should be encouraged to associate itself with the moral and social fabric of the nation. Overall, this has been lacking for a number of years. There has been a lack of trust between the public and private sectors. However, a government that is able to maximize the allocation of resources and improve basic social amenities will help to bridge this gap. Taxes should be seen to be put to good use.

At the same time, the private sector in Indonesia should acknowledge the importance of contributing to this process; training programs, scholarships to study overseas, the provision of basic health and social security amenities, and ensuring that the company itself adopts a performance-oriented environment are crucial.

For foreign direct investment (FDI), it is not sufficient to consider Indonesia as a resource of cheap labor or as a statistic in comparative productivity levels. There should be long-term commitment from the companies concerned to developing the social fabric and the overall welfare of the nation. Maximizing profits from the comparative advantage that we possess should go hand in hand with a responsible social and welfare policy for employees.

Relocating from Indonesia (such as we have seen recently) simply because of increasing labor costs or declining productivity levels is not an ethical practice when one considers the livelihood of the employees concerned. It would not arise if the companies concerned were associated with the social welfare of the nation.

All these initiatives are intended to create the cement in which ethical standards can develop. Yet in a society in which basic amenities are not assured and hardship is common, it is very difficult to encourage social and moral behavior to underpin business ethics.

Creating an ethical environment

While recent problems in the West have shown the difficulty of maintaining business ethics in general, problems in developing countries are far more acute. It is unrealistic to expect a developing country to be able to apply strong business ethics where the livelihood of the general population is poor. In Indonesia, even the middle class have problems making ends meet. Young graduates entering a profession have starting salaries of around US$80–100 per month. Job vacancies often attract applications from hundreds, if not thousands, of well-trained Indonesians. Salaries in general remain low, while living costs continue to increase.

The issue is how to generate prosperity at the private-sector level in order to increase the capacity of companies to provide more adequately for the workforce. In this context, it is appropriate to address the question of why Indonesian business in general failed to broaden national prosperity during periods of double-digit growth. In this respect, the short-term perspective of many Indonesian industries resulted in a lack of resources being devoted to investment in the future. There are still today very few Indonesian companies that are geared to securing a leading edge in the future. Little investment is devoted to research and development and the focus on marketing remains inadequate. Large sectors of the Indonesian economy continue to compete on high-volume, low-margin products.

For example, while the textile industry remains very vibrant internationally, large sectors of the Indonesian industry continue to compete in relatively low-value segments of the market. In many cases, Indonesian companies are producing goods with very low margins. Footwear is another example where Indonesian industry is hard pressed to even cover labor costs, let alone generate the funds to contribute to the social and welfare fabric of the nation.

If anything, the competition now unleashed in the global economy is making the situation much worse. Where Indonesian industry does not possess a comparative advantage in raw materials, we are forced to try to keep labor costs at a minimum in order to compete globally. At the same time, the lowering of tariffs is unleashing competition on the domestic market. As a result, Indonesian industry is under intense competitive pressure.

A number of measures can be taken to try to improve wealth generation. In specific cases, the government of Indonesia may encourage the development of research and development or improved marketing skills in certain sectors, or encourage investment in value-added sectors. In other cases, we may wish to encourage investment in those sectors where Indonesia possesses a comparative advantage other than simply cheap labor costs. Development of our own fishery and agricultural resources is an obvious example. Woodworking and furniture, and the paper and pulp industries are also important.

Such initiatives are unlikely to succeed without the general commitment of the international community. Unless markets are opened to Indonesian products in general, it is unlikely that Indonesia can generate the wealth to be able to establish an effective social and welfare system that would underpin sound business ethics in our society.

Indonesia has increasingly opened its markets to foreign competition. There is no doubt that the hidden hand of the market has improved efficiencies within the Indonesian economy. The process may, however, also have reduced the ability of the nation to generate income for social needs. The positions of conglomerates and state enterprises are being challenged and their ability to meet social and welfare objectives for their employees is increasingly being threatened.

While, on balance, the opening of the Indonesian market is irreversible as part of the process of globalization, it should be stressed clearly that sound business ethics in Indonesia will not just emerge on the basis of strengthening laws and accounting principles. Such ethics can only be underpinned through the generation of wealth. The private sector in Indonesia should not just be considering the bottom line of profit or maintaining favorable labor costs, but should also accept responsibility for improving social and welfare conditions. To do so, it must be able to generate the income required. Access to foreign markets is therefore of crucial importance and lack of market access will not provide the wealth needed for Indonesia to institute favorable social and welfare conditions.

Regionalism

Western-inspired efforts to reinforce the rule of law, combined with, for example, the introduction of competition policies such as has occurred in Indonesia, have been repeated in a number of Asian countries, particularly those that sought assistance from the International Monetary Fund (IMF) following the Asian crisis. Bearing in mind the importance of foreign investment to the prosperity of the region, we are often reminded that the rule of law, good governance and sound business practices are prerequisites for attracting foreign investment. However, these efforts do not address the issue of business ethics. In this context, I believe that it is important for the Asian region to have a common understanding on the broader definition of business ethics and, in particular, the efforts required to create a climate in which business ethics can thrive.

On the basis of a broad definition of business ethics to include participation in the social and welfare development of a nation, the following needs to be considered:

Attracting foreign investment

A number of countries in the ASEAN region have very similar economies. We compete with them to attract foreign investment, either by highlighting our lower labor costs and claims of productivity or by providing various tax incentives. At a government level, we are not particularly ethical in our approach in that we are selling our working populations short and we are also reducing the tax base by providing incentives. This is not a particularly ethical approach to attracting investment.

While it is necessary and desirable to attract FDI, I would recommend that the region should adopt common standards for FDI to ensure that companies also understand the importance of contributing to the social and economic welfare of the countries in which they operate. We should draw on the experience of companies such as Siam Cement and the Tata Group and perhaps adopt their standards for FDI. This will also help to encourage FDI that does not simply see a country in terms of low labor costs and the ability to maximize profits, but which also sees itself as a partner in contributing to the nation in which it operates.

Although it could be suggested that such an approach would be unattractive to foreign investment, I do not believe this is so. The ASEAN region has a lot to offer. A significant proportion of FDI is either designed to exploit the resources of the region or aims to be an actor in markets which still offer considerable potential for growth. The region is not without leverage, but we have to use this leverage to improve the social welfare of our countries.

I also believe that FDI should welcome such an initiative in that the political and economic stability of a country ultimately depends on the welfare and social conditions of its people. Governments showing responsibility for their people will be well received and, in return, we must endeavor to improve transparency in business practices and adherence to the rule of law.

Encouraging domestic investment to support the ideal

The responsibility of the private sector is not limited to FDI. I would like to see the introduction of voluntary codes of ethics at a regional level. While it may not be possible for all companies to adopt standards such as those exemplified by Siam Cement, they are worthy of being laid out as objectives to achieve.

For domestic investment, we should consider the means by which this can help companies become more competitive and achieve greater prosperity in the global economy. This could involve intensifying larger regional initiatives at industry level.

Codes of conduct at the regional level

I fully support institutionalizing codes of conduct for business at the regional level, and primarily within the AFTA region. The guiding principles relating to, for example, an adherence to fairness, a belief in the value of the individual, a concern for social responsibility and a dedication to excellence should be developed within our respective private sectors.

Above all, we must draw lessons from the Western economies, particularly regarding the pressure exerted on publicly listed companies to support share prices by generating profits and dividends. While the approach in the West is to tighten accounting principles, we should encourage greater understanding from, among others, shareholders and investment bankers of the importance of rating companies in accordance with their social and welfare roles.

Developing regional initiatives for research and development, transfer of technology

While wealth creation allows for the introduction of ethical standards, the Asian region has for too long been considered as either a supplier of basic raw materials and commodities or as a cheap production outlet in the global economy. Quite often, Indonesian companies produce to order according to specifications and designs. They are told where to source raw materials and they may not even know the final destination of the goods concerned.

I am not against such industrial practices, which form part of an interdependence in the global economy. However, these practices do not sustain economic progress in the long term. There is therefore a need to intensify initiatives such as the pooling of research and development resources at regional level. Furthermore, there is a need to add value to our products by, for instance, moving along the distribution and marketing chains. For example, we should be more willing to share and develop trading houses abroad as a way to penetrate markets. It is unethical that the region simply be considered as a production outlet because of cheap labor. We have to be able to reverse this process.

Common position at the global level

It will be increasingly important at the global level for the region to adopt common positions. It is important for members of the World Trade Organization (WTO) to understand that ethical standards should be met in trade negotiations. In particular, it is important that the Doha Declaration concerning benefits for developing countries be respected by full implementation. The mercantile approach to market access wherein the most sensitive sectors of Western economies, such as agriculture, remain protected will not result in an equitable distribution of wealth in the global economy. In such circumstances, it is unrealistic to expect much progress on ethical standards in business at the global level.

Global initiatives

- ## Market access for developing countries is indispensable

Ethical standards in business also need to be considered at the international level. The strengthening of the rule or law or of accounting practices does not address issues at the global level. In the Asian context, there is a need to ensure that developing countries are able to participate more fully in the benefits of globalization. As I have stressed before, business enterprises must be encouraged to think beyond short-term profit and to embrace the social and welfare aspirations of the employees and countries in which they operate. The prospects of achieving this in Indonesia depend on wealth creation. In a global economy, this depends on securing market access for Indonesian products.

Indonesia has already chosen the path of participating in the global economy. The benefits of the Indonesian market are increasingly opened to the outside world. Industries from the West are present in most of the prominent sectors of Indonesian industrial manufacturing activity and finished goods continue to flow to our market both in sensitive and non-sensitive sectors. Bearing this in mind, we must be able to secure market access for our products abroad. Continuing to put forward obstacles designed to maintain protection for agricultural products denies the developing world access to sectors in which it has comparative advantage. It is not ethical to be given access to markets for products in which we can barely compete. This approach to trade negotiations is unethical and should change.

- ## Adopting international standards for working conditions

I fully support the need to adopt basic international standards governing appropriate working conditions. While the International Labor Organization (ILO) has a key role to play, the desire to integrate labor standards into the WTO framework is of deep concern, as it appears to be an attempt to defeat the competitive edge that developing-world companies may possess in lower labor costs.

On the issue of labor, I would like to see the ILO further develop codes of conduct to be adopted in business communities internationally. It should be acknowledged that business ethics includes social and economic considerations and not just regulatory controls. A broader understanding is essential.

- ## Standards of ethics

It should also be conceivable to develop an international standard system whereby the good practice of companies operating internationally could be acknowledged and highlighted, with all the possible marketing advantages that this could entail. This will help promote ethical standards in the business community. Here, the code of ethics of the Siam Cement Group is a good example.

- ## International controls on lending

The banking community appears not to have learned lessons from the past. While lending remains invaluable as the fuel for industrial growth, banks must also be able to assess more adequately the risk of loans granted and investments made. The ASEAN crisis was, to a certain extent, due to the foolhardy manner in which banks were eager to encourage companies to accept loans to diversify from their core businesses. The financial community should contribute to laying the foundation of ethics in the financial sector.

Conclusions

The development of ethics in business depends on the society in which we operate. The emphasis on profit dilutes ethical standards and it is therefore important to link the pursuit of profit with other goals, such as contributing to the social and economic welfare of employees in addition to contributing to the social fabric of the nation in which the company operates.

There is a significant number of companies that do adopt policies that are not solely directed at maximizing profits. There are a number in Asia that I would call flagship companies that have adopted their own code of ethics without any prompting from government. However, the overall development of ethics depends on economic growth and prosperity. In Indonesia there are a number of flagship companies but they are few and far between.

A major problem in developing countries is the lack of wealth generation to support social and welfare development, at both government and private-sector levels. There are additional problems associated with maximizing the allocation of resources and encouraging a performance-oriented environment.

In the global economy, the level of competition has intensified and this has accentuated the problems of developing countries. The environment is not conducive to the widespread adoption of ethical standards simply because they cannot be afforded.

Ethics is not only an issue of the way in which a company operates; it also involves the behavior of government in economic and trade relations. In this global economy, commitments made by governments should be respected and implemented. In this context, the Doha Declaration supporting a Trade Round for developing countries is yet to materialize. On the contrary, the developed world continues to protect sensitive sectors of its economies while using the trade system to prise open the economies of other markets. This approach is not ethical, but rather reflects the mercantile attitude of old.

At the regional level, Asian countries should group together and adopt a common position on trade negotiations. We should also encourage a more ethical approach to attracting foreign direct investment. We should encourage the wider adoption of codes of ethics at the private-sector level. Social values should be disseminated and companies encouraged to work with employees to achieve common goals.

At the international level, the role of international organizations such as the ILO should be enhanced. However, the voluntary adoption of standards should be encouraged, with companies who adopt the standards rewarded with appropriate certification. Such ethical standards should also cover financial houses and banks, a number of which precipitated, if not caused, the Asian crisis.

In closing, let me state that the "Asian values" that are displayed in many traditional family-run companies do offer a path for the development of ethical standards within the wider context of modern business. The concern of this type of company for the welfare of its employees represents not only a humanitarian approach to business, but a formula for long-term strength. The combination of such an approach with modern management systems, including provisions for future investment for development, does offer a useful model. It is also clear that such values require support from government in creating a conducive environment in which such values can thrive. Ultimately, though, attempts to create a society based on responsible and ethical policies will only succeed with the granting of ethical business conditions by the developed world. A cooperative regional approach offers possibly the only means of persuading the developed world that the development of sustainable communities based on ethical values is beneficial to all.

8

LABOR
Business, Ethics and Labor

Lim Boon Heng

Secretary General of the National Trades Union Congress, Singapore and Minister, Prime Minister's Office, Government of Singapore

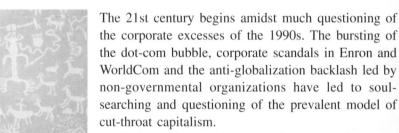 The 21st century begins amidst much questioning of the corporate excesses of the 1990s. The bursting of the dot-com bubble, corporate scandals in Enron and WorldCom and the anti-globalization backlash led by non-governmental organizations have led to soul-searching and questioning of the prevalent model of cut-throat capitalism.

Unions play a role in shaping and defining the ongoing debate about a more ethical or sustainable form of capitalism. Unions have a role in building such a form of "ethical capitalism."

Ethical capitalism at its heart is not exploitative or adversarial, but collaborative and consensual, seeking to build wealth that is equitably shared, not amassed wealth for the privileged few.

Unlike the dog-eat-dog world of cut-throat capitalism, ethical capitalism is characterized by a sense of common values. Instead of exploitation, trust and values-based regulation lubricate transactions.

It is not only ethics teachers or priests that should bother about ethics. Ethics has practical advantages in business. Trust and integrity lower transaction costs. They create positive externalities that are enjoyed by all in the market. Proper, values-based regulation too is a component of business ethics. Some economists have concluded that there is a cost to poor corporate governance regulation, reflected in a discount of the share price.

Investors mauled by the spate of corporate fraud are demanding more rigorous regulation. What they want is not more rules, but better rules. Workers want rules that will protect their interests, not sacrifice them to shareholders' interests.

The basic framework of ethical capitalism is a perspective based on common values, not adversarial relationships. Corporations serve stakeholders, not only shareholders. Stakeholders include employees, customers, business partners and the community.

Within this framework, unions advocate an equitable sharing of profit with workers, in line with value-added productivity and contribution from workers.

Ethical capitalism is not an emasculated form of capitalism. It is robust, involving all stakeholders in responding to the challenges of globalization such as the widening income disparities within and across nations.

Stakeholders

First, an elaboration of the importance of stakeholders, which will help shed light on the true purpose of business.

We have become so enamored of the prevalent perspective of the 1980s and 1990s that shareholders' interests must be paramount because of the risk they shoulder, that we forget how aberrant such a view is in history.

For millennia, there has been a strong line of thinking that businesses have responsibilities beyond their shareholders. Ideas that are precursors of the "stakeholder" theory have been with us since ancient times. In classical Greece, businesses were expected to be of service to the community. In the medieval period, a good businessman had to be honest in intention and actions and was expected to use his profits in a socially responsible way. The ideas of "noblesse oblige" (the responsibility of the rulers to the ruled) and the Confucian concept of benevolent rule, represent an analogous concept of social responsibility among European aristocracy and Confucian leaders. Several British businesses subscribe to the Quaker ethic, which subscribes to the same thinking.

In the 20th century, debate that businesses should adopt broader responsibilities revived in the 1930s, with Chester I. Barnard's *The Functions of the Executive* arguing that the firm serves society, and putting forward the position that corporations are means to larger ends, rather than ends in themselves. In 1953, Howard Bowen's path-breaking book *Social Responsibilities of the Businessman* argued that businesses are "servants of society" and that "management merely in the interests (narrowly defined) of stockholders is not the sole end of their duties." In other words, businesses exist to serve society, not stockholders.

This is not to deny corporations their right to make profit. Just as schools serve society by educating children, parliaments by making laws and politicians by aggregating diverse interests, so corporations serve society by making and selling goods and services for profit. This profit oils the economy; it is the currency of exchange by which corporations pay workers, and workers pay schools to educate their children, and both workers and corporations pay taxes for the benefit of society. Without businesses, there would be no commerce; and without commerce, no profit; without profit, no wages; and without wages, there is only indentured labor, not labor that is mobile and free.

Thus businesses serve society by making profit. But profit is the means, not the end. In his book *Not for Bread Alone*, Japanese business guru Konosuke Matsushita put it this way:

> "Some people think that the purpose of an enterprise is to make a profit. Indeed, profit is indispensable for conducting proper enterprise activities...However, profit in itself is not the ultimate goal of an enterprise. More basic is the effort to improve human life through enterprise management. Profit becomes important and necessary only to better pursue this basic mission."

Once we realign our perspective, many things fall into place. Corporations make profit in order to serve society better. Making a profit is thus a means, not the end.

Forces of globalization and Singapore's response

The excesses of capitalism are magnified a hundred-fold by the openness of markets and the rapid flow of finance, technology, information and labor that are the result of globalization. Few societies can insulate themselves from the global commercial markets nowadays, although not a few desire to. Rapid movements of goods, and interactions of finance and information, have created porous borders, limiting nation states' ability to determine the fate of their economies and that of their peoples. As the recent, rapid spread of the severe acute respiratory syndrome (SARS) shows, what happens in Guangzhou leads to consequences all over the world, from Hong Kong, Beijing, Hanoi and Singapore, to Toronto and Taipei.

Globalization and the rise in international trade and investments are fundamentally altering the employment relationship and present unions with new challenges.

Harvard economist Dani Rodrik points out in *Has Globalization gone too far?* that globalization has made the demand for labor more elastic, as workers in domestic economies become more easily substitutable by foreign workers. This has widened the skill premium and depressed wages at the bottom end of the workforce, widening income gaps between different skill levels. At the same time, it has also widened income disparities within skill groups. Economists estimated that trade contributed to between 10% and 20% of the wage differential between high school dropouts and other workers in the 1980s.

While capital has become more mobile, labor — especially low-wage labor — has not. This reduces the bargaining power of workers vis-à-vis employers and, in turn, erodes labor's ability to press for a fair share of enterprise profits. Economists studying wage inequality attributed a significant role to declining unionization, with one study estimating that about one-fifth of the rise in wage inequality in the United States is due to this decline. In Western Europe, where unions have remained stronger and the policy environment more supportive, the wages of the less skilled have not collapsed. But the price has been an increase in unemployment.

As demand for low-skilled labor has become more elastic, so has supply of high-skilled talent, resulting in depressed wages for the former, and bidding up wages of the latter. This increases the income disparity among groups of workers.

Employers' ability to substitute workers and their ability to shift capital and move to lower-cost countries, result in increased volatility for workers. Workers are more likely to face job loss or a fall in wages as a result.

Such insecurity leads to greater demand for both broadening and deepening social safety nets. Rodrik notes that countries which are most open to international trade and most exposed to external risk, have the highest levels of government spending, as governments in these countries seek to provide a buffer from international economic forces. He shows that throughout the 1980s, in the United States and Japan, where trade forms a low percentage of GDP, government spending as a percentage of GDP was low, at 10–20%. This contrasted with government spending levels of 40–50% in small, trade-dependent countries like Luxembourg, Belgium and the Netherlands (whose trade-GDP share was between 100–200%).

In this, as in many other empirical studies, Singapore bucks the trend. We are highly trade-dependent, with a 278.63% trade-GDP ratio in 2002. However, government spending is modest by OECD standards — 17% of GDP. Singapore may not be able to continue in this fortunate situation indefinitely, as globalization widens income disparities and raises demand for income transfers, subsidies and other relief measures, at the same time that it reduces the government's ability to finance such transfers through taxation. As governments have reduced ability to tax capital, which is highly mobile, a greater share of the tax burden shifts from capital to labor. This is documented by Rodrik in the creeping up of labor income tax rates from about 27% to 35% in France, Germany, the United States and the United Kingdom between 1970 and 1991. In Singapore, corporate income taxes have been trending down, and the tax burden has shifted from direct taxation on income to indirect taxation. For example, for FY2002, 31.7% of the estimated Singapore $21.11 billion tax revenue came from corporate income tax, and just 18.6% came from personal income tax. The other 49.7% came from contributions by statutory boards, asset taxes, motor vehicles taxes, custom & excise duties, Goods and Services Tax, fees & charges, betting taxes, stamp duty and miscellaneous revenue.

What is the labor movement's response to the twin driving forces of increasing job volatility and increasing demand for deeper and broader social safety nets?

In Singapore, our approach is not to fight globalization, but to ride its waves. For example, we will not try to protect employment, but will promote employability. We will push for a deeper social safety net, not by demanding more benefits that simply raise the cost burden of companies and government, but will advocate for restructuring of benefits that help workers cope with job volatility. We view globalization and greater economic integration as inevitable for Singapore, and as an opportunity for workers to raise standards of living.

The response of the Singapore labor movement is grounded in some values held since our independence in 1965.

Chief among these is the belief in the dignity of work, and the importance of self-reliance. In Singapore, receiving handouts is viewed as demeaning if one is able to work. Welfare assistance is reserved for the needy or those unable to work.

When help is needed, the community will offer its support. A strong tradition of self-reliance and mutual help within the community has developed from colonial times and continues today.

We also place a premium on education and skills-acquisition. Education is geared towards producing innovative, productive workers in the economy while allowing each child to maximize his potential.

Another foundational value is a voice for workers. After independence, Singapore broke with the adversarial Anglo-Saxon union tradition and established a tripartite framework. In 1972, the National

Wages Council instituted tripartite wage-bargaining at the highest level. The founding members of the People's Action Party (PAP), the party which has won every general election in Singapore since 1959, included union advocates. From its inception, the PAP has been pro-labor, and the party was instrumental in setting up the National Trades Union Congress (NTUC), Singapore's federation of trade unions.

These foundational values guide the Singapore labor movement's response to the challenges of globalization.

Building consensus

We respond by building a consensual, not adversarial, relationship between labor and government. This does not mean there are no contending views, but that these views are reconciled through collaboration and consensus.

This is in line with Singapore society's norms of a communitarian, consensus-seeking polity. The government is expected to rule with moral leadership, and citizens in general demonstrate high trust in authority. Unions advocate for workers' interests within the context of building consensus with government, not in opposition to it, working towards the common goals of economic development and social cohesion.

The NTUC believes the best way to advance workers' interests is to continue with its symbiotic relationship with the People's Action Party government, and to maintain it as a consensual relationship. PAP members of parliament are sent to unions as advisers or executive secretaries to keep politicians in touch with workers' concerns. Such appointments must, however, receive the consent of the unions. Indeed, it is the unions that appoint them upon recommendation. The NTUC secretary-general is also a Cabinet Minister; ensuring workers' views are represented at the highest decision-making level. This unusual arrangement is achieved only when the incumbent passes two independent electoral processes — election by the union body as secretary-general, and election to parliament representing a constituency.

Such an alignment between trade unions and political party is by no means unique. In the United Kingdom, the British Trade Union Congress is aligned to the Labor Party. In the United States, the AFL-CIO is aligned to the Democratic Party. Neither of these, however, goes as far as Singapore.

Within a collaborative framework, unions then work with government to figure out how best to help workers adapt to the changing workplace. We begin by asking the fundamental question: What is it that workers and employers need in a globalizing world, amidst fundamental shifts in the labor market?

The key requirement is the need for flexibility, from both firms and employees. Firms need flexibility to respond to changes in the business cycle, to outsource processes and adapt products. Workers need to be flexible to respond to changes in demand for their services. This means adapting to changing work conditions, to take on contingent jobs and to learn new skills. To create such a flexible workforce requires fundamental changes in labor-market institutions.

Portability of employment-related benefits

To ensure that mobile workers are supported by a robust social safety net, employment benefits have to become portable, and no longer tied to the employer. In particular, retirement, medical and unemployment benefits should be designed to aid mobility. In Singapore, the mandatory retirement savings scheme, the Central Provident Fund to which both workers and employers contribute, is already portable, as the funds are held in individual accounts not tied to an employer. Health benefits are, however, still largely tied to the employer, and the labor movement has been a strong advocate for incentives to persuade employers to shift to portable benefits. In the recent Budget, the government raised tax incentives for companies that introduce portable medical benefits. Unemployment benefits are not provided, as Singapore has had a tight labor market for three decades. As the economy undergoes a restructuring, resident unemployment has crept up gradually. The labor movement believes there is scope to introduce a savings scheme to help tide workers over periods of unemployment, and has been an advocate for this.

Annual Average	Residents Unemployed*	Resident Unemployment Rate (%)
1998	54300	3.5
1999	61000	3.8
2000	59600	3.7
2001	62800	3.8
2002	82400	4.9

*Data for annual average derived from non-seasonally adjusted figures.

Flexible organizing structure: seamless membership

The very organizational structure of unions will have to evolve to meet the needs of a more mobile, flexible workforce. Instead of recruiting from their core constituencies of employees in large industrial organizations, unions will have to make themselves relevant to the large pools of workers in the professional and managerial class, among the contingent workforce, and among the low-wage and low-skilled most in need of protection.

Instead of organizing into central unions along company or industrial lines, unions may have to offer membership in a network of employee organizations or professional associations that are able to represent workers at different stages in their career moves. Already, professional groups are evolving to offer collective bargaining. New York-based Working Today, with about 93,000 individual members and associations, brings together a range of white-collar workers including journalists, translators and artists. For annual dues of US$25, they get group-rate health insurance, legal advice and a range of discounts.

If unions are unable to meet the needs of the new labor force, their relevance will be eroded. In Singapore, we have introduced two important changes to our organizing structure to ensure that unions continue to be the main representative of workers' interests in a changing workforce. First, we aim to provide seamless, portable membership to workers, so that a worker who joins a union is a member for life, regardless of changes in employers. In the United States of America, there are nearly twice as many former union members as there are union members, as union members who leave a union job have to be organized again in future jobs. Providing seamless lifelong membership will help unions retain and broaden their membership base.

Another initiative we have undertaken is the promotion of a category of membership called "general branch," which is targeted at employees who work in companies where the union does not yet have the right to engage employers in collective bargaining — for example, in smaller establishments. General branch members receive all the benefits of traditional union membership, including grievance management but excluding collective bargaining. As employment contracts become more individualized, we have started extending services for general branch members to include consultation and legal advice on their individual employment contracts.

Changes in the way unions organize members will require changes in legislation. Labor laws in many countries, including Singapore, were enacted during a time when jobs were meant to be lifelong and the pace of change gradual, when organizations were large and industrial and when there were clear demarcations between manager and employee. Thus in Singapore, a secret ballot is required whereby at least 50% plus one employee must say yes before a union can be formed at the workplace. This worked well in an industrial workplace with few and large employers, each employing thousands or tens of thousands of members. But the secret ballot becomes cumbersome in small companies with a handful of bargainable staff.

No one-size-fits-all approach will be able to meet the needs of the diverse groups in the workforce. For example, professionals and managers may be organized along the lines of professional or craft guilds of yore, pooling resources and risks. On the other hand, contingent workers may prefer to band together to form labor councils to bargain collectively or to improve employment conditions, as the South Bay Central Labor Council in San Jose, California, has done. Low-skill workers need basic employment safeguards and skills training to escape from the low-wage trap. Despite the different groups of workers, some needs will be generic: unions will have to facilitate or offer labor-market intermediary services, such as job matching and job search, training provision, mediation and conciliation services between workers and employers, and associations to promote a greater voice for employees.

Whether unions continue to be effective in their societies in the 21st century depends to a large extent on how they respond to the needs of the new workforce, and how well they are able to forge partnerships with government and community bodies to meet workers' needs in the areas outlined above. Partnership and consensus-building, not militancy and adversarial relations, will characterize the responses of successful labor movements.

Promoting employability

To be truly flexible, workers have to re-skill and re-tool themselves to meet changing demand for their labor. Skills training and lifelong learning are essential. Unions have a special role in facilitating or providing skills training because of the coordination problems in training provision in a traditional free-market economy. This is analyzed by Peter A. Hall and David Soskice in their book *Varieties of Capitalism*. The problem can be summed up thus: employers have a disincentive to invest in training in the absence of assurances that others will not poach their newly-trained employee. Workers have no incentive to invest upfront in company- or industry-specific skills, in the absence of guarantees of jobs in these sectors. The result is an under-investment in industry-specific technical skills of the kind most needed by companies.

The problem is most acute in liberal market economies such as America, Britain and Singapore. In these economies, the provision of training is left pretty much to the employment market, in contrast to coordinated market economies with centralized vocational training systems that make the school-to-work transition seamless, such as Germany. Still, there is no satisfactory model able to cope with the faster pace of change. Liberal market economies typically under-invest in technical skills training, as there is little incentive for students to spend years acquiring technical skills in the absence of job guarantees. Instead, young people have a high incentive to differentiate themselves in the job market by getting a tertiary education. The wage premium for a university degree is thus high. Not surprisingly, there is a correlation between wage inequality and incidence of vocational training: wage inequality is highest in countries like the USA, Canada, Ireland and UK, which have the lowest proportion of young people in post-secondary vocational training compared to countries like Belgium, the Netherlands and Germany, which have lower wage differentials and a high incidence of vocational training.

Singapore's labor market has many of the features of the liberal market economy. The wage premium for graduates is high, although it is narrowing in recent years as we improve our polytechnic education. In 2001, pay surveys show that a university graduate earns a premium of 62%, or about US$550 a month, over a polytechnic graduate. Workers show a greater propensity to invest in broad-based higher education than in technical skills.

To correct the market failure problem inherent in training, Singapore offers generous subsidies to induce workers to receive training in growth sectors. Low-skilled workers receive highly subsidized training, as well as make-up pay to compensate them for lost hours at work. A variety of training programs are in place. One is the Skills Redevelopment Programme (SRP). After five years, as at the end of February 2003, a total of 1,830 companies participated in SRP training, with 114,114 SRP training places being taken up since 1998. NTUC aims to forge closer collaborations with the various industry partners, including employer groups, unions and training providers to identify training needs and define the training roadmaps for the various industries. It expects to achieve some 20,000–30,000 training places this year. A total of $67.3 million funding was provided by government, with $28.7 million disbursed as of February 2003.

Subsidies are available not only for low-skilled workers, but also for professionals, under the Manpower Conversion Programme, which trains people for growth sectors like logistics, social services and the info-communications and e-learning sector. In all these, the labor movement has been an advocate and partner. For example, unions raised over $20 million for the NTUC Education and Training Fund for members.

A new statutory board to promote lifelong learning is being formed to spearhead efforts to help workers retrain. Unions will continue to advocate for innovative programs to bolster training. For example, we have mooted the idea of creating individual skills-training accounts that will allow workers to pay for training over their careers. Another measure we support is the use of tax laws to support lifelong learning and the use of matching grants to private institutions that offer re-skilling programs. Unions advocate that training and retraining must be closely linked with job creation.

Unions as a social partner

Unions have to rethink their modus operandi in the globalized world. Instead of casting themselves as opponents of capital and champions of labor, unions have to see that they help workers best by developing a good relationship with capital, and with the state. A consensual rather than adversarial relationship is the bedrock of the tripartism that Singapore's NTUC practices. The NTUC shares the same core purpose of all trade unions in the world: to protect and enhance the interest of workers by raising their skills, productivity, and real wages in a sustainable manner. We adopt a consensual approach to pursue our interests, the most effective approach within the socio-political context in Singapore.

In Singapore, unions see themselves as a social partner working to generate wealth, not just to share wealth. Wage negotiations are thus based on realistic assessments of macro-economic and business-cycle considerations. Only when companies are profitable will they locate their wealth-creating activities in Singapore. Where necessary, wage restraint or even wage cuts will be supported by the unions to save jobs. In the 1985 and 1998 recessions, for example, unions supported wage cuts in a bid to restore Singapore's wage competitiveness.

Singapore unions are mindful of the lessons from labor history. Unions elsewhere often saw their roles eroded, marginalized and excluded from social dialogue. In adopting a narrow view of what constituted workers' interests, union leaders sometimes missed the woods for the trees, and militantly pressed home a tactical advantage only to lose the larger battle. John L. Lewis (1880–1969) led his coal-miners' union, the United Mine Workers of America, into a coal-miners' strike in 1943, rebelling against the wage freeze imposed during World War II. He refused to heed pleas by President Roosevelt, whom he had supported throughout the 1930s, to heed the national interest and call off the strike. "The President of the United States is paid to look after the national interest. I am paid to look after the interests of the miners", Lewis said. As recounted in Peter Drucker's *Post-Capitalist Society*, the war economy was fueled by coal and the country could not afford to lose even one day of production. Lewis won the strike. But public opinion turned against him and the union and the coal-miners' strike became a byword for labor excesses. It was a Pyrrhic victory, marking the beginning of the decline of unionism in the United States.

In Britain, faced with militant unions that disrupted enterprise, Margaret Thatcher changed the institutional environment governing the relationship between the state, the employers and the trade unions, diminishing the influence and organizing power of trade unions.

The Anglo-Saxon practice of having an adversarial labor-government relationship is not the only model there is. Social pacts, where labor works with government to save jobs, are a feature of the European political landscape, including Italy and Sweden. In the Netherlands, unions pushed for wage moderation twice to save jobs in two economic crises: in 1982, when one in 25 manufacturing firms went bankrupt and 300,000 jobs were lost, and in 1993.

In Singapore, we believe workers' top priority is to have a means of livelihood. Only if a worker has a job can the union help to secure growth in real wages, in line with growth in the worker's productivity. Workers in Singapore are competing with workers elsewhere for international capital, trade and jobs. Wage costs must be internationally competitive. In many developed countries, unions try to protect workers' interests by fighting for a living wage or a minimum wage. However, the living wage in a developed country may be many more times that in a developing country, for a worker with the same level of productivity. This is the fundamental reason for a global shift in jobs, both manufacturing and services, from the developed to the developing countries. Some unions in developed countries have tried to fight this global shift in jobs by advocating for more stringent labor practices and higher wages in developing countries.

In Singapore, we do not believe that this is the right approach. Each country will evolve and improve its own labor practices, in pace with its level of economic development. This has been the experience of the developed countries. Life in industrializing Britain was famously summed up by Hobbes as being "nasty, brutish and short." It is doubtful if Britain then could have industrialized so effectively if it had been forced to adhere to labor standards today's labor advocates want to enforce on developing countries.

Instead of taking an ideological position on a living wage, Singapore unions believe that if wages have to stay competitive, then the cost of living in an economy has to match the purchasing power of workers. Unions do not advocate that government subsidizes incomes or legislates minimum or living wages. Instead, unions advocate government subsidies to keep the basic cost of living affordable. Hence, in Singapore, the government subsidizes public housing heavily, and about 90% of the population lives in public housing. Education is compulsory and almost fully subsidized. In health care, there are large direct subsidies to providers of basic health-care services, as well as compulsory health-care savings (Medisave), opt-out individual insurance (Medishield), and subsidies for the indigent (Medifund).

In Singapore, unions continue to be strong, with membership rates growing from the mid 1990s to 19.2% in 2002, and with unions continuing to be an effective bargaining partner in the tripartite relationship. We consider it important to press to maintain workers' share of enterprise profits, not by militant bargaining but within a context of enlarging the pool of profits for all.

Deepening/broadening safety nets

New safety nets have to be put in place to deal with the very real pressures that globalization brings to workers. Globalization is changing the employment relationship faster than governments can restructure safety nets to deal with the changes. But there is only so much that governments can do, especially as they face budget constraints as their ability to raise taxes becomes more limited. Individuals, families and the community must do their part to save and set aside earnings for the inevitable periods of unemployment.

Rather than foist all the pressure for deeper safety nets onto the government, we should recognize that creating safety nets in a volatile work environment is a shared responsibility. Rather than thinking that more money will solve the problem, we should be strategic and focus efforts on what will offer practical help.

The key lies in creating a support infrastructure that smoothes the transition between jobs for workers. As far as social benefits go, this means making health and retirement benefits portable, rather than tied to the employer. It means that establishing saving schemes for those retrenched or out of work will also help tide workers over periods of unemployment. Unions in Singapore continue to advocate for these changes.

In addition, unions have a role in reducing the friction workers face when they change jobs. There are real economic gains to be reaped if workers can move from job to job seamlessly. Independent contractors are estimated to spend nearly one-quarter of their time searching for and landing their next project opportunity. Union organizations can use networks with employers and workers to match jobs with people and projects with talent.

Apart from offering job-search assistance, unions can also play a role in organizing and bargaining on behalf of independent contractors. To ensure that workers can move from job to job, unions should create opportunities to work, and reduce discriminatory practices that prevent re-entry into the workforce. For example, we have worked with employers and regulators to reduce discrimination against older workers, against women, and, in some societies, discrimination against youths.

Social leveler

Singapore's labor movement plays an important role in moderating price increases and helping workers stretch their dollar through its network of cooperatives, covering insurance, housing, supermarkets, child care, and health and dental care. We also provide affordable recreational facilities, including a golf course, for workers.

Each of our cooperatives sets the benchmark for quality at affordable prices. NTUC FairPrice, our supermarket chain, is ubiquitous in Singapore. It offers fresh groceries at prices competitive with those of low-cost wet markets. Additional rebates are given to members. In uncertain economic times, or whenever there are concerns of profiteering, FairPrice plays a role in steadying the price of basic essentials. For example, FairPrice absorbs the Goods and Services Tax (consumption tax) on key basic essentials in difficult times, to help households. When there is a crisis-induced shortage, it assures the consumer by maintaining price levels, and thus preventing for-profit supermarkets from profiteering.

Our cooperatives help ameliorate discontent arising from widening income disparities, and reduce the risk of social exclusion. We believe such concrete measures to improve the standard of living of workers is a more meaningful response to wage disparities than the push for a minimum wage. Cooperatives are a counterweight to winner-take-all market competition. Given the current world-wide focus on maximizing shareholder value, cooperatives can play a significant role through maximizing stakeholder value.

Ethical capitalism

Looking ahead, there is a real risk that anti-globalization movements will gain currency among international grassroots organizations, especially if the ethical deficit continues to mount. Workers are dissatisfied with astronomical compensation packages not tied to performance. Investors are angry at fraud committed by companies, abetted by auditors who are supposed to be the watchdogs. An alliance at the grassroots is massing against globalization.

Rather than joining the anti-globalization movement, a more effective response is to press for changes to reduce the excesses of globalization. This requires innovative solutions and a rethinking of traditional relationships. In the Singapore labor movement, we believe the solution lies in helping workers cope with the realities of globalization, while advocating for a more sustainable, equitable kind of capitalism.

9

LEADERSHIP
Business in Society: Leading by Example

Jaime Augusto Zobel de Ayala II
President and CEO of Ayala Corporation

 In Asia today, the subject of corporate citizenship and corporate social responsibility is laden with paradox. In this setting, where government resources are in many ways inadequate to meet society's development needs, it is a tradition that private enterprises have also contributed to social betterment and public welfare. At the same time, ethical norms are not as well defined as they are in the West, and corporations sometimes fall short of even their basic responsibility to pay the right taxes. Thus, where so much poverty abounds and the private sector is so critical to the achievement of economic and social progress, corporate behavior can range from the heights of altruism to sheer indifference to society.

Corporate citizenship — the sense of membership of corporations within a community with its attendant rights and responsibilities — has not evolved in Asia in the same way it has in the West.

In Europe and America, it was born out of intense debate between two camps amidst the growing power and influence of large corporations in the post-war era. At one end, proponents of responsible citizenship contended that a private corporation has responsibilities to society that go beyond the profit motive, that it has a broader constituency to serve than shareholders alone, and that it must take an enlightened view of self-interest and help solve social problems in order to create a better environment for itself. At the other end, laissez faire advocates maintained that the sole mission of business is to produce goods and services at a profit. In so doing, it is already making its maximum contribution to society and is therefore being socially responsible. As the debate has developed over the decades, however, momentum has swung in favor of those who advocate a broader involvement. Business leaders who once were loath to recognize any social burdens for their organizations have more and more accepted the idea of corporate citizenship.

This debate did not surface prominently in the Asian scene because it has long been part of tradition and expectation that Asian corporations should be socially responsible and should contribute substantively to social progress and national development. In our part of the world it is rare to find a business leader or economist espousing publicly the arguments of the profit-maximizing advocates. The key reason for this is that in most Asian societies, and especially Japan, the relationship between business and society seems to have been far closer than it has been in the West. Most Asian cultures in one way or another reflect this cooperative spirit, though practice may fall short of the ideal. In Japan, for example, a corporation and society are very closely linked — so much so that some feel that the two are virtually synonymous, and that for a business to profit it must benefit the whole of Japanese society.[1]

Governments have likewise played a prominent role in Asian business life, with many of the biggest Asian corporations owned or partly owned by the state. In these circumstances, business was definitely seen as an integral part of society's drive towards progress. Even with the trend towards privatization of state-owned companies during the '90s, the corporate practice of social engagement remained.

The advent of a new international business environment towards the close of the 20th century and early in the 21st century is bringing these variant traditions of Asia and the West closer together. The very same forces that herald "a new way of doing business" around the world are also fueling the new interest in corporate citizenship across the continents.

One of these key forces is globalization, which more than anything has fueled changes in the relationship between business and society. In the new global economy, corporations do business across nations with the minimum of barriers and have become more important in deciding how we all live, wherever we are in the world. Consequently, the private sector has had to face new challenges and demands on its behavior. Companies are asking themselves again what are the fundamental values they stand for.

---

[1] Suzuki, Hideyuki, *Corporate Responsibility and Environmental Management in Japanese Business*, 1996.

A palpable change in attitudes is taking place because of two basic developments: (1) business operates today in a more transparent world and it is therefore difficult to escape scrutiny; and (2) business is accountable to a wider range of stakeholders.

In a global economy, multinational companies (MNCs) have become aware that inconsistencies in their operating practices across the countries in which they operate can make them vulnerable to severe market backlashes. Several famous brands have faced harsh international criticism for the use of child labor and other less-than-praiseworthy practices in the manufacture of their products in developing countries. Similarly, local companies are facing analogous challenges as a result of the greater competition being provided by MNCs. Besides the pressure to live by international standards, they are finding social responsibility and accountability as a new barometer for public judgment.

Equally influential in spurring the corporate-citizenship agenda is the environmental movement, which preceded globalization by several decades. Over the last 30 years, environmental activists have been hammering away for greater business responsibility in conservation efforts. Driven by pressure from both consumers and legislation, these finally began to produce far-reaching results in the 1990s, with the convening of the Earth Summit in Rio de Janeiro and the worldwide acceptance of the principle of sustainable development. Many companies now acknowledge that environmental responsibility has become a strategic issue in their plans and operations. Because governments, the private sector and the general citizenry have come to recognize that they all have a moral responsibility to protect the environment, earth-friendly practices and the principle of sustainability now feature very prominently within the corporate-citizenship movement.

Other factors that have helped to fuel the movement are human rights and child-labor issues. The discovery of human rights abuses and child labor in the manufacturing practices of several notable global companies has highlighted the need for companies to be mindful about conditions in the workplace, not just in their own backyard but also in their supply chains. The great disparity in working conditions between affluent first-world nations and those in developing countries underlines this challenge. Almost half of the world's working children are found in South and Southeast Asia, where child labor is rife because of mass poverty.

All these factors and issues have set the stage for what some observers describe as the new paradigm for corporate citizenship in our time.

A new paradigm

By its very name, corporate citizenship is analogous to individual citizenship in society. Just as the citizen has rights and responsibilities as a member of a broad community, so a corporation has rights and responsibilities as a functioning part of society. While corporate rights are enshrined and clear in law, corporate responsibilities are not as well defined or recognized. Hence the debate over the years as to what constitutes responsible corporate citizenship.

At its most basic level, corporate-citizenship theory sees the corporation as having certain economic, legal, environmental and social responsibilities to fulfill as a member of society. Its primary responsibility is that it has to be financially and economically viable and must operate within its constitution and articles of incorporation. It has a legal responsibility in that it must work within the boundaries of the law and should pay its fair share of taxes to the government. It has an environmental responsibility in that it must ensure that its operations and products do no harm to the environment. And it has a social responsibility in that it should contribute to the uplifting and development of the communities in which it does business.

Historically, the response of business to the challenge of citizenship at first tended to be minimalist: a corporation is a responsible citizen as long as it obeys the law, pays taxes diligently, and does its part in helping to grow the economy, which in turn fuels social progress.

A subsequent response to the citizenship challenge was the exercise of corporate philanthropy, through which business organizations actively help to improve the welfare of various sectors of society and assist in the development of public education and other necessary public services. Related to this work is the concern for public relations, which seeks to enhance the image and reputation of the company. This is exemplified by the outstanding work of foundations all over the world bearing the names of their corporate parents.

The new view of corporate citizenship takes the concept to an entirely new level by proposing a more proactive and strategic approach that includes enriching the company's relationships with stakeholders and enhancing the overall quality of life in society. The new model explicitly integrates the social dimension into corporate strategy and planning. Many feel that business must adopt this forthright approach to social responsibility because it is the prime beneficiary of the new international business environment. As every country adopts market economics, it is up to business (whether it involves domestic companies, multinationals or truly global enterprises) to take the lead in social-development initiatives that protect the environment and build healthy local and global communities.

At the heart of the new corporate-citizenship model is the belief that in an increasingly globalized environment, the role and scope of business in world affairs is greater now than it has ever been and, in many major economies, governments are finding that their roles are being dramatically reshaped. In addition, it has become increasingly clear that businesses thrive in societies that are progressive and where there is a high level of trust and mutuality between the two. The conclusion to be drawn therefore is that corporate citizenship is not just about philanthropy, nor should it be merely a fringe activity. Corporate citizenship should be a mindset and a philosophy which is viewed as integral to corporate strategic planning.

One key element of the new thinking is the belief that there need not be a conflict between profitability and shared values and that being socially responsible is a win-win situation. The notion that by doing some good in society, a company will also do well in its business has actually been around for some time now. As early as the 1950s, early proponents espoused a "do well by doing good" business philosophy and believed that corporate contributions for charity purposes were insufficient to demonstrate that a firm was a good corporate citizen. This is consistent with the modern thinking that responsible citizenship means devising corporate strategies and building a business with society's needs in mind. Today, there are still those who believe only in the profit motive but, in my view, the mandate for business-society cooperation is clear, and the earlier business acts on it the better.

The interest in corporate citizenship is undeniably gaining more momentum, growing as the role of business in society increases and the role of government shifts from being a provider to more of a facilitator and regulator. At the same time, public awareness about the issue has been ignited by the massive accounting scandals in the United States and business failures in Europe, and business today is being challenged to prove that it is a responsible partner in social progress.

The Asian experience

In the midst of the Asian economic miracle in the late '80s and early-to-mid '90s, there was a rising trend in corporate Asia towards responsible corporate citizenship. Success made many Asian companies more ready and willing to take on a larger social role. But the Asian financial crisis of 1997 and Japan's deep slide into economic stagnation have stemmed this tide, as attention shifted in most companies toward sheer survival. As crony capitalism was unmasked as one of the culprits behind the crisis, the focus in recent years has been more on corporate-governance issues and how corporations are run rather than on issues of social responsibility.

Consequently, and this is particularly true of the Philippines, corporate citizenship is still largely a matter of individual choice within the private sector, rather than an institutional trend. For some, the exercise of responsible corporate citizenship is a strategic commitment that is integral to success. For others it is merely an extracurricular, add-on activity.

The sterling examples of corporate citizenship and corporate social responsibility across the Asian region are cases of companies leading by example. They embody a genuine commitment to contribute to national progress and improve the quality of life in their countries. And they reflect creative and innovative ways of enabling these companies to make a difference.

Likewise, long before corporate citizenship and corporate social responsibility became buzzwords in the West, many of the oldest and most respected Asian companies already recognized social involvement as sound business practice. They endowed all kinds of social institutions and projects to improve the quality of life in their societies. They clearly understood that their business would thrive with a healthier, better-educated and more-productive populace.

In developing countries like the Philippines, there can hardly be any debate about the issue. The private sector must be part of the solution to our social ills. Because mass poverty is part of the very air we breathe, we must be involved in its eradication. Because unemployment is high, we must play a leading role in relieving the problem. And because good public policies and good governance are so critical to solving these problems, we cannot be indifferent to the making and implementation of public policy.

Two organizations that reflect the Asian thinking on corporate citizenship are the Keidanren in Japan and the Philippine Business for Social Progress (PBSP) in the Philippines.

Keidanren is Japan's largest and oldest business association. It has far-reaching political and economic influence in its home country and has been the pace-setter in promoting corporate citizenship in Japan. In April 1991, it created a Global Environmental Charter and, in September 1991, in the wake of scandals involving some securities firms, it established its Charter for Good Corporate Behavior, whose seven key principles are outlined on the following page:

1. Endeavor to offer excellent goods and services that are useful to society.
2. Strive to make it possible for employees to lead comfortable and plentiful lives, and respect them as human beings.
3. Conduct corporate activities in a way that takes environmental protection into consideration.
4. Endeavor to make a contribution to society through philanthropic and other activities.
5. Work to improve social welfare in the community through business activities.
6. Firmly refrain from behavior that is counter to social norms, including having anything to do with organizations that have an adverse influence on social order and safety.
7. Always promote communication with consumers through public-relations activities and open hearings, and strive to make the principles of corporate behavior conform to social norms.

With Japan as one of the largest economies in the world and with many of its firms doing business in many countries, Keidanren was keen to show that Japanese business operates according to internationally agreed norms of behavior. The Charter is primarily aimed at senior executives and managers who, it says, have to "examine and discipline their own behavior and exercise leadership in keeping moral standards high in their corporations… [these] must not only obey the law but also bring in social conscience to bear on their undertakings."[2]

Reflecting a similar thrust is the work of PBSP in the Philippines. PBSP is a foundation with many of the country's top companies as members and contributors. It sees its mission as one of "making strategic contributions to improve the quality of life of the Filipino poor; promoting business sector commitment to social development; and harnessing resources for innovative programs that lead to self-reliance and social development."[3] Its statement of commitment includes the following:

"First: Private enterprise, by creatively and efficiently utilizing capital, land and labor, generates employment opportunities, expands the economic capabilities of our society, and improves the quality of our national life.

---

[2] McIntosh, Leipziger, Jones & Coleman, *Corporate Citizenship*, Pitman Publishing, London, 1998.
[3] Excerpts from the Charter of the Philippine Business for Social Progress. Website: www.pbsp.org.ph

Second: The most valuable resource in any country is the person. The higher purpose of private enterprise is to build social and economic conditions which shall promote the development of the person and the well-being of the community.

Third: The growth and vigorous development of private enterprise must be anchored on sound economic and social conditions.

Fourth: Private enterprise must discharge its social responsibility towards society in a way which benefits its unique competence. It should involve itself more and more in social development for the total well-being of the nation.

Fifth: Private enterprise is financially and technologically equipped to participate actively in social development. In terms of scientific technology and managerial competence, private enterprise can help provide the total approach for social development in our depressed communities.

Sixth: Private enterprise, together with other sectors of society, shares obligations and responsibilities which it must discharge to the national community. The ultimate objective of the enterprise is to help create and maintain in the Philippines a home worthy of the dignity of the person."

PBSP reflects a long tradition of business involvement in the problems of our national life. In the two major political upheavals in the Philippines in 1986 and 2001, which saw two presidents toppled from office by people power, Filipino companies and business leaders stood shoulder to shoulder with social and political reformers in raising the flag of reform and change.

Private-sector involvement in the resolution of social issues in our country has been influenced in part by our closeness to Western corporate practice. It has also been heavily influenced by the existence of a very active civil society in our country. Non-government organizations often work hand in hand with private foundations in engaging themselves within the local communities so that critical problems and issues can be resolved.

What we do in the Ayala Group

In the case of our own Ayala Foundation, we have tried to focus our work on certain issues and areas which we consider vital to national life and where we think we can be of help. These are: poverty eradication through grassroots development for children and the youth sector (with initiatives involving education and ICT as social enablers), environmental conservation, and cultural development. And everything we try to do is kept consistent with the fundamental values we profess as an organization. While it is not for me to say whether we are succeeding in this work or if we should be viewed as an example to others, I can say that we try our utmost to make a positive difference in the lives of as many Filipinos as possible.

When we were trying to determine how and where we could make the most significant impact, given limited resources, we were guided by several powerful realizations:

- The youth sector makes up a very significant portion of the Filipino population, represents the future of our country, and must therefore be nurtured.
- Filipinos are inherently creative and are, we believe, among the most talented in the world. The quality of our education has been a key competitive advantage over the years but the reality is that this has been eroding. While some of our universities and institutions of higher learning are still competitive and can still be considered world-class, most of these are private and out of reach from the majority of the population. Decades of under-investment in the Philippines' public school system, particularly at the elementary level, has meant that the talent and potential of underprivileged Filipino children are not being developed properly.
- Information technology is a powerful enabler and can be a platform for social development and mobility.

With these in mind, the Ayala Foundation, together with some local and international partners and NGOs, has been running several critical and innovative programs.

In 2000, Ayala launched its CENTEX project — the Center of Excellence in Public Elementary Education. The project is designed to help bright children from poor families receive the quality of education that they deserve. With the help of some experts in early-stage children's education, we have opened two CENTEX schools — one in a poor urban community in Manila and another in a provincial site. These have been joint undertakings with the national government through the Department of Education, Culture and Sports, and the respective local government units. With the Ayala Foundation taking the lead role in managing the project, we involve ourselves in curriculum design, make modern technological facilities available, assist in training the teachers, and oversee the growth and holistic development of the children.

Another program which we have been conducting yearly since 1999 is the Ayala Young Leaders' Congress (AYLC). Leadership is something that we feel needs to be identified early and nurtured. Every year, we identify some 70 student leaders from private and public schools all across the Philippines and bring them together for a three-day congress where they are given a chance to interact with their peers and learn from sterling examples of leadership in government, business, media and the arts. We believe that this is an ideal way to inculcate the ideals of social commitment and servant leadership in our nation's future leaders, as well as to forge strong bonds among them.

The Ayala Foundation has also recently launched several initiatives which harness the potential of information technology for youth development. These include the Youth Tech project, where we have helped provide public schools with computer labs and Internet access; as well as programs such as iLink and Computer Clubhouses, where we partner with companies such as Mitsubishi Corporation and Intel in providing information technology and Internet facilities and training to out-of-school youths in depressed areas.

The Ayala Group also joined the government's poverty-alleviation program, *Kalahi*, where companies such as Ayala Corporation, Globe Telecom, the Bank of the Philippine Islands, Ayala Land, Manila Water and the Ayala Foundation pooled their resources to help improve the lives of residents in a poor community in Metro Manila. Together, the group provided a revolving livelihood fund, installed free water connections, constructed a sewage treatment plant, donated books and a Youth Tech lab, and trained residents on Internet usage and local-area networking.

These are only some of the major initiatives that Ayala supports and we take our role as corporate citizens seriously. We plan to continue supporting these initiatives, hopefully bring in more partners and sponsors, and replicate them wherever possible. We believe that corporate organizations that last cannot be concerned merely with maximizing short-term profits or creating an effective corporate image. Whether working with government agencies, NGOs or other corporate partners, the Ayala Group has always tried to build and nurture a relationship of trust with a broader community, recognizing that our constituencies operate beyond our shareholders, employees, suppliers and customers.

To this end, we encourage all our companies to integrate social-development issues into their business plans. We have also organized the Ayala Business Club, an organization of managers across the different

Ayala companies, to spearhead community outreach and local-government assistance programs in their localities. We are very heartened by the overwhelming response from our employees to calls for support and participation in various civic activities. Many of them, on their own, are likewise actively involved in community-outreach activities.

I believe that promoting social development is a task that needs to be borne by the private sector in developing countries where government institutions may not have sufficient resources or capabilities to provide for the needs of society. We see this happening now in many large corporations in our country and across the region, and it is encouraging that many CEOs have already made it part of their broader mandate.

Business leadership by another means

In a sense, responsible corporate citizenship is really the exercise of business leadership by another means. Corporations generally measure success in terms of earnings, market share, balance-sheet resources or some other financial measure. Corporate citizenship introduces another dimension by which we can measure our leadership in society. As society has a multitude of needs, the forms that this kind of leadership can take are countless and the limits are only those imposed by the imagination and the level of commitment.

One example is the Thai Business Initiative in Rural Development (T-Bird)[4], which seeks to relocate migrant workers in Bangkok to their home provinces and communities. Through the program, Thai and multinational companies adopt rural villages, providing rural communities with marketing expertise, financial resources and training to promote job creation. Over 35 companies have adopted rural villages. One of the most promising initiatives is the one of Bata, the world's largest manufacturer of footwear. It adopted a village in Buri Ram province and assisted in the establishment of four factory cooperatives employing 140 people and manufacturing 8,000 shoe-uppers per day. Three-quarters of the workers are reverse migrants, who have returned to their home province from the metropolis.

Another is a Unilever project in Uttar Pradesh, India[5]. Hindustan Lever, a Unilever subsidiary, had a dairy in this part of India that was

---

[4] Leipziger, Deborah, "Canadian Companies on the Cutting Edge: Bata Promotes Development", Research report, 1996, New York, Council on Economic Priorities.

[5] McIntoshet al, op. cit., pp. 216–217.

losing money. The reason was that the farmers were too poor to feed and care for their cattle adequately. Hindustan Lever decided to take a radical step — to invest in the development of the rural community. The company provided interest-free loans to the farmers, to feed and care for their cattle, so as to improve the quality and quantity of the milk they produced. It developed a five-year plan to improve human and animal health in the community. Within just a few years, the dairy was making considerable profits, which were being reinvested in the community. The development initiative now covers 400 villages in the state of Uttar Pradesh.

These are only two examples of the corporate social initiatives in the developing countries of Asia today. Each country has a number that stand high for both breadth of vision and practical impact. To speak of them as examples worthy of emulation is not to suggest that the project should be copied or adopted in another setting. There are no set models for the social initiatives that a company may take on. And the needs in Asia are so numerous that initiatives can range over a very wide and varied area. What is worthy of emulation is the degree of commitment and social conscience that drives these initiatives.

Toward global standards

Of the three continents — North America, Europe and Asia — Europe has gone farthest in developing standards for corporate citizenship and social responsibility and spearheading innovative approaches to the field. America has started to develop its own systems for monitoring and evaluating citizenship performance. And Asia is just beginning to stir to the challenge. One positive sign that the movement toward improved corporate citizenship is gaining momentum is the development of social-accountability standards and social auditing.

In recent years, international standards such as Social Accountability 8000 have emerged. SA8000 provides a benchmark for monitoring and evaluating the performance of companies on key social issues such as human rights, workers' rights, and health and safety and can be applied internationally across all commercial sectors. In much the same way that ISO 9000 established a management system standard for quality-control assurance, SA8000 is able to assess whether companies and organizations are meeting basic standards on core social issues.[6]

---

[6] SA8000, Council on Economic Priorities Accreditation Agency, New York, October 1997.

Complementing the development of standards is the rising popularity of social auditing as a means for measuring business performance in the field of corporate citizenship. Social auditing was developed in the late '90s by European companies as a result of the success of environmental auditing as a measure for evaluating a company's performance in protecting the environment. It is designed to assess the social impact and ethical behavior of an organization in relation to its aims, and those of its stakeholders. Through social auditing, companies can gain legitimacy in the eyes of society, ally increased profitability with social concerns, improve management performance through informed decision-making and provide feedback to stakeholders on the company's achievements. The fact that systems of social auditing are being developed by the largest accounting and consulting firms today is a clear indicator that social accountability is coming of age.

In addition to these two standard-setting programs, there is significant work being done by other organizations in establishing social and environmental sustainability indicators and reports. Clearly, responsible corporate behavior is becoming more important as a measure of overall corporate success and, because of globalization, these trends in the West have increasingly stirred interest in Asia as well. Multinational companies, in relocating many of their operations to the region, have increasingly had to deal with criticism on the non-uniformity of business practices. Similarly, local Asian companies are under pressure to measure up to international standards in helping improve quality of life and other social concerns. I personally believe that this is an area where Asia will begin to show substantial improvement in the coming years, especially as social pressures continue to mount amid our present economic challenges.

At the end of the day, responsible corporate citizenship is really a question of values — the values the company, its leaders and its employees live by. Whether one operates in the developed or the developing world, corporate and personal values dictate the way one engages in business. Time and again, ethical choices will have to be made between taking the moral high road or pursuing "practical" business practices. While companies can sometimes get away with evading their broad responsibilities to society, I believe that they end up hurting themselves and the country in the long run. Ethical and socially responsible companies, on the other hand, may end up sacrificing some possible business advantage, but these are only in the short term. Ayala, for example, is the oldest business house in the Philippines and we therefore have inherited a unique legacy of managing for the long haul. Responsible companies, those that want to endure and succeed through time, should manage themselves as if they were running a marathon and not a sprint.

Looking ahead, I have much confidence in the future prospects of corporate citizenship in Asia because social involvement is a traditional practice of Asian private enterprise, and there is an emerging focus on corporate ethics and values and social responsibility in the wake of the recent crisis. Asian business at its best has always been both a dynamic economic engine and a caring social institution. The goals of maximizing profits, growing shareholder value, and contributing in a meaningful way to social progress are, in the long term, all inextricably linked and without conflict.

10

MANAGEMENT
New Japanese Business Culture

Karuna Shinsho

Karuna Shinsho, freelance journalist, Tokyo
In discussion with Joichi Ito, Founder & CEO, Neoteny, Japan
Oki Matsumoto, President & CEO, Monex Inc, Japan

 In the 1980s, doing business the Japanese way might have seemed like a roadmap toward corporate supremacy. The international community marveled at Japan's economic prowess, exemplified by its gravity-defying stock market. That admiration nearly turned to fear in some alarmist quarters as calls to "contain" Japan's economic system grew. But in 1990, the façade of its economic superiority came crashing down as Japan's bubble economy burst. Since then, Japan has been in the hot seat, pressured by internal and external forces to drastically change the way it does business. But more than a decade later, the country has yet to pull itself out of recession.

In the meantime, the bright, brash youth of Japan have been carving out a new path toward business success, most evident in the rapidly changing world of information technology. What ideas do these "entrepreneurs" bring to Japan's business landscape? And in the wake of recent global corporate scandals, what lessons have Japanese businesses learned, if at all?

In a country that historically respected conformity and tradition, Oki Matsumoto — president and CEO of the publicly-listed online securities company Monex, Inc. — and Joichi Ito — founder and CEO of venture-capital firm Neoteny — represent a new breed of businesspeople in Japan. They are masters of their own fate in a market dominated by corporate giants. Matsumoto is an investment banker-turned-CEO of one of Japan's first e-brokerages. And Ito, a college dropout, went on to create numerous

Internet companies and is now in a position to give the Japanese government tips on technology. They have been hailed in the media as "rising stars" and "the next generation of global leaders." But they also see their future success and those of others as being dependent on what kind of business practices ultimately prevail in Japan.

Matsumoto first pinpoints the overwhelming presence of the company in Japan as a problem. "When I see the scandals happening with Japanese corporations these days, whether it's a bank or Tokyo Electric Power, I bet that each individual had strong reservations about doing those bad things. But nobody can say no to the corporation. And even if he's a board member, he can't really turn a project down. So I think there's a huge gap between individual ethics and those of the corporation."

It may not be surprising to hear such a statement from Matsumoto, who has for the most part made career moves that, until recently, had been considered "individualistic." After graduating from the renowned Tokyo University law department (which usually sees its graduates seek positions in government or blue-chip corporations in Japan), Matsumoto joined Salomon Brothers as a bond trader, and then jumped ship to Goldman Sachs to eventually become its youngest Japanese partner ever at the age of 30. And then, in 1999, Matsumoto reportedly left a fortune in stock options at Goldman to start his own Internet brokerage firm, Monex.

Ito's career path has also been unconventional in traditionally conformist Japan. After dropping out of the University of Chicago, Ito launched a slew of businesses, including Eccosys (Japan's first web-production company), Digital Garage (a web marketing and solutions provider), PSINet Japan (the nation's first commercial Internet Service Provider), and Infoseek Japan (one of the country's largest search portals). Now he concentrates on using his bicultural experience as a bridge between Japan and the United States with Neoteny, his venture-capital firm focused on personal communications and enabling technologies. And Ito's insights on Japan's business culture reflect that bicultural background. He particularly stresses the importance of historical context and role definition. "Even if you have the same names like *shacho* (president) or board member," he says, "they mean very different things. For instance, most of the Japanese presidents are actually the chairmen of their labor unions. That's kind of ridiculous from an American perspective, but from the perspective of a Japanese company where the president represents the employees' interests, it's not. If you look at Japan's *zaibatsu* [giant financial groups] and *iemoto* [head family].

Differences in such corporate responsibilities may also lie in the difference between who is considered a stakeholder of a company in Japan and in other countries. "In the United States," Matsumoto says, "it's very clear; it's basically the shareholders. In Japan, it's the society, employees, clients and shareholders. And the shareholders tend to be ranked lower than other stakeholders. If you compare Gross Domestic Product (GDP) versus summation of market capitalization of listed companies, in the United States, GDP is about US$12 trillion, and the summation of market capitalization is equal to that. But in Japan, GDP is 500 trillion yen and market capitalization is 250 trillion yen, just half. Japan represents 13% of worldwide GDP, but Japanese corporations represent only 8% of worldwide market capitalization. So there are gaps between the real value of corporations versus market capitalization. That is probably rooted in how corporations regard shareholders."

Ito also argues that the kind of priorities companies set regarding shareholders can lead to problems. "It's very easy to be ethical when your shareholders and customers and your employees are all the same and they're all telling you one thing. But if your shareholders tell you one thing, your partners tell you another thing, the government tells you another thing, and society tells you another thing, then you get into a moral and ethical dilemma. I think one of the key things Japan is experiencing is a disconnect between stakeholders in different sectors of society. For instance, there is foreign money coming into the market, an aging propulation with a different set of moral values amidst the spread of globalization, and the necessary shifting of resource allocation in Japan from manufacturing to services. We need to resolve the conflicts that each shift creates – I think that this resolution is very important."

For Matsumoto, addressing the issue of stakeholders was important when he started Monex. "Many Japanese corporations' shares are closely held. If you look at them, usually 60% or 70% of each company's shares are held by other corporations. In that kind of set-up, you don't have to worry about shareholders' interests because everyone is holding each other's share. In Monex, which we started in 1999, 50% of the capital was injected by Sony and 50% by myself. Later, it changed to 51% by me and 49% by Sony. This is a very rare case in Japan — that a big corporation and an individual set up a joint venture together. Currently we have more than 220,000 clients, everyone online, and we have 23,000 shareholders, over 98% of them individuals. This number of shareholders is quite large. Even if you look at section one of the Tokyo Stock Exchange, there are many companies with fewer than 5,000 shareholders." And it's that kind of shareholding structure which, Matsumoto says, also prevents Japan Inc.

from taking corporate governance seriously. He cites a recent scandal at a Japanese company as an example: "*Yukijirushi Shokuhin* (Snow Brand Foods) was hit by scandals about its beef just half a year or a year after its parent company, *Yukijirushi Nyugyo* (Snow Brand Milk), had a huge scandal over its milk. Both were listed companies at that time and now *Yukijirushi Shokuhin* is de-listed. There's no governance or control. People asked why it happened and what were the shareholders doing. The reality is that 80% of *Yukijirushi Shokuhin* was held by *Yukijirushi Nyugyo*, 16% was held by an agricultural bank called *Norin Chukin*, and only 4% was in flotation. So this is the biggest problem in why corporate governance doesn't work in Japan. We have to dissolve or unwind this kind of shareholding structure."

Ito also sees similar problems in other areas of corporate Japan, including in his own business of venture capital. "People in charge of running other people's money in Japan often tend to be lifetime employees, with no bonus attached to the returns, so there are no incentives. So when we invest in the U.S., whenever the value of a company goes down, then it's quickly marked down to reflect that and to manage expectations of investors and reflect transparency. But, in Japan, nobody wants a mark-down. In fact, the person in charge would often tell us to mark it down only after the person in charge has been transferred to another group and the successor is in place.

Such reported corporate behavior in Japan is often believed to be the result of the country's lack of black-and-white commercial rules and its reliance, instead, on tacit knowledge. Matsumoto, for example, finds the practice of choosing board members in Japan "very, very strange". "In many cases," he says, "a board member is already decided on five years or ten years in advance. Board members should be decided on by the shareholders. To decide these things years ahead only lowers the functionality and efficiency of a company and I think that puts up a huge barrier for outsiders to come in from overseas or even from inside Japan."

But Ito sees some advantages to using tacit knowledge in, for example, car companies. "To a certain extent, tacit knowledge makes sense because it's more efficient. If you keep using the same engineers, you have what's called *anmoku no ryokai*, you understand without communicating, so the efficiency of communicating is higher, but the efficiency then breaks down the moment you open up the network and you have to create process." Ito also believes that this lack of transparency is a product of a common business practice in Japan. "Japanese at an individual level have a lot of personal indebtedness to each other and doing favors for each other is a really important form of Japanese business. I think in Asia, it's also like that. And the problem is because people don't have money, the transactions are all favors for each other. And these favors are not codified. So you owe a lot people favors and they owe you favors and what happens is that those favors are also not in the corporate balance sheets, but they affect the governance of the company. This happens to a certain extent in other cultures, but it's huge in Japan."

Yet, at the same time, Ito admits that things are slowly changing. "Many companies in Japan are starting to use IT (Information Technology) to structure purchasing, for instance, and to lower costs. And what they're finding is that they're unearthing a lot of tacit relationships and making it more difficult to exchange personal favors. They found that people who sell power tools give kickbacks to the people who buy power tools. After the end of every construction project, construction workers used to throw all the power tools in the concrete, so many buildings in Japan had power tools embedded in the walls. When the construction industry began to institute checks into where everything went and what was paid for, they began to question the disappearance of the tools. With the downturn in the economy, people are being forced to focus on costs and they can't afford to waste anymore and as you start pushing through the waste, you find a lot of Japanese ethics and business practices that can't survive the scrutiny and transparency. This is going to force change in Japan."

Change is something both Ito and Matsumoto have called for — Ito on one occasion suggesting a "wholesale revolution" to make Japan a functioning democracy, and Matsumoto pushing for more transparent and democratic markets. Yet, they also realize that such changes won't come easily or quickly. Matsumoto feels Japanese companies haven't addressed their inefficient ways because of different perceptions of the country's economic problems. "Japan is like a lake. On the bottom of the lake, there are the ruins of broken buildings and gas pipes. On the surface, though, everything is calm and even if you throw a stone into the water, there may be a wave, but after two minutes, it's calm again. We need to either put a light into the water or wait for all the water to go down before we can see what is on the bottom. Some people will look at the surface and say Japan is alright, that it's beautiful, at peace, and under control. Others say Japan is in trouble if you look at the bottom. Both observations are actually true. As the bad economic situation continues, the waterline will come down and people will start to try to change things." But Matsumoto also warns against rapid change: "Japan is very big. We represent close to 20% of GDP worldwide. We cannot afford radical changes. Somehow the Japanese system has been made to accept only very gradual changes. Also, I think our type of feeling is all over the place. When you listen to the whole situation, we're reaching a threshold or peak of a mountain. Once we reach the peak of the mountain, things will change."

Ito also sees that Japan is trying to change, but he cautions that the kind of change being considered isn't so clear. "I agree that Japan is trying to get over this hump and see what the problem is. But I don't know, for instance, whether Japan is moving to globalization. I think Japan needs to become a part of the global community. And opening up the Japanese markets is a very different topic from building democracy inside Japan for the Japanese by the Japanese. The Japanese haven't yet embraced the idea that they have to change their fundamental ethics and thinking across culture." However, regardless of the debate over what constitutes the ideal type of change, Ito asserts that change itself is an urgent matter for Japan. "Asia's much younger than us. They have much lower costs. We have no service sectors that are really strong. The population is aging. And we're expensive. But we still have cash in the bank so it's like being a retired sports guy who's got $2 million in the bank and is totally unmotivated to learn anything else. He still thinks he's popular. He still thinks he's rich. And he still thinks that maybe he should go back into manufacturing again. But in fact, he's never going to win against the Koreans, the Taiwanese or the Chinese."

Matsumoto concurs that the Japanese way of thinking must change, cautioning against Japanese isolationism. "People call North Korea an aggressive isolationist. I tend to call Japan a moderate isolationist. It's very bad in today's world being a closed nation. It's risky and very strange and it's not good for growth in Japan as well as in the worldwide economy. We don't accept diversity and diverse values. It's rooted in education or our homogenous country."

Yet, one would expect the Internet, which is indispensable to both Ito's and Matsumoto's businesses, would help to change all that. But according to Ito, in many ways, it hasn't. "Information technology is a tool for restructuring the company and making it more efficient. So if there's no will in the company to restructure or change the governance or to be transparent, it doesn't help you at all. Most Japanese companies bought huge IT systems and kept their process the same. The systems failed to add any value and so what's interesting for Japan is that so far IT has had much less impact than originally anticipated."

If Internet technology truly hasn't made a huge difference in corporate governance in Japan, what does that mean for the future direction of the country's business culture? Business, for all intents and purposes, is about making money. Capitalism thrives on self-interest and greed. Can corporate ethics ultimately exist hand in hand with a market economy? Matsumoto and Ito believe it is possible. "Business is business with people," Matsumoto asserts. "So if you are a very bad person trying to be very profitable, then you can make money for the moment, but you can't sustain profitability. At the end of the day, business is how you get paid by your clients so I think that in the long run, profitability and ethics converge. It's the same thing because we do business with people."

"If you're doing something that has value and creating value for society," Ito says, "the business model is how you should get paid for the value. So if you think about business from the approach of 'how do I create a service that adds value and how do I get paid for it and how do I do it efficiently?', that's the kind of right ethics for a company. I think the old way of doing it was that 'I'm important so I deserve a piece even if I'm not adding value'. It's like the old Chinese saying that the person who finds the well should be paid forever." But Ito also believes that there is more to an ethically sound business model than that. "We need to start to think about developing social ethics. Basically, in your life you have a certain number of things that are connected with money, like your family and culture. In Japan, after the Second World War, when you couldn't feed yourselves, then money was the primary focus in many cultures. Once you get beyond where you have enough money, then you start spending time on other kinds of ethical or spiritual things that aren't corporate things."

And perhaps that is the crux of the matter: that corporate governance isn't just about whether a business itself is run ethically or not, but how other components that support it — the people, society, country, and the world — are cognizant of, and in agreement over, ethics in general.

11

MEDIA:
The Media in China: Open Questions

Hu Shuli

Managing Editor, Caijing Magazine, Beijing

Here I am going to give an overview of the Chinese news media, which, in recent years, has expanded very rapidly in depth and breadth. In fact, the transformation of the Chinese media industry has paralleled the transition of China's economy, so that today both stand as Big Stories of our time. Of course, for me as a participant in this "race to develop," it has been both exciting and challenging.

Telling this story is a multi-step process. First we review the historical context of the industry's development. Then follows background on the development of the organization with which I am directly affiliated, *Caijing* ("finance" in Chinese) *Magazine*, and some of the ethical and other dilemmas of reporting financial news in China. Finally, I will review some of the events of the recent past, such as SARS (Severe Acute Respiratory Syndrome), which have posed a particular challenge to the industry's development. We then are able to chart the way forward, ethically and in a broader sense.

The historical context

During the 1980s, there were a limited number of newspapers and magazines and all were directly owned and controlled by the government. Along with the great economic and social changes that were taking place, journalists were trying very hard to work as watchdogs and to tell the truth when possible. However China was far more isolated from the world than it is now; so, not surprisingly, journalists didn't fully understand how an independent press worked.

The media industry saw great changes in the 1990s. Very rapidly, the single system of official newspapers sponsored by the Government or the Communist Party was joined by thousands of semi-official or fringe newspapers and magazines. Many of these dealt specifically with issues related to the transition in the Chinese economy and the resulting changes in society.

But even in the semi-official business newspapers in the early 1990s, the size of the editorial budget made it impossible to assert full journalistic independence in matters of news policy. There simply was not enough money to support investigative reports, which require many more resources than reporting official news. Newspapers could not support budgets for travel to the places in which stories were happening. Often, reporters had to rely on their news sources for funding travel expenses, making it impossible to remain independent and unbiased.

As the stock market grew and finance was reformed in China it was clear that financial reporting would be the most amenable path to the kind of "real journalism". Business topics in China, unlike political ones, have always been arguable in the past twenty years, and the transition of economy has offered the largest part of news which can really impact the world. It was clear that this field was open and receptive to independent and investigative reporting not available in official news organizations.

At the beginning of 1998, I was given the opportunity to launch a high-quality financial news magazine with what was then an extraordinarily large editorial budget. More importantly, the investors were willing to give complete editorial control to my fellow editors and me, thereby separating management from the editorial side of the publication. This division, which seems standard in other parts of the world, was a first for a Chinese news magazine. Thus, Caijing was born. Although it was only a monthly magazine at that time, and therefore offered a much smaller platform than I was used to, we appreciated the opportunity and were excited at the prospects.

China's shift to a market economy has created an environment that demands a new level of openness and accountability when dealing with financial news. Since our very first day, Caijing has been confronted with the need to enforce transparency and accountability in the news-gathering and reporting process. It is a process that has helped us both to elevate our own level of journalistic integrity and to serve as an independent watchdog of the markets.

Making news, making a difference

In April 1998, our very first cover story was a comprehensive and up-front report on a real estate company, Qiong Min Yuan, that was listed on the stock exchange. The company was a dark horse in the market, a little-known company whose share price at one point skyrocketed 400%. But, suddenly in 1997, it was suspended for inflating profits. A few insiders had been tipped off before the suspension and, by the time of the discovery, had already dumped their shares on the market. Naturally, when the malfeasance was discovered, the share price crumbled, leaving some 50,000 small, individual investors stranded with shares that were now worth only a fraction of their original value.

As with many other cases of insider or connected-persons trading on the markets, no one dared to report the story. So, we decided to break this self-imposed silence and explain the full story to our readers in a report simply entitled "Who is Responsible for Qiong Min Yuan?". It was our first issue of the magazine: it contained no new investigative scoops, but simply put what everyone knew on paper and in public. It caused a huge stir. In response, the magazine was banned - but not before the print run of 50,000 copies had been sold.

Ever since that first issue, Caijing has been vigilant in honoring the public's right to know. The language and behavior of the financial sector can be very confusing to the general public, so we made it our special mission to explain, in clear and thorough terms, all the activities of the market. We have made authoritative reports on what we consider to have been the major events in the markets in the past five years. The most notable of these was a cover story in October of 2000 - "The Inside Story of Fund Management."

The article, based on a suppressed analysis by an official of the Shanghai Stock Exchange, exposed how many of China's investment-fund management companies engaged in illegal and irregular trading in the securities market. It was the first time a serious magazine had criticized the fund-management sector and, by implication, the stock market. Needless to say, a lot of people got mad: ten of the companies mentioned in the report attacked us in the media and even threatened to sue.

However the fund-management story was a watershed for Caijing — and for the Chinese press in general — because the government left us entirely alone, neither criticizing our coverage nor banning our report. Since then, the Chinese financial media have been even more willing to take risks in criticizing the market and its abusers, and thereby providing a sort of supervision by the people. We've exposed price manipulators and cases of falsified profits. Ten hours after we made an on-line posting of our August 2001 story, the "Yinguangxia Trap" — a story that revealed how the company had faked 700 million RMB profits — authorities suspended trading of Yinguangxia's stock and within a week had launched an investigation. When the Enron case exploded in the US, it was called the "American Yinguangxia" in the Chinese media.

The ethics of reporting the irregularities and corruption in capital markets can be debated, mainly with the vested interests, which attacked us as not caring for the development of newly established markets. However, I have always believed that it is the duty of the financial media to ensure transparency in the markets - whether in the activities of its players or the terminology that they use. We are not "against" any particular group, but are merely standing for the public's right to know. Our role as a third voice on the markets, we believe, makes all the players - especially those without privileged access to government or information - better informed. A level playing field is crucial to China's development into a complex market economy, and the financial media has a role to play in this. (Besides the three categories, there are some small newspapers and magazines, not considered as main stream news media, focusing on niche markets.)

Developing the media sector

With Caijing's success came a more general awareness of the opportunities and possibilities that existed within the Chinese financial news market. In short, people and companies woke up to the fact that it was possible to practice real journalism. Since 2000, even more independent newspapers and magazines have been launched, and there is now an unprecedented level of competition in the Chinese media.

While both the electronic and print media are booming in business and financial news, it is still the case that their reach is limited because of the way the market has developed thus far. The case of printed media, which is still a main source of news for millions of urbanites, is somewhat more complicated.

In China, the news-oriented newspapers and magazines are divided into three main categories. The first is the official papers, such as People's Daily and Workers' Daily, which are used to disseminate propaganda and are studied by government and party officials. The second category is what might be termed the tabloid official newspapers, such as Beijing Evening News and other evening or local newspapers, which are partially responsible for broadcasting propaganda while catering to the general public. The third kind of printed news comes in the form of commercial papers covering mainly the financial and business fields.

In recent years, the first two groups of newspapers and magazines have been devoting more stories and pages to economic and financial information. However, what is most remarkable about the printed media is how, since 1998, many new publications focusing on financial and business news have started. Aside from Caijing, the market has received *21st Century Business Herald*, *The Economic Observer* and *New Fortune China Business Post*, among others, all marked by updated ideas and modern eye-catching layouts. In the face of this new competition, the older financial and business newspapers, such as *China Security Journal* and *Security Times*, have had to reinvent themselves to maintain their status. All these news publications are now clamoring for an audience that, while expanding, is still quite limited. Competition is intense.

Similarly, the news websites also give considerable room to the financial news. Compared with the traditional media, news websites have the advantage in providing a platform to potentially unite the much-divided media market. As an example, one just has to look at one of the most influential news websites, Sina (www.sina.com). In addition to releasing thousands of stories from the Xinhua News Agency and other domestic and foreign agencies every day, it also has developed special columns, such as "Finance Magazine Cover Show," "Everyday Top News of Finance Papers" and "Top News of International Finance Papers," which collect and highlight not only the financial news, but also stories that are covered in the finance media. In essence, they are reporting on the media. To the average observer comparing the situation that existed in 1998 with the current situation, the market has developed immensely, and the resources being devoted to building up the financial and business media are huge.

However, we should not fall into thinking that the market as it is today is good enough. With the market prospering, new problems have formed, and some of the old ones still exist.

With the information boom supplied by an increasing array of media outlets have come mistakes too. For instance, some of the news is not accurately reported, is reported in the wrong context, or with incorrect or vague references. If the problem in the past was that too few dared to publish something sharp, today it may be that too many overstep the mark in doing so. If there was a lack of choice before, the problem now may be to find a source of news that is reliable, accurate and truthful amongst so many choices. Today's readers must hone more critical and careful reading skills, to be able to discern what is true and what is not.

Eventually, China needs to develop independent, authoritative and professional media that take on roles similar to those that are played by the *Wall Street Journal* in the U.S. and the *Financial Times* in the UK. The market has moved from being monolithic to very heterogeneous, with a plethora of choice. The whole industry still has to undergo a consolidation and integration, out of which will emerge the true, lasting leaders.

However, this is not an easy process in China because of the limitations of the current system in managing publication and distribution on a national scale. This is a legacy of the planned economy. China's newspapers and magazines must be licensed to publish and distribute. The licensing is represented by the unique ISSN number issued by General Administration of Press and Publishing, PRC. Only government units or agencies are eligible to own an ISSN, and the license can be revoked if the direction of news coverage is found not to be in line with the national news broadcasting policy.

What's more, since the mid 1990s, some popular newspapers could be sold through post offices or newsstands, as well as through subscriptions. The serious national daily newspapers, however, are still sold only on subscription and distribution through the postal network. As a result of this centralized control, it is very hard for the new business-oriented print media to grow. In addition, the overabundance of news-stand publications have caused the market to become highly fragmented. Therefore, there is a long way to go in integrating the Chinese news market.

Rites of spring

Which brings us to spring 2003. If Caijing's five-year experience tells us a great deal about the recent transitions in both the Chinese economy and media, then the handling of the Severe Acute Respiratory Syndrome (SARS) outbreak in China tells us much about both where Chinese media is at this critical moment, and where it is capable of going. SARS can be seen as a turning point and bellwether for the development of the media.

Starting in early April 2003, SARS drew tremendous media attention from both international and national media outlets, including Caijing. We covered the story from its earliest stages, devoting a great deal of time and effort to charting the course of the epidemic.

The story began in the middle of February, when SARS, originally called "atypical pneumonia" when it first erupted in Guangdong province, was still being dealt with primarily in the local regional press.

The SARS outbreak in Guangdong caught us off guard. Though Caijing is a business magazine, and SARS is, technically, a health issue, we could feel the weight and importance of this medical crisis. In this complex economy, we saw the epidemic's potential to have a far-reaching impact on the economy and on society. We had an obligation to follow it.

Therefore, our double issue for February 20 told the whole story of SARS in Guangdong, in a lengthy analysis titled "Guangdong Disease Crashing Against the National Disease Control System." Our coverage pointed directly to the weaknesses that riddled China's disease-control system, weaknesses that were becoming ever more apparent with the SARS outbreak. We wanted to send a warning to the nation.

After February, the SARS situation in Guangdong began to quieten down and we, just like everyone else, thought that it had ended. However, in late March our Hong Kong Bureau chief, Haili Cao, reported to work and found herself in the middle of a city that was wearing masks.

Though Haili's report surprised us, we were able to confirm — from the website of the World Health Organization in Geneva — that SARS was still spreading. On March 26, when the Guangdong government reported that 792 SARS cases had been recorded by the end of February, we decided that we needed to turn our attention back to SARS in China. Immediately, our reporters headed out to interview MOH, the Beijing Bureau of Health, the Guangdong Bureau of Health, and WHO officials, among others. By that time, a WHO expert team had arrived in Beijing.

Some questioned whether we should be reporting on an outbreak which, at that stage, had reached only a low level of magnitude. We believed, however, that this was important news and that our readers needed to know about the situation, not least because of the huge impact it could have on a frail national health system. We did a series of stories and analysis about SARS in China and the world, producing a 10-page special report in the issue of April 5. Minutes after our story was sent to print, Zhang Wenkang, the Minister of Health, went on State television to announce the epidemic in China. We retrieved the magazine from the printer to update the numbers.

This part of the story was simply a prelude to what would follow. SARS spread through Beijing and other places throughout April, reaching its peak at the end of the month. As the epidemic grew, so too did the news story. Caijing was right on track. In early April, we streamlined our reporting on SARS, weaving separate strands of coverage into a cover story for our April 20 issue titled "Where the Dangers Come From?"

April 20th was a critical moment in China's management of the SARS situation. Zhang Wenkang and Meng Xuenong, the mayor of Beijing, were both fired, just days after they had declared that the epidemic was under control. Accurate information on the disease suddenly became easier to obtain, enabling us to publish more detailed reports.

Caijing placed great emphasis on completing in-depth investigations and explaining the situation thoroughly. In particular, we focused on the migrant workers in the cities and the Midwest as they encountered the infection. For instance, we asked how less-privileged groups could respond to SARS, and how they could protect themselves against the spread of the disease. It was part news, part public service.

With this new concentration, we printed another series of stories in our May 5 issue. It was titled "SARS Spreading Westward" and covered the public health system in Shanxi, Sichuan, Gansu and the Midwest. The same issue included both our story "Migrant Workers Under the Shadow of SARS" and several reports about the impact of the disease on the economy. Our reporting uncovered a large problem with the government's strategy to deal with SARS. The so-called "intense within, loose outside" policy didn't work, and the less-privileged groups were likely to be the biggest victims.

As we reported on the Midwest, it became increasingly clear that readers wanted not only new information on SARS but also reflections on how China had dealt with the rise and containment of the disease. In order to draw a complete picture about SARS, we decided to print a supplementary weekly magazine for the duration of the epidemic.

So we ran four special magazines. Ten editors and reporters focused on concrete incidents, major events and on-the-spot investigations in an attempt to piece together an accurate and complete picture of the crisis. In such articles as "Finding Out About Infections in the Hospital," "Peasants and Migrant Workers in the City," and "The International and Domestic Affected Areas," we tried our best to uncover the truth.

Recently I read a story from an American newspaper criticizing China's media for being only "patriotic" in its coverage of SARS. While I'm not a specialist in the study of news transmission, I have to take issue with such a simplified accusation. I think that, despite all the difficulties, Chinese journalists have tried their best to cover the crisis — they dug out the truth, reflected over the available lessons and, in later cases, warned the population. They did what they saw as their duty as journalists, rather than as patriots. Pride in country is one thing, but it takes much more to replace one's role as a journalist. While it is true that there were official and unofficial views on SARS, many Chinese journalists reported on the outbreak honestly and forthrightly, and I believe that Caijing was among them. We tried our absolute best.

Now we are in the post-SARS period, Caijing has finished its supplements and returned its focus to general business and financial news. As SARS brought with it irreversible changes, there is a long way to go for China to have its media reformed in line with international standards and the requirements of its own market economy. As part of a market in development, journalists and editors in China are forced daily to review their ethics as they reach for viable business models. Going against the grain in the early years of the market's development was not easy, and decisions that we made could have broken us financially. The market has turned a corner, but there will still be tests of faith and ethics. Indeed, the rewards are great for the media organizations that emerge from this stage of the industry's development, and this raises the ethical bar for those involved.

I say, keep watching the Chinese press. The next generation of Chinese journalists is a group of well-educated, independent thinkers who are fully aware of the media's international stage. They are high-quality minds that bring with them a vibrant enthusiasm for the growing freedom of our press, and entertain a world of ever-increasing possibilities for responsible, investigative journalism. This is the future of journalism in China.

12

PUBLIC RELATIONS
Branding and Corporate Responsibility go Hand in Hand in Asia

Shelly Lazarus
Chairman and Chief Executive Officer, Ogilvy & Mather Worldwide
and
Matthew Anderson
Chief Executive, Asia Pacific & EAME, Ogilvy Public Relations Worldwide

 Great brands meet or exceed consumer expectations. This has always been true. But as the marketplace has gotten more sophisticated and competitive, marketers have realized that what motivates people to buy products is far more complex today. It is not just function, efficacy or availability. Nor is it simply price or positioning. It is a host of contacts, impressions and emotional connections, along with function, that drive consumer behavior. We call this 360 Degree Branding. In our experience, everything that touches the consumer creates the brand: from style and design, to packaging, news coverage, delivery trucks and service experience. Everything from hearsay to history counts.

Since everything counts when building brands, it's an obvious step to consider the ethical dimensions of brands. This is especially important here in Asia, where a holistic view of branding is relatively new, but social responsibility has long played a role in corporate behavior. For brands to be successful in Asia, they have no choice but to consider their ethical dimensions.

Why 360 demands ethical thinking

Branding in Asia has never just been about traditional, straight-at-the-consumer advertising. Consumers in many developing markets have experienced such inconsistency in quality that they have rarely taken product promises purely on their word. This puts accountability front and center. A recent survey across Asia found that making quality products and taking full responsibility for their performance contributed most to consumer trust in business.[1] Customers expect companies to stand by their products. When something goes wrong, Asians want brand owners to take responsibility, to fix the problem and ensure it won't happen again.

To market in Asia, in fact, is to enter a social contract. What's new is that this social contract is rapidly moving beyond the promise to make good things and provide reliable service. Nowadays, customer expectations encompass other areas of corporate responsibility, such as safety and health issues, environmental practices and labor relations.

Clearly, this moves brand building beyond just typical marketing. It entails taking responsibility for the way your entire business affects society and understanding, in turn, that the fate of your brand can depend on people who may not use your products or services at all — stakeholders as diverse as government officials and regulators, analysts and editors, NGOs and activists, community and religious leaders.

If you are reading this book, chances are you already think corporate social responsibility is important. But recognizing that a meaningful, coherent and cost-effective corporate social responsibility (CSR) program is a branding exercise may be entirely new.

Brands are it

We believe that branding and CSR have been on parallel but separate tracks in Asia. There are explanations for this. Many executives in the region equate branding with selling. They are understandably, and often rightly, reluctant to trumpet good works or exploit marketing programs with social agendas. Moreover, much corporate philanthropy has traditionally been associated with company founders and generally based on the sort of close-knit relationships that characterize Asia's family-controlled corporations.

Considering branding and social responsibility as separate activities not only misses the point, it is missed opportunity. In a 360 world, where everything counts, branding activity and corporate behavior are already intertwined in the minds of the stakeholders and consumers — and they should be.

Brands should be purposefully enriched with ethics and community values for the simple reason that brands are the most important and

---

[1] "Drivers of Brand and Company Trust" — Wirthlin Asia.

unique asset a company has. If the last tumultuous years of globalization, media explosion, SARS and roiling economies have taught us anything, it's the value of a strong brand. There is plenty of compelling economic evidence that having a strong brand is what is needed to succeed in today's marketplace — to be profitable, build market share and secure customer loyalty, to face down rivals, move into new markets and across borders, and to remain relevant to increasingly demanding consumers. For any CSR program to be meaningful, it must take into account the value of the brand, and its inextricable link to it.

Responsible brands are Asia's future

Since Asian consumers demand accountability — it's that social contract we mentioned — it is easy to make the jump from product quality to transparency, to care and concern for health, safety, the environment, and the treatment of employees. Corporate behavior counts. And it counts with an array of people beyond the actual consumer.

Increasingly, government representatives, decision-makers and opinion leaders want brands to multiply the efforts and money they can commit to strengthening their countries. Asian leaders want help building confidence in economic performance. They want progress, with Asian characteristics of course, and are eager to see companies sustain Asia's ethos of hard work and entrepreneurial drive. They know that few governments can tackle the big issues — poverty, pandemic disease and the infrastructure required for economic growth — without private-sector support.

In China, for example, companies from Boeing to BP are not only providing foreign travel, exchanges, symposia and training to develop talent, but are also backing initiatives to protect the environment and raise operating standards, as well as an array of volunteerism and community involvement.[2]

This parallels customers' desires for brands that make them feel good at a deeper level than mere consumption. They want brands that are in tune with their deepest aspirations and beliefs about the world. Today, one in five Hong Kong consumers says he has avoided a brand whose parent company was not a good corporate citizen. In other parts of Asia, as many as three out of four consumers say they would switch to a brand

---

[2] "Corporate Social Responsibility in China: Practices by U.S. Companies" — The Business Roundtable. A number of the companies listed are Ogilvy clients.

associated with a good cause. Imagine how much purchase behavior will change as these consumers have more information about business and more options to choose from.

Sticks and carrots

Corporations that ignore the growing interest in their behavior do so at great peril. Stakeholders — whether they be government officials, employees, community leaders or pressure groups — have both the ability and incentive to reward and punish corporate behavior. It's not just the controversial categories of business that must pay heed.

Ten years ago, it was the oil, automotive, spirits and tobacco companies that had the most active responsibility programs, often driven by a concern over regulation or activism. Now, CSR is a proactive consideration, because there is no longer just a stick, there's a carrot as well. Research shows that shares of so-called stakeholder-balanced companies outperform peers. Well-crafted social responsibility programs help win and retain customers, keep employees happy and positively influence their behavior, and engender goodwill with important stakeholders. Goodwill is the big carrot that is prompting companies to be smarter about ethics and responsibility.

Who you are can equal where you are

There is another CSR consideration that is unique to the region. For many businesses in Asia, distribution is the *sine qua non* of growth. Outside of the urban centers, there is a huge potential consumer base that is not serviced by the same kind of distribution infrastructure typical of highly developed markets. Penetrating this frontier requires a different mindset than just "channel" thinking. You have to consider the stakeholders — often including powerful officials, local NGOs, activist groups and village-level political institutions — who can determine where and how a brand operates. The importance of having these groups as allies cannot be overstated.

In India, where more than 70% of the population lives in the countryside, we see an increasing recognition that business can and should shoulder aspects of rural development. This requires thinking more broadly about community involvement. Castrol, for example, helped communities in the Indian states of Gujarat, Rajasthan, Madhya Pradesh and Maharashtra cope with severe drought, which had crippled agriculture and reduced the availability of safe drinking water. Under the banner of its Castrol CRB Plus brand, the company worked with villagers, farmers' groups, NGOs and village councils to improve irrigation and promote water conservation and harvesting. A vital corporate-community partnership was created, to the benefit of the Castrol brand, and it resulted in a successful water-management and agricultural-renewal solution for the community. As agriculture recovered, the demand and preference for Castrol's products increased.

Create goodwill: without it, millions of customers and untold opportunities could be out of reach. With it, the potential to expand is enormous. Quite simply, who you are can mean where you are and how far you will go.

Easier said than done

The common difficulty all companies face in executing CSR is that it is easier said than done.

Some companies rely on ad-hoc projects or philanthropy, rather than formulating a CSR framework that matches the character of the company and its business. They fail to prioritize the range of the company's stakeholders. And they forget to link corporate responsibility to return on investment — or at least they lack ways of demonstrating its effectiveness.

They also struggle to communicate what they're doing. People are skeptical, as is the media. As responsible behavior becomes expected, trumpeting environmental and social credentials also becomes more risky — the bigger the company, the greater the risk of sounding arrogant or self-congratulatory. And the more kinds of CSR activities a company undertakes — especially when employees or divisions nominate projects without clear guidelines — the harder it is to communicate them without sounding unfocused.

Many companies rely disproportionately on stand-alone advertisements to tell their CSR story. Frequently, they fail because they are, all too often, formulaic and forgettable. We recently looked at nearly 100 different CSR ads running in Asia, and found that two-thirds were essentially interchangeable, using a similar layout, tone and copy. Millions of dollars are spent to promote projects using ads that fail to make a memorable link between the sponsor and the cause.

Even worse, stand-alone CSR advertising backfires into cynicism: "It's great that this company supports a good cause, but I wish they hadn't spent so much money telling me about it."

The brand as a starting point

We believe that one of the best ways to navigate the difficulties of CSR is to use the brand as a guide. If the brand is an organizing principle for all of a company's activities, then its application to CSR is a logical step. We are not talking about a logo, a slogan or a rallying cry. Rather, we are suggesting you create a framework that captures the essence of your brand's social meaning. Your brand itself can help reconcile conflicting aspirations and priorities. On a basic level, the brand should determine what individual projects or philanthropic programs a company supports. This legitimizes them and simplifies communications.

For example, it might not seem relevant for an IT company to get involved in tree planting, but it would make sense for that company to help provide children with educational materials or Internet access — especially if the company's expertise is connecting people and its higher promise is helping them reach their potential. That's, of course, a much easier story to tell and understand.

Several of Asia's largest banks contribute to financial education programs at universities around the region. Such work is on target with their brands, reflects true expertise and allows employees to take pride in their contributions to their community.

But CSR goes deeper than charity or philanthropy, however appropriate. A company's CSR activities need to be ingrained into every area of its business — everything from its labor policy, to the ingredients in its products, to how much pollution it creates, to whether its products are accessible to the poor, to its partners, and to its vendor and consumer relationships. CSR is about what a company does, not just what it says. None of this lessens a company's duty to shareholders. In many cases, the best avenues or responsibility involve areas where the company's resources and expertise can be uniquely and efficiently applied for social gain and the well-being of consumers. When a company is thinking about these issues, the brand and the larger idea it represents can help determine both what to do and what to avoid.

Six steps to increasing the effectiveness of CSR

Using the brand as the essential guide, there are six common threads that run through companies that have embraced and implemented CSR successfully in Asia. If you want to increase the value of CSR at your company, and, more important, use that commitment as a platform for your brand to build equity across stakeholders, these guidelines may help.

First: Commit from the top down

The first step is to make very clear to the whole company that responsible behavior involves every area of the business. It's not a communications program or a marketing strategy — it's about making sure that the growth and evolution of your company reflects the principles you have embraced. That's tough, but it has to be done. Because if it's not, you run the risk of having a disconnect between the company's public face and its private actions. For example, you can't be a company that gives money to environmental charities and then pollutes rivers. Hypocrites get the worst reviews.

To achieve institutional commitment to CSR, the message has to come from the highest level. Usually the chairman, the CEO or the board has to take responsibility for it, and it has to be made clear to the rest of the company that CSR is a central business priority. Unless the entire company is given that message, then responsible actions and ethical standards will languish. That means achieving internal consensus before you start, and then articulating a clear CSR vision, so that everyone in the organization understands how and where your company is going and what their role will be.

Nestlé's history of community involvement is rooted in this principle. CEO and vice chairman Peter Braebeck-Letmathe has been an outspoken advocate of Nestle's Nestlé CSR vision, in the belief that it directly contributes to the sustainable long-term growth of the company. Nestle's Nestlé corporate brand promise — "Good Food, Good Life" — means that the company goes beyond providing quality things to eat. Nestle Nestlé contributes to life through sports, arts and education, in addition to working with NGOs that are involved in nutrition and the environment. In Malaysia, for example, Nestle Nestlé conducted a nationwide survey on the nutritional habits and needs of Malaysian children. Based on the findings, Nestle Nestlé is now working in partnership with the Ministry of Education and various health and nutrition groups to improve the well-being of school children.

Second: Involve all your assets

By examining the company as a whole, you will find the areas where responsible practices can have the greatest impact. It starts within. A particularly Asian dimension to corporate responsibility is the need to ensure the integrity of business suppliers and supply chains. The actions and behaviors of these organizations are critical to the credibility of your CSR initiatives and the perception of your brand. Thus, business partners at all levels need to be carefully integrated into your CSR vision.

This dimension of corporate responsibility is fundamental to international brands with extensive manufacturing interests in Asia. They must strive to align all suppliers and business partners behind their social-responsibility agenda in order to satisfy audiences back home. Indeed, most major sporting goods and apparel brands now have stringent social-responsibility requirements for their suppliers, distributors and sub-contractors. Full compliance is the goal.

Third: Engage employees

One of the biggest dividends a corporation can reap is in the area of employee relations. A good corporate reputation can make staff more enthusiastic and productive, more likely to stay with the company, and bigger advocates for the brand. It's important that companies choose issues that their employees and their families can support, and even take an active role in delivering.

A number of Asian businesses and multinationals have developed meaningful programs with employees volunteering support. For example, the Nokia "Helping Hands" program works with local authorities to identify the top issues facing a community. Nokia employees then volunteer their time to address these issues in community-level programs. Such programs reflect the spirit of their organizations. They have a measurable impact on employee morale and enhance the sense of community engagement.

Fourth: Establish meaningful partnerships

Working with NGOs and other groups can often deliver benefits more efficiently and enhance credibility. These partnerships not only deliver services, but they can also check, certify and endorse your activities. Doing this often means establishing dialogue with people and organizations that you're not used to talking to. Dialogue with stakeholders is a fundamental skill that businesses now need to perform.

In 1979, a man with 50 rupees (about US$1) and a dream to mobilize community action for child rights started an NGO in India called CRY. Over the years, CRY has grown, both in size and in the number of groundbreaking partnerships, with such companies as British Airways, ICICI, Tata Group and Titan. When working with corporate partners, CRY

Chief Executive Pervin Varma warns of over-simplifying complex development issues in the search for easy-to-grasp results. In the area of goodwill, she stresses the importance of creating credibility for corporate claims. Brands must not be seen as using NGOs to build their image, but rather they should show that they are vital partners involved in good works that then get talked about.

Harry Hodge, Chairman Asia Pacific of Quiksilver, believes that today's consumer is far more intelligent than people assume. Quiksilver takes its responsibilities as a market leader seriously — its vision of a responsible, healthy and committed company sets the standard for the surfing industry. Quiksilver takes its CSR cues from its customers' perspective, merging their interests into the corporate agenda. Quiksilver has developed the sport and brought along young talent. It also addresses the ethics and labor practices of business partners via a program called QUEST (Quiksilver Ethical Standards of Trade). Moreover, Quiksilver supports Reef Check, the environmental organization dedicated to saving coral reefs. While the company has received recognition from the United Nations for its efforts, its management may be even happier knowing that they are running a top brand in ways that their customers approve.

Selecting the right partners is crucial. Just as companies are evaluated by third parties, companies need to rigorously assess their partners to ensure their credible, effective long-term associations.

Coca-Cola's commitment to youth has led it to support education in Asia Pacific. This commitment is brought to life in dozens of meaningful and effective partnerships with governments, multilateral bodies and NGOs. For example, in partnership with Vietnam's Ministry of Education-Training and the National Youth Union, 40 Coca-Cola Learning Centers have been set up in secondary schools and youth centers across Vietnam. In Malaysia, Coca-Cola and the United Nations Development Programme (UNDP) have teamed up to spearhead efforts to bridge the digital divide. The new partnership and pilot project, called "e-learning for life," was launched by the Malaysian Ministry of Education, Coca-Cola and UNDP.

Fifth: Tell your story in interesting and credible ways

You have to be able to measure your progress, both anecdotally and in detail. If you can't provide evidence of what you've done, with data that proves that it's had a beneficial effect, you probably won't be believed.

GSK recently published *The Impact of Medicines*. This corporate and social responsibility report for 2002 complements the company's annual report and annual review. The document, which is easy to find on gsk.com, begins with the chairman and CEO affirming that corporate responsibility is integral to GSK's business and expressing GSK's commitment to constructive engagement with stakeholders. The report then provides an overview of GSK's contribution to society, medicines for the developing world, community investment, R&D, employment practices, environment, health and safety, and ethics.

The involvement of external partners should make it easier to collect and disseminate relevant information. Remember that this is an ongoing task. Good CSR communication is about managing expectations. That means maintaining a regular dialogue with all stakeholders, so they can let you know what they expect from you, and understand what is likely to be achieved in a given timeframe. Meaningful dialogue with stakeholders, while still a new concept for many companies, offers great opportunity to bridge even larger differences.

At the consumer level, a visit to Starbucks in Asia will show you a creative approach to telling the corporate citizenship story. Look first at your coffee cup. You'll see that as much space is given on the cup to describing their CSR vision as to their world-famous logo. At the sales counter, you will find brochures describing programs to protect the environment and the communities of their coffee growers. These themes are central to new Starbucks branded coffees, such as the "Fair Trade" and "Shade-Grown" blends.

Sixth: Visualize

Crisp design and a clear corporate identity can make your company's story come alive. Think visually. Use video, photographs and images, not to mention third-party endorsement and involvement. Tell your CSR story with compelling and consistent visuals that resonate with your stakeholders. As David Ogilvy once quipped: "Tell the truth, but make it interesting."

BP does it well. This is a company willing to engage the world on the issues of energy needs, uses and alternatives. BP does this with a compelling, consistent and recognizable campaign. Their television ads feature real consumers asking hard questions about the environment, and the future of energy. Beyond TV, there are print images of solar-powered gasoline stations, and BP coffee cups that convey the message that the contents were heated by solar energy. All of this helps illustrate that BP is fulfilling its brand promise of being Beyond Petroleum. BP is a broad brand: one with ethical dimensions to its marketing communications, and a willingness to address and discuss openly the responsibilities of energy companies.

Committing to CSR

Companies are increasingly willing to commit significant long-term funding to CSR. They are recognizing that they need to talk to an array of different stakeholders, that they need their actions to be highly visible and measurable, and that they need to be committed from the top down. They're recognizing that CSR is not a cosmetic issue, but one that cuts to the very core of the corporation.

The question for them is not whether CSR is important, but how to actually do it with the same degree of professionalism and accountability expected from the organization as a whole. Companies that use their brand as their guide will not only be more effective, they will produce the highest return on their investment.

In practice, that means putting the six ingredients for a successful CSR program into place. It means doing it in a rigorous and committed fashion, and it means doing it right now. In a 360 Degree world, where everything counts, doing anything less just won't do.

PART
4

Transformations

INTRODUCTION

The two preceding parts of this book reflect pieces of an overall design for Total Ethical Management (TEM) for corporations in Asia. The discussion of the main religions and philosophical schools of thought lay the foundations for ethical business practice in Asia, while the examination of the most relevant applications of business ethics show the need for adjustments which can be made in a relatively short time.

We are now approaching the heart of the issue — the imperatives for change and the necessary transformations which need to be achieved in a holistic and sustainable manner in diverse aspects of public activity and life. This long-term agenda also draws from the cultural heritage of Asian wisdom, mainly from the four Asian religions discussed in Part 2.

Corporations which follow the guidelines of TEM will, of course, enjoy strong global competitiveness and good financial management. They will be able to deliver superior value to their customers, shareholders and employees. To achieve these benchmarks, however, corporations can no longer rely solely on the orthodox development model — straightforward economic growth. A transformation of the ethical basis of economic activity can reposition companies, leading to improved competitiveness and financial sustainability.

Corporate leaders should focus on the following transformations, which are at the heart of TEM.

Social development

The conventional development model applied by corporations and nations was traditionally focused on mere economic aspects. This model generated significant inequities and proved to be unable to achieve long-term sustainable growth. The first imperative of Total Ethical Management is to focus on social development; that is, to provide social structures that effectively propagate and sustain the values that people wish to live by. Social development should be placed on an equal footing with economic development — people need both adequate material standards of living and adequate social structures.

Mutual trust

The next imperative is mutual trust. The fact of the matter is that mutual distrust between corporations and other stakeholders and between corporations themselves has become deeply embedded in global economic interactions in recent years. This distrust increases the possibility of unethical behavior — along the lines of Thomas Hobbes'[1] pessimistic view of a world where mistrust reigns: Homo homini lupus — Man is a wolf to man. Total Ethical Management implies, however, that individuals and organizations be mutually worthy of trust. Mutual trust must be earned and then sustained with a behavior based on high ethical standards. Establishing a level of mutual trust, respect and understanding of each other's needs is a requirement for any interaction leading to long-term sustainable growth.

Societal governance

In the attempt to engender trust between all players in the social development process, it should be emphasized that the so-called civil society — self-organizing communities of common interest, such as non-governmental organizations (NGOs) — can act as a catalyst for social development, as NGOs are based on voluntary participation. The state and the world of business, however, may be seen to be based on coercion. Societal governance which is linked to an active role for the civil society will lead to reduced social atomizing and the unsettling effects of market forces, ultimately enforcing social development.

Global citizenship

Every corporation will be a citizen, taking an active role in social, environmental and community concerns. Corporate citizenship can be

---

[1] British philosopher, 1588-1679.

defined as the contribution a corporation makes to society through its core business activities, its social investment and its engagement in public policy. The manner in which a corporation manages its relationships with different stakeholders — in particular, shareholders, employees, customers, business partners, governments and communities — determines its impact. Corporate citizenship should be applied globally, not only in a limited regional or national context. Corporations that adhere to regulations in their home countries often abuse labor, human rights and the environment in other countries, especially poor countries. Global citizenship is a genuine approach to applying high standards of social engagement on a global scale.

Public accountability

By being global citizens, corporations are becoming accountable for their policies, actions and use of capital. Accountability is about power and enabling stakeholders to have a say both in making official decisions and in holding corporations to account. In the past, corporations often escaped public accountability unless faced with public pressure and negative publicity. Accountability should apply in all situations to which corporations are exposed — not only in situations of crisis.

Corporate governance

Public accountability will lead to a system of corporate governance — the system of relationships a corporation has with its shareholders or, more broadly, with society at large. It is the system by which corporations are guided and controlled. The structure of corporate governance defines the distribution of rights and responsibilities among different participants in the corporation (such as the board, managers, shareholders and the public) and sets the rules and procedures for making decisions on corporate affairs.

Industrial renewal

Finally, by applying all earlier steps of a Total Ethical Management, corporations may be enabled to renew themselves and their respective industries. The process of industrial renewal is fundamental for sustainable economic growth and employment as corporations consciously and voluntarily decide to renew themselves. Industrial renewal is linked not only to entrepreneurship and innovation, but to a fundamental "ethical change" — the underlying principles and philosophical *weltanschauung*, why and how corporations are engaged in economic activity.

Many elements of these transformations are in line with the fundamental tenets of Confucianism, Buddhism, Hinduism and Islam. Business ethics based on Confucianism may spell out the need to exercise *jen* — and not merely pursuing selfish business interest. Business ethics requires sacrificing self-interest for a higher interest of society. The self is always to be seen in relation to the whole, even when pursuing business interests. Buddhist business ethics may aim for non-aggressive, non-violent business practices through trying to create win-win situations for all market participants. Buddhist business ethics embrace sustainable development and corporate citizenship as a sort of corporate nirvana. Hindus, on the other hand, are free to pursue their individual ends so long as they also do their dharma. Hinduism gives everyone the right to pursue economic gain — as long as the ultimate goal of sustainability is respected. In Islam, ethics govern all aspects of life. Muslims, generally, are not allowed to cheat others, or to pay or receive interest, in particular.

Managers of companies in East Asia and other emerging markets may have lost these "good" foundations of business conduct and think that "Western" imperatives of ethical management should not apply to them. The Asian financial crisis was the culmination of a period in Asian economic development in which the sublime visions of sustainability and citizenship were largely neglected. Even traditionally hard-working business people were snared by the lure of easy money. Traditional value builders ended up arbitrating — with disastrous results when the local currencies collapsed.

Often, Asian corporate executives have picked only some elements of the ethical value chain because they feel that others (for example, a comprehensive system of corporate governance) are not achievable. As more and more Asian companies are being listed overseas, they are forced to comply with global best practices in this specific field. Turning a collection of independent endeavors to raise ethical awareness and practices into one integrated ethical platform presents one of the stiffest challenges for Asian managers today. Indeed, being able to develop and implement an effective integrated ethical strategy is the acid test of a well-managed company, not only in Asia but elsewhere in the world today.

Until the shock of the Asian financial crisis of 1997, there may have been a certain preoccupation with pure commercial concerns, at the expense of moral principles. In many cases, this resulted in the active pursuit or tacit condoning of corrupt practices, exploiting employees, neglecting safety provisions and other activities — all justified by a narrow definition of the "bottom line." With family and cultural networks being relatively strong, independent NGOs and other civil society organizations have been relatively weak and not institutionalized. Governments in Asia have exercised a strong influence over economic and social priorities, but remain weak in implementing social safety precautions. Many of Asia's large corporations still have a large private shareholding and many are not subjected to the same public pressure on their behavior as public companies in Europe and North America.

Despite these differences, now, with the definition of an ethical value chain, Asian companies are able to tackle the ethical void in their operations by participating in efforts to incorporate the perspective of social development into their planning and operations activities. The whole corporate culture is to be aligned with and transformed into social development, mutual trust, societal governance, global citizenship, public accountability and corporate governance. Finally, by focusing rigorously on these areas, corporations may achieve sustainable industrial renewal. While there has been growing concern about ethical malpractice, these heightened concerns need to be more explicitly integrated into the analytical framework so that Total Ethical Management can provide the holistic and balanced approach necessary for creating genuinely sustainable corporations and societies.

- Asian companies have to transform their root assumptions of economic activity towards social development.
- The transformations have to be conceived and realized in a holistic and inclusive manner, incorporating mutual trust, societal governance, global citizenship, public accountability and corporate governance to finally achieve an industrial revival.

13

SOCIAL DEVELOPMENT
The Role of Corporations and
International Institutions

James Wolfensohn
President, The World Bank, Washington DC

Introduction

The World Bank has as its primary goal the alleviation of poverty, particularly in the many developing countries throughout the world. Half the world is living on less than US$2 a day; one-fifth of the world on less than US$1 a day. We have a planet today of six billion people, five billion of them living in developing economies. These countries have over 80% of the people, but only 20% of the world's GDP. And of the five billion people living in developing economies, three billion live in Asia.

As the World Bank confronts the challenge of reducing poverty, it must address the root causes of poverty and focus on conditions necessary for sustainable development. It has become increasingly apparent that to be effective, development programs:

- Require the full engagement, and sense of ownership, of governments and members of the civil society and corporate officials in the developing countries
- Require partnering by many institutions from both the public and the private sectors
- Must be scalable to a large number of people
- Must be sustainable over the long haul.

Sustainable poverty alleviation also requires that successful economies generate long-term employment opportunities. Without jobs, it is not possible to deal effectively with the inequity of three billion people living at under US$2 per day.

Successful economies can best be achieved by a dynamic private sector in a market-based system. As market-based systems have evolved, companies increasingly have recognized that it is in their best interest to operate with high standards in the areas of corporate governance, labor, the environment and ethics.

Empirical evidence supports the assertion that corporate governance matters. For example, a recent McKinsey survey shows that institutional investors are prepared to pay a premium for good corporate governance. These investors are willing to pay a mark-up of more than 20% for shares of Asian companies that demonstrate good corporate governance. The highest premium (27.1%) among the six Asian countries included in the survey is reserved for Indonesia, which is considered by those surveyed to have the lowest standards of corporate governance. By comparison, the premium is 18.3% for U.S. companies and 17.9% for U.K. companies. Asian corporations have much to gain from strengthening investor confidence by making the transition to sound corporate governance.

A system of corporate checks and balances increases the likelihood of equitable treatment and equitable opportunities for all market participants. It also increases the likelihood of responsible corporate standards on issues such as human rights, health and safety, labor and the environment. This system of checks and balances constitutes the framework of corporate governance at the company level.

Over the past decade, a growing number of countries and companies have also recognized the benefits of corporate social responsibility (CSR) policies and practices in business. Developing a CSR strategy based on integrity and sound values with a long-term approach offers both business benefits to corporations and positive contributions to civil society as a whole. This is an area in which major challenges need to be addressed.

At the country level, developing countries must introduce reforms to strengthen market forces and create a favorable environment for good corporate governance and social responsibility. Specifically, the governments must (i) improve their legal and regulatory systems to protect rights and address grievances equitably, (ii) deal with the challenge of financial-sector reform to promote the efficient allocation of capital in a transparent way, and (iii) meet head-on the challenges of good governance, including the issue of corruption. Enhanced corporate governance and corporate social responsibility are unlikely to occur if the government does not address these essential reforms. These reforms are unlikely to have an impact unless they lead to changes in behavior and actual practices of individual companies in the private sector.

The World Bank's efforts to improve corporate governance and corporate social responsibility have been to support (i) legal, regulatory, and financial reforms to improve the environment in which the private sector operates; (ii) the building of capacity and strengthening of institutions and market forces; and (iii) increased transparency and accountability in the public sectors.

The World Bank has been explicitly talking about corruption in the context of its development strategies since the mid 1990s. In preceding years, global concerns about corruption had intensified and evidence of how corruption undermines development had begun to accumulate. At the 1996 Annual Meetings, we vowed to fight the cancer of corruption. Subsequently, our procurement guidelines were amended to specifically address corruption in Bank projects. In September 1997, the Board approved a comprehensive anti-corruption framework for the Bank.

Anti-corruption is now an integral part of public sector reform supported by the Bank. Over the past six years, the World Bank has supported more than 600 specific anti-corruption programs and governance initiatives in nearly 100 borrowing countries. Nearly one-quarter of new projects now include public expenditure and financial reform components. The impact of corporate governance and good governance on poverty alleviation is widely recognized. Empirical evidence has demonstrated a strong positive causal relationship between better governance and higher per-capita income.

World Bank initiatives to enhance corporate governance and CSR

The World Bank has supported initiatives in many Asian countries to enhance corporate governance and corporate social responsibility. In many cases, the programs involve the joint efforts of the Bank and other multilateral and bilateral institutions. In all cases, the programs require the close engagement of local institutions or private-sector entities.

These initiatives are generally designed to support the introduction of best practices while at the same time recognizing that there is no single set of rules. One size *does not* fit all in the diverse cultural and corporate practices of Asian countries. Governments and business entities are encouraged to tailor best practices and to change the incentives for adopting or implementing good practices.

The programs often include country-specific assessments of corporate governance and social-responsibility policies and practices. These generally result in policy dialogues with senior government officials on recommendations as to how to comply with, and the costs/benefits of complying with, international best practices. Efforts then begin to build government and corporate institutional capacity, frequently through technical assistance (TA) projects, support for government agencies and professional institutions, and, in most cases, training of key government/ private sector officials. See Box 1 for a description of these country-specific assessment programs.

Box 1

Country Assessments of Corporate Governance The ROSC/FSAP Initiatives

Working closely with the IMF, the World Bank has developed a standardized methodology for assessing country-specific corporate governance policies and practices. The approach is based on the OECD Principles of Corporate Governance. These universally accepted principles are founded on four fundamental concepts — responsibility, accountability, fairness and transparency. The joint initiative, known as "Reports on the Observance of Standards and Codes" ("ROSCs"), actually covers a set of 11 internationally recognized core standards (including the OECD Principles of Corporate Governance) relevant to economic stability and private- and financial-sector development.

Participation in the ROSC/FSAP initiative is voluntary. The assessment has proven to be most effective when the country under assessment is committed to a reform agenda and agrees to the publication of the resultant report through the World Bank ROSC website. Policy recommendations included in the reports offer alternatives about how to comply with OECD Principles through the effective enforcement of the existing legal and regulatory framework. Sometimes the recommendations include the modification of existing laws or rules or the adoption of new ones. The recommendations also focus on how companies can improve their internal governance structures. The endorsement and ownership of the reform program by the private sector is essential for corporate governance reform to be successful. Therefore, policy recommendations may include measures to encourage the development of private-sector associations such as institutes of directors, not-for-profit shareholder associations or

> other business associations, which operate in parallel with existing public institutions and provide private solutions to information dissemination.

The Bank-sponsored anti-corruption programs seek to find champions in the country who can lead the process of institutional change and help them identify needed reforms. In this connection, the Bank has recently conducted country-specific expenditure-tracking surveys and public-official surveys in 30 countries throughout the world including Bangladesh, Cambodia, Indonesia and Thailand.

With respect to corporate social responsibility, the challenge has been to instill this philosophy into multinational corporations and the domestic corporate and public-sector fabric of developing countries on a large scale. See Box 2 for a description of a web-based training course on CSR.

Box 2

Training in Corporate Social Responsibility

The World Bank Institute has developed a web-based course "Overview of Corporate Social Responsibility." The overall objective of the course is to provide participants with an introduction to the fundamental rationale, design and implementation of CSR programs. The course focuses on:

- key elements of the policy and business environment that support CSR and how these elements function as an integrated system
- providing a strong justification on why CSR should be incorporated in corporate business strategy and country development strategy
- facilitating access to relevant research and data, and dissemination of best practices.

The course is aimed at high-level government officials, business, public-sector and civil-society leaders, academics, business students and journalists in developing countries.

In Asia, a number of recent initiatives have been undertaken to expand the focus on CSR, including the use of this web-based course. For example, in the Philippines, approximately 200 students and young leaders participated in online conferences and the CSR course. A group of students recently presented their ideas for corporate responsibility and a more inclusive development agenda to the Philippine President. At the University of Asia and Pacific, the web-based CSR course is being incorporated into a business school course.

In Thailand, the Director of Graduate Studies at Shinawatra University's business school and a number of his colleagues have taken the course and plan to use the course as a guide to incorporating CSR into their new MBA program.

In Indonesia, a framework for collaboration on CSR projects is under development with the Jakarta affiliates of the Kenan-Flagler Institute of Private Enterprise.

A key target for the course is business students — the future leaders of the corporate and public sectors of developing countries. The challenge is to maximize scalability, impact and effectiveness.

At the corporate level, governance TA projects in Asia have covered a wide range of important topics. Most are designed to enhance institutional capacity through the introduction and implementation of international best practices or through the training of key officials. They have included:

- directors' training in China, Indonesia, the Philippines, Thailand and Korea
- implementation of international accounting and auditing standards in Thailand, Indonesia and Korea
- a strengthened capacity of the courts through the training of judges and related staff in Indonesia.

See Box 3 for a description of a bank turnaround project in Mongolia that resulted from improved corporate governance by the bank's board of directors.

Box 3

The Turnaround of Agricultural Bank (Ag Bank) of Mongolia

Ag Bank was established in the early 1990s following the breakup of the mono-banking system. The state-owned bank was the only Mongolian financial institution with an extensive rural branch network. Since its inception, the bank had undergone a number of reforms, including one privatization attempt. In the late 1990s, however, the bank failed and was put under the receivership of the Bank of Mongolia. Some advisors within and outside the country were calling for its shutdown.

The World Bank carefully reviewed the situation and agreed with the government that Ag Bank could be re-capitalized and kept open, but only if a comprehensive set of safeguards was put in place to prevent further haemorrhaging. Ag Bank restructuring became an important part of the Bank's Financial Sector Adjustment Credit program (FSAC). Through the concerted efforts of the World Bank, the International Monetary Fund, the USAID and the government, an Ag Bank restructuring plan was adopted which had three primary objectives: (i) restore financial soundness; (ii) return financial services to the rural areas; and (iii) prepare for privatization. For this purpose an external management team composed of two American banking specialists and several Mongolian executives was hired for a period of two years with funding support from USAID.

In August 2000, the new management team took over and, within the first 12 months, Ag Bank eliminated bad assets and registered rapid growth in deposit-taking, loans and cash. It was again able to pay income taxes. The achievements were consolidated in the second year and by the time the government announced the international competitive tender for Ag Bank privatization, the bank's capital adequacy ratio reached 13%, and its return on equity 10%. In January 2003, the privatization process was successfully concluded.

The World Bank has been involved in a number of management contract arrangements, but not many as successful as the Mongolia Ag Bank case. The key to the success was an important arrangement under the restructuring plan for the management team to report to an independent board of directors that had two foreign board members. And the board was required to ensure that the government would not interfere in the operations of the bank. The following factors contributed to the maintenance of this management independence: the Bank's FSAC, the USAID's funding and guidance, the government's strong commitment, close coordination among donors who met regularly over the issue, and the willingness of the management team to defend its independence.

This arrangement could be viewed as a departure from general corporate-governance principles as the government was the owner of the bank. However, in transition economies, such an arrangement might enhance corporate governance of SOEs, and the state's best interest was assured when the troubled institution was turned around.

In the case of the World Bank's private-sector arm (IFC), assistance to specific privately-owned companies often begins with an IFC equity investment. Concurrent with the investment, the company is requested to introduce specific reforms in corporate policies and practices, including corporate governance. IFC frequently arranges for supporting TA projects to assist in the needed reforms. See Box 4 for a description of the impact of IFC's investment in a Chinese bank on the bank's corporate-governance practices.

Box 4

Corporate Governance at the Bank of Shanghai

One of the challenges facing IFC when it made an equity investment of US$22 million for appropriately 5% of the Bank of Shanghai in 2000 was to help this commercial bank enhance its corporate-governance practices. The bank is owned 30% by the City of Shanghai, but also has 38,000 individual shareholders who previously were depositors or employees in 100 separate urban credit cooperatives that were merged in 1995 to form what then became the Bank of Shanghai.

Before making the investment, IFC insisted on an audit of the bank in accordance with international accounting and auditing standards by an international firm of auditors. This practice has since become an annual event for the bank. Another important part of IFC's investment strategy was to request a seat on the bank's board, which it was granted. IFC arranged for a recently retired Western senior banker, who had worked in Beijing for three years and was fluent in Mandarin, to fill the seat.

Much progress has been made since IFC's representative began attending board meetings. For example, an Audit Committee was formed, with IFC's board member as chairman. The committee meets regularly with the outside auditors. In fact, the auditors conduct an annual workshop for the full board, not only on the results of the audit but also on how the bank's operations measure up to international standards.

The Audit Committee also holds frequent meetings with the Internal Auditor, reviewing its annual audit program as well as the results of its internal audits. As is the case generally in China, the internal audit function is in need of substantial upgrading and enhanced professionalism if it is to become a positive force in the bank's governance structure.

More recently, Hong Kong Shanghai Banking Corporation purchased an 8% interest in Bank of Shanghai and was likewise granted a seat on the board. By joining forces, IFC and HSBC have been able to complement each other's efforts to introduce best practices to the bank. These include the creation of a Compensation Committee that has established a performance-based compensation structure for top management, as well as a Risk Management Committee that has begun to monitor the credit risk policies of the bank. The IFC and HSBC directors have also been instrumental in educating other board members on the importance of limiting shareholder dividends in order to build capital to fund the future growth of the bank. As a result of these efforts, the board has become much more engaged in discussions with management on the strategic development of the bank.

While much has been accomplished, much remains to be done, especially in further educating and convincing the board as to its proper role in an effective corporate-governance framework.

Challenges for the future

In East Asia, we see progress across the board. A number of significant challenges remain, however, as efforts continue to strengthen corporate governance and corporate social responsibility — and thus to alleviate poverty on a sustainable basis.

• Public-sector reform

Efficient and effective governments are generally thought to have certain important characteristics in common. They are accountable to the citizenry and reasonably efficient in the delivery of public services. Their decision-making processes and the resultant decisions are, in general, transparent and predictable. Checks and balances exist to guard against arbitrariness and to ensure accountability, while not eliminating the flexibility and delegation needed to respond quickly to changing circumstances. In sum, they are accountable and results-oriented.

Most governments in East Asia have recognized that non-transparency, a lack of accountability, excessive intervention and a lack of delegation contribute to corruption and poverty. These are fundamental challenges that need to be met. Supporting public-sector reforms will remain an integral part of our future work.

• Capacity-building

A significant constraint on the introduction of corporate-governance reform in most Asian countries has been the lack of qualified professionals or weak institutions. There generally is a dearth of trained accountants, lawyers, judges and other professionals necessary to carry out the desired reforms.

As a result, emphasis must continue to be placed on the development of professional institutions, such as institutes of directors and accountants, with rigorous accreditation and ethical standards, and on the training of professionals on international best practices.

• Scalability of training initiatives

In order to meet the massive training needs, it is important to conduct training in an increasingly scalable manner. Given the size of many of the developing countries in Asia (for example China, India, Indonesia, Pakistan, Bangladesh — each with more than 100 million citizens), training must be provided to very large groups of public- and private-sector individuals in order to achieve the desired impact.

This requirement places a premium on leveraging traditional training initiatives, including using technology to reach large groups of geographically disbursed students. The Bank's GDLN program has been and continues to be an important vehicle for providing these types of training.

• Sustainability of reforms and partnership

Historically, some of the reforms supported by the World Bank and other multilateral and bilateral institutions have been discrete and limited in duration. Not enough attention has been paid to the sustainability of the reforms after project completion. Institutionalizing the reforms and more effective local partnerships can help to ensure sustainability.

• Family-owned/controlled companies

A challenge somewhat unique in East Asia results from the family-owned/controlled companies that are prevalent throughout the region. A study was recently conducted of publicly listed companies in nine East Asian countries stretching from Japan to Singapore. Of the nearly 3,000 companies reviewed, more than half are controlled by families. The 10 largest family-controlled businesses in the Philippines, Indonesia and Thailand control half of the corporate assets that were surveyed in their respective countries.

This prevalence of dominant family-controlled businesses raises unique corporate-governance issues. The controlling families generally have seen little benefit in transparency to minority shareholders. Such shareholders are kept in the dark regarding important corporate activities; key decisions are made by the controlling families with little awareness, let alone input, from the other owners of the business.

Because the families are fearful of losing control, more often than not they end up relying too heavily on bank financing for raising capital to support and expand their business operations. Empirical evidence has shown that highly leveraged companies are more vulnerable to external shocks and that a high degree of leverage is associated with less profitability in the case of family-owned businesses.

A key challenge is to move from relationship-based systems to rule-based systems of corporate governance. This transformation must include measures such as the election of independent or outside directors, the establishment of audit committees, and the separation of the oversight function provided by the board from the management function provided by the CEO and operation officers. These and other similar measures will continue to be of particular significance as long as family-controlled companies remain so dominant in the private sector in East Asia.

Conclusions

Improving corporate governance and corporate social responsibility while fighting corruption have become integral components of the reform supported by the World Bank to alleviate poverty. And as it has refined and expanded its corporate-governance initiatives, the Bank has recognized the need to partner with other multilateral and bilateral agencies as well as with private-sector entities.

A key to success is the identification and support of public and private-sector officials who are committed to reform. Buy-in to corporate governance, corporate social responsibility and the fight against corruption is essential for sustainable reforms. Buy-in follows from an understanding that strengthening corporate governance is in the best interest of corporations.

In the private sector, enlightened multinationals are in a position to leverage their own efforts to strengthen corporate governance by introducing compliance systems and requiring equally high standards of ethics from their suppliers and others with whom they do business.

The challenge, therefore, is to support implementation of reforms that build institutional capacity, expand the supply of qualified professionals through scalable training programs, and maintain and enhance momentum in the good times when the pressure for reform dissipates. For its part, the World Bank is up to the challenge and committed to the long-term fight for sustainable poverty alleviation.

14

MUTUAL TRUST
From a Chain of Distrust to a Chain of Trust

Motohisa Furukawa
Member of the House of Representatives, Japan

Introduction

After the defeat of World War II, Japanese society was devastated by economic hardship. Yet, within less than two decades, the island country surpassed the world's expectations. People's diligence and hard work earned great economic success that culminated in the economic boom in the 1980s. A host of internal and external factors aided in Japan's phenomenal rise, and it is difficult to credit one factor as having exclusive responsibility for the miraculous recovery. However, without the Japanese people's ethical values, the country would not have enjoyed a fast revival and attained its status as the world's second-largest economic power today. Japanese ethics, thus, played a crucial role in the country's recovery. In Japan, trust between people has historically been an important ingredient in ethical business dealings. This trust derives from *rinri,* which concerns itself with human relationships and roles as outlined by the Confucian code of ethical conduct. For the Japanese, all human relationships, including relationships within the family, community, workplace and school, succeed only if trust exists. Through *rinri,* concerted efforts could be made in reconstructing the economy. It linked people together in a network of human relationships that abided by the roles and respect dictated by *rinri*, thereby creating a strong chain of trust in society.

The economic boom of the 1980s, commonly known as the Bubble Era, did not last forever. In 1989, the bubble economy crashed and, since then, Japan has suffered a lengthy depression. Besides economic woes, social problems began to plague society. Japanese society lost track of its traditional ethics. Relationships of trust started to deteriorate during the Bubble Era but the symptoms were not obvious until after the bubble burst, when the deterioration rapidly worsened. Consequently, the decade following the Bubble Era is often referred to in Japan as "the lost decade." The misconduct of politicians and bureaucrats, scandals within corporations and repeated disgrace involving teachers, doctors and police followed one another in quick succession. For many companies, profit replaced ethical responsibility as the guiding principle of business practice. For example, in 2000, Snow Brand Foods Co. was caught in the spotlight in a scandal involving poisoned milk products arising from unsanitary conditions in its production facility. The company followed this up in 2002 with another embarrassment involving the deliberate mislabeling of imported beef in order to qualify for a government repurchase program.[1] Besides the offenses of public institutions and corporations, the integrity of the very basic unit of the Japanese society, the family, is being tested. Shocking news of child abuse by parents and murders by juveniles are becoming regular fixtures on the news. Most recently, Japanese citizens have been outraged by reports of a 12-year-old boy who abducted and brutally murdered a 4-year-old boy in Nagasaki.[2] All of these scandalous events have initiated a chain of distrust in society. People no longer trust their government, companies, schools, or even their own families.

Over a decade has passed since the bubble burst, and the Japanese economy remains haunted by depression. Revitalizing the Japanese economy will be impossible without first curing many of its economic and social maladies. It is time for Japan to reflect on its society and identity in order to restore confidence amid appalling misdeeds. Among many changes that need to be made, Japan must embed its traditionally high ethical standards back into its businesses, government and society. In this paper we will examine Japanese ethics, mainly from the viewpoint of business, and attempt to explain how they were lost and how they might be recovered. In the course of this examination, we will see that Japanese ethics embodies principles that could serve as ethical business standards applicable to global businesses. Certain features may have universal value

---

[1] "HEAVY STAKES: Loads of Bogus Beef in Mad Cow Buyback", *Asahi Shimbun*, April 7, 2003, available at: <http://www.asahi.com/english/national/K2003040700227.html>

[2] "12-Year-Old Admits to Killing Boy in Parking Lot", *Asahi Shimbun*, July 10, 2003, available at: <http://www.asahi.com/english/national/K2003071000342.html>

or appeal. In the aftermath of Enron, today's global community cries out for more ethical business practices. Japanese ethics could be introduced as an alternative ethical conduct for consideration. Thus, Japan can become the force that presents it to the rest of the world.

Rinri of Japan

To understand Japanese ethics, it must be appreciated that, as they derive from traditions different from those of Western ethics, they do not necessarily convey the same concepts as their Western counterparts. Historically, Japanese morality is influenced by Confucianism from China, while Western morality is founded on Judeo-Christian traditions. The former defines morality as interaction between people, whereas the latter intertwines morality with religious beliefs.[3]

Under Western traditions, the terms "virtue," "morality," "values" and "ethics", despite their separate meanings, overlap to some extent in concept. Japan, however, does not distinguish between these various representations of ethics. For centuries, Confucian teachings were widely adopted as the guiding principle in the daily actions of the Japanese people. Confucianism promotes *rinri*, which addresses human roles and relationships. Under *rinri*, identity and responsibilities are closely related to one's designated role. Confucius had emphasized family as the foundation of the society, and identified five crucial relationships: master and subject, father and son, older brother and younger brother, husband and wife, and friend and friend. In these crucial relationships, the subordinate must obey the superior, whereas equals must respect each other. If a member recognizes his/her role and acts in accordance to his/her responsibilities, the member would gain the trust of the community. Members must think for others in the family in order for the family to function as one unit vis-à-vis the larger society. Although originating in China, *rinri* was localized and certain Japanese values were incorporated into it. Included in *rinri* are the Japanese concepts of respect and shame. Ruth Benedict mentions in her great book, *The Chrysanthemum and the Sword*, that both respect and shame are characteristics of the Japanese. Respect in this sense means feeling in awe of heaven and the greatness of existence, and this feeling encourages people to be humble and accepting. Those who lack a sense of shame are seen as lacking the

3 "What Happened to Japanese Business Ethics", Koyama Hiroyuki, *Look Japan*, August 1997, available at: <http://www.lookjapan.com/LBecobiz/97AugEF.htm>

minimum quality of a human being. The existence of *rinri* meant a basic consensus and expectation that people would not act against their expected roles and responsibilities. That is, there was a sense of trust that people would not engage in unethical behavior. The consensus and expectations were the fundamental conditions on which people established and maintained relationships of trust.

The word "family" was adopted by the Japanese in a more symbolic sense to describe all crucial relationships. Unlike the rest of East Asia, the family consciousness of the Japanese applies to non-blood relations as well. It is a metaphor and thus the concept of *rinri* is applicable not only to the family but also to the larger community and all the sub-communities (for example, the family, the company, and so on) that comprise the larger community. For any member of society, the starting point is the smaller community. A natural extension of this type of philosophy is a worldview that focuses more on the group, and the individual member behaving in harmony with group interest. Thus, within this group orientation, there is a constant but fluid demarcation between the insider (*uchi*) and the outsider (*soto*), depending on the surrounding circumstances. For example, a class of students might think of themselves as insiders of one group when facing another class in the same school; however, during a soccer match, all classes in the same school would view themselves as insiders in the same group when their soccer team's opponents came from another school.

The notion of *uchi* and *soto* do not really exist in Western societies. Western societies, unlike Japanese society, start with the individual. The sense of ethical responsibility towards society is formed less from the standpoint of a group identity. Some commentators have noted that the relationship seems to be one between the individual and God, and that Western ethics has religious undertones.[4] In this sense, then, Japanese ethics differs from Western ethics (or even from other Asian ethics because of localization). As such, the Japanese term *rinri* is used for the rest of this paper to articulate Japanese ethics.

Rinri in business

Historically, Japanese businesses were founded on *rinri*. As early as the Edo period (1600–1867), *rinri* was already a deeply-rooted business principle. Ethical business activities incorporating *rinri* suggest that

---

[4]   Ibid.

employees and employers must recognize their respective roles and responsibilities in the workplace. It also requires that the business entity itself recognizes its role and duties toward the public. Trust then exists in two spheres: within the business; and between the business and the public. Baigan Ishida, an educator who lived during the middle of the Edo period, developed a philosophy for merchants known as the "Way of the Merchant" (*Shingaku,* literally translated as "the science or learning of the heart"). During Ishida's time, merchants belonged to the lowest social rank since acts of commerce were considered menial labor. Ishida encouraged merchants by instilling confidence and by teaching them that: "Commercial acts are not menial. There is no substantial difference between a merchant earning profit and a samurai earning a salary. However, merchants must not pursue profit through dirty or unjust deeds. A true merchant shall act so as to make profit both for him and for others." His teachings were widely respected and implemented as guiding principles for business conduct. For example, merchants of the Omi district who were well known to be the most capable Japanese merchants of that time followed the famous "10 Commandments on Business," which included the following notable ethical business rules:

- To do business is to serve society and its people, and profit is its just reward.
- A good location is more important than size of the store, and product quality is more important than good location.
- Do not force customers to buy. Do not sell products that customers like. Sell products that are beneficial to customers.

The concept of *rinri* as a fundamental business practice continued into the Meiji period (1868–1912). This is evidenced by the philosophy of the famous Meiji Era capitalist, Eiichi Shibusawa. Shibusawa established the first stock company and the first bank in Japan. He is generally considered to be the founder of Japan's modern business world. Based on cordiality and compassion, the spirits of the Analects of Confucius, Shibuzawa proposed "an integration of morals and economy." He also endorsed the belief that "the duty of merchants is to consider the public's interest and make efforts to bring about happiness to other people rather than unnecessarily pursuing one's own interest." He advocated that businessmen should embrace the Analects of Confucius in one hand while holding the abacus in the other. Under this tradition, there is great emphasis placed on trust. Trust surpassed money in importance during business dealings.

In more recent history, examples of *rinri* can be found in the philosophy of familiar business leaders such as Konosuke Matsushita (1894–1989), the founder of the multinational electronics giant Matsushita Electric Corporation. In 1946, Matsushita established a think tank, the PHP Institute, with the vision of bringing peace and happiness to the world through prosperity. PHP Institute publishes a quarterly magazine that discusses and analyzes Matsushita's business philosophy. In one of the issues, Matsushita described the businessmen of the past who treated commitment with great seriousness. Even on holidays, he noted, businessmen stayed as late as necessary in order to complete any requisite calculation and payment for loan settlement. In the event that a loan could not be repaid, the great sense of responsibility was such that one would give away one's daughter in order to honor the commitment.[5] Although this is extreme by today's standard, such practices demonstrate the importance people had placed on building trust in business as well as the significance of living up to one's responsibility.

For Matsushita, the role of corporations today is to be the "public's tool." He explained that as the public's tool, the responsibilities of a corporation are, first and foremost, to pay taxes in order for the government to build public infrastructure. In this way, profit is viewed mainly as the counter which helps measure how much tax a corporation must pay. By implication then, for Matsushita, profit was not for the purpose of fattening shareholders' pockets. Under his philosophy, unprofitable businesses should rethink their roles and responsibilities in society. They should not operate when they contribute nothing in terms of taxes and therefore fail in their duty as the public's tools.[6] In addition, for Matsushita, the central focus of his products is how they could be beneficial to the people. His philosophy remains greatly admired today and continues to be a part of his company's vision, as can be seen in the Matsushita Electric Corporation's management objective:

> "Recognizing our responsibilities as industrialists, we will devote ourselves to the progress and development of society and the well-being of people through our business activities, thereby enhancing the quality of life throughout the world."[7]

---

[5] *Konosuke Matsushita Studies*, PHP Institute, Fall 2002, p. 40.

[6] "Reading the Fifty Keywords of Konosuke Matsushita", *The 21*, PHP Institute, July 1993, p.34.

[7] Matsushita Electric, Basic Management Objective, available at: <http://www.panasonic.co.jp/global/profile/gp_0001.html>

Why has rinri been lost?

Notwithstanding its central importance to society, *rinri* has been lost in Japan today. The is primarily because Japan's economic success led the Japanese to become conceited. Material desires have become the driving incentive in all spheres of life and activities today. The United States was the epitome of the wealthy society, and the Japanese, positioned as they were in a devastated land after the war, aimed to be like the Americans. In the second half of the 1980s, Japan caught up with the United States and then, beyond the world's expectations, proceeded to overtake it. During the Bubble Era, traditional ethical business practices, under which contribution to society was an important responsibility, were gradually replaced by a *carpe diem* philosophy of earning as much money as possible, or doing everything for the interest of the company, even if to the detriment of the public. This philosophy came about when the company became the new family. Traditional *rinri* did not exist in this new family. To make matters worse, all opportunities to learn traditional *rinri* were lost, leaving a dearth of sources for ethical education.

Company replacing the concept of family

During the period of economic growth, the concept of "family" started to change. Before the defeat in World War II, the Japanese had viewed themselves as members of one big household, the Empire of Japan, with the Emperor as head of the household. The nation was their family. This national household disappeared in 1945 when the Emperor announced the surrender. It was during this time when the nation felt the urgency to rebuild its shattered economy. Industrialization was rapid, and many companies were established. Without the Emperor as the head of the national household, people had to search for a new group identity. Companies filled that void and became the new family. In part due to industrialization but also due to people's loyalty towards their companies, urbanization was inevitable. Urbanization drove traditional Japanese families with larger extended members, usually consisting of three generations under the same roof, into smaller nuclear families. People left their village lifestyle behind and migrated from rural to urban regions to pursue the corporate life. The new, loosely formed communities based on work-relations, missed much of the closeness of the old communities. Smaller nuclear families tended to be composed of younger members. As a result of these changes, people lost the traditional concept of family at both the micro level (for example, a large village community was changed to small, unconnected, independent nuclear families) and the macro level (for example, national family consciousness became national corporate consciousness).

Postwar Japan focused single-mindedly on becoming a great economic power.[8] This sole focus, together with the transformation of the family structure, resulted in a breakdown of traditional communities with which identity and values had once been so strongly associated. *Rinri* became limited to the interaction with members of the same company rather than with society as a whole because the focus was to make the companies rich and powerful. In the international arena, Japanese corporations did indeed become rich and powerful, further reinforcing the link between people's identity and the corporations to which they belonged. Like the head of a household, a company took care of an employee for a lifetime. Practices such as lifetime employment and promotion-based seniority rather than meritocracy were features of this new family. Under this system, when a worker entered a company, his life was secure and his employment guaranteed. However, the security did not last long. When the bubble economy collapsed in 1989 companies had to abandon unprofitable and ineffective business practices, including lifetime employment. As a result, employees could no longer rely on the company. Slowly, companies stopped serving as the family for employees. Once again, people were faced with an identity crisis. This void has yet to be filled as, at present, there is a lack of consensus on what factors should determine human relationships. The consensus based on *rinri*, where people trusted that everybody would behave according to their designated roles and responsibilities, is still missing.

Lack of sources of ethical education

Exacerbating the problem of the disappearance of *rinri* is the fact that almost all environments for learning *rinri* have been eliminated from Japan. It is neither available in educational or religious institutions nor preserved in local communities today. Before World War II, under government policy Japanese received rigid moral education in schools, which emphasized moral education as part of the curriculum. However,

---

[8] "In Search of Lost Ethics", Funabashi Haruo, *Look Japan*, June 2002, *available at*: <http://www.lookjapan.com/JV/02JuneEF.htm>

after the war, moral education was criticized as being connected with emperor worship and thought of as having contributed to the prolonged and agonizing war. Consequently, moral education was deliberately eliminated from the curriculum. Were all Japanese religious, as for instance devout Christians in the Western world, this would not be a problem, because such education would be available through religious institutions. However, most Japanese are not very religious and, furthermore, the indigenous religious traditions of Shinto and Buddhism do not incorporate *rinri* per se. In addition, the family's ability to pass on the concept of *rinri* to the younger generations has been fading. In the past, *rinri* was common knowledge for families and communities. It was naturally taught by older members to younger members, and it was generally practiced by all members, who abided by it. However as the composition of families and communities has changed in the ways described above, fewer people are able to teach *rinri* to children.

How can Japan recover rinri?

The disappearance of *rinri* is taking a toll on the Japanese economy. Individual cases of corporate violations (such as the Snow Brand Foods Co. scandals) are rampant. Additionally, financial institutions are in a dilapidated state, dragged down by a significant number of non-performing loans. The disease eating away at the Japanese financial institutions remains unchecked. To keep the banks afloat artificially, public funds are injected and, once again, the public is hurt. Some leaders in the financial sector whose personal interests get in the way of the sector's recovery have continued to defy repeated calls for their resignation. Without good and effective leaders, the health of the economy remains uncertain, reinforcing the truth of the old saying, "Fish rots from the head down." A number of commentators have questioned whether Japan can re-establish its competitive edge in the global scene without regaining the traditional ethics which had previously helped make it strong.[9] Many people are realizing that *rinri* is precious and should be rediscovered.

In the past, it took a great deal of time and effort to establish *rinri* in Japanese society and it will undoubtedly take as much time and effort to re-establish it. Society has to start again, and should begin by first firmly planting the concept of *rinri* in the school curriculum to provide a basic

---

[9] See, for example, Funabashi.

foundation. Children should be taught *rinri* from a long-term perspective as the benefits and effects of *rinri* are felt by society over time (it is not a quick fix, but a long-term correction to core problems). Additional efforts ought to be made to guide adults who are unfamiliar with *rinri* on appropriate behavior that complies with *rinri* to the greatest degree possible. This might be accomplished through public educational programs on television and in newspapers, books, magazines and so forth.

In addition, ethical education in business could be achieved directly via specific education programs. Japanese businesspeople are becoming increasingly aware of the necessity for this. For instance, Kazuo Inamori, the founder of Kyocera Corporation, a major Japanese international manufacturing company, has established a unique business school called Seiwa Juku for SME executives.[10] Seiwa Juku emphasizes the importance of ethical business practice and attracts numerous business students throughout Japan. As of 2002, it has over 3,000 members. Among its teachings, Seiwa Juku encourages companies to be involved in philanthropic activities. This type of educational center is a major step toward the recovery of *rinri* for the business world.

In pre-war Japanese society, compliance with ethics was a matter of common sense as it was integrated in school and in the behavior of any community. *Rinri* was taken for granted and nobody felt the need to spell it out in clear, written rules. There was a social consensus that Japanese people shared, understood and abided by the same ethics. When such social consensus diminished over time, the lack of written rules meant that traditional *rinri* could be easily forgotten as its concepts were not readily available in the new communities. By nature, *rinri* is best enforced through voluntary observation rather than strict imposition of written laws. The most effective means to increase awareness is for people to learn *rinri* out of free will. However, given the deepening identity and moral crisis, it is not sufficient to rely solely on people's willingness to learn. Today, it is necessary to construct visible ethics from conventionally invisible ethical standards. *Rinri* should be provided as concrete codes. Behavior that does not appear to be voluntary in the beginning may, in due course, encourage voluntary behavior. For example, companies could incorporate ethical concepts in their work rules for employees. These new work rules should be carefully drafted so that they do not result in undesirable ethical behavior vis-à-vis the larger society (specifically, these rules should not focus solely on activities that increase the profits and benefits of the company to the detriment of the

---

[10] See, for example, Seiwa Juku *available at:* <http://www02.so-net.ne.jp>

public). In the public sector, ethics is already being constructed into visible codes. An illustration of this can be seen in the National Public Service Ethics Law, which was established four years ago in the wake of repeated scandals involving government bureaucrats. This law provides the code of ethical conduct for civil servants. Since the code is written and readily available to the public, the public can always learn about the code as well as check on whether the provisions are appropriate. In the course of making the rules of ethics more visible, the two keywords required in modern society, transparency and accountability, will at the same time be satisfied. If these efforts can be implemented across all sectors of the Japanese society, *rinri* will return and members of society will behave ethically once again.

Conclusion

As we have seen, Japanese ethical standards are different from their Western counterparts. Under *rinri,* Japanese ethics is concerned with the fulfillment of designated roles and responsibilities. For centuries, *rinri* infused and informed Japanese business practice. Furthermore, it was the guiding principle for interaction between people. People trusted each other since *rinri* meant that all could be trusted to behave ethically. But this chain of trust was weakened after World War II with the breakdown of traditional family and community structures and values. The focus shifted away from the individual as a member of society, with all its attendant duties and responsibilities, towards the primacy of the company. Relationships became much more unpredictable and a blanket trust that people would behave ethically became impossible. The chain of trust was damaged further during the Bubble Era, weakening the bond of trust.

To rebuild this chain of trust, Japan should take action to restore *rinri* in society to help revitalize both the ailing economy and society. In rebuilding the chain of trust, Japan must start from the beginning, introducing the concept in classrooms so that children can have a foundation of ethical behavior on which to rebuild society. In addition, businesses that provide education on ethical business activities should be promoted and supported (by the public and the government). At present, Matsushita's PHP Institute and the Seiwa Juku, established by Inamori, could serve as educational models for large corporations or for business schools to emulate. While these are certainly not the only institutes that educate the public on business ethics, more are needed. Moreover, there is a need to increase public awareness regarding the necessity of ethics education and in this regard *rinri* could be made visible through the establishment of written codes. Cases such as Enron illustrate that the chain of distrust is not confined to Japan. Written codes will also enable the presentation of Japanese ethical standards abroad. The transparency and accountability enshrined in a written code of conduct, coupled with the re-introduction of *rinri* in the educational system, will allow *rinri* to penetrate society more fully. Finally, with the understanding that even written codes sometimes cannot achieve the desired effects, business and political leaders should take the initiative to make *rinri* a guiding standard in their conduct. They should set examples for people to follow. Leaders must be aware of their social roles and duties. It is essential that they implement noblesse oblige. In this way, "subordinates" will follow and "equals" will trust and respect their leaders. Implementation of *rinri* will strengthen society and will reinforce the chain of trust.

15

SOCIETAL GOVERNANCE
NGOs as Catalysts for a Better Society

Christine Loh

Former member of the Hong Kong Legislative Council
CEO, Civic Exchange, Hong Kong

 Today's global managers have to view the world differently. Business is no longer just about more sales and higher profits but also, increasingly, about ethics, responsibility, and the interests of stakeholders. Depending on how a company runs its business, stakeholders can be possible allies or adversaries. Stakeholders include a broad church of folks; from employees, agents, licensees and customers, to governments and public agencies, as well as local and international non-governmental organizations (NGOs).

This chapter discusses the delicate relationship between companies and one sector of stakeholders, the NGOs, and examines whether and how NGO activism is forcing business to integrate more deeply into society, and to elevate ethics in managerial practice.

The rise in NGO global activism is a response to the rapid and unprecedented pace of globalization. Since the end of the Cold War, globalization has become the prime focus of international economic affairs in addition to political affairs. The anti-globalization movement led by key NGOs is having an impact on the multinational corporations (MNCs) and corporate Asia. They pose difficult questions for governments and authorities on how development should take place in the future. NGOs are unlikely to let up and Asian companies and governments are going to have to consider their social and environmental responsibilities alongside the quest for profits and GDP growth, whether they like it or not.

Moreover, globalization's sister-trend of urbanization, where cities act as magnets drawing population away from rural areas, is also demanding that governments and business acknowledge NGO demands for better ways to ensure harmonious and healthy living in Asia's still-growing metropolises. Indeed, we are beginning to see early signs that MNCs, Asian business and local governments now see socially responsible practices as a business advantage. Indeed, governments are realizing that they can improve governance by working closely with NGOs. In any event, the authorities simply do not have the resources to take care of all the many problems they are expected to deal with, and thus, working with civil society is a way for governments to get things done that benefit their communities. There is a gradual symbiosis developing among governments, companies and civil society that could lead to a more just global system.

Anti-globalization movement

The anti-globalization movement has many sub-movements — some are indigenous whilst others are regional or international, such as those whose primary interests lie in the areas of sweatshops, human rights, fair trade, environmental economics, genetic engineering, Aids/HIV, and the World Trade Organization (WTO). Since September 11, there are also groups working against war with Iraq as well as to promote religious tolerance.

In recent years, the NGOs have discovered that they are part of one global campaign challenging the dominance of the MNCs over world economy and challenging governments for their failure to protect the public interest. This is how a seasoned activist from the West, Juliette Beck, summarized the globalization problem:

> "Multinational corporations control almost every aspect of modern life, from the food we eat to the news we learn from to the government we live under. In the last few decades, multinational corporations have grown so huge that 51 of the 100 largest economies in the world are corporations. The role of governments has been relegated to implementing policies that help corporations increase their profits, even when these policies are detrimental to workers, the environment, community well being and future generations. Countries in the global south are forced to participate in the global economy according to the rules set by corporate-dominated institutions, like the World Bank, International Monetary Fund (IMF) and the WTO ... Under corporate globalization, progress is defined by expanded

economic growth (GDP), as measured by profit-generating activity. This growth, the corporations argue, is best achieved by allowing corporations unrestricted access to cheap labor, natural resources and consumer markets. To achieve, this, governments have now created both a sophisticated legal framework that gives unprecedented new rights to private investors and institutions that have the power to enforce these rules, even when they conflict with popular will. Also, corporations' insatiable appetite for growth and the consumerism created to feed this system, have created an environmental crisis of epic proportions that may soon prevent 80 percent of humanity from being able to meet its most basic human needs."[1]

A view from the East is equally sobering. The Malaysian NGO, International Movement for a Just World, states in its membership form:

"For what is emerging in the name of globalization … is an unjust global system. It is a system which allows a privileged minority located largely in the North to dominate and control the world. It is a system in which the vast majority of humankind will remain poor and powerless. It is a system which panders to the unbridled greed of a few and fails to provide for the basic needs of the many. A system which allows greed to grow and selfishness to spread is a threat to humanity. It undermines the spiritual and moral basis of civilization. It would be a tragedy if such a system becomes the inheritance of our children."[2]

Rise of the MNCs

From the mid 1980s, MNCs and foreign direct investments (FDI) began to have a profound impact on the world economy as MNCs began to rapidly expand internationally. Between 1985 and 1990, FDI grew at an average of 30% per annum, which represented four times the growth of world output and three times the growth rate of trade. The annual flow of FDI has doubled since 1992, to about US$350 billion. Of the world's biggest 500 corporations by revenue in 2002, more than 130 are American, more than 80 are Japanese, more than 120 are European and

---

[1]   Juliette Beck, Coordinator of the Global Democracy Project for Global Exchange, *Doing Democracy: The MAP Model for Organizing Social Movements*, Bill Moyer, JoAnn McAllister, Mary Lou Finley, Steven Soifer, New Society Publishers, 2001.

[2]   www.just-international.org

the rest are from around the world, with just a handful from Asia other than Japan.[3] Much of world trade is actually their inter-company trade (trade among subsidiaries of the same company). For example, about half of the trade between the U.S. and Japan is actually inter-company trade. In other words, the MNCs and their inter-company activities dominate world trade.

During the 1990s, there was a significant shift in the distribution of world industry away from the developed economies — the U.S., Western Europe and Japan — to the developing economies. Whilst the developed economies still possess the largest share of global industry and wealth, their share has declined in relative terms, whilst the developing economies, particularly China, have advanced in economic importance. Indeed, one of the most important changes in the world economy has been the internationalization of industrial production and services, made possible by advances in communications technologies and falling transportation costs.

Development-model controversy

The role the MNCs play in the world economy is a controversial one. Whilst most governments and businesspeople believe the economic development that MNCs generate is beneficial for the world as a whole, critics charge that corporate strategies, the internationalization of production and FDI are undermining communities around the world. Critics argue that the MNCs are accountable to no one and their strategies essentially seek to turn citizens into consumers, to increase consumption and therefore generate higher sales and greater profits.

The most ferocious critics are the NGOs. It may be said that the anti-globalization campaign really took off at the Seattle WTO protest in 1999, when more than 50,000 people took to the streets to launch the movement. Politicians and corporate leaders were clearly caught off guard as they had underestimated the power of NGO activism in the age of the Internet. It may be easy for companies to accuse the NGOs of rabble-rousing but it is harder for them to counter convincingly the alternative view. Essentially, the NGOs see the current development model favored by governments and business as one that is environmentally threatening, socially divisive in causing unemployment and widening the divide between rich and poor, and economically counter-productive. They are calling for:

---

[3]   Fortune Global 500.

"...a shared commitment to building a peaceful, environmentally sustainable and socially just global society. Progress would instead be measured by ecological health, the advancement of human rights, and community-defined quality of life ... Trade in goods and services would be done in a way that raises living standards when workers and farmers are fairly compensated."[4]

Sustainable development

The anti-globalization movement's rallying banner can be summarized in the concept of sustainable development, first articulated in 1987 by the Brundtland Commission.[5] It was recognized then that the current model of development based on consumerism comes with not only a very high environmental price but also pushes at the limits of the Earth's carrying capacity and threatens our continued existence over generations. The Brundtland Report noted that there should be justice in the distribution of scarce resources on both an intra-generational as well as an inter-generational basis. The former refers to the right to equitable access to the world's resources today, and the latter refers to the right of future generations to have the resources for their development needs. The NGOs argue that it is necessary to re-examine the world's resource distribution because the present economic system of the developed economies based on capitalism and the free market can promote an *efficient* allocation of resources but not a *just* allocation.

In their march forward, environmental protection and social factors have not always been seen as top-policy priorities for Asian governments. Their argument was that once their countries were sufficiently well off, they could then afford to clean up and provide better social conditions. They pointed to the history of the West to justify their case — after all, they argued, the West messed up first and then became more environmentally and socially conscious. It was even argued that it would be unfair for developing countries to be asked to observe higher environmental and worker-safety standards when the West did not have to and got rich thereby. In the early 1990s, for example, Indonesia and Malaysia defended their rights to logging against international pressure, arguing that it was a part of their national patrimony.

---

4   Juliette Beck op. cit..
5   The UN-sponsored Brundtland Commission's report is also known as *Our Common Future.*

Today, Asian governments have, by and large, bought the rhetoric of sustainable development. Indeed, at the U.N.-sponsored Johannesburg Summit in 2002, most governments around the world acknowledged sustainable development as a policy priority and were even prepared to note that progress was too slow. The challenge is whether Asia will find a way to reconcile economic development and environmental protection with human and social factors properly accounted for. The jury is still out.

So, how should Asia develop? It has become impossible for anyone to deny today that economic growth brings environmental degradation and a host of other social challenges. Examples abound. In Northern China, people are facing severe water shortages, which has resulted in government plans to divert water from the Yangtze River in central China to the North at a cost of billions, which may as yet cause other types of environmental problems. Air quality is a problem in many parts of China and the developing world. For example, 29% of China suffers from acid rain; only 3% of the cities have excellent air quality whereas over 65% of the cities have poor air quality. Each year, some 180,000 Chinese die prematurely as a result of air pollution. In Southeast Asia, the continuing burning of forests in Indonesia has become a symbol of the region's resource-depletion problem, and when air streams carry the haze to neighboring Singapore, Malaysia and the Philippines, air pollution becomes a matter of regional diplomatic concern as well. Moreover, the delicate ecological balance everywhere is under threat.

The question is whether more development within a short space of time will push the region's natural carrying capacity to collapse, and what might be the consequences. The carrying capacity relates to the Earth's capacity to absorb pollution and continue to perform ecological services such as the water, carbon and nitrogen cycles, which are critical to all life. These challenges are not easy to resolve. They clearly have political, economic and social impacts of significant magnitude. Whilst they require government leadership and even regional and international cooperation in many instances, the role of NGOs in contributing to to the search for solutions is critical.

"Shifts" since the Asian financial crisis

Since the Asian financial crisis (1997–1999), three significant "shifts" have taken place in the region, which have made the authorities and companies more willing to work with NGOs. The political, economic and ethical "shifts" have coalesced and are important to how Asia develops in the future, particularly if they can be mutually reinforcing in helping the region find alternative development paths. There is urgency for Asia to experiment with alternatives because the intensity of development is likely to be phenomenal with the substantial population involved. It could make or break environmental conditions, which will in turn have an impact — positive or negative — on social conditions in the region.

- ## Shift 1: Political

The first "shift" is political. Over the last six years, many regimes have been challenged and various reforms have been instituted, particularly with regard to providing greater transparency. The crisis opened up a larger political space for civil society to participate more actively in the governance of the respective countries. The demands to root out corruption and calls for political change have, in general, helped Asian NGOs to promote their causes. In any event, governments are acknowledging that they cannot cope with all the challenges and they need the civil sector to pitch in. Asian NGOs are a mixed bag, like their brothers and sisters elsewhere. Their motivations and agendas are diverse, reflecting the particular issues and political circumstances of their countries. Coupled with the rise of the international anti-globalization movement, both governments and business have had to respond much more positively to NGO demands.

- ## Shift 2: Economic

The second "shift" has to do with a change in Asia's consumption patterns. The Asian financial crisis slowed development momentarily but the fashionable view today is that Asia has re-emerged to drive world economic growth for the next decade or two. Many Asians, and notably the urban Chinese, have a general sense of optimism for the future, with perhaps the exception of Japan. For example, China's Development Research Center has forecast that FDI could reach US$100 billion every year from 2006 to 2010, up from around US$50 billion in 2002. The forecast may turn out to be overly optimistic but what is clear is that China's optimism is attracting substantial outside investments. Rural dwellers might not be so optimistic but some economists are predicting that higher Asian consumption in the cities is what will underwrite growth for the foreseeable future.

Asia had a population of 3.5 billion in 2000, with 1.3 billion in China and another billion in India. Within rising per-capita incomes and a detectable change in attitude to spending, the younger, better-educated population is already showing signs that they are much less frugal than their parents. Greater consumption on the part of Asians will have a profound impact on the environment, such as resource depletion and pollution. Even with, say, zero-emission cars, there will be more congestion on the road. Moreover, all the consumption that supposedly powers the world's economy may not help the less fortunate to meet their most basic needs for clean water, sanitation, electricity and education.

Thus, both sound public policy and building consumer awareness — neither of which can be achieved without the active participation of the civil sector — are critical to achieving sustainability. NGOs are working on a quiet revolution to get consumers to be more conscious of how they consume and to give their dollars to more socially responsible companies.

• Shift 3: Ethical

The third "shift" is with business ethics. Note how corporate language has changed. Since Seattle, corporate leaders have started to speak about the need to promote "compassionate globalization" and "globalization with a human face." MNCs, including Asian companies, have signed on to the U.N.'s Global Compact to explore how to be a better global corporate citizen. The CEOs of some of the world's largest companies have signed on to the World Economic Forum's Framework for Action, which calls upon corporate chiefs to develop strategies for managing their company's impact on society and its relationships with stakeholders. Likewise, the junior members of the World Economic Forum, known as the Global Leaders for Tomorrow, have developed a pilot environmental sustainability index. Slowly and, with luck, surely, the corporate world is at last beginning to acknowledge that ethics has a place in business.

NGO activism

The extent and variety of individual and NGO initiatives are diverse and numerous — too numerous to note here. It is, however, useful to note two examples, one in India and the other in China, that have had or could have a major long-term impact. While neither of these is a usual NGO suspect, they are, nevertheless, part of civil society in their respective countries, and through using available channels skillfully, they have already made substantial contributions.

In India, lawyers such as M.C. Mehta and a number of judges have developed a unique environmental jurisprudence that allows citizens to take public-interest cases directly to courts. The development is significant because it represents a departure from the English common-law tradition that requires a litigant to have a direct interest in a case before being able to institute proceedings. Furthermore, judicial intervention, whilst controversial, has introduced a way to achieve social justice where the political system fails.

In China, some of the best young minds are going into the environmental sciences. For example, Peking University has created a new College of Environmental Sciences by combining a number of schools. The College's creation comes just as authorities are realizing that the current model of development, especially in fast-growing industrial provinces like Guangdong, may damage the environment irrevocably. Thus, the College has been appointed to help Guangdong province to build a strategy for sustainable development, even as provincial leaders forecast a doubling of GDP by 2010 and again by 2020.

The College is also assembling an expert team — including international experts — to articulate a new paradigm for sustainable economic development. This includes exploring ideas on dramatically increasing resource efficiency for industries, which could improve both technology and management. The idea aims to eliminate waste, which serves no economic purpose while creating undesirable externalities. Other ideas include "capping" pollution levels and eventually trading emissions. It is also likely to recommend that leaders prioritize "leap-frog" industries, such as zero-emission vehicles. Every major car-maker is seeking to develop energy-efficient vehicles for the future and the Ministry of Science and Technology is already supporting research into electric cars and other fuel efficiency efforts to kick-start local industry.

The good news is that this sort of exploration for an alternative growth strategy should increase the intellectual capital on what sustainable development could mean. In turn, this could bring numerous business and investment opportunities for far-sighted entrepreneurs.

Corporate social responsibility

At the corporate level, a sobering thought for any company must be the example of what happened at Bhopal. The lesson from this is that past irresponsibility can come back to haunt you.

In 1984, gas spewed from the Union Carbide pesticide plant in Bhopal, India, killing 2,500 people instantly and eventually resulting in up to 20,000 deaths. The International Campaign for Justice in Bhopal claims that an additional 120,000 to 150,000 have suffered from chronic illnesses, including respiratory infections, gynecological disorders, cancers, and neurological damage as a result of the accident. In 1987, India's Central Bureau of Investigation revealed that the disaster was the result of decisions taken by top management to scale back safety and alarm systems in order to cut costs. In 1992, a warrant for the arrest of Warren Anderson, the then CEO of Union Carbide, was issued for "culpable homicide" (manslaughter). In 2001, Dow Chemicals acquired Union Carbide. In 2002, the Indian court called for the extradition of Anderson to India to face charges. Thus, the saga is far from over.

As in the case of Bhopal, corporate denials have become impossible with the publication of numerous studies pointing to MNC activities that are causing substantial damage to the environment — deforestation, soil erosion and desertification, water pollution and the creation of toxic wastes. MNCs have also been accused of moving old industrial plants or products that would not pass environmental standards in developed economies to developing nations.

Today, there is a growing consciousness among companies that corporate social responsibility (CSR) matters. For example, corporate reporting on the social and environmental activities has never been so widespread. How should companies give an account of the economic, environmental and social impacts of their activities? One method gaining international acceptance is the Global Reporting Initiative (GRI), which is an NGO that promotes a common disclosure framework. There are approximately 140 companies worldwide using the GRI approach and they are contributing to building up a set of standards for reporting on environmental impacts, corruption policies, supply-chain issues, human-rights policies and labor practices.

According to a report in June 2002 from the consultants Context, 103 of the FTSE 250 companies now have stand-alone reports, with 50 of them having published CSR information for the first time.[6] According to another survey by international accounting and consulting firm KPMG, Japan has more than 70% of its largest companies producing CSR reports of one kind or another. Whilst NGOs have rightly criticized the quality of some of these and other CSR reports, there is hope that the reporting process will improve as the call for independent verification by the NGOs is likely to become the trend.

An example to emulate is that of Hong Kong's MTR Corporation, which operates subway services. Its 2001 Sustainability Report uses the GRI guidelines and stands head and shoulders above many of the reports

---

[6] www.context.co.uk

produced by the MNCs. The British-based Association of Chartered Certified Accountants (ACCA) gave the MTR Corporation's 2001 report the top award for environmental reporting. It should be noted that the ACCA, an NGO, has taken on the role to promote environmental protection by providing an annual prize, for which it received recognition in the Queen's Award in 2002. The MTR Corporation's 2002 Sustainability Report published in April 2003 again broke new grounds in the area of risk assessment.

Since 2001, the FTSE, published by London's *Financial Times*, has had a new index for socially responsible companies — the FTSE4Good. Dow Jones also has a sustainability index — the DJSI, as fund managers are slowly responding to investors' demands for socially responsible investments. A new NGO, the Asian Sustainable & Responsible Investment Association (ASrIA), was set up in Hong Kong in 2001 to promote socially responsible investment in the region and, by all accounts, interest is gradually taking hold.

Ethics is good for business

Business now says CSR is good for business. To be admired, a company has to not only create value for shareholders, but also display strong environmental and social practices. Every year, the *Financial Times* newspaper surveys the world's top 1,000 corporate executives and asks them to nominate three companies in the world they most respect. Since 2002, the executives have also been asked to nominate three companies they think managed environmental resources best. In 2003, they were also asked to nominate three companies which will make the most impact over the next five to 10 years on economic and social issues in emerging economies and their reasons for choosing them. NGOs were also asked for their nominations on environmental resources and emerging economies in order to provide a fuller picture.

But, what are companies doing on the ground to be good citizens? Beyond getting certification for ISO14000 for continuous environmental improvements, and signing on to SA8000 to improve conditions for its workers, Reebok offers a courageous experiment that could lead to more democratic processes in workplaces across Asia. In 2001, what is believed to have been the first free elections to a factory's trade union took place in Guangdong Province at a factory owned by a Hong Kong company making shoes for Reebok. In October 2002, a similar election took place at another shoe factory owned by a Taiwanese company in Fujian Province. The management of the two factories arranged the elections at the behest of Reebok. What is most encouraging is that the local authorities have allowed these elections. The Chinese Government had been wary of free trade union activities. The new election procedures, which took months to negotiate, were based on proportional representation to reflect the number of workers in each of the factory's seven units.

According to Reebok, its aim is to produce sustained improvement in working conditions by promoting better communication between management and the shop floor. By experimenting in this way, Reebok hopes to empower workers to ensure compliance with labor standards and prevent abuses. Because the MNCs cannot directly ensure the compliance of their subcontractors on a day-to-day basis, empowering workers to stand up for their rights is the best way to produce the desired results. Reebok believes other MNCs may well follow their lead in pushing for similar reforms. Reebook's director of human-rights programs is guarded about the results to date, noting: "I don't know that anybody has bought a pair of Reebok shoes because of its human rights program. But we are a global corporation and we have an obligation to give back to the communities in which we live and work."[7] Whilst it costs money to promote democracy in the workplace, the benefits include lower labor turnover and fewer accidents. Reebok has arranged training for workers' representatives to learn how to handle union matters, such as conducting meetings and recording grievances. The two new unions are officially affiliated with the state-controlled All China Federation of Trade Unions.

What is most interesting about the Reebok experiments is that the local officials in Guangdong and Fujian no longer see providing cheap land, a large labor pool and tax breaks as the only way to woo investments from MNCs. A commitment to improving environmental and labor standards can be a new competitive factor that differentiates one manufacturing area from another. After all, many of the top international brands produce premium-priced products and are thus not looking for the cheapest manufacturers but those who can help them maintain their brand premiums. This is a wise strategy for the more developed provinces such as Guangdong and Fujian which are losing price competitiveness in manufacturing consumer products, because they can continue to go up scale by producing higher-end products.

Despite many positive improvements, the NGOs are not letting up in their efforts as there are still too many examples of poor practices in

---

[7] "Sewing a seam of worker democracy in China", *Financial Times*, 12 December 2002.

factories. The Hong Kong Christina Industrial Committee (HKCIC), for example, specializes in labor investigations in China and keeps a close watch on the MNCs to make sure they practice what they preach. The latest HKCIC report, published in February 2003, argues that the MNCs are paying too little to enable factory owners to make the workplace improvements required by the MNCs. Through continuing to point out publicly such things as low wages and long working hours, the NGOs are forcing the MNCs to respond. After the release of the HKCIC report, representatives from Disney, Toys "R" Us and McDonald's all felt compelled to say they would look into the allegations made.

Whilst the above examples show how MNCs are buying into continuous improvements in factories in the developing world, Hongkong Land, a developer of high-end commercial properties in Asia, shows how improving dialogue with its immediate stakeholders is good for business and the corporate soul. A key component of workplace responsibility is improved communication between employer, employees and stakeholders so that each feels its views and concerns are heard and that the relationships are placed on a more equal footing. The old fashion top-down command formula is now seen to be sub-optimal in creating good management. The new process adopted by Hongkong Land in its dealings with all of its contractors and sub-contractors in constructing Chater House in the Central district managed to improve communication, reduce friction between the parties, improve site management, and reduce on-site injuries and accidents. All the stakeholders felt that the process helped them to improve their management skills, which can be adapted for future use. Indeed, the main construction company, Gammon-Skandia, which is partially owned by Hongkong Land, was able to win a new contract with another developer based on the positive experience from Chater House.

Challenge of urbanization

This chapter would be incomplete without a mention about urbanization and how the authorities cannot cope with urbanization without help from NGOs. By 2007, more than half of the world's population will reside in cities. In the next 30 years, the global population is expected to grow by two billion and demographers project that cities in developing countries will attract most of that growth. Many of the fastest-growing cities are in Asia. There are many issues relating to such a rapid and intense pace of urbanization but one of the most important is that of water and public hygiene. To put things in context, it would cost US$200 billion to supply clean drinking water and sanitation for every village, town and city on the planet. This is roughly the same sum that is spent on advertising in the U.S. every year.

The results of uncontrolled urbanization can be seen in the slums that are the feature of most cities in the developing world. The authorities are clearly directly responsible for this and conditions could be a lot worse were it not for the work of the NGOs. In Mumbai, for example, through the National Slum Dwellers' Federation of India (NSDFI), substantial improvements are being made to public toilets. The NSDFI is part of Slum Dwellers' International (SDI) that now has members in India, Nepal, Cambodia, Thailand, and the Philippines, as well as in Africa and South America. SDI's mission is to create a platform for the urban poor to take responsibility for improving their own lives. Some 40% of Mumbai's 18 million people live in slums or some kind of degraded housing. As many as 5% to 10% of the city dwellers are street sleepers. A key problem in Mumbai's slums is the awful state of the communal toilets managed by the municipal authorities. In India, public lavatories are more than just toilets. They are social focal points, where people come together to exchange news about what is happening in the community. Jockin Arputham, the president of NSDFI, noted that "the only difference between middle-class people and the urban poor is that the former go to the toilet alone."[8] The NSDFI has been successful in getting the authorities to allow slum communities to plan, design, construct and maintain public toilets. As a result, it is now building toilet blocks — totaling 10,000 toilet seats in Mumbai.

Bangladesh has a different water problem. With its high population density and lack of sanitation infrastructure, surface waters are perpetually contaminated, and waterborne disease is a leading cause of widespread illness and premature death among infants. Whilst governments and international bodies are involved in improving conditions, the NGO Forum for Drinking-Water Supply and Sanitation takes on the task of testing water contamination. Its laboratory in Dhaka has become one of the country's most sophisticated testing authorities and has analyzed more than 25,000 samples for the government and international aid agencies. By doing accurate testing, it is able to assist the government in developing evidence-based policies.[9]

---

[8] *World Watch*, "Toilet Power", Vol. 15, No. 6, November/December 2002, pp. 26–27.
[9] *World Watch*, "Poisoned Waters", Vol. 16, No. 1, January/February 2003, pp. 22–27.

Conclusion

The challenge is clear — Asian governments and corporate Asia cannot afford to shy away from taking action to help build a new world that can be both prosperous and sustainable. Without a healthy natural environment, there can never be the kind of development to provide a fair deal and a just world for this or future generations. The growing gap between rich and poor in Asia needs to be acknowledged and dealt with if long-term instability is to be averted. In this, individuals, NGOs and companies can succeed where government bureaucracies fail. The NGOs can be relied upon to continue to push the envelope to demand concrete actions and timetables from politicians and companies to make positive changes because they see themselves as shareholders in a much wider enterprise — that of human civilization.

16

GLOBAL CITIZENSHIP
The Asia challenge for the global company

Uwe R Doerken
CEO, DHL, Belgium
and
Alyson Warhurst
Professor of Strategy and International Development
Warwick Business School, UK

 This chapter explores the DHL view of the imperative of corporate citizenship in Asia. It discusses how the region presents special challenges for international companies such as DHL on account of its various levels of democracy, different approaches to labor standards, different social and environmental priorities and different business traditions. It suggests that where such diversity flourishes and where conditions are fast evolving, global business should work in accordance with its own best standards, with those recommended by international law and with universally recognized codes of conduct, guided by local cultures and conditions. The challenge for companies such as DHL is to embed the values of corporate citizenship within the company and to ensure that employees worldwide, in Asia and elsewhere, are empowered through fair conditions of work, training and management support to act in accordance with those values and local needs. Corporate citizenship is only partly about philanthropy and community development programs — although, harnessing core competencies to contribute to social development in poor regions of the world, especially in times of crisis, is an important responsibility that DHL embraces. Corporate citizenship is also about being efficient and competitive, as well as financially stable. Companies can best behave as good global corporate citizens if they are themselves healthy and thriving as business enterprises.

For a global company like DHL, this includes the employment it creates and sustains, the conditions of work provided and improved upon, the environmental protection promoted and the stability and benefits generated for business partners, host governments, community neighbors and shareholders. The latter benefits flow as a result of making a profit, paying taxes, engaging in productive business-to-business relationships and following strategies of expansion and growth in line with business values that emphasize social responsibility and environmental stewardship. The positive impact of those contributions in society can only grow as business grows and becomes more profitable. This chapter is not intended to be an exhaustive survey of corporate citizenship in Asia. It reviews some of the issues, raises some challenges, analyzes some of the implications and aims to illuminate certain aspects of DHL's thinking on the subject. It then goes on to describe the DHL approach as an example of one possible way forward. In so doing, it discusses the DHL belief that corporate citizenship is about the "way we work" and that responsible business practice is about harnessing core competence alongside efficient business enterprise to contribute on a broad basis to society and its economic, social and environmental sustainability.

Corporate citizenship in Asia — some background

Some suggest that corporate citizenship or corporate social responsibility (CSR) is primarily a Western concept. They suggest that decision-making in companies in Asia tends to be more centralized and less consensual than in companies in the Western economies, and that Asian companies have different cultural expectations regarding working terms and conditions and approaches to environmental protection and resource use. At a workshop organized by the U.N. Research Institute for Social Development (UNRISD) in 2000, it was argued, for example, that in the case of Indonesia, "while concepts like corporate social responsibility have become more fashionable they have essentially been introduced from abroad."

However, in some parts of Asia, CSR and corporate citizenship have been on the agenda a long time. For example, in India, politicians from Gandhi onwards have stressed the role of business in social development. As early as 1965, Prime Minister Lal Bahadur Shastri chaired a national-level seminar held in Delhi on the "Social Responsibility of Business" for policy-makers, business leaders, thinkers and trade union leaders. It called for regular dialogue between stakeholders, social accountability, openness and transparency, social audits and corporate governance. The seminar reported that:

"[CSR] is responsibility to itself, to its customers, workers, shareholders and the community. Every enterprise, no matter how large or small, must, if it is to enjoy confidence and respect, seek actively to discharge its responsibilities in all directions ... and not to one or two groups, such as shareholders or workers, at the expense of community and consumer. Business must be just and humane, as well as efficient and dynamic ... An enterprise is a corporate citizen. Like a citizen it is esteemed and judged by its actions in relation to the community of which it is a member, as well as by its economic performance."

It is interesting to note that the dramatic events surrounding the fall of Enron, WorldCom and Tyco, and the consequent concerns in the West about corruption, fraud, governance and accounting standards, have not been strongly felt in Asia, despite the fact that the repercussions were global. The region, although associated with corruption, has not experienced a reputational and financial crisis on the same proportions as Enron. Moreover, some commentators suggest that higher standards in Asia are the result of, for example, the requirement in some countries to conduct environmental reporting and of the strong sense of loyalty to customers, business partners and employees that Asian companies so openly demonstrate. Furthermore, although CSR is practiced "in name" by only a few firms in Asian countries, this does not mean that there is a comparative lack of social and environmental responsibility demonstrated by business within the region. For example, the provision of shelter, health care and schooling for workers and their families (sometimes sponsored by deductions from pay) is more characteristic of CSR in developing countries. Other research highlights how CSR is part of the way some Asian companies work on a day-to-day basis. For example:

- The UK's Department for International Development supported the Resource Centre for Social Dimensions of Business Practice, which carried out research into the relationship of business and poverty. This highlighted the significance of approaches by national companies in countries such as Singapore and India, where the tradition of business involvement in social issues is exemplified by family businesses and where businesses of every size have seen social reform as part of their contribution to nation-building. Often this is linked with local commitment and religious affiliation. Community involvement is still largely through trusts and foundations — there are over 200,000 private-sector trusts to help local communities in India, most of them set up by businesses.

- Indian CSR has traditionally involved providing financial support for schools, hospitals and cultural institutions. However, some have observed that this philanthropic drive has been driven by business necessity. With minimal state welfare and infrastructure provision in many areas, companies had to ensure that their workforce had adequate housing, healthcare and education, so that employees were well enough for productive work.

- Business Associations play an important part in promoting more responsible practice by companies. In the Philippines, the Philippine Business for Social Progress (PBSP) and the Asian Institute of Management (AIM) have, for a number of years, developed and promoted CSR in the country, addressing such issues as the provision of micro-credit, disaster relief, corporate giving and environmental stewardship.

As elsewhere in the world, corporate citizenship in Asia is not just about support for local workers and communities; rather it has become, by necessity, a mainstream business issue — it is about how business goes about doing its work and its broader contributions in society. However, it seems that the concept of corporate citizenship is still very much in the early stages of its evolution. Many challenges now face companies in Asia, both local and international, in making corporate responsibility an integral part of business strategy without diverting resources to the extent that the profitability of the overall business enterprise is undermined. Having said that, it is the failure to put in place strategies to address the concerns of local communities or work against the environmental degradation that can result in costly retrospective mitigation or ultimately lead to bankruptcy or the need for withdrawal from a country or business relationship. These events can turn out to be more expensive for business in the long run.

Challenges for global corporate citizenship in Asia

There are a number of key challenges that working in Asia poses for a socially responsible global business. Six key challenges identified by DHL are explored here: ethical supply-chain management and labor standards; investment and human rights; public consultation and the "social license to operate"; working in zones of conflict and security; corruption and the lack of law enforcement; and environmental protection.

• Ethical supply-chain management and labor standards

In manufacturing and agriculture, two areas of particular concern to DHL, as to all responsible global businesses, are child labor and "bonded" labor, as well as excessive working hours and overcrowded and unhygienic working conditions. The legal age of workers in some countries is 14 years old. The International Labour Organization's ILO Convention 138 recommends the abolition of child labor, and stipulates that the minimum age for employment shall not be less than the age of completion of compulsory schooling, specifying that this must be 15 years unless there are exceptional circumstances. In addition, ILO Convention 182 and Recommendation No. 190 on the Worst Forms of Child Labor is directed at eliminating, for people under 18, slavery, prostitution, drug trafficking and any other work that generates health and moral hazards for children. High-profile cases involving the use of child labor in some factories in South East Asia have received a great deal of media attention and pose challenges for reputational management, particularly in the retail sector. These issues pose further challenges of, first, reconciling the income-generation needs of poor people and the need for business to increase competitiveness as new supply options become available and, secondly, of ensuring access to the education and humane conditions of work that are stepping stones out of poverty.

The provision of services to workers is often thought of as constituting a paternalistic approach, and social audits in respect of labor standards today would likely investigate whether this is a benefit to employees on top of their wages or a debt that is imposed regardless of whether they had chosen to accept specific welfare support. Working to repay a debt — debt bondage — especially a debt that is imposed by a company through "compulsorily" providing goods or services, may be considered to contravene ILO Convention 29 on Forced Labor. Forms of bonded labor are found all over the world, but have been shown to be more prevalent in parts of India, Pakistan and Nepal, on farms and plantations, in brick-making and in quarrying, where its roots are to be found in the caste system or in feudal agricultural relationships.

- ### Investment and human rights

Global companies are increasingly facing criticism about where they invest. Indeed, there are some single-issue interest groups, as well as some Western governments, that discourage investment in certain countries on account of documented poor human-rights records — in Burma, Sudan and Iraq, for example. Some companies have pulled out of those countries on account of such public or shareholder pressure. But there are also companies that have sought to use the opportunities that their investment affords to make positive contributions to society in those countries. Rather than withdrawing, these companies have instead followed a strategy of constructive engagement. For example, they have provided human-rights training and engaged in health-promotion projects or, as is the case with DHL, have contributed to restructuring in post-conflict situations through the provision of such assistance as including transporting humanitarian aid and supporting development agencies in some of the associated logistics.

Working in such countries clearly brings with it a special set of responsibilities, and corporate citizens are expected to play a positive role in promoting the protection of human rights and ensuring that their activities are never misinterpreted as constituting complicity in any human-rights violations that take place. Indeed, this is one of the elements addressed by the Secretary General of the United Nations, Kofi Annan, when he calls upon global business to sign the U.N. Global Compact, a voluntary agreement by business to promote the protection of human rights, labor standards and the environment. DHL is a signatory to the Global Compact and participates in the Global Compact Learning Forum, which aims to help business share experience about the challenges of implementing the Compact's nine principles in their operations in different countries and contexts.

- ### Public consultation and the evolving concept of the "social license to operate"

In countries such as India and the Philippines, laws exist that oblige companies to engage in prior consultation with local communities before making an investment. There is now a body of evidence that strongly indicates that if a company does not engage in such dialogue with host communities they might not acquire what is now referred to as a "social license to operate" — the informal agreement of their neighbors. They might find that they are not able to recover predicted returns on their investment because they do not have the support of their local host communities. The case of the extractive sector, in particular throughout Indonesia, Papua New Guinea, Pakistan and India, bears this out. So too does the experience of establishing airports, with communities, for example, lobbying to restrict night flying or preventing the construction or use of access roads. The issue of ensuring that local communities are supportive of new transportation infrastructure, mines, factories or farms is relevant, whether in Asia or elsewhere. Notwithstanding this point, it is important to note that the "license to operate" does not only grant permission to invest but may be vitally important throughout the life-span of an operation. Since infrastructure investments in developing countries, and particularly in the poorer regions, have been poorly maintained, this represents an area of concern for the logistics and transportation sector.

- ## Working in zones of conflict and war-prone areas, and the challenge of security

Many Asian countries have been engulfed in internal conflict or are locked into confrontation with neighboring states. A notable example is the recent resurgence of hostilities between Pakistan and India over Kashmir. There are also countries that are occupied by a neighboring state or in which there are disputes about sovereignty and government allegiance. Afghanistan, Indonesia, East Timor, Papua New Guinea, the Philippines, Thailand, Tibet and Nepal are examples of such countries.

Again this sets up a specific challenge for the responsible practice of business, and one of which DHL is acutely aware given its global logistics and transportation business. While DHL works in accordance with the business concept of "first in, last out and first back in," it must recognize that this carries with it many responsibilities, not least of which is the responsibility to ensure that its business activity does not in any way contribute to inflaming tensions in fragile post-conflict situations.

An example of a response by DHL to such a post-conflict challenge is that of its support of the U.N. in Afghanistan, a country to which DHL, with its long-standing policy of being first back in again, returned in March 2002 after a 15-year absence due to political unrest. From the first flight on March 15, DHL has been providing a valuable contribution to the rebuilding and development of the Afghan economy. Three times a week, DHL's shipments include humanitarian aid, diplomatic cargo and office equipment destined for aid agencies and diplomatic missions operating in Kabul. DHL has also been helping with the rebuilding of the war-torn country. In spring 2002, the U.N. asked DHL for help with reestablishing its offices in Kabul after a seven-year absence. Via diplomatic pouches, DHL has shipped bulk office supplies and computers for the U.N., saving transit time for the organization by providing a more direct route to Kabul than the previous route through Islamabad. The tradition of providing humanitarian assistance in times of crisis stems back as far as 1985, when DHL Mexico provided logistical support to victims of the September earthquake. Another example from Asia of DHL's commitment to humanitarian assistance is the support the company provided when a tidal wave hit Papua New Guinea in 1997. Then, DHL Australia flew in 20 tonnes of emergency goods, including one tonne donated by DHL staff.

• Corruption and the lack of law enforcement

Although Asia has not had any corporate scandals on the scale of Enron, in recent years it has had its own serious cases of alleged public-sector embezzlement reportedly linked to corporate sources. Credible sources show that in countries across the region, corruption is part of political, economic and social life.[1] The perception is that corruption clearly remains a serious problem in most countries in Asia, with Bangladesh and Indonesia seen as the countries in which corruption is considered most prevalent. Some have undertaken measures to improve transparency and enforcement standards, and this has helped them to attract investment, with Thailand, Malaysia and South Korea ranking among the top ten performing stock indices in Asia in 2002. However, there is still a long way to go for some countries. Working in such countries in a socially responsible way presents a major challenge for global business. It places the burden on companies to develop policies and procedures proactively to ensure that they do not inadvertently become complicit in fraudulent business practice. Increasingly, new guidance being developed at the international level by, for example, the OECD and by the NGO Transparency International suggests ways for this subject to be addressed, and some companies are putting in place confidential helplines to support their employees.

One area of law enforcement that DHL is particularly well placed to support both in Asia and globally, and for which it has won praise, is that of combating fraud. Globally, DHL complies strictly with the regulatory requirements regarding inspections designed to prevent the entry of explosives, narcotics and other contraband into the DHL Network. In its Asia Pacific operations, the importance of these inspections is regularly emphasized, as is the importance of liaison and lobbying with

---

[1] Transparency International: Global Corruption Report 2001.

governmental, law enforcement and regulatory bodies. DHL Thailand has managed to combine both of these. During 2001, DHL Thailand's strict shipment-inspection policy resulted in the interdiction of hundreds of forged passports. Bangkok is a location that has been associated with the production of fraudulent documentation, and the events of September 11, 2001 highlighted, among a great many other things, the dangers of forged travel documents. Following these seizures, DHL Thailand informed the relevant embassies and liaised with Thai Police and immigration officials in an effort to assist with their ongoing efforts to combat this form of criminal activity. In recognition of this work, DHL Thailand was presented with a special award from the U.S. Immigration and Naturalization Service for its work in combating human smuggling and trafficking. DHL Thailand is the only commercial organization to have received such an award.

In the field of high-value freight security, DHL Asia has been supporting an initiative developed in 2000 by Technology Asset Protection Association (TAPA), a non-profit organization. The association was created to guarantee high security standards in the freight transportation of high-value technology products to minimize monetary or asset losses incurred due to theft during the shipment process. The issue of freight security has gained increased impetus since the launch of the global war on terrorism. DHL has now received certification for nine of its facilities in Hong Kong, the Philippines, Singapore and Thailand following an audit by TAPA. The facilities were evaluated in the areas of warehousing, site security (including security in and around the facility, security work instructions, training, access control, secure storage, alarm control, closed-circuit video security systems) and road transportation.

• **Environmental protection**

The lack of effective environmental legislation and regulatory frameworks, compounded by both lack of capacity and weaknesses concerning enforcement in many Asian countries, has resulted in many serious negative environmental impacts, with resultant protests from community and public-interest groups. The Bhopal disaster in 1984, involving a gas leak from Union Carbide's chemical plant, with its aftermath of deaths and injuries continues to receive a high profile in the media and from environmental and human-rights organizations. The export of waste to countries such as India, Pakistan and China (largely from the U.S. but also from Europe, South Korea and Japan) and of other hazardous materials from rich to poor countries also calls into question the issue of ethical business behavior, particularly in light of the Basel Convention (1994) banning such exports — already applicable to European business but as yet to be adopted by the U.S. Again, the lack of a level playing field in respect of regulation and a growing societal expectation in respect of waste prevention mean that it makes sense for global companies to develop their own strategies and best-practice guidelines where local regulation is weak.

DHL is a global transportation company and therefore generates emissions that must be both reduced and managed proficiently. In 2000, DHL introduced a global tracking and monitoring system to monitor fuel use, measure fuel burned by various aircraft and meet the new ISO14001 environmental standards to which DHL is committed. Capturing this data enables DHL to measure efficiency by monitoring operator, fleet or specific aircraft fuel usage; set budgets and run economic analysis on various aircraft types and plan network routes more accurately; assess the environmental impact of its fleet; and help DHL maintain its ISO14001 certification. In 1999, DHL Aviation resolved to implement a company-wide Environmental Management System (EMS), providing a framework for responding to the environmental challenges before them. This was a strategic business decision with real business benefits measured by working towards — and achieving — a single multi-site certification to ISO14001 for both ground and air operations. The benefits of adopting an effective EMS policy and achieving the ISO14001 standard are many. Notably, it secures the prosperity of DHL's global community by reducing waste, costs and inefficiencies and preserving natural resources. There are commercial benefits including improved operations and customer relations, legal and regulatory compliance, better performance management, increased staff motivation and attractiveness for investors.

The business case for corporate citizenship in Asia

While the six challenges described above represent a major challenge to multinational companies, such as DHL, that operate in Asia, at the same time there is a growing body of evidence that suggests that, on top of the moral imperatives, there is also a strong business case for acting as a global corporate citizen in Asia, and indeed anywhere in the world.

The key business benefits of corporate citizenship include:
- Enhanced reputation, which contributes to being the partner or "supplier of choice" in a growing range of business transactions,

or in new markets. Increasingly, other global companies with CSR strategies are requesting that DHL demonstrate its ethical credentials
- Increased ability to recruit, develop and retain staff, and a better-motivated workforce
- Better relations with government and other partners, which can contribute to enhanced future business relationships
- Keener anticipation and enhanced management of risk
- Operational cost savings through environmental efficiency methods that create "win-win" solutions for society and business
- Enhanced learning and innovation that can contribute to wider competitive advantage.

Ways forward: Corporate citizenship baselines

- Guiding principles and standards and their relevance for DHL

There is now a range of principles, codes and standards providing frameworks and guidelines for international best practice in corporate citizenship, and it is suggested that most of these are applicable in an Asian context.

The U.N. Global Compact addresses at the global level some of the challenges posed by working in Asia through its nine principles covering human rights, labor and the environment (see boxed information).

Available statistics[2] show that over one-third of the 601 companies signed up to the U.N. Global Compact Principles are Asian, notably from the Philippines (91 companies) and India (85), with a smaller number (11 companies or fewer) from China, Indonesia, Japan, Korea, Nepal, Pakistan, Sri Lanka or Thailand.

The UN Global Compact

Human Rights: The Secretary-General asked world business to
1. Support and respect the protection of international human rights within its sphere of influence; and
2. Make sure its own corporations are not complicit in human rights abuses.

---

[2] Source: www.unglobalcompact.org 'Global compact participants by country: Dec 19, 2002'.

> **Labor:** The Secretary-General asked world business to uphold
> 3. Freedom of association and the effective recognition of the right to collective bargaining;
> 4. The elimination of all forms of forced and compulsory labor;
> 5. The effective abolition of child labor; and
> 6. The elimination of discrimination in respect of employment and occupation.
>
> **Environment:** The Secretary-General asked world business to
> 7. Support a precautionary approach to environmental challenges;
> 8. Undertake initiatives to promote greater environmental responsibility; and
> 9. Encourage the development and diffusion of environmentally friendly technologies.

Alongside the Global Compact, there is also a growing body of other standards and initiatives emanating from the U.N., NGOs and also businesses in OECD countries.

The international framework of human rights establishes international law relating to corporate citizenship and socially responsible business practice. This comprises three main items: the Universal Declaration of Human Rights (U.N. 1948); the Labor Standards embodied in the Fundamental Conventions of the International Labor Organization (ILO 1930–1999); and the Rio Declaration on Environment and Development (U.N. 1992). These are binding for states.

However, as the U.N. Commission on Human Rights changes its focus from development to implementation and as society demands increased accountability from companies, national laws, codes of conduct and voluntary initiatives are being developed that interpret the international framework of human rights in terms of "norms" for responsible business practice. Business and industry groups, concerned to ensure that so-called norms of best practice are indeed relevant and feasible for the specific circumstances of their business, are developing some of these voluntary initiatives.

Three main codes of conduct are relevant to a company like DHL. First, the Human Rights Principles and Responsibilities for Transnational Corporations and Other Business Enterprises (U.N. Sub-commission on the Promotion and Protection of Human Rights 2002); second, the Tripartite Declaration of Principles Concerning Multinational Enterprises and Social Policy (ILO 1977); and, third, the OECD Guidelines for

Multinational Enterprises (OECD 2000). At DHL the last of these is considered extremely useful as the company begins to develop its policies and programs for promoting good corporate citizenship, particularly in respect of the challenges faced when operating in developing countries. From the perspective of DHL and of many other companies with global operations, the most helpful and highest-level "voluntary initiative" that builds on these codes, and on the international law referred to above, is the U.N. Global Compact.

Two other initiatives are important to DHL in that they provide guidance at the global level. The first is the World Economic Forum's Corporate Citizenship "Framework for Action" (2002), to which DHL is also a signatory. This calls for a four-point action plan, which DHL is following. For example, step one is to "provide leadership," and the importance of business principles are noted in this regard; step four is "be transparent," which underlines the DHL commitment to report to stakeholders on performance in respect of its social and environmental responsibilities. Indeed, as a demonstration of leadership, DHL has established a dedicated Corporate Citizenship Unit (CCU) within the office of the CEO. The second initiative that DHL considers relevant to its work is the Global Reporting Initiative (GRI). DHL plans over time to report on its corporate citizenship performance in accordance, where relevant, with the principles and indicators suggested by the U.N.-convened multi-stakeholder GRI framework. It will also be interesting to see whether ISO develops a standard for responsible business practice, as DHL found the discipline of meeting ISO 14001 accreditation in environmental performance a useful exercise and considers it part of its commitment to upholding the U.N. Global Compact Principles on the environment.

Partnerships

More recently, DHL has learned that harnessing its core competence in partnership with others can generate greater development impact. Therefore, within the framework of a number of WEF initiatives, DHL is working with other business and civil society partners within the Global Disaster Resource Network and the Global Health Initiative, as well as within the Global Digital Divide Initiative. In all three of these networking programs, DHL applies its core competence of logistics and transportation, together with the expertise of others, to help address problems that are so great in scope that each partner could not hope to address them alone. The Global Disaster Resource Network is a global network of companies in the engineering, construction, logistics and transportation sectors that are committed to assisting humanitarian organizations in their efforts to reduce human suffering associated with disasters by acting as a clearinghouse for companies to offer a defined range of their resources free of charge. The Global Digital Divide (GDDI) builds partnerships between the public and private sector to bridge the divide between those who can make effective use of information and communication technology (ICT) to improve their lives and those who cannot. The Global Digital Divide Task Force was launched in 2000 with a three-year mandate to develop and transmit creative public and private-sector initiatives to transform the digital divide into an opportunity for growth. The Task Force has initiated and supported education and entrepreneurship projects, as well as raising awareness of the issue through its policy advocacy efforts. Led by the business sector in partnership with the not-for-profit and government sectors, the Task Force has undertaken projects in the fields of education, entrepreneurship, policy and strategy, and resource mobilization. The Global Health Initiative's mission is to increase the quantity and quality of business programs fighting HIV/AIDS, tuberculosis (TB) and malaria. The GHI partners with the Forum's 1,000 member-companies, the World Health Organization, the Joint United Nations Program on HIV/AIDS, Roll Back Malaria (RBM) and Stop TB. DHL's role is to support the transportation of medicines and the logistics surrounding its distribution to patients in developing countries.

Ultimately, however, we believe that it is the individual CSR strategy of a company like DHL, together with the issue of how that company has positioned itself within the different societies within which it works as a corporate citizen, that can make the difference in contributing to economic and social development and protecting the environment. This suggestion is applicable wherever a company is operating in the world — whether in the West or Asia.

The boundaries of business responsibility

Corporate citizenship can never be a replacement for the rightful role of democratic governments to set up regulatory frameworks for the benefit of society. However, for Asia, more immediate priorities often limit the role of the state in distributing more widely the benefits of business in the face of poverty and inequity and in providing safety nets for those who are adversely affected by business or government decisions.

It can therefore be argued that in developing countries there is a greater responsibility for global business to be aware of some of the more indirect as well as immediate implications of an investment decision, and to address these impacts responsibly within the local communities in which they operate. We should remember that employees of business are also members of local communities, which is another reason to emphasize approaches that look at business "in society" — not business and society, as if society is a separate entity. It is also worth noting that banks, whether private or multilateral, and in particular the World Bank Group, increasingly attach environmental and social conditions to the provision of credit, equity or insurance, and do so primarily in order to protect predicted returns on their investments and ensure that public monies do not contribute to a worsening of poverty.

The jurisdiction of states is limited to national boundaries and international law is binding only on states, not on business. Where national law does not exist or is weak, there exists a responsibility on the part of large multinational companies such as DHL to respect established voluntary codes of conduct that give a practical interpretation of international law for business. Moreover, how companies apply these responsibilities as corporate citizens, as well as the competitiveness of the services they offer, will increasingly be the basis upon which customers and business partners will make their purchasing and business decisions.

The challenge of corporate governance

Corporate governance is increasingly considered to be a key component of corporate citizenship and particularly important in Asia, since poor corporate governance was identified as one of the root causes of the Asian financial crisis in the 1990s.

It has been suggested that the absence of effective discipline within the managements of some corporations, coupled with apparently complicated relationships between corporations, their owners, finance providers, auditors and consultants, severely affected investors' confidence in the region's corporate sectors. Economies that took early steps to improve corporate governance have been recovering from the crisis at a more rapid pace than those which have not addressed this issue. The Asian crisis showed that good corporate governance is important not only for individual corporations that wish to raise capital but also for an economy looking to realize sustainable growth.

Companies in Asia have sometimes claimed that Western-style corporate-governance standards do not apply to them. However — and with some Western standards now shown to be severely lacking — it is clear that high standards of corporate governance are a necessary prerequisite regardless of market sector or economic region. Again, this is a challenge for all global companies in their worldwide operations, not just for those in Asia.

To achieve good corporate governance across the region, it is suggested by some observers that more needs to be done. However, apart from Hong Kong and Singapore, where corporate-governance systems have been considered sound for some time, most Asian countries have achieved discernible and significant progress in reforming their corporate-governance systems during the past few years. This is of particular note given the scale of the problems in corporate governance shared by these countries and the short time in which this progress has been made.[3]

The following examples indicate the nature of current momentum in Asia in corporate governance as outlined in a recent report entitled "Leading Social Investment Indicators Report 2001" (SRI World Group, Inc. 2001):

- **China** (China Securities Regulatory Commission — CSRC) has taken a number of steps to enhance transparency and the independence of directors. It has also stated that it will routinely examine for truthfulness in accounting and financial and corporate-governance reporting. Codes of best practice are being developed.
- **Hong Kong** (Society of Accountants — HKSA) has published guidelines that encourage transparency and corporate governance.
- **Malaysia** (Kuala Lumpur Stock Exchange — KLSE) conducted a major overhaul of its listing requirements in an effort to increase the credibility of the market, with a focus on improved corporate governance and mandatory training for directors.
- **India** (Securities and Exchange Board of India — SEBI) has issued a mandatory code for corporate governance and disclosure with quarterly compliance reports.

---

[3] Source: This section draws on "Comparative corporate governance trends in Asia", Chong Nam, Yeongjae Kang, Joon-Kyung Kim. July 2001.

- **Indonesia** has established a Forum for Corporate Governance in Indonesia (FCGI) to disseminate information, encourage sharing of best practice and provide benchmarks.
- **Japan** (Ministry of Justice) has proposed changes to its commercial code to bring corporate governance in line with International Standards, with specific emphasis on board composition and structure and audit processes.
- **Pakistan** is working with the Asian Development Bank to develop an institutional capacity in corporate governance, to increase efficiency through governance standards, strengthen the regulators' ability to promote good corporate governance and enhance shareholders' understanding of international best practice.
- **The Philippines** has established a governance Advisory Council to develop and align Philippine companies and government agencies with international standards of corporate governance, particularly in transparency, business ethics and integrity of business and financial transactions.
- **Singapore** has recently adopted its first code of corporate governance, which focuses on disclosure and board structure and composition, together with a system to monitor compliance. Legislation is passing through government to develop a disclosure-based regime with stock market enforcement.
- **South Korea** (Ministry of Commerce Industry and Energy and the Federation of Korean Industries) has set up a corporate-ethics evaluation system. Government incentives are to be offered to companies conforming to a new definition for corporate governance, with increased emphasis on transparency and consumer protection. Problems inherent in the financial institutions are to be addressed by insisting that banks factor in a company's corporate-governance performance when determining credit rating.

Finally, it should be noted that transparency in procurement practices by government agencies and relevant capacity building and training, which was an agenda item at Doha, is a priority for Asia and is being followed up on by the WTO, by regional development organizations and banks and by national governments.

DHL's experience of corporate citizenship and responsible business practice

DHL's definition of corporate citizenship is drawn from the World Economic Forum. It provides the sort of generic guidance that we believe can help a global company act responsibly wherever it is working in the world — Asia or elsewhere. It states:

> "Corporate Citizenship is about the contribution that a company makes to society through its core business activities, its social investment and its philanthropy programmes, and its engagement in public policy. It is determined by the way a company manages its economic social and environmental impacts and its relationships with different stakeholders, in particular shareholders, employees, customers, business partners, governments and communities ...[It] is not just a 'nice-to-have', charitable add-on, but [is] a fundamental element of good business practice and effective leadership."

> (World Economic Forum, Global Corporate Citizenship, The Leadership Challenge for CEOs and Boards, 2002)

DHL's very fast growth, characterized by autonomy at the local level, has brought benefits in corporate citizenship terms such as the local sourcing of services and the employment and training of local managers who understand the cultures in which they are working. But it also poses challenges in some areas, as the company strives to combine cost-efficiency measures, such as centralized procurement, with responsible business practice. Sometimes DHL needs to make trade-offs, and there are no simple solutions. Rapid local growth also means a rise in local solutions to fit customers' needs. At the same time, DHL has been working hard to standardize functions globally, such as operations and "e-purchasing." DHL will therefore always need to find a balance between the respective advantages of local and global solutions.

DHL's approach to corporate citizenship is consequently a reflection of its close relationship to the local communities in which it operates and the skills it can most effectively apply as a global transportation company. Should disaster strike — for example, earthquakes, floods or conflict — DHL has always done all it can to help those affected and the humanitarian agencies that support them. DHL has done this as an extension of the logistics and transportation activities that are core to its business. By focusing on this type of assistance, DHL is able to bring appropriate expertise and to incorporate delivery of humanitarian aid into DHL's existing transport operations, thereby making it more cost-effective. This is not philanthropy; it is corporate citizenship; it is the application of core business competence more widely in society.

DHL is in the process of consolidating the community-investment "strand" of its CSR work. This involved looking at existing work as well as initiating new projects in response to need. Although charitable giving will always be considered important and initiatives by DHL employees will continue to receive good support, and indeed are considered to contribute to team building, the future work of DHL's community investment programs will either, as mentioned above, be the extension of the business that DHL does, or will contribute to capacity-building within the next generation. The latter is in line with one of the outcomes of the Doha Development Agenda meeting, which emphasized capacity building in developing countries. Examples of work in these two areas include the case of post-conflict humanitarian assistance provided in Afghanistan outlined above and the provision of food aid to needy people in Singapore and DHL's new partnership with AIESEC, a student organization, to promote capacity-building among young people in the Asia-Pacific region.

Looking first at the provision of food aid, DHL Singapore, as part of its CSR activities, launched a weekly delivery service of fresh vegetables to 415 needy and elderly citizens for a year. "Veggie Express" is a charitable service: DHL buys the vegetables, with staff volunteering to sort and distribute the produce. Internal response has been overwhelming as employees take up the opportunity to work for a day outside of normal duties to make a difference in the community through this scheme. This charitable work is an extension of the business that DHL does every day.

As a contribution to capacity-building, DHL has recently invested in a new partnership with AIESEC, the largest student organization in the world. The sponsorship provides traineeships that DHL will open up for selected AIESEC members, beginning in Asia Pacific. Through this, DHL supports AIESEC in its mission of helping young people develop into individuals able to meet the challenges of the international business world. DHL will offer internships in a wide variety of disciplines, giving young people the opportunity of working closely with senior managers and the experience of a truly multicultural environment. AIESEC International President Evrim Sen said he was delighted to have found in DHL a partner with the same vision:

"It has always been our goal to contribute to the development of people and of communities by serving as an agent of positive change in the world through education and cultural exchange. The new relationship with DHL will be a significant boost to our efforts."

Again, this is an example of DHL's CSR work being an extension of the way the company works. DHL intends to take the program global, from its regional starting point in Asia, introducing young talent to the company everywhere and across all functions, as well as significantly increasing the number of positions made available within the scheme.

The imperative of corporate citizenship for DHL also flows from working in countries where democracy is weak. DHL operates in 41 out of the 42 countries categorized as "high risk" by the U.S. State Department. This means that DHL has a special responsibility to ensure that its activities are undertaken with reference to best business practice when working in countries with poor human-rights records. DHL's commitment to corporate citizenship, demonstrated by being a signatory to the U.N. Global Compact, means that DHL will over time need to put systems in place to ensure that its business activities are monitored and reported accurately.

Corporate citizenship poses a challenge in balancing responsiveness with responsibility. As noted previously, DHL has a history of being first into a country, last out when there is trouble, and first back in again afterwards. While DHL's presence may facilitate delivery of much-needed humanitarian assistance, as well as help in the re-establishment of the infrastructure needed to support the renewed operation of both business and government, working in such countries brings with it a special set of responsibilities. Corporate citizens are expected to play a positive role in the protection of human rights and to be ethical in their business transactions in line with new codes of conduct such as the OECD Guidelines for Multinational Enterprises (2000) and the U.N. Human Rights Principles and Responsibilities for Transnational Corporations and Other Business Enterprises (2002).

DHL therefore adopted the World Economic Forum's Corporate Citizenship "Framework for Action", published in February 2002, to shape its global approach to addressing these wide-ranging business responsibilities. In brief, under the Framework a practical four-point plan is proposed:

- Provide leadership
- Define what it means for the company

- Make it happen
- Be transparent about it.

The corporate-citizenship management system that DHL is developing will introduce a range of performance-monitoring tools. This will help the company demonstrate that the commitment to corporate citizenship is one that the company is prepared to measure and report on to its stakeholders. In addition, "Corporate Citizenship Champions" are being identified within DHL and trained through coaching programs to ensure that corporate citizenship is effectively embedded into the culture of the company. There will also be a strong focus on dialogue with internal and external stakeholders, which is also recommended by the World Economic Forum framework and GRI.

DHL's current view is that its work in the area of corporate citizenship should cover the following three work streams:

- **Internal CSR** — social justice in the workplace for employees, including fair terms and conditions of work, equal opportunity and business integrity, and governance frameworks for ethical business practice including supply-chain management.
- **External CSR** — responsible relationships with external stakeholders, which would include a business-practice strand and a community-investment strand. The latter is an area that is important to DHL, given that the company operates in a great many of the world's under-developed and conflict-ridden countries as well as the highly developed, rich ones. There are therefore two key criteria that DHL employs within its community-investment work: first, that the CSR work DHL supports must be an extension of the business that it does (for example, transporting humanitarian assistance); and, second, that DHL's CSR work must aim to contribute to capacity-building (such as skills, education, health and well-being, for example) within the next generation.
- **Environmental stewardship** — minimizing the impact of DHL's operations on the environment, for example, through reducing noise pollution and fuel emissions, promoting the protection of the environment and recognizing that living species should be protected and treated with respect whenever DHL's work involves their transportation.

Conclusion

In this chapter we have looked at the special challenges for international companies such as DHL of working in Asia. The challenges vary across the region in the face of various levels of democracy, different approaches to labor standards, different social and environmental priorities and different business traditions. Where such diversity flourishes and where conditions are fast evolving, DHL feels that global business is best advised to work in accordance with global business's own best standards and those recommended by international law and universally recognized codes of conduct, informed by the knowledge of local staff.

The challenge for business is to embed the values of corporate citizenship within the company and to ensure that employees worldwide, not just in Asia, are empowered through fair conditions of work, training and management support to act in accordance with these values. And although, as we have argued, corporate citizenship is not just about philanthropy, contributing to social development in poor regions of the world, especially in times of crisis, is an important corporate responsibility. Corporate citizenship is also about being a healthy business enterprise and thriving. It is about undertaking community projects in areas of core competence — logistics and transportation in the case of DHL — so that optimal value-added can be generated in society.

DHL believes that corporate citizenship is about being efficient and competitive and about ensuring the business is financially stable. If these conditions are met, guided by a CSR strategy and robust management system, performance indicators and risks review process, such benefits should flow as meaningful employment, good conditions of work and sound development opportunities bring stability and economic opportunities to employees, business partners, host governments, community neighbors and shareholders. The benefits are generated as a result of making profit, paying taxes, engaging in productive business-to-business relationships and through following strategies of expansion and growth in line with business values that emphasize social responsibility, good governance and environmental stewardship.

Engaging in meaningful CSR programs that are aligned to core business purpose, and following the strategies that will keep the business itself in good health are the corporate citizenship challenges facing Asia and the entire world.

17

PUBLIC ACCOUNTABILITY
Transparency, Accountability and Governance in Asia

Samuel A. DiPiazza Jr.
Global CEO, PricewaterhouseCoopers, USA

 Transparency and accountability are without question top-of-mind issues among Asian business leaders. PricewaterhouseCoopers' fifth annual global CEO survey released in January 2002 reported that corporate governance and transparency issues continue to grow in priority for Asian chief executives. The survey found that 76% of Asian CEOs consider corporate governance to be a key factor in attracting foreign capital and investments, and 80% view corporate governance as an important consideration when selecting business partners.

The reasons are clear and lie in the benefits of increased transparency and accountability. These include increased management credibility, more long-term investors, more awareness among industry analysts more access to capital at a lower cost, reduced share-price volatility, and a higher likelihood of realizing a company's true potential value.

Yet, despite these benefits and widespread support from Asian CEOs, some view Asian business, particularly in South East Asia, as lagging behind in terms of transparency and accountability. One measure is the perception of corruption in a particular country. On a scale of 1 to 102, where 1 indicates a low level of corruption, Transparency International's 2002 Corruption Perceptions Index ranks Singapore as #5. Malaysia, however, is placed at 33; South Korea, at 40; China, at 59; Thailand, at 64; the Philippines, at 77; and Indonesia, at 96.[1]

---

[1] TI Corruption Perception Index at www.transparency.org

Besides the perception of corruption, other perceived and actual impediments to greater transparency and accountability in Asia include the possibility of an economic downturn, an "information-transparency-accountability infrastructure" that is still in its infancy, and "a culture of family-owned empires where boards of directors tend to be chaired by the head of the management team and where non-executive directors are often not as independent, powerful or indeed as well qualified as they should be."[2] In addition, some point the finger at "Asian values", which, ironically, were once first praised as the drivers of the so-called Asian Economic Miracle, only to be later identified as a critical weakness in governance during the Asian crisis.[3] Still others cite the negative impact of state-led companies and a lack of both "global standards of behaviour" and "global management talent."[4] All of these are complicated by the ever-present possibility of an economic downturn.

Finally, and perhaps most importantly, many observers continue to believe that corporate transparency is, largely, limited to financial information. However, to be truly effective, the spirit of transparency must embrace all aspects of an enterprise, including the reporting of non-financial but critically important information such as strategies, key value-drivers, and market opportunities. Companies must provide a reasonably holistic view that goes beyond the information that financial reporting regulations currently require. Gathering, preparing, and publicly communicating this broader range of information with integrity is likely to be a criterion of good corporate governance in the 21st century, both in Asia and worldwide.

With this trend as a background, this chapter discusses transparency, accountability, and other matters of governance in major Asian economies, proposes recommendations where appropriate, and presents views on how best to achieve a holistic approach to transparency that goes beyond the narrow confines of financial disclosure.

The chapter approaches these complex topics from two directions. First, we look at five major business environments — Malaysia, Singapore, Hong Kong, Japan and China — to examine the current reality and emerging trends in corporate governance. Each is a different dynamic

---

2   Fran van Dijk, "Letter from Hong Kong", at www.sustainability.com

3   This is a hotly debated topic. For a definition of Asian values, see Han Sung-Joo, "Asian values: An Asset or a liability," in Han Sung-Joo (ed.), *Changing Values in Asia — Their Impact on Governance and Development*, Japan Center for International Exchange, Tokyo, 1999, p.4.

4   Andrew Sheng, "Transparency, Accountability and Governance in Asian Markets", The 21st Tunku Abdul Rahman Lecture 2001, April 17, 2001.

environment with clearly drawn needs and issues. Second, we then look for alignment between new ideas on governance and corporate information in the West, with the Asian environment. If those ideas have broad validity, as I think they do, they will find applications in Asia. They will be recognized as not just Western but *global* ideas that can be successfully adapted into different environments and cultures.

Substantial progress in Asia

While generalizing is difficult, the realities of Asia, in my opinion, are both dynamic and progressive. There is truth in much that has been said about the lack of transparency and accountability in Asia, but we also need to acknowledge that tremendous progress has been made and continues in some Asian nations, particularly since the Asian financial crisis. Asia's substantial progress can be contrasted to the relative inactivity on governance issues in the U.S. until the Enron crisis of 2001.

• **Malaysia**

Malaysia is a good example. Even before the financial crisis, the government formulated an approach to financial reporting backed by the force of law, replacing the previous system under which accounting standards were issued by the accounting profession and enforced by auditors. The new framework, enacted under the Financial Reporting Act of 1997, mandates an independent standard-setting structure that includes representation from all interested parties — preparers, users, regulators and the accounting profession. Under this new framework, all financial statements in Malaysia must comply with standards issued by the Malaysian Accounting Standards Board (MASB), which are aligned with International Accounting Standards (IAS). This ensures comparability of financial statements.

Since its formation, the MASB has issued 31 additional standards and is currently on track to reach full alignment with IAS in the next year or two. To ensure compliance, regulators such as the Kuala Lumpur Stock Exchange (KLSE), the Securities Commission (SC), the Companies Commission of Malaysia, the Central Bank and the Malaysian Institute of Accountants are empowered to enforce compliance.

Since 1996, the SC has worked to implement a market-based approach to regulating the Malaysian capital markets. The SC's plan focuses on the quality of information disclosed by issuers of securities so that investors can make informed decisions. Surveys conducted in 1999 and 2002[5] revealed that the market, in general, supports the SC's approach, which is now stimulating greater transparency and accountability among market participants.

As part of its capital market development plan, in 1998 the government established a High-Level Finance Committee, with participation from the private sector, to advise on the best means for enhancing corporate governance and for setting best practices. At about the same time, the KLSE, in conjunction with PricewaterhouseCoopers, conducted a survey to determine the state of corporate governance in Malaysia and made proposals on how to protect stakeholders' interests. The survey results were then used by the High-Level Finance Committee to formulate its Report on Corporate Governance, which made specific recommendations on raising corporate-governance standards.

The Report covered the development of the Malaysian Code on Corporate Governance (the Code); legal and regulatory reform; and training and education to expand the pool of persons qualified to be company directors. Many recent initiatives in Malaysia derive from recommendations that first appeared in this Report.

The Code was based on principles adopted in the United Kingdom, including the Cadbury Code of Best Practice and the Hampel approach. Issued in March 2000, it was mainly private-sector driven, based on principles of self-regulation that were accepted by those likely to be affected. The Code aimed to establish best practices within the structures and processes already existing in companies, thereby achieving the optimal governance framework. Issues covered include the composition of boards, the recruitment of new directors, the remuneration of directors, and board committees.

The Code's approach allows for a more flexible response to corporate-governance issues than that allowed under statutes or regulations. It recognizes that, for some aspects of corporate governance, statutory regulation is necessary, while for others, self-regulation, complemented by market regulation, is more appropriate. Thus, in February 2001, the KLSE mandated some of the Code's recommendations, including those concerning independent directors, directors' training, and annual reporting.

The Capital Market Masterplan — which charts the strategic positioning and future direction of Malaysia's capital markets for the next 10 years — is another major program championed by Malaysia's SC. First

---

[5] Commissioned by the SC, the survey was conducted by Pricewaterhouse Coopers.

announced in 1999, this plan was approved by the Minister of Finance in December 2000. It encourages transparency, accountability and a performance-oriented corporate sector. It also promotes shareholder activism and encourages greater participation in corporate governance for institutional investors. In fact, many of the underlying principles of the Masterplan built upon the recommendations of the Finance Committee Report on Corporate Governance.

Among other steps, the plan recommends enhancement of the disclosures published in annual reports by publicly listed companies, particularly in the quality of non-financial information. It also provides for the newly established Minority Shareholders Watchdog Group (MSWG), formed by major Malaysian institutional groups in 2000, to support proactive participationby shareholders in publicly listed companies. The Group aims to harness the strength of large (albeit minority) institutional investors and to monitor and institute changes in the companies in which they invest, and it is already making its presence felt through key decisions.

Although Malaysia's corporate-governance framework is substantially in place, challenges do remain. The main challenge for Malaysian companies is not only to embrace the underlying principles, but to do so in a holistic manner.

• Singapore

Singapore has also made great strides over the last several years. Historically the recipient of positive rankings with regard to low perceptions of corruption, Singapore has a strong track record of undertaking corporate-governance initiatives and is no stranger to reform. Even before the Asian financial crisis, requirements for independent directors and audit committees were in place. Following the crisis, an even greater impetus was felt among regulators to quicken the pace of development in corporate governance.

Businesses in Singapore operate in a robust regulatory environment, with the government taking a proactive approach to regulation. Although not long ago regulators in Singapore were very proactive in delineating what companies could and could not do — even going so far as to pronounce on whether a company seeking IPO was a good investment opportunity — more recently, regulators have moved towards a more disclosure-based and market-driven approach.

Singapore's business environment reflects a cultural leaning toward conformity. This, and the nation's compactness, has eased the way for the government to enforce new rules with virtually no opposition from the corporate sector. Unlike some countries in the region, Singapore is relatively free of politically motivated vested interests, making it relatively easy for new regulations to take hold.

For instance, the Ministry of Finance, together with the Monetary Authority of Singapore and the Attorney-General's Chambers, spearheaded a comprehensive review of matters related to corporate regulation and governance, particularly those affecting listed companies. As part of this exercise, it appointed three private-sector-led review committees, one of which examined and made recommendations on corporate governance. The Government then accepted all of the recommendation of this Corporate Governance Committee (CGC).

Such significant movement toward improved corporate governance has had a considerable impact on Singapore's accounting practices and its businesses. Singapore's accounting standards are based on IAS and each new Standard is, after an 18-month period for an exposure draft, adopted as a local standard. The government has taken an active role in reducing the time delay for adoption, and has also encouraged the local Institute of Certified Public Accountants to adopt new IAS as soon as possible. In addition, in August 2002, the government established the Council on Corporate Disclosure and Governance (CCDG), an entity much like the Financial Accounting Standards Board (FASB) in the U.S.

Singapore's movement toward improved corporate governance has affected each of the three types of companies doing business in Singapore.

The first group, government-linked companies, operate with their own boards and managements on a commercial basis. Thus far, there has been little, if any, criticism regarding the protection of minority shareholders' interests. However, anecdotal evidence suggests that these companies have not only performed well on their own merits, but also are mindful of the interests of independent shareholders and careful to avoid any allegations of compromising the interests of minority shareholders.

The second group — larger corporations or conglomerates that were once family-owned — has also taken steps to improve governance. For example, many have hired professional managers who are given relatively free reign to manage based on their own judgments.

The third group — small and medium-size enterprises (SMEs) — has only in recent years begun to come to the market as listed companies, encouraged to do so by the relaxation of listing requirements by the stock exchange. Because of their size, their short histories and the close involvement of their owners, many of these businesses are still in the process of learning to behave as public companies.

In Singapore the regulations once were one-size-fits-all. But a new approach has taken hold, under which the primary regulations contain only the general and core requirements across the board. The new Code of Corporate Governance takes a balanced approach that specifies best practices, but allows for deviation, subject to appropriate disclosure.

Even prior to the issuing of the Code, a self-regulating market mechanism enabled Singapore to achieve a surge in transparency. In 2000, the *Singapore Business Times* introduced a disclosure scorecard — the Corporate Transparency Index (CTI) — to measure the quality of disclosure in companies' earnings announcements. At the first round of scoring, approximately 85% of the listed companies fell short of the perceived average score, which generated a great deal of public discussion. Six months later, virtually every company had improved its score, with many voluntarily disclosing more relevant information.

The results were startling. Under a prescriptive approach, many companies — particularly the SMEs — focused only on meeting minimum requirements based on regulation. In contrast, a market-driven approach, which included favorable publicity for good corporate behavior and public embarrassment for a poor showing, has been both effective and cost-efficient in bringing about desired outcomes.

• Hong Kong

A relatively mature economy, Hong Kong has historically been very proactive with regard to promoting standards to enhance corporate governance. The Stock Exchange of Hong Kong Limited (SEHK) has been the driving force behind a number of such initiatives, including revising the Listing Rules (1991), introducing a Code of Best Practice for directors and requiring independent non-executive directors (1993), and expanding disclosure requirements in financial statements (1994, 1998 and 2000). Such efforts have been complemented by company and securities legislation aimed at enhancing the corporate-governance regulatory framework.[6]

Perhaps one reason for Hong Kong's steady progress is the spirit of open debate fostered by the SEHK through Consultation Papers such as the one in 2002, in which the SEHK invited views from a diverse group of respondents on a number of controversial proposals related to shareholders' rights, directors and board practices, and corporate reporting and disclosure of information. After considering the views of all respondents, proposals were adopted, revised or dropped. The thorough

---

[6] "Consultation Conclusion Report" issued by the Hong Kong Stock Exchange Limited, available at www.hkex.com.

consultation ensured that the recommendations met the interests of all parties. This process of give and take, of considering advantages and disadvantages, has had a very positive influence on improving governance in Hong Kong. A look at the evolution of two of these proposals will best illustrate the point.[7]

For instance, with regard to quarterly-disclosure requirements, the Exchange proposed that Main Board issuers (like their peers listed in the Growth Enterprise Market) be required to publish quarterly results within 45 days of the quarter end. Most respondents disagreed, citing, among other factors, that such a requirement might increase time and costs, cause an undue emphasis on short-term results, and result in the publication of misleading information. As a result, the SEHK did not mandate quarterly reporting but, rather, encouraged it as a best practice.

With regard to directors' remuneration, the Exchange proposed that companies should "disclose directors' remuneration and compensation packages in their annual reports on an individual, named basis." Again, most respondents disagreed, citing privacy and safety concerns among other reasons. In response, the SEHK amended its proposal to require disclosure on an individual but "no name" basis.

Not all governance-related issues in Hong Kong, however, have benefited from this beneficial process of input and debate. One such issue is the protection of minority interests. Even though companies are required to disclose related-party transactions, the interests of minority shareholders are not explicitly protected. Significantly strengthening the protection would require changes in company law that would, for example, allow minority shareholders to actively engage in company governance.

Thus, although Hong Kong has made significant inroads toward improving the level of transparency and disclosure, we must continue to ask what will drive the continuation of these efforts in the future. The fact that the economy is dominated by large family-owned enterprises tends to dampen any urgency in this regard. The answer to this conundrum is twofold, and involves both the long-term impact of China and the future growth of local institutional investment.

Historically, Chinese companies seeking access to international capital markets have turned to Hong Kong as their first choice, although recently this has been mitigated by the preponderance of State-Owned Enterprises (SOEs) and greater P/E rations on the exchanges in China. Over the long term, Hong Kong must compete for Chinese companies with China's

---

[7] For a full discussion, see Ibid, pp.31–35.

domestic markets, which are opening to foreign investment. Hong Kong and PRC domestic markets will be attractive because they provide access to a larger pool of capital and avoid more rigorous requirements in other international markets. These are all powerful incentives for Hong Kong to continue to raise its levels of corporate governance.

The second issue involves the growth of institutional investment. Until recently, most individuals in Hong Kong did not benefit from pension funds, and pension-fund investment in Hong Kong was lower than in other markets, such as the U.S. and Europe. However, after the establishment of the Mandatory Provident Fund Schemes Authority (MPFA), the proportion of institutional investment in Hong Kong is likely to increase. These investors will likely bring added pressure for better corporate governance.

Such trends bode well for the future of Hong Kong but steady progress in improving transparency, accountability and governance will be required. To accomplish this objective, Hong Kong, like many of its Asian neighbors, should adopt a more coordinated approach. Currently, the lack of coordination between different bodies which influence governance — including accounting regulators, the SEHK, the Securities and Futures Commission, and the Institute of Directors impedes accelerated reform. Synchronizing the efforts of these groups to avoid overlap and eliminate inefficiencies will do much to accelerate the progress of corporate governance.

• Japan

A review of the literature on governance in Japan suggests that, like many of its Asian neighbors, Japan is moving toward becoming more transparent and accountable.[8] Japan has had a formal set of governance principles in place since the late 1990s. In 2001, the Japan Corporate Governance Forum revised these principles to reflect changing attitudes toward corporate governance, the growing power of institutional investors and changes to Japan's Commercial Code. In 2002, Japan's Commercial Code

---

[8] The following is typical: "...first, Japan is adopting the global accounting standards; second, Japan is moving from the bank-centred system to the capital market-based system, and from the system with concentrated investor ownership to the system with more dispersed investors; and third, Japan is experiencing a comprehensive overhaul of its legal and regulatory infrastructure on capital markets." (Hideki Kanda, "Disclosure and Corporate Governance: A Japanese Perspective", at Corporate Governance in Asia: A Comparative Perspective, Seoul, 3–5 March 1999 at www.oecd.org

was revised to state that, as of April 1, 2003, companies could opt to adopt a more Western style of governance, which would include, for example, the formation of boards with a majority of non-executive directors.

However, as of today, only a few Japanese companies have announced that they will take advantage of this option. The 20 or 30 large Japanese companies that are also listed in the U.S. have, for obvious reasons, made greater progress. But the majority of Japanese companies have been reluctant to change, despite many of the same pressures that have induced companies in other Asian nations to move ahead. The reason behind this, I believe, lies in the differences between the Japanese and Western views of governance and of the roles of public companies in general.

Under the Anglo-Saxon view, public companies exist primarily to increase shareholder value, although this view is gradually changing to accommodate concepts of sustainability and corporate citizenship. This view contrasts with the Japanese view, in which the roles of public companies are much wider and broadly defined around general social and economic good. In addition, because the largest shareholders in Japanese public companies have historically been banks and financial institutions, the interests of individual investors or minority shareholders have had a low priority. Lastly, the Japanese custom of mutual shareholding between companies and between companies and banks (*mochiai*) essentially neutralizes the power of shareholders through "I own you, you own me" relationships.

Such differences in outlook have led to the development of fundamentally different systems of governance. Where the Western system requires independent audit committees and boards, the traditional Japanese system consists of a statutory auditor that reports on management's performance to a board of directors. However, because the CEO/president has the right to choose the auditor and board members, governance is less independent.

There are other factors working against accelerated change in Japan. The recent scandals in the U.S. were the subject of widespread media attention in Japan, leading many to conclude that for Japan, U.S.-style governance was weak and non-workable. There is also a prevailing attitude among Japanese managers that autonomy is preferable to supervision, and it is only recently that institutional investors have pressed for greater transparency and accountability. The largest impediment, however, involves the concentration of power in the hands of CEOs/ presidents in the traditional system, under which directors often lack the power to replace top management even when appropriate.

Such impediments, however, are gradually giving way before the economic realities of an increasingly global business environment. Under economic globalization, Japan's economy cannot remain isolated from the other economies of the world and still expect to prosper. Therefore, in addition to changes to the Commercial Code mentioned above, Japanese accounting standards have been dramatically revised over the past few years — for example, to attempt to move closer to a fair-market-value basis for financial statements. Under pressure from foreign investors, many Japanese companies are now publishing their financial statements in English as well as in Japanese. The English versions, while still based on Japanese GAAP, have the look and feel of financial statements issued under U.S. GAAP.

In addition, Japanese banks are gradually relinquishing their positions as majority shareholders and focusing on transaction support; there is a movement away from *mochiai* toward relationships that are more adaptable to fluid market conditions; foreign institutional investors are applying increasing pressure for greater disclosure; and domestic shareholders are becoming more demanding. These all reflect a general increase in attention to shareholders' rights.

The question for Japan, then, is not "When?" but "How?" or "What are the best ways to improve governance?" Thus far, the Japanese have relied on optional measures, such as changes to the Commercial Code, compliance with which is strongly advocated but not mandatory. Given the strong attachment to traditional Japanese business practices among Japanese investors, managers and employees, such an approach may be slow in bringing about change. The Japanese will need to decide, given the demands of the global marketplace, whether to give changes for improved governance the force of law.

• China

In his remarks at a press conference releasing the Annual Report of the U.S. Congressional-Executive Commission on China, the Commission's Chairman, U.S. Senator Max Baucus, summed up well the sweeping changes that have occurred in China over the past two decades:

> "...the last 20 years has seen a period of profound change inside China — economic reform and the development of a market economy, decentralization of power, individual Chinese citizens gaining more individual autonomy and personal freedom."[9]

---

[9] October 2, 2002 at www.cecc.gov/pages/annualRpt/baucusComments.php

Perhaps the major change, however, has been the government's refocusing of its priorities. Once concerned primarily about the distribution of resources and the provision of basic social services, today the Chinese government has as its highest priority economic development. China is in transition from a socialist economy to a socialist *market* economy with strong elements of both socialism and capitalism. The state has retained key socialistic elements such as central planning and control, and state ownership of assets in key sectors. However, it has also stimulated competition in other sectors that it feels are productive and that pose a minimum of risk to the state. Controlled competition has paradoxically decentralized much of the control of economic and commercial activity down to the provincial and municipal levels, thus placing control of resources in closer proximity to actual operations.

Such a system might seem to contain irreconcilable tensions. But from the Chinese perspective, the dynamic contradiction between market forces and central planning leads to creative change. This view is possible, in part, because of the unique relationship between the central government and the provinces. Unlike the federal system in the US, where a clear set of obligations govern the relationship between the states and the federal government, the Chinese system is characterised by individually negotiated bilateral agreements between the central government and each province.

Given its distinctive environment, how has China fared with respect to moving forward in complying with global standards of accountability and transparency? In my view, the answer is, quite well. In China there is a vocal, visible and genuine movement toward improving the governance of state-owned assets, developing more accurate and transparent reporting, fighting corruption, and becoming more accountable to the public and to minority shareholders. Laws addressing these ends are being developed, formally accepted and implemented.

For example, the China Securities Regulatory Commission (CSRC) has developed and published volumes of new legislation on various aspects of corporate governance, including the protection of minority shareholders, accounting standards, transparency and reporting. In addition, it has created a complete commercial code in less than two decades and has made very considerable progress in reforming an antiquated accounting system into one which is nearly compliant with International Accounting Standards. The Chinese government has consulted widely with organizations like PricewaterhouseCoopers and others to broaden its understanding of recent developments in global standards. The result has been a body of regulations and other achievements that deserves respect.

New laws and regulations also provide detailed prescriptions concerning other governance-related matters. For example, regulations now require all banks to have boards of supervisors and boards of directors. The boards of supervisors tend to represent the state's interests, while the boards of directors tend to represent the interests of management. Under new regulations, the right to appoint auditors and the committee that supervises the audit, as well as the required participation of the auditors in board meetings, has shifted from the board of directors to the board of supervisors, vesting responsibility for these activities in the state. This is widely viewed as a serious effort to control the potential for corruption.

These efforts and others like them have resulted in some highly desirable changes.[10] However, many challenges remain. The most important center on (1) issues related to state-owned assets, (2) a phenomenon that might be termed "fragmentation," and (3) the evolution of Chinese attitudes toward private property.

With regard to transparency, accountability and other matters of corporate governance, the single largest issue for China is to determine how best to manage the influence and impact of state ownership of assets on independent regulation and on the fair exercise of regulatory authority. The mandate to protect state assets affects regulators across the board — securities regulators, foreign-exchange regulators, tax authorities, environmental regulators and labor regulators. Balancing public and private interests will be complex, and this places regulators in a difficult position with regard to creating a level playing field. It is also difficult, where state-owned assets are involved, for regulators to be strict in their enforcement of regulations, especially where it pushes against local interests.

---

[10] As PricewaterhouseCoopers partner and China authority Ken Dewoskin points out, "China's banks, bureaucracy, SOEs [state-owned enterprises] private sector, and courts are all moving forward with ambitious reform agendas…For example, the large state banks are restructuring their governance mechanisms, being obligated to provide annual reports on their performance and subject to more intense audits, and generally they are being forced to manage their funds in a commercial and responsible way…Against a history of unstable and non-commercial behavior, business practices throughout the economy are moving steadily toward international norms…Foreign-investment restrictions, which have been ad hoc, non-transparent and subject to different interpretations in different jurisdictions, are moving toward clarity, stability and uniform application." Kenneth Dewoskin, "China in the Next Three to Five Years," *Issues*, at www.pwcglobal.com

China must also address the high level of regulatory fragmentation facing the business community. Frequently, the national, provincial, and municipal regulatory bodies may be at odds with each other. Since local companies are regulated by the municipal governments, a retailer, for example, seeking to create and carry out a national plan, might face confusion with regard to which authority grants permission to build stores. National licensing rules may contradict regulations at local levels, or, as in the auto sector, partnerships and joint ventures are tied to specific locales. Companies operating nationally require regulations with a national scope. However, the market in China is still very much characterized by a provincial set of natural economic territories (NETS) that do not easily fit together on a national basis.

China's economic development has also created a gradual shift in attitudes toward private property. From 1949 to 1979, the prevailing doctrine was that accumulation of private property was evil. With the beginning of economic reform in China, that attitude was revised to allow the release of some distribution and marketing activity to individuals. By the mid '80s, it had become clear that some individuals had learned to leverage labor and accumulate capital. The government sanctioned this development, and these so-called rich peasants were held up as examples of the power of individual industry. By the 1990s, this movement had accelerated and wealthy individuals and private companies began to emerge. Slowly but surely, this newly activated private sector began to exceed the productivity of the state-owned sector.

The problem, however, is that the emergence of a productive and successful private sector has done little, if anything, to loosen the grip of power exercised by the Communist Party in China. There are no independent watchdog agencies in China. The Party can intervene in courts to influence the outcome of a case if it feels that national interests are at stake. The Party plays a role in the decisions of all regulatory authorities. And the Party remains a key factor in deciding whom the government appoints to run the major regulatory agencies and major businesses. If serious governance reforms are to continue to take hold in China, a reasonable balance must be struck between the interests of the Party and those of the private sector. The system must work to create genuine independence for key regulators in banking, securities, insurance, telecommunications, aviation and other core sectors. A small step in this direction would give powerful new meaning and importance to all of the hard work Chinese authorities have accomplished over the last 20 years in creating a robust canon of commercial laws and regulations.

Given China's incredible success and the prospects for that success to continue, it is clear that the obstacles to improving transparency, accountability and other matters of governance are not insurmountable. Powerful incentives to continue to improve are in place. They include the impact and force of domestic market activity, the emerging and important government-led campaign in China to encourage Chinese enterprises to acquire foreign assets, and China's accession to the World Trade Organization.

Domestic market activity and proximate market activity, such as that occurring in Hong Kong, are putting a great deal of pressure on China to improve governance. Moreover, exposure to global capital markets has been a powerful force for change within Chinese enterprises. In search of capital, large Chinese companies have had to comply with International Accounting Standards in a comprehensive way. This change in how financial activities and results are being reported is filtering down and penetrating company operations. In addition, to succeed, these companies must become more competitive and this requires improved earnings, growth and product development within a context of greater transparency and accountability.

Transparency will also be enhanced by an emerging and significant campaign on the part of the Chinese government to encourage Chinese businesses to acquire assets abroad. This type of acquisition has been occurring for about a decade with a focus on natural resources, such as gas or mineral rights, paper-pulp and even agribusiness.

Chinese businesses, however, have now begun to look beyond natural resources as prospects for acquisitions. They are, for example, interested in acquiring technology companies in order to bring manufacturing capability back to China, where manufacturing is less expensive. They are looking at distribution and retail capability in advanced markets like North America in order to gain more control over brands and channels to market. Such initiatives force companies to operate more transparently. They are under pressure to achieve a level of compliance higher than any currently required in China. Chinese companies expanding into closely regulated foreign business environments, where regulators are more strict and even-handed than in China, are subject to powerful, positive pressure to improve their understanding of what it means to operate successfully in a well-regulated environment.

Lastly, China has committed to a higher level of transparency by virtue of its accession to the World Trade Organization (WTO). After a little over a year, some would say that China's report card is mixed. However, none would deny China's progress when considering that it is its first foray into an environment that requires compliance with an international set of rules and regulations. While some trading partners have complained about China's interpretation of provisions on agriculture, telecommunications and financial services, overall, its compliance efforts have been laudable. In response to WTO requirements, China significantly rewrote its trade regulations, reorganized its Ministry of Foreign Trade and Economic Cooperation (MOFTEC), and then merged MOFTEC and the former State Economic and Trade Commission into a new, streamlined Ministry of Commerce. In addition, a newly established State Bank Regulatory Commission has taken over responsibilities from the People's Bank of China to regulate banking. This represents a strong push to address banking-sector solvency, governance and reporting problems. China's membership in the WTO, which exposes the country to the glare of the international spotlight, will only support China's long-term move toward significant enhancements to corporate governance.

What does the future hold with respect to transparency, accountability and other governance matters in China? China, like its neighbors, will need to continue to make progress. It will need to strengthen its judicial function so that commercial issues can be litigated and arbitrated in a way that is less political than it is today and more responsive to commercial realities. As long as politically driven preferences continue to trump legal remedies, progress will remain at a slow pace, and could even threaten economic growth.

Luckily, the likelihood is that commercial law in China will be strengthened and reporting will be improved. However, while China will evolve toward a new model of capital aggregation, corporate governance, transparency and accountability, it is not likely that China's model will resemble in all respects those of the U.K. or the U.S. More likely, China's model will evolve in the direction of its more transparent neighbors — Hong Kong, Singapore and Japan. In these economies, transparency — or the lack thereof — is influenced by complex structures of public and private entities, known as Bamboo Networks. The challenge will be to achieve a level of transparency within an environment that has inherent conflicts of interest owing to its very structure.

A global issue

While Asia has unique opportunities and problems, improving corporate governance and public reporting is not strictly an Asian issue, nor is it exclusively a U.S. or European issue. It is a truly global concern. As Tunku Abdul Aziz, of Transparency International, has cogently observed:

"The information age has arrived, and societies that are unwilling to accept this new reality, as part of the global business equation, are inflicting serious economic injury upon themselves. The floodgates of global information are opening, and no power can reverse the process."[11]

Nor, I suspect, would any society want to. The globalization of business has created a common set of goals to which all business enterprises aspire, regardless of geographic location. All companies doing business globally want increased share value, better management, access to new capital and more long-term investors. Achieving these objectives means embracing global standards and regulatory reform, increasing credibility, protecting investors and understanding concepts of sustainability such as the triple bottom line (financial, environmental and social). In short, achieving these objectives requires becoming more transparent and accountable.

A global solution with regional implications

At PricewaterhouseCoopers, we view transparency and accountability as global issues that each economy will approach in its own unique manner based on their own characteristics. However, we view transparency and accountability as integrally related to public trust and investor confidence in corporate information, which are the basis for healthy capital markets. For this reason, a common framework is needed to ensure a positive response.

Less than a year ago, I published a book that introduced two new models designed to strengthen public trust in corporate information.[12] While this book responded to the crisis in investor confidence caused by several dramatic corporate and audit failures in the United States, my co-author and I had the longer term in view. It will take some time for these models to become widely known, discussed, adapted as necessary and put to use. I believe that they have a strong future in Asia as in other parts of the world, but only Asians can decide to use them.

---

[11] Tunku Abdul Aziz, "Strengthening Integrity: The Importance of Transparency and Accountability in Economic Sustainability", Resource Material Series No. 56. 113th International Training Course Visiting Experts' Papers.

[12] Samuel A. DiPiazza Jr. and Robert G. Eccles, *Building Public Trust: The Future of Corporate Reporting*, New York: John Wiley & Sons, 2002.

• The Corporate-Reporting Supply Chain

Figure 1: The Corporate Reporting Supply Chain

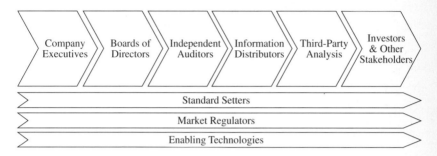

The first of the two new models is the Corporate-Reporting Supply Chain (Figure 1). Not a revolutionary proposal, it is better described as a clarification. The model addresses the roles and relationships of the various groups and individuals involved in the production, preparation, communication and use of corporate-reporting information. The diagram strongly and conceptually illustrates what may be commonly known by those in business and government.

There is a flow forward. Company executives initiate and take responsibility for corporate information intended for public use. In most countries, the board of directors reviews, questions and approves the information, thereby taking its share of responsibility for its correctness, breadth and depth, and relevance. Independent auditors ascertain the quality of information according to local regulations. The information then moves beyond the corporate boundary to be distributed in various forms and channels by professional information packagers. Third-party analysts explore the information and add it to the information base underlying their investment recommendations to clients. And, finally, investors and other stakeholders use the information for decisions ranging from investment to employment.

The Corporate-Reporting Supply Chain is critical to making markets work, and I believe that it has become critical today to perceive the Supply Chain as a whole, in its interdependence and mutual responsibility. In the United States, we have seen what can happen when one or another member of the sequence fails to perform to a high standard. The result was business failures, audit failures, disgraced executives and boards, disruptions to employees' careers and pensions, and the rapid passage of new legislation to address the problems.

Much of this chapter has been dedicated to discussion of new rules, issues and trends in Asia that fit somewhere in this diagram. Cultural and political factors, as well as the relative maturity of individual economies, will naturally affect how the various participants and their roles evolve. But they will all remain embedded in the Supply Chain, and thus are likely to evolve together.

- **The Three-Tier Model of Corporate Transparency**

Figure 2: The Three-Tier Model of Corporate Transparency

The second model, the Three-Tier Model of Corporate Transparency, embodies a set of far-reaching proposals designed to take reporting and auditing to new levels of excellence. It is neither Western nor Asian; it is global in its potential application. But business leaders, regulators and other participants in the Corporate-Reporting Supply Chain in each country will naturally need to explore its implications and practicality in their specific environment.

The Three-Tier Model addresses three related levels of corporate information.

Tier One: Global GAAP

Today's world of global capital markets, global companies, global competition and global investors unquestionably needs one set of truly global generally accepted accounting principles (Global GAAP). If Global GAAP existed, investors could more easily compare the performance of any company, in any country, in any industry. Developing and implementing a principles-based Global GAAP will not only require collaboration among the world's major accounting standards setters, but will also require mechanisms for creating interpretative and enforcement functions that work on a global basis. Information technology and the underlying processes of globalization reshaping corporate management are themselves powerful drivers and enablers of more-uniform accounting practices.

Global GAAP will most likely come about as the next step following the current movement toward adoption of International Accounting Standards (IAS). In Asia this movement is highly visible, as outlined above. For Asia, this progress at the Tier-One level is extremely positive.

Tier Two: Industry-based standards

Tier Two encompasses industry-specific and industry-developed standards for financial and non-financial information, provided in addition to the basic financial information at Tier One. Tier-Two information addresses intangible assets such as human and intellectual capital, as well as non-financial value drivers such as customer-relationship management and the product-development process. Because value drivers differ so greatly between industries, the corresponding measures and standards will necessarily be industry-specific.

In a global business environment, industries in Asia and worldwide are likely to develop along the same lines and to have much the same value drivers at comparable levels of development in terms of size, markets and internal complexity. It is likely, therefore, that industry-based standards will eventually take hold in Asia, and a sign that this is so is already evident in Malaysia's Capital Market Masterplan, which argues for the development of industry-specific, non-financial information.

Tier Three: Company-specific information

Information at Tier Three is unique to each company. It includes information on strategy, projections and plans, risk-management practices, corporate governance, compensation policies and performance metrics. While well-defined external standards cannot be developed for Tier-Three content, general guidelines for content, as well as external standards for formatting such information, certainly could be developed.

In Asia, the Tier-Three concept faces significant challenges. Though gradually changing, political pressures and traditional business approaches and company structures still serve as impediments to greater transparency in this dimension of corporate activity in many Asian economies. However, pressure from foreign investors and intensified scrutiny resulting from increased globalization will inevitably bring about greater transparency at the Tier-Three level.

A more integrated, fuller information set

The Three-Tier Model of Corporate Transparency advocates that companies evolve toward providing investors and other stakeholders with a much broader range of information than financial-reporting regulations currently require. It also argues that these key users of corporate information will benefit only if companies communicate the information in an integrated fashion that provides a holistic view of the enterprise.

But it is important to note that the Three-Tier Model is not a one-size-fits-all solution for every country. Specific economies will always have unique characteristics and country-specific needs. As earlier pages of this chapter have stressed, there is no Asian trend or Asian perspective as such. Rather, each economy is moving toward greater levels of disclosure and improved governance in different ways at different speeds, according to their particular circumstances of culture, politics or economy. Western economies are also subject to their own timetables.

I do argue, however, that the notion that lies at the core of the Three-Tier Model of Corporate Transparency — the free flow of accurate information — is universally desirable and, as countries develop, prerequisite to the formation and maintenance of stable, peaceful, productive and prosperous societies.

Three values: Transparency, accountability, integrity

Good governance and improved corporate reporting can be achieved only in an environment that encourages a spirit of transparency, a culture of accountability and people of integrity. In my view, these three values support and enable all of the progressive efforts discussed in this chapter.

• Spirit of transparency

Every member of the Corporate-Reporting Supply Chain must embrace a spirit of transparency. All must agree to be as forthright in their own communications as they can, keeping in mind the true purpose of such communications. For example, rather than using communications to attempt to manage market expectations and outcomes, company executives should report on all important value drivers honestly and completely. All other Supply Chain participants should do the same.

• Culture of accountability

Every member of the Supply Chain should try to create a culture of accountability. Each group must hold itself accountable for fulfilling the responsibilities it has to all others: management, for producing relevant and reliable information for shareholders; boards of directors, for ensuring that management (and the board itself) lives up to this obligation; independent auditors, for ensuring the objectivity and independence of their audit opinions; and analysts, for producing high-quality, unbiased research. Investors and other stakeholders must also hold themselves accountable for the decisions they make.

• People of integrity

None of this will work without people of integrity. Practicing the spirit of transparency and establishing a culture of accountability cannot happen without individuals who are truly committed and up to the task. Rules, standards, frameworks and theories can go only so far. Ultimately, what truly matters are the decisions and actions of individual people. When individuals demonstrate personal integrity, that integrity will be reflected across entire economies and in society at large.

18

CORPORATE GOVERNANCE
The Role of the Board in Improving Management

Chang Sun
Managing Director, Warburg Pincus, Hong Kong

 The issue of corporate governance generated a great deal of attention following the bursting of the speculative stock market bubble of the late 1990s and early 2000. During this period, a number of business executives had substantially enriched themselves while their companies witnessed precipitous drops in performance metrics and equity values. This negligent, if not outright criminal, behavior went largely unchallenged by boards of directors.

Corporate governance is a generally accepted set of institutional guidelines that oversee the direction and performance of corporations. The principles of corporate governance ensure the protection and equitable treatment of shareholders, enforce disclosure and transparency of financial performance, establish independence from management, stipulate accountability to shareholders and outline responsibilities of the board of directors.

This chapter describes some of the consequences of ineffectual corporate governance and offers suggestions to strengthen the role of the board of directors in enforcing these policies.

The concept of corporate governance evolved with the development of capital markets and the growth of the modern corporation, which emerged as the preferred business organization during the Industrial Age. Owners of growing family enterprises embraced the corporate model as a way to maintain control over increasingly large and distant operations, and to accommodate the eventual transition of ownership without disrupting operations. Individual or family owners used the corporation to seek increasingly larger amounts of equity capital from thousands of individual investors, who wanted full equity participation but complete freedom to trade their shares, even if it meant they had no say in the management of corporate affairs.

In highly developed capital markets such as the United States, the insatiable appetite for funding and the emergence of large public corporations led to the wide distribution of fractional ownership of companies. This was facilitated by financial intermediaries, who sold large amounts of corporate bonds and stocks to tens of thousands of individual investors.

The job of managing business affairs was left to corporate officers, who assumed greater strategic and operating responsibilities as shareholders increased in number and became more geographically dispersed.

This separation of management from share ownership through the securities market created what became known as the "agency problem." Although professional managers are hired to act as the agents for business owners in managing the corporation, the objectives of the two groups often conflict. Adam Smith observed this divergence as early as 1776 in *The Wealth of Nations*:

> "The directors of such companies, however, being the managers rather of other people's money than of their own, it cannot well be expected that they should watch over it with the same anxious vigilance with which the partners in a private copartnery frequently watch over their own."

With little or no ownership interest in the corporation, a manager's reward for working at the company is derived mainly from salary, bonus, perks and recognition by others. Some managers who feel that they are underpaid relative to their contribution might try to use their management positions to maximize their own compensation, often at the expense of the owners' interest.

The fact that a number of managers took advantage of lax corporate governance to benefit themselves at the expense of shareholders was vividly illustrated in a 2002 study conducted by the non-profit advocacy group United for a Fair Economy and the Institute for Policy Studies. The study covered 23 U.S. companies, including Qwest Communications International Inc., Global Crossing Ltd., Enron Corp., and WorldCom, which had their accounting practices investigated by regulators. The study showed that the chief executive officers at the 23 companies made an average of US$62.2 million or a total of US$1.4 billion from 1999 to 2001, the period covered by the study. At the same time, the value of shares at the companies fell by US$530 billion, or 73%, from January 1, 2001, to July 31, 2002. Dennis Kozlowski, CEO of Tyco International, took home total compensation of US$331.7 million during those three years, and Bernie Ebbers, founder of WorldCom, made US$44.1 million in cash compensation and arranged US$400 million in personal loans from WorldCom. Garry Winnick of Global Crossing made US$20.8 million plus US$508 million in selling company stock during the three years covered by the study.

In stark contrast to this rich executive compensation, from January 2001 to July 2002, CEOs at the 23 companies laid off 162,000 workers. Among the companies reviewed in the study, Enron, WorldCom, Tyco, Qwest and Global Crossing wiped out a combined US$460 billion in shareholder value while their companies succumbed to bankruptcy.

In Asia, the challenge of corporate governance is different: companies are less beholden to management but under the control of small groups of powerful shareholders because of high concentrations of corporate ownership in the hands of families or individuals. A study conducted by the Asian Development Bank showed that between 1997 and 1998, the cumulative holdings of the top five shareholders in publicly listed companies averaged between 57% and 65% for Indonesia, Malaysia, Thailand and the Philippines, and 38% for South Korea. Compared to a figure of over 80% in the United States, only 4% to 13% of the listed non-financial corporations were widely held in Indonesia, Malaysia, the Philippines and South Korea, according to a World Bank study in 1999.

With their large ownership positions, it might be assumed that the interests of controlling shareholders of listed companies would be aligned with those of the minority shareholders. Although this is true for shareholders with most of their wealth and assets tied up in the publicly listed entities, conflicts of interest often arise when the controlling shareholders conduct business or financial transactions between two or more public companies, as well as private entities under common ownership. If controlling shareholders abuse their dominant positions to take advantage of minority investors, nothing can be done to stop them. Because of the nature of the Asian markets, the voice of minority shareholders is even weaker than those in the United States.

For example, in August 2002, shareholders of Hong Kong-listed Boto International Holdings Ltd., a manufacturer of artificial Christmas trees and leisure furniture, met to vote on a proposal to sell 70% of its highly profitable, proven business to a buyout firm. The deal would allow the controlling shareholders to keep a 30% interest in the privatized core business while swapping that asset for a money-losing, start-up computer-animation business. Opponents of the sale, including the company's own independent financial advisor, argued that the deal was unfair to the minority shareholders because of the risky nature of the animation business and the low price offered for the business being sold. But the bigger issue from a governance standpoint was how regulators defined "independent investors," the only shareholders eligible to vote on the proposal. Two senior executives of Boto, one a nephew of the head of the family and reportedly holding 60% of the company, were both cleared by stock exchange authorities to vote on the proposal, which passed by a narrow margin.

The independent shareholder who led activists opposed to the sale seemed disappointed but was not surprised. "We would have won if management-related votes were excluded...Until the Stock Exchange and its Listing Committees reflect investor interests and give the benefit of the doubt to independent public shareholders, Hong Kong will continue to be a minefield for investors."[1]

Even when minority shareholders muster ownership equal to or slightly greater than the controlling shareholders, they are often thwarted in their efforts to be heard in key corporate decisions. This is because many listed companies are controlled through pyramid-holding or crossholding schemes. This is where one publicly listed subsidiary is majority-controlled by another listed entity, which is majority-owned and controlled by another entity, forming a pyramid with an ultimate holding company at the top. These schemes allow the owners to use limited amounts of capital to control a number of companies without direct majority ownership in each company.

An example can be found in the Jardines group of companies. With only a 7% stake, Britain's Keswick family has maintained its iron grip on the Hong Kong-based and Singapore- and London-listed Jardines empire, which has extensive interests in Asia and elsewhere. Through Jardine Matheson (Holdings) Ltd. and Jardine Strategic (Holdings) Ltd, the family's takeover-proof crossholding structure controls real estate (Hong Kong Land), hotels and travel interests (Mandarin Oriental and Trafalgar House), food distribution (Dairy Farm, a supermarket chain), a car distributorship (Cycle & Carriage), construction, and financial and other interests.

---

[1] *Finance Asia*, August 20, 2002.

Twice the Keswicks have thwarted attempts by shareholder Brandes Investment Partners of San Diego, California, to break up the crossholding. In its second bid "to unlock shareholder value," in May 2001, Brandes claimed that were it not for the Keswicks' crossholding riddle, it effectively held 32% of Jardine Matheson and 37.5% of Jardine Strategic.

In practical terms, the fund manager still held more than anyone else — with 10.5% of Jardine Matheson and 2.3% of Jardine Strategic — but its proposal to merge the two Jardine units was voted down, as was a proposal calling for shareholders to elect compensation and nomination committees. The merger would have left the Keswick family with up to 25% of the combined company, but vulnerable to a leadership challenge from larger stakeholder Brandes. U.K. fund manager Marathon Investments, which had a combined 1.5% stake in both entities, had supported Brandes for a number of reasons. "Apart from disenfranchising the majority of shareholders," Marathon said, "the crossholdings between JM and JS confer considerable commercial disadvantage on both firms."[2]

Other complaints regarding ineffective corporate governance at Asian companies include limited financial disclosure and insufficient operating information, rude and arbitrary decision-making with little regard for minority shareholders' opinions, and murky dealings with related companies. In addition, controlling shareholders often have businesses outside listed entities, and transactions between listed and unlisted units can create sharp conflicts of interest at the expense of minority shareholders.

Although symptoms vary from Asia to America, the abuse of corporate control by management or powerful factions of shareholders has the same root cause: the separation of ownership from control. If corporate control is in the hands of honest, hard-working people, everyone benefits. If it falls into the hands of greedy, unscrupulous management or powerful ownership factions, then defenseless minority shareholders suffer the most from either a wealth transfer from corporate coffers to those in power and/or a decline in the value of the company's equity.

---

[2] *The Times of London*, May 19, 2001; *Business Times*, Singapore, February 28, 2002.

How should corporate governance be strengthened?

A wide range of reform proposals are being discussed in boardrooms and securities regulators' offices around the world. Suggestions proffered so far by government, regulators, legislators, academics and others tend to fall into three broad categories: (a) for government and legislative bodies to tighten laws, rules and regulations setting out responsibilities of corporate officers and boards; (b) for financial intermediaries and service providers, such as accountants and investment bankers, to shoulder more responsibility and share liability (for example, through a separation of research departments from investment banking); and (c) for corporations themselves to find ways to better align the interest of management with that of the shareholders, and to implement more stringent internal procedures to monitor and regulate executive behavior.

The United States has taken the lead in the campaign to strengthen rules for corporate governance, most notably through the Sarbanes-Orxley Act. However, this legislation has received mixed reviews. "The most noteworthy feature of the new Sarbanes-Oxley law is its nearly total silence on the subject of how corporate boards should do their jobs — and the penalties that directors would face if they don't do so," complained one critic.

Certainly, government action can pressure management and board members to treat their fiduciary responsibilities more seriously, even if Sarbanes-Oxley comes up short.[3]

However, with no universal standard, it is difficult for government entities or securities regulators to go much beyond toughening the existing rules of disclosure and handing out harsher punishment to people who commit fraud, market manipulation or embezzlement. The Sarbanes-Oxley law apparently didn't stop Richard Scrushy, chief executive officer of HealthSouth Corp., the biggest rehabilitation hospital chain in the U.S, from signing statements certifying fraudulent financial statements that artificially inflated earnings by US$1.4 billion since 1999, in an attempt to not miss Wall Street analysts' earnings estimates. The SEC filed civil charges alleging fraud against Scrushy on March 19th, 2003, and HealthSouth's former chief financial officer, Weston Smith, pleaded guilty to fraud charges. But this gives little consolation to the shareholders of HealthSouth who have lost much of their investment in the company,

---

[3] Jeffrey Byron in *Red Herring,* September 23, 2002.

which has already been removed from the S&P 500 index and is at risk of being de-listed from the New York Stock Exchange.[4]

But what can legislation do to protect the interests of minority shareholders when there is no blatant criminal offense?

The obvious solution would be for minority shareholders to stand up for their rights, band together to wage proxy fights, install their own representatives on the board and strike down unacceptable proposals. But with company shares traded on a daily basis, there is a constant shift in the ownership base, making it almost impossible to organize a group of activist shareholders. The only exception is institutional shareholders such as mutual funds, pension funds, insurance companies or private equity funds, which today own about half of all publicly traded stock in the United States.

Ironically, most institutional investors are active traders of company shares, but passive when it comes to corporate governance. They value liquidity and stock-price performance above anything else. The managers of these large funds, which can easily control 10–15% of a company's outstanding shares individually and over 50–60% collectively, focus on short-term financial-performance indicators, but seldom bother to spend time pushing for ways to improve management practices or corporate governance if they detect problems in those areas. Even when they discover problems, fund managers typically "vote with their feet" and move on to their next investment selection rather than using their sizable ownership positions to participate in the resolution of governance issues.

Although not morally correct, fund managers can hardly be blamed for paying attention to stock performance rather than corporate governance — they are compensated according to the daily, monthly and quarterly performance of their funds, not on how well they uphold minority shareholders' rights.

This phenomenon points to a key problem with the governance of publicly listed companies: shareholders want ownership without commensurate responsibility. The majority of public equity market participants want share ownership with limited liability, high liquidity and other people (management) to look after the underlying assets. In other words, they want all the benefits of corporate ownership and none of the responsibilities associated with it. They want to own stocks and want those stocks to perform well — whether they appreciate or not — and they want to be able to buy or sell them at a moment's notice. In order to avoid restrictions on insider trading, they don't want to have their

---

[4] *Asian Wall Street Journal* and Reuters, March 21st, 2003.

representatives on the board, even though they may own a large percentage of the corporation's shares. Thus, they leave the care of their ownership interest completely in the hands of management or controlling shareholders. The rationale behind this approach is that investors believe that they influence management thinking through stock market participation. If management is doing a credible job, investors buy more stock and push up share price. If management fails, or there is a corporate-governance issue, investors sell their stock and let the market signal its disapproval of the company.

It is precisely this kind of "market dynamic" attitude that has created shareholder apathy regarding corporate governance — everyone thinks that somebody else will somehow look after everyone's interest and, in the end, no one does anything. To safeguard their interests, shareholders must become more active in monitoring management's performance, and the group to best champion this role is the board of directors. Some large shareholders, such as private-equity and venture-capital funds, play this role in their portfolio companies and may even continue to do so after their investments become publicly listed. These funds understand the importance of active involvement and accept the lack of liquidity associated with large ownership positions. They typically have their own representatives on the board of directors with a strong voice in corporate decisions.

Unfortunately, the role of active minority shareholders may be severely constrained by what is known as the "independent director" rule. This stipulates that representatives of shareholders owning more than 10% of the outstanding shares cannot serve as independent directors. Since independent directors must constitute a majority on key committees of the board, active shareholders are often ruled out of the most crucial decisions.

The dilemma impeding effective governance is that the majority of individual and institutional shareholders reject taking an active role in managing corporate affairs. A minority of shareholders wants to be involved in the process but is restricted by the independent-director rule. Most shareholders look to members of the board to guard their interests, since the board is the highest authority in the corporation and charged with the task of upholding standards of governance and management performance.

In today's market, one seldom finds the board of directors of a publicly listed company, whether in the United States or in Asia, that adequately meets this standard, particularly as it relates to independence from management and majority shareholders. All too often, the boards are either too pro-management or too weak to act forcefully on behalf of shareholders. Outside board members are usually CEOs who sit on one another's boards, bankers or lawyers who render professional services to the companies and so-called "independent" directors with no business, ownership or other ties to the company.

It is unlikely that directors will favor shareholders when boards consist of CEOs of major corporations who belong to the same business and social circles. They share the same agency problem and have a common interest in protecting their jobs and compensation. At renowned retailer Gap, the chairman sits on the board of Apple Computer, and Apple's CEO Steve Jobs sits on Gap's board. Two other Gap directors sit on the Charles Schwab board, while Chuck Schwab sits on Gap's. With interlocking directorships, it would be all too easy for the clubby CEOs to play the game of "you scratch my back and I will scratch yours." Gap's board, for instance, did nothing about contracts with the chairman's brother to build and remodel stores, and a consulting deal with the chairman's wife.

To guard against boardroom cliques, in 2002, General Electric Company announced new governance policies and stopped the practice of putting CEOs of other companies on its board. Sun Microsystems CEO Scott McNealy and Paolo Fresco, the chairman of Fiat SpA, both retired from the GE board as a result of these changes. GE planned to begin 2003 with 17 directors, of whom 11 were to be independent. The company has also said that, in future, only independent directors would sit on the board's audit, compensation and governance committees and receive no fees other than standard director's compensation.

Recruiting board members with business ties to management creates numerous conflicts of interest, and often leads to an inbred, entrenched elite. At Walt Disney & Co., half of the 16 directors have ties to the company or its CEO, Michael Eisner. It should come as no surprise that the company's compensation committee has made Michael Eisner one of the few CEOs in U.S. corporate history to earn more than US$1 billion over the course of his career. Before his death in February 2002, William Dillard, chairman of Dillard's, one of America's biggest department store chains, presided over a board that included seven directors with ties to the company, including four of his children. Dillard had no nominating committee, which allowed the CEO to hand pick directors. Two-thirds of Dillard's board was elected by holders of privately held Class B shares, making the retailer exempt from NYSE governance rules.[5]

---

[5] Louis Lavelle, *BusinessWeek*, 7th October. 2002.

With close business and personal ties, the executive directors and non-independent directors on the board cannot be reasonably expected to challenge management or controlling shareholders on questionable actions. The job of protecting the interests of outside shareholders, therefore, largely falls to the independent directors.

There are three aspects to the issue of independence. The first is how it is defined — independent of whom and independent to what degree? Securities regulations in many countries define independent directors as individuals that have no financial dealings with or significant ownership in the companies that they serve. In the United States, directors representing shareholders with 10% or more of a company's outstanding shares are not allowed to sit on audit committees, which are required to be composed of independent directors only.

This definition of independence is flawed and needs to be modified since it disqualifies representatives of non-management minority shareholders whose interests the authorities are trying to protect. Independence should be defined as being autonomous from management, not of shareholders. For example, a listed company may have 10% to 20% of its shares owned by a large mutual fund or private-equity fund, which, by virtue of their ownership positions, are naturally motivated to protect and promote the interest of minority shareholders. If the representatives of such a fund cannot serve on the key committees of the board, their ability to counterbalance the power of controlling or management shareholders is severely restricted.

This argument is gaining acceptance. Securities regulators in Singapore have indicated that significant ownership by itself does not destroy a shareholder's independence; issues such as financial dealings and frequent business transactions are much more relevant to the question.

Rather than being restricted in their ability to serve on the key committees, significant minority shareholders should be encouraged to play an active role in enforcing high standards of corporate governance, in monitoring and evaluating management performance and in setting management compensation in accordance with board-approved goals and objectives.

Being financially connected to shareholders is actually a good thing — only by having capital at risk can the directors truly care about shareholder value. Without an ownership link, motivation falls into very short supply. A director who is totally independent of management and owners is left almost wholly dependent on those around him when it comes to making choices on complex and crucial decisions.

The second aspect of the independence issue relates to how, in practical terms, to ensure the existence of true autonomy on the board, even with the "right" definition of independence. Independent thinking and decision-making require a high degree of integrity and strong will-power on the part of independent directors, particularly on controversial issues with personal wealth and reputation at stake.

It is not easy to find and recruit directors who exhibit these qualities and meet the tough standard of independence. With small, individual shareholders too dispersed to organize themselves and propose their own slate of candidates, the job of nominating directors, independent or otherwise, typically falls on the shoulders of management or controlling shareholders. Human nature dictates that they would first consider candidates from their own circles and with whom they feel comfortable. Rather than having direct financial or business dealings with management or controlling shareholders, those candidates usually have close personal or family ties. For these directors to directly challenge or oppose the proposals put forward by the very people who put them on the board, they must overcome strong emotional barriers. If the board seat carries prestige and handsome financial rewards, maintaining a truly independent position at all times will be even more difficult.

It is obvious that the selection of independent directors should not be the responsibility of management or the controlling shareholders. Ideally, the widely dispersed shareholders (the "silent majority") should be united to nominate their own representatives. However, this is difficult, if not impossible, to accomplish for all but the best organized shareholder groups. The only shareholder groups that can attempt to perform this duty are mutual funds, insurance companies, pension funds, endowments or private equity funds with substantial ownership positions in public companies. They should be encouraged to play an active role in corporate governance by nominating their representatives to serve as independent directors.

If they are excluded from serving as independent directors because of the current definition of independence, at a minimum these shareholders should be allowed to form an independent nominations committee that is charged with the mission to identify candidates with no financial or personal ties to management or controlling shareholders. Such a process can certainly produce truly autonomous directors.

Having truly independent directors, however, could lead to the third issue of independence. With neither financial interest nor career development at risk in the outcome of board decisions, independent directors may lack a strong motivation to research the issues at hand thoroughly and make truly informed decisions. They are motivated only by their sense of duty and responsibility to shareholders. Since they are not directly elected by the shareholders and receive no instructions from anyone as to how they can reach "independent decisions," these directors can only rely on their own sense of right or wrong. And there are no penalties or adverse consequences for making the wrong decision or even simply staying away from board meetings. For a large proportion of directors on publicly listed companies, whether in Asia or in the United States, missing board or committee meetings is quite common. Many companies have similar experiences to PepsiCo's, where all three members of its audit committee missed at least 25% of their meetings in 2001.

Assuming they do have a strong commitment to come to board meetings and to devote their attention to crucial business issues, independent directors still need a sufficient amount of information and time to make their voting decisions. This information usually is under the control of management majority shareholders, who are not obligated to pass it on to the directors. It is again up to management's or majority shareholders' sense of duty to give independent directors all the necessary information to make their decision. Even assuming that independent directors do get sufficient and timely information, there is still the question of available time and resources on their part to process, analyze and digest the information provided in order to reach the correct conclusions. As almost all independent directors have other full-time jobs or commitments (directors' fees are quite low compared to their other sources of income), it could be difficult for them to devote the time necessary to conduct independent reviews of the facts in order to arrive at impartial conclusions. Furthermore, since independent directors are unlikely to have their own staff to conduct research and fact-finding, they usually rely on management and majority shareholders for analysis and other information.

Today, consciously or subconsciously, people think of a management team as essential for the success of a corporation. The board of directors is not considered in the same context, but almost as an afterthought, assembled around inside, ex-officio directors, partly to meet regulatory requirements and partly to dress up the public image of the company. In the search for outside directors, therefore, too much attention is focused on the academic and business background of candidates and their compatibility with existing directors. Minimal consideration is given to candidates' organizational, analytical and communication skills.

The system for selecting directors, reviewing their performance and determining their compensation is in need of overhaul. Indeed, it is surprising that a minimum time commitment for directors hasn't been more widely discussed, given the more stringent penalties board members now risk for legal or regulatory lapses. With little monetary inducement, the only pressure on directors to perform derives from whatever sense of responsibility they might have towards shareholders — which may not be much pressure at all. Directors too often, either because they lack the time or the interest, skip meetings and simply go along with management's recommendations, without doing the investigative work required to reach their own informed conclusions.

To ensure that they do perform their duties, directors should be subject to periodical performance reviews and evaluations just like the management team they are supposed to supervise. The directors' degree of financial reward and length of tenure should be based on the results of performance reviews. Negligence and dereliction of duty on the part of directors should be punished in accordance with company by-laws and securities regulations.

Directors should be held accountable, hired and fired in much the same way as other top executives. Choosing good ones requires the same care that companies apply to selecting their CEOs. Directors must also be compensated adequately so that they can afford to devote the time and resources required to discharge their duties properly. To enhance the board's independence and effectiveness, it is advisable to separate the role of the chairman of the board from that of the chief executive officer, with the chairman representing the shareholders and the CEO representing the management team. A separate period of time should be set aside for discussion among the outside (non-management) board members, coordinated by a lead director elected by the outside directors.

Making fully informed and independent choices requires the time and effort that independent directors with outside preoccupations cannot reasonably offer — without either commensurate incentives or the qualities of a saint. Today's complex organizations need independent directors who have the analytical skills and the time to put them to work on behalf of shareholders. Hiring and retaining the right ones requires stringent selection procedures and performance reviews — and the budget to compensate them appropriately. This applies to Asia as much as anywhere else.

A board of directors composed of high-caliber, highly committed people who will devote a substantial amount of their time to the company's affairs can be costly in terms of compensation and company resources. However, if shareholders are serious about enforcing a high level of corporate governance, they must recognize that it is critical to treat the cost of maintaining a high-quality board of directors just like any other business expense. The board is the highest authority in, and an integral part of, the corporation, not a rubber stamp for management or a bouquet of flowers to decorate the walls of corporate corridors.

Markets and human beings being the competitive creatures that they are, the perfect governance regime will probably remain elusive until the end of history. But raising membership standards of boards and redefining the role of independent directors will go a long way toward empowering investors who have been long ignored and, at the same time, restore confidence in our markets.

19

INDUSTRIAL RENEWAL
Reform, Restructuring and Ethical Management

Duk Hoon Lee
Chairman & CEO, Woori Bank, Korea.

 Korea's state-driven development policy since the early 1960s led to an economic system where the *chaebols* became the main engine of the country's economic growth. While lauded for its outstanding success in generating rapid developments in Korea, the *chaebol* system caused a lopsided concentration of economic power. For this reason, the *chaebols* have been held largely responsible for the financial crisis of 1997. With an economic crisis of unprecedented severity, the Korean government has, under a set of corporate-reform programs, implemented various measures to improve the transparency of corporate management. Such regulatory measures, however, may not be completely effective if they are not accompanied by voluntary and practical reform efforts at the corporate level, which includes compliance with fair rules in the marketplace. In other words, corporations must practice ethical management in order to bring ultimate success to *chaebol* reforms.

This article focuses on three issues: first, the role of the *chaebols* in the Korean economy; second, the corporate restructuring program as an institutional setting for the reform of the *chaebols* and ethical management as a practical tool; and third, how to establish ethical management to complete the reform of the *chaebols*.

Understanding the chaebols

• **The chaebol and its growth**

The term *chaebol* is now widely known and generally refers to the large Korean business conglomerates. In general, a *chaebol* can be defined as a large conglomerate with many affiliates involved in different industries and under the management control of a certain individual or family.[1] In Korea, the term usually refers to the 30 largest conglomerates, around which economic power is concentrated.

The aftermath of the Korean War (1950–1953) and the subsequent lack of physical and financial resources presented fundamental difficulties to Korea's economic development. In the 1950s, Korea's industrial production was largely dependent upon aid and official loans from abroad. During this period, economic policy was often driven by non-economic considerations rather than market principles. It wasn't until the late 1950s that a foundation for economic growth was laid out with investments in the light manufacturing industries, which, in turn, began the formation of the *chaebols*.

The first and second economic development plans (1962–1971) were implemented throughout the country. In an underdeveloped and monopolistic market structure, profit-making was first made possible by increasing market share, through which the *chaebols* began to grow and diversify. The *chaebols* also benefited from the export-promotion policies of the government and the subsidized bank loans and foreign capital that were available during this time.

The 1970s was a period of accelerated growth for the *chaebols*. To spur economic growth, the government adopted policies to make direct investments to heavy and chemical industries along with export-promotion policies. By maintaining a close relationship with the government and benefiting from the government-directed credits, the *chaebols* virtually monopolized the markets and accumulated significant amounts of capital during the decade.

The stable economic environment of the 1980s, characterized by low oil prices, low interest rates and a depreciation of the dollar, enabled the Korean *chaebols* to forge new business opportunities. Rather than the wide expansion and diversification strategies that characterized their

---

[1] Dong Sung Cho, *The Korean Chaebol*. *Chaebol* refers to an individual or family that has control over a major Korean conglomerate group with diverse businesses across key industries.

growth in the 1970s, they focused more on fostering existing businesses and entered into the high-tech and financial industries.

In the era of open and global competition that came with the Uruguay Round and the WTO system in the 1990s, the business environment for *chaebols* began to change structurally: current-account deficits increased, oil prices rose along with interest rates, and the dollar appreciated. However, regardless of the circumstances, the *chaebols* kept expanding into the IT and distribution industries instead of consolidating and restructuring unprofitable businesses.

• Their role in the Korean economy

The *chaebols* played a critical role in stimulating rapid development in the Korean economy: a phenomenon often referred to as the "Miracle at the Han River." Overcoming the inefficiency that came from inadequate market mechanisms, the *chaebols* accomplished economies of scale under the state-led economic development policies, and led the rapid growth of the Korean economy, to the point where Korea eventually became one of the Four Dragons of Asia.

It was the *chaebol* system which enabled Korea to overcome its lack of economic resources and achieve economic growth. Within a relatively short period of time, the system transformed the light industry-oriented economy into a more value-added, heavy and chemical industry-oriented structure. The success of the export-oriented growth policy was also made possible by the *chaebol* system. By utilizing trade corporations, the *chaebols* formed an international network to open up new business opportunities in foreign markets. Throughout the recessions and oil crises of the 1970s, the *chaebols* made a significant contribution to improving the balance-of-payment problems and creating employment opportunities. Some *chaebols* were able to develop themselves into globally competitive firms by differentiating themselves with unique technologies and competitive products. These firms have become widely recognized in the international market place and have contributed to creating a positive image of the Korean economy.

• Recognizing the system's problems

A capitalist market economy can be described as a system that maximizes economic efficiency through the allocation of resources based upon market principles. Under the state-led development plan, the *chaebol* system evolved into a mechanism that mobilized scarce savings to the strategic industries. It, therefore, faced limitations in efficiently allocating resources as the economy grew and became more diverse. While the *chaebols* could create wealth relatively easily through diversification when the country's economic system was immature, it became increasingly difficult to create such values under a mature and more competitive economic system.

Since the 1980s, the world economy has been pursuing freer and more open markets. Thus, competitiveness could not be achieved through the *chaebols*' existing management systems. The *chaebols* had expanded the scope and scale of their business by increasing the number of their affiliate companies. This expansion had been achieved through widespread intra-group transactions and cross-debt guarantees among affiliates. The resulting concentration of economic power led to crony relationships between the government and businesses, uncompetitive small and medium-sized enterprises and an inefficient financial system. The problems associated with the *chaebol* system also included the formation of monopolies, rising costs and inefficient investments. Concentrated ownership enabled a small number of major shareholders to monopolize the benefit of business activities and growth, causing an unfair distribution of returns among shareholders and other concerned parties.

• The need for reform

In order to address the negative effects of this concentration of economic power in the hands of the *chaebols*, the government shifted its policy stance from the mid 1980s to achieve a more balanced growth among the economic sectors. For instance, various measures to control the extension and use of bank credits to *chaebols* were introduced. However, the legacy of government-led corporate controls and market intervention made it difficult to fundamentally resolve the problems of the *chaebols*.

Moreover, the partnership between the government and the *chaebols*, which stemmed from the state-led credit policies of the 1960s and 1970s, began to change with financial deregulations in the 1980s. With accelerated liberalization of capital accounts in the 1990s, the *chaebols* began to have direct access to the capital market and ownership of non-bank financial institutions, such as insurance companies and merchant banks. However, in the absence of effective financial supervision and market discipline, the investment behavior of the *chaebols* was not always ruled by market principles. The legacy of implicit government guarantee and the belief that the *chaebols* were "too big to fail" encouraged moral hazard among the chaebols and related parties. The financially weak conglomerates' short-term loans dramatically increased, while excessive investments were made throughout the late 1990s. Indeed major terms-of-trade shocks hit the economy in 1996 and 1997 and the profitability of the *chaebols* deteriorated sharply, which ultimately led to an economic crisis.

With the insolvency of financial institutions and the foreign-exchange crises plaguing the Korean economy, the practices of the *chaebols* came under severe criticism and they were singled out as the main cause of the disastrous economic situation. As it became clear that the crisis could not be resolved under the existing corporate-management scheme, the need for structural and behavioral reform of the *chaebols* became even more urgent.

The reform of the chaebols

• The principles of corporate-sector restructuring

Until Korea was hit by the economic crisis in 1997, the *chaebols* failed to recognize that a new paradigm had been forming in the Korean economy. As a result of the continued focus on volume-oriented growth, the Korean corporate sector was plagued by unprofitable companies with high costs, low efficiency and excessively leveraged financial structures. As these companies started to lose competitiveness against firms in other emerging market countries, the Korean corporate sector began to see the need for greater fundamental restructuring and reform.

To resolve this situation, the Korean government entered into a five-point agreement — a basic corporate-restructuring scheme — with the top five *chaebols* in January 1998, and presented three additional principles of agreement in August 1999. In short, a full-fledged corporate restructuring policy was enforced after the financial crisis to improve corporate transparency and accountability and to reform the structural weaknesses of the Korean corporate sector.

The first main principle of corporate restructuring was directed at improving the transparency of corporate management and emphasized the internal corporate governance mechanism of corporations; the rights of minority shareholders; and the reliability of corporate accounting practices. To strengthen the internal monitoring mechanism, independent outside directors, an independent audit committee and a cumulative voting system were introduced. The rights of minority shareholders were strengthened by easing the prerequisites for exercising the rights and enabling those shareholders to voice their opinion when appointing independent outside directors. Also, a company's obligation to disclose information was strengthened, combined financial statements became mandatory, and strict external audits were exercised in order to enhance accounting transparency.

The agreement to improve transparency in corporate management has obliged corporations to appoint more independent outside directors and increase the ratio of outside directors on boards of directors. As a result of these reforms, the attendance record of outside directors has continuously improved, which has led to enhancing the functional role of the board of directors. Also, the results of corporate accounting audits after 1998 suggest that boards of directors no longer act as a rubber stamp — which again points to the fact that corporate transparency has improved significantly.

The second principle relates to the elimination of mutual-debt payment guarantees. The *chaebols* borrowed excessively from the financial market by obtaining debt-payment guarantees from highly credited affiliate companies. This imprudent practice of mutual-debt payment guarantees among affiliates was the reason why a single case of insolvency could lead to a chain of bankruptcies for a corporation's affiliates. Subsequently, the Fair Trade Law was revised to prohibit this practice and existing guarantees were settled with the exception of amounts subject to extensions according to the Fair Trade Law. The abolishment of such interwoven debt-payment guarantees has been the key to achieving *chaebol* reforms.

The third principle deals with improving the financial structure of corporations. The government believed that the excessive borrowing of large corporations was the main cause of the economic crisis and therefore concluded that the most effective way to restore the competitiveness of Korean corporations was to significantly decrease their debt-equity ratio. For this purpose, the government urged corporations to reduce their debt-equity ratio to below 200% by the end of 1999. To comply with this policy, corporations issued new equity and sold assets, which changed their conventional practice of raising funds through debt issuance.

The fourth principle that the government laid out was the strengthening of corporations' core competence through a firm focus on the core business. To promote this, the government made efforts to eliminate excessive and duplicative investment by *chaebols* and reorganize their business structure according to their core competencies using "Big Deals," the swap of businesses among *chaebols*.

The last principle of the agreement was focused on strengthening the accountability of the controlling shareholders and managers. The government viewed that the management's tendency to overly focus on business expansion was an outcome of a governance structure that had an almighty controlling shareholder who was exempt from monitoring and surveillance. With this in mind, the government emphasized the accountability of the controlling shareholder by establishing a "fulfillment of duty" clause and strengthening the conditions regarding the details to be included in the board of directors' minutes. This was designed to allow the board of directors to function in a more pragmatic and efficient manner.

In addition to the five main principles of corporate restructuring, the government introduced three complementary principles. The first of these was to improve the corporate-governance system of non-bank financial institutions. After the economic crisis, the market share of *chaebol*-affiliated investment-trust companies and insurance companies rose significantly, leading to sharp increases in their assets. The government feared that these institutions would direct their excess funds to affiliate companies. With the new regulation, non-bank financial institutions have to appoint at least half of the board of directors from outside of the company, and introduce compliance-officer and audit-committee systems. In conjunction with this, the rights of minority shareholders were strengthened. Also, the limit of stock investment by investment-trust companies to their affiliate companies was lowered from 10% to 7% of their trust assets, while the investment and loan limit of insurance companies was lowered from 3% to 2% of total assets.

The second complementary principle was the moderation of cross-shareholding and illegal intra-group transactions. In conjunction with the continuous restructuring of the *chaebols*, a restriction on total equity contribution was reinforced in April 2001. Also, a system of public disclosure was introduced so that minority shareholders and creditors could effectively monitor and challenge any unreasonable intra-group transactions and eventually help eliminate them. Furthermore, when the intra-group transactions of affiliates of the top ten *chaebols* exceeded a certain amount, they became subject to the vote of the board of directors.

The third complementary principle that the government laid out was the prevention of illegal inheritance and donations by major shareholders. In order to prevent major shareholders from utilizing new financial techniques to cover up any dealings in illegal inheritances and donations, the government imposed greater transfer income tax on major shareholders' securities trading. A tax was imposed on gains arising from the listing of non-listed shares, while the trading of shares by a major shareholder with over 3% of total shares was subject to a transfer tax of between 20% and 40%, depending on the length of time of possession.

The government's efforts to reform the *chaebols* were effective in that they enhanced the conglomerates' financial soundness by significantly reducing their debt-equity ratio and financial costs. The enforcement of these principles also helped to establish a profit- and cash-flow-oriented management. Furthermore, facilitating corporate restructuring through a main creditor bank can be marked as the beginning of corporate restructuring through market forces. However, the continued delay in the liquidation of insolvent *chaebols* such as Daewoo, and the enforcement of the Big Deal, which turned out to be a poor reworking of old-fashioned industrial policy, proved that the government's corporate restructuring efforts were not yet complete.

Corporate restructuring led by creditor banks

Financial institutions led the corporate restructuring in accordance with the principles outlined above. Financial institutions strengthened their corporate-monitoring function and undertook corporate restructuring to improve and stabilize the chaebols' unprofitable financial structure, which was overly dependent on external debt financing.

• Agreement to improve financial structure

The 64 largest *chaebols* entered into a comprehensive financial restructuring contract with their main creditor banks to reduce their debt-equity ratio to below 200% by 1999. The main creditor bank was then responsible for monitoring whether the agreement was being followed. If the debtor companies failed to reduce their debt-equity ratio to below 200%, the main creditor bank could penalize them by collecting existing loans or denying new loans. Through such aggressive efforts, the debt-equity ratios of all top five groups, excluding Daewoo, decreased from 400% to 200%.

• Implementation of workout programs

In order to assist the rehabilitation of viable companies under workout programs, financial institutions offered debt rescheduling, partial debt forgiveness, debt-equity swap, and injection of fresh loans. The companies themselves made efforts to improve their financial conditions by selling assets, divesting themselves of troubled affiliates, reducing their workforce, and consolidating various subsidiaries. In addition, to share the burden of losses, shareholders agreed to equity write-offs and the issuance of new shares, and major shareholders contributed their private property as well.

Companies that did not perform well during the workout period and failed to meet their management targets were subject to a rigid reinvestigation of their viability. Companies deemed non-viable were liquidated or put under court receivership, if necessary. From June 1998, 83 companies were placed under the workout programs. Of these, 47 were normalized, 15 non-viable companies were liquidated or put under court receivership, and 21 are still under the workout procedure.

- **Establishment of a market-led restructuring system**

In response to the autonomous monitoring of debtor companies' credit risks and disposal of bad debts, financial institutions accumulated significant amounts of loan-loss provision in accordance with the Forward-Looking Criteria (FLC). In addition, the Corporate Restructuring Promotion Act was enacted in August 2001 to stimulate market-led corporate restructuring. The corporate-restructuring vehicle (CRV) and corporate-restructuring company (CRC) laws were also enacted as a market-based mechanism of corporate-sector restructuring, while the pre-packaged bankruptcy system introduced in April 2001 allowed creditors to hand in a previously approved rehabilitation plan immediately after they applied for the liquidation process. The M&A fund was also introduced in March 2001 to facilitate market-led corporate restructuring.

Corporate restructuring by Woori Bank

The government's corporate restructuring efforts, including the implementation of the principles of *chaebol* reforms, were greatly aided by Woori Bank's lead. Woori Bank is the main creditor bank for 16 of the top 35 companies in Korea. As the main bank of these large companies, Woori Bank is striving to establish a transparent corporate-management system by eliminating asymmetries in its information and promoting healthy investment behavior through strengthening the monitoring and screening functions of its management.

Woori Bank has also established an ongoing corporate-restructuring system based on current market information and dynamic, forward-looking factors. The bank is operating an "early-warning system" to detect potential insolvencies at an early stage, using its internal and external resources to collect comprehensive company information.

Woori Bank has been implementing various methods of corporate reform, including management assessment, monitoring, special contracts and a corporate credit-risk assessment system to screen for potentially insolvent companies. Additional methods such as workout programs, court receivership, composition procedures, M&A, and sales have also been used to deal with insolvent firms.

From 1999 to 2002, Woori bank eliminated 16 trillion won (approximately US$13 billion) of non-performing loans from its book through outright sales, collection of loans, and debt-equity swaps. Out of this total amount, outright sales accounted for 6.7 trillion won, write-offs accounted for 5.9 trillion won, collection accounted for 2.1 trillion won and debt-equity swaps accounted for 1.3 trillion won.

Unfinished reform and the imperative of ethical management

• Unfinished chaebol reform

If one were to assess the success of the measures taken by the Korean government to reform the *chaebols*, it would be fair to say that they have only been partially achieved thus far. The existing principles of corporate restructuring focus on establishing an institutional setting that would enhance business transparency. However, it is not possible to complete a more fundamental corporate reform without firmly establishing management practices that are devoted to transparency and fair competition.

To facilitate economic activities and maximize efficiency, companies should strive to establish an institution that can enhance transparency by improving corporate governance, establishing transparent accounting procedures and practices, and establishing a management system that values its shareholders. However, we will only be able to achieve ultimate success when management, shareholders and employees abide by this institution. In this regard, ethical responsibility has become as important as economic or legal responsibility. Ethical management is now regarded as a new code in business strategy.

• Ethical management as a core business strategy

The supplier-oriented economy has recently been transformed into a customer-oriented market, where companies with limited transparency and those that do not abide by market principles lose the trust of investors, consumers and the market. Consequently, such companies must bear the brunt of plummeting stock prices and borrowing difficulties that could result in a failure of their business. Transparency affects a company's continuing viability and ethical decision-making is now considered to be as important as economic decision-making.

We are now in an era where companies must strive to be socially responsible, committed to changing business practices and decision-making structures in accordance with ethical standards. Ethical management is now an essential element of corporate competitiveness and a necessity for enhancing corporate value.

• Ethical management of Korean companies

Korean companies have increasingly begun to realize the importance of ethical management as a tool to maintain corporate values and as a survival strategy. The demand for management transparency in the global market has driven corporations to adopt a management strategy centered on ethics.

A recent survey on corporate ethics conducted by the Federation of Korean Industries (FKI) showed that 49.7% of the 292 respondents had already established and were following a corporate-ethics charter. The survey indicates that the market value of firms that practiced ethics management was significantly higher than that of firms that did not. For instance, the four-year average stock price growth rate of corporations that have an ethics-management department was 46.3%, while the growth rate of corporations that neglected to establish an ethics charter was only 22.1%. This shows that the long-term stock price of corporations who aggressively implemented ethics management exceeded the average market price. Indeed, the capital market pays a premium for transparent and ethical management.

Case Study 1: Shinsegae Co., Ltd.[2]

Shinsegae is a distribution specialist and the leader in its field. It offers various online and offline services to customers through department stores, a discount-store chain, and a cyber shopping mall, based on a strong logistics infrastructure.

During the economic crisis in 1997, Shinsegae experienced mounting difficulties managing its business. Although Shinsegae continued to restructure its businesses, profitability declined substantially in 1997. Faced with the unstable business environment, Shinsegae viewed ethical management processes as a core element that could engender a robust and stable income structure, and put them into practice in 1999.

As a first step, Shinsegae consolidated its business contracts with partner companies to establish a fair-trade system and then went on to implement a self-regulatory fair-trade operations plan, voluntarily enacting 10 general principles for fair and transparent trade. From January 2000, Shinsegae began to monitor cases of bribery as part of its aggressive corporate ethics policy. In February, the management held corporate-ethics workshops to raise the employees' awareness of best practices. In December 2000, Shinsegae encouraged employees to practice ethical management by rewarding those who were exemplary in the area. In March 2002, it established a separate department with responsibility for implementing detailed plans of ethical behavior and management.

As a result of these measures, work procedures have become more transparent and have led to increased business productivity. Another benefit that Shinsegae reaped from its efforts to promote fair trade has come in the form of higher-quality services and products from partner companies. Such developments have greatly heightened the employees' sense of pride, while performance-based incentives have increased their satisfaction with the company. Shinsegae has also succeeded in attracting new investment from shareholders by

---

[2] Source: White Paper on Shinsegae's Ethics Management (July 2002).

providing them with transparent investment information. By adopting an openly ethical approach to its management, Shinsegae has enhanced its image and credibility among its customers, shareholders, employees and partner companies. This, in turn, has helped the company to significantly enhance its competitiveness and corporate value.

Case Study 2: Yuhan-Kimberly[3]

Established in 1970, Yuhan-Kimberly manufactures paper and sanitary products and is renowned for its environmentally friendly products, in-depth marketing research, profit reinvestment and sound financial structure. Since its establishment, Yuhan-Kimberly has pursued "quality, service and fair trade" as the fundamental principles of all its business activities. Yuhan-Kimberly realized that these ethical principles could only be achieved when the code of conduct for the whole company was aligned with the values of its employees. Therefore, Yuhan-Kimberly published a code of conduct as a guideline for its employees' behavior when dealing with co-workers, customers, counter-parties and competitors.

In implementing this policy, the company introduced a "Team of 4" duty shift system, which allowed employees more leisure time to recharge themselves and receive training and education. In living up to its ideology of respecting human dignity, Yuhan-Kimberly also achieved increased productivity and improved financial performance.

In addition, for the past 20 years, Yuhan Kimberly has, through its Green Campaign, enjoyed a reputation for being an environmentally friendly company. The Green Campaign has succeeded in educating consumers on the value of environmental, cultural, educational and recreational functions of forestry, an industry which is well worth over US$50 billion per year. This in turn has resulted in creating a deeper interest and more investment in forestry of Korea, which takes up more than two-thirds of the peninsula.

---

[3] Source: Yuhan-Kimberly Investor Relations Department.

Case Study 3: Woori Bank

Woori Bank, the second-largest bank in Korea, is a sound and profitable bank with assets of 101 trillion Korean won (approximately US$81 billion) as of December 2002. Moreover, Woori Bank is among the first financial institutions to adopt advanced financial systems such as RAPM (Risk-Adjusted Performance Measurement), BPR (Business Process Reengineering) and KMS (Knowledge Management System).

Woori Bank is also a leader in ethical management. Woori Bank recognizes that ethical management is a prerequisite for the bank's continued success and respectability. It, therefore, established an ethics-management system, which consists of an internal governance system and an external program to promote the bank's contribution to society. With the management's emphasis on ethics, the bank has established and disseminated a corporate ethics charter, which has contributed to the reform of its corporate culture by reinforcing the ethical behavior of employees and stressing the company's social responsibility.

To ensure its effective implementation, the role of the compliance department has been expanded to monitor the behavior of employees in complying with the laws, regulations and social ethics, to educate management and employees in ethical behavior and to develop strategic plans to implement corporate ethics.

Furthermore, Woori Bank supports various social-service programs created voluntarily by employees. Woori Bank also established the "Woori Sarang Fund" to provide prompt support in the event of natural disasters and is fulfilling its duties as a corporate citizen by contributing a part of its profit to the community. Such practices encourage employees to practice ethical behavior and enhance the bank's image in the community.

Woori Bank is planning to implement a detailed and systematic ethics-management program whereby individual employees can regularly monitor themselves to see whether they are complying with the rules, and under which all details of ethical activities performed by employees can be quantified and fed into an incentive and penalty system.

Establishing ethical management as corporate culture

Transparency in corporate management, which has been promoted as a key measure of *chaebol* reform since the 1997 crisis, can be achieved through establishing ethical management processes and parctices in corporate culture. The key task of a company in a new business environment is how to achieve both economic efficiency, which is related to a company's profit, and social ethics, which is related to a company's social responsibility. Companies must not stop at simply stating the principles of ethics management for the sake of formality. They must first set out a detailed corporate-ethics charter and then establish an independent monitoring scheme to supervise whether their employees abide by the established criteria. Furthermore, if such a system is to be effective it must be understood by, and have the support of, employees. This can be achieved through ongoing education and training in the workplace.

While a voluntary code of practice can work, the effectiveness of ethics management can be maximized when social monitoring and evaluation are brought together. Non-governmental organizations must recognize that corporations are important members of society and require them to fulfill their ethical role as leaders of the society. In addition, financial institutions and credit-rating agencies must place more emphasis on qualitative criteria such as corporate governance and the CEO's management philosophy when evaluating companies.

Conclusion

The Korean economy is currently undergoing a paradigm shift in its economic structure, management schemes and market institutions. In this context, the Korean government has striven to increase the transparency of *chaebols* by continuously improving the regulatory environment and infrastructure and by actively implementing corporate-restructuring programs.

As a result of such efforts, significant progress has been achieved in the corporate sector's financial structures, corporate governance and accounting transparency. The task ahead of us now is to have companies move beyond the government-led reform and continue self-initiated and autonomous restructuring efforts in line with market principles. When efforts to enhance market competitiveness are combined with the implementation of ethical management practices, a truly successful reform of the *chaebols* can be achieved. In this regard, having a level playing field is crucially important, but so too is the ethical behavior of management and employees in implementing a free and competitive market system.

Recently, Korean companies have begun to recognize the critical importance of ethical management in their businesses. However, they have yet to practice it fully. As going concerns, companies should not regard ethics management as a temporary trend but must recognize it as a core strategy for survival. The existing relationship-based financial system is currently in transition towards a capital market-based system. As a result, it is increasingly important for corporations to provide market participants with transparent information and to upgrade management accountability.

For ethical-management principles and processes to be fully integrated into the corporate culture, the CEO's full commitment, vision and leadership are crucial driving forces.

Second, any ethics-management action system must be detailed and systematic. As can be seen from the case studies, it is crucial to establish an organizational unit that is wholly responsible for ethics management to facilitate training and effective internal control. It is also important to establish an infrastructure where the practice of ethical management is such that it is compatible with the values and aspirations of the company's employees.

Third, companies that practice ethical management require society's support. Society must create an environment that encourages and enables companies to fulfill their social responsibilities. The capital markets and the media, too, have a role to play in this, highlighting and rewarding best practice in the area of ethical behavior.

Fourth, financial institutions and credit-rating agencies should differentiate between companies that actively practice ethical management and those that do not. Emphasizing ethical management in this way would also provide greater incentives for companies to practice ethical management.

In conclusion, corporate reforms based on ethical-management practices are critical to the sustained development of the Korean economy as a whole. Only when there is appropriate infrastructure in place that takes full account of this paradigm shift, and only when companies comply voluntarily with the fair and transparent rules of the market, will *chaebol* reform be achieved.

PART 5

Total Ethical Management

20

THE GLOBAL VIEW
Cultural Factors in Cross-National Business: Mitsubishi Motors and the Turn Around

Rolf Eckrodt

President & Chief Executive Officer, Mitsubishi Motors Corporation, Japan

With over 37 years in the automotive business, spent primarily in Europe and South America, I feel privileged to now experience what is perhaps the most fascinating challenge of my career – that of integrating the strengths of Mitsubishi Motors Corporation (MMC) and DaimlerChrysler (DC).

It all started when, in January 2001, the so-called Turnaround (TA) Team arrived at MMC. The aim of these two dozen managers from DaimlerChrysler was to stabilize and then develop MMC, after DaimlerChrysler had acquired a 34% stake in the Japanese auto manufacturer in 2000.

The job of the TA team was neither to "Japanize" DC nor "Westernize" MMC; but, rather, a little in the manner of traditional Asian marriage matchmakers, define the path and the goal that would not only satisfy both partners, but also ensure that this Alliance itself would be fruitful and long-lasting. The aim was to link the benefits each partner can bring into the Alliance and so, in consequence, strengthen it.

Mitsubishi Motors, of course, is a typical example of the phenomenal development of the Japanese auto industry, while DaimlerChrysler is the result of a merger between a German (Mercedes-Benz) and an American (Chrysler) auto manufacturer. But I feel that the attitudes of the two members of our partnership partly typify those of their greater geographic areas.

When, three years ago, our multinational team arrived at MMC, we were told that the first basic difference Western business people would encounter when working with an Asian company was the actual atmosphere of the workplace itself. Asian companies are said to stress the importance of organizational-social relationships; whereas Western corporations prioritize individual tasks and goals.

Mitsubishi, for example, has a long history, stretching back to 1884, when our founder, Yataro Iwasaki, entered the shipbuilding business in Nagasaki, and included the beginning of automobile manufacturing in Japan with the "Model A" in 1917. This was the first mass-produced passenger vehicle in Japan. Since that time, the company has followed the traditional Japanese management system of guaranteeing lifetime employment and organizing promotion by seniority. As a result, when the DC team arrived in Japan we found an organization run along *batsu*, "group" lines. While this system had certain advantages in periods of rapid growth, it had to be re-evaluated in light of the current, global market and its fast moving pace.

Although the Japanese word batsu is usually translated as "group", it has a rather deeper meaning than would normally be recognized in the West. In Japan and Asia as a whole, belonging to a group affects the everyday lives of most people from birth, through school, university, career and even into retirement. Japanese, for example, often emphasize such relationships much more than individual connections.

Non-Japanese have been known to confuse the batsu with a Western-style club, but this is wrong. In Europe and America, for example, people tend to join clubs or societies for enjoyment, comradeship or even personal gain; but in Japan and throughout most of Asia, groups are the very foundations of almost all social functions, and members work for the development of the group rather than simply for the success of the individual. Of course, this bettering of the group is eventually also a bettering of the individual and so can be fully rational even from an individualistic point of view.

One of the things that we had to understand when we joined forces was that a company such as MMC does not consist of one batsu but, rather, a combination of many. This means that individual workers had tended to work toward the success of their own individual groups and without necessarily always considering the success of the company as a whole. What is more, decisions were generally made by all group members, with little responsibility being held by a single person. In other words, the groups were a means of saving face if anything went wrong, so that no single person could be held responsible.

Our first major tasks were business-oriented; namely, to put down a TA plan to bring MMC back to profitability by reducing costs, optimizing processes, finding new markets and re-establishing a line of products, such as the COLT or the GRANDIS in Japan and Europe, or the OUTLANDER in the U.S. We established transparency concerning costs, debt and quality. The result was a company dedicated to new processes, products, a new people-spirit and, finally, profitability.

To achieve this meant strengthening individual responsibility and accountability. The new spirit at MMC made it clear that it is acceptable to make mistakes on an individual basis, as long as everyone learns from those mistakes, and that there is a much stronger feeling of success if a worker can say, "I achieved that," rather than "I was one of the team that made that possible." It was necessary, therefore, to instill a sense of daring and individualism. Our motto is based on an old Japanese proverb which goes: "He who fights may win. He who doesn't fight has already lost.

Another challenge faced when adjusting the management culture at MMC was the traditional formality of relationships, even within a company. In general, Japanese tend to have two forms of communication. The first is called *tatemae*, which means the formal, polite face one shows to whoever one is communicating with. The second is *honne*, wherein lie your true feelings. Under normal circumstances, Japanese employees tend to use the formal, polite method of communication when talking to management and often hold back their true feelings — sometimes until it is almost too late to find solutions to their problems.

As a result of this, MMC now has a policy of encouraging everyone to speak their minds. When, for example, I did my first rounds of factories and offices, I made it a point to put my arms around people, draw them close and ask what they really thought. This kind of behavior had long been considered taboo in Japan, as it was uncommon to touch colleagues in such a direct manner and even to get someone to say something that had not been checked by the batsu. However, the rewards were great and almost instantaneous. Being a *gaijin* (foreigner) in Japan has certain advantages. Most Japanese do not expect gaijins to act in a traditionally Japanese way and, in certain respects, they seem to be saying to us, "Go ahead! Break the taboos and show us what you can do."

On a personal basis, my way of communication has always been to be direct and not hide my real feelings or expect the employees to do so, either — and it has borne fruit. Consequently, our Japanese colleagues in our factories, now even express some kind of disappointment if I do not always go for close, direct and personal contact. As a result, many workers now feel safe in expressing their opinions on an individual basis. Our key words in this respect are "openness" and "transparency."

Another challenge was a sense of isolation that many of my Japanese colleagues — particularly middle management – experienced when faced with rapid and comprehensive change. Masuyasu Kitagawa, a former member of the Lower House and former governor of Mie Prefecture, now Professor at the School of Public Management of Waseda University, recently wrote in this context that Japan must "reject the basis mentality that has shaped postwar politics and dare to aim for a new sphere by welcoming 'discontinuity'". This does not mean the end to tradition; rather, it means re-inventing oneself, a strong Japanese tradition in itself.

Before the DC team, composed, incidentally, of more than 10 nationalities, arrived at MMC, the path from joining the company to retirement was relatively smooth if you didn't rock the boat. Promotion would come according to years served, with the result that many middle managers in their 40s and 50s were very satisfied with their jobs for life and their cozy "salaryman" existences. It was, therefore, a challenge when they were suddenly exposed to changes imposed upon them by a management team that had not come up through the ranks.

There is an old proverb in Japan that says that "the nail that sticks up has to be hammered down." That is to say, one individual cannot be allowed to act differently from all the others because it will cause discomfort. I believe, however, that one of the major tasks of any management team, wherever one works, is to explain that, although the "nail story" may be true for shoes, it is not necessarily so for companies and societies. In fact, it can often be said that the nail that sticks up (and hurts!) causes people to think about other possible solutions. Being different is, I believe, an advantage and being an irritation can result in success. We wouldn't, for example, have pearls if tiny grains of sand didn't cause oysters to take action to stop the irritation.

In regard to the problem of lack of individual initiative, we established a system of payment based on ability rather than seniority, making us a pioneer in the Japanese auto industry. Salary and promotion are now based on individual performance and less influenced by factors such as age or time spent with the company. We introduced this system for managers in 2002 and extended it to all company employees in April 2003.

At MMC we develop leaders who not only stand up for what they believe, but who are also capable of making decisions by themselves and who, in effect, surprise other people with innovative market- and customer-driven ideas. Traditionally in Asia, decisions have been reached by consensus. Conversely, in the West decisions are made by the majority, and although some people may be bitterly disappointed, even more will be satisfied. One point I found interesting in MMC, and which showed that Japanese individualism is on the rise, was that when we asked (in a company-wide survey) about the willingness to move ahead, most people said that they were willing to change, but that they didn't think their colleagues were. This shows that on an individual basis, Japanese employees are willing to face new challenges, but, because of the old group philosophy, some might be reluctant to discuss ways of doing so with their close comrades, and, therefore, assume that those fellow workers would resist change.

Regardless of the actual final decision, one other difference that the Western team at MMC has faced is simply the style of discussion. In Japan, there has traditionally been a form of continuous informal communication between all levels, from managers to salaried employees, with each group eventually promoting a stance that would then be further discussed with other groups, with a formal meeting basically only "rubber-stamping" a consensus. In the West, on the other hand, in more formalized meetings, all participants express their views, with a decision actually being made at a particular meeting.

Both of these systems have advantages, but the Japanese method suffers from some specific shortcomings. Opinions are not aired in open session, so misgivings by individual members of small groups are never heard by all involved in the process.

To enable us at MMC to make the most effective decisions, however, we now have a policy that encourages all views to be brought into the open. We are breaking down the wall of intuitive, nonverbal communications in the hope that it will lead to a more innovative management style. Fujio Mitarai, President of Canon Inc. and Vice Chairman of the Japanese Business Federation (Nippon Keidandren) recently put it this way: "Management boils down to communication. Senior managers have heavy responsibilities. They should speak up, listen carefully, and determine whether their message is being effectively conveyed."

Another important point is the use of symbols. Japan puts a strong emphasis on slogans, rituals and gestures, a fact seen, for example, in the use of bright-colored flags with paroles at cultural events and in front of shops. The new MMC has started using them in a new fashion. For example, we handed out to all employees so-called Quality Cards displaying the figure "110%", a green card everyone can put in his or her wallet or breast pocket. What it reminds us of is to improve and "give" more than 100% concerning all our processes and products.

A further enigma of Japanese middle management, particularly with the seniority-based promotion system, is that those at the top have sometimes acted as "brakes" on radical change, as Masao Hirano, head of McKinsey's Tokyo office put it. Having served their time, so to speak, in the channels of promotion, they traditionally did not want to be seen as the directors who introduced radical change. This has resulted in a stifling of fresh and often innovative ideas from younger employees who are much lower on the ladder of power. As a result, we are fast-tracking a number of young employees who have proven original thinking and won over the proven, elder managers. It is not a question of "old" or "young," but one of an open vs. a closed mind.

So far, I have been discussing some of the challenges that our Western team faced in understanding traditions at MMC. There is, on the other hand, much that Westerners can learn from Asia and its way of doing business. Japan, for example, has an extremely long and strong history of craftsmanship and innovation — one has only think of such skills as simplification ("Walkman"), modules (from architecture to car building), minimalism (from stone gardens to processors) or portability (from 12th century *yatata* carrying cases for brushes to today's PDAs — "personal digital assistants"). "Japanese design" is nothing less than a brand in itself, and *kaizen* and "just in time" are concepts developed by the Japanese auto industry and copied by other manufacturers the world over. The simple fact that the Japanese car industry is now the second-largest in the world, and has become so in a matter of a few decades, proves the point. Just as important are the sense of politeness, fairness, pride and the style of doing business, something partially lost in the harsh reality of, say, the U.S. business world.

We have to change our mindset. We could begin by halting our geographical specificity. On American maps, for example, the East Coast of the U.S. is in the center; on German maps the center is a line running through the middle of my home country, and, of course, on Japanese maps the Japanese islands are at the heart. We all tend to be geocentric, and this can result in an inability to value the abilities and standards of those who appear on the edges of our own individual maps. In other words: It's time to refocus!

At MMC, we are trying to get all employees, both Japanese and non-Japanese, to take a global view that allows them to understand the values and cultures of their partners. Japan, for example, is a very crowded country where it is very difficult to create one's own extensive personal space. The result of this, of course, is that the Japanese have developed a social code that allows them to live in close proximity without encroaching too much on private space. There are, therefore, rules of courtesy. Typical of this is bowing. Such as rules on how low one should bow to another, depending mostly on position and seniority.

I have a personal view of bowing, which I have explained to my employees: "Bowing, yes! Bending, no!" This means that I will always bow to others as a form of courtesy, but I will not submit to someone simply because of seniority, or, even more important to me, expect them to lower their self-esteem by submitting to me.

What this example tries to prove is that the key to personal relations between the East and the West lies in remaining true to one's self while accommodating others. This is especially true because we have very different traditions and perspectives. It would be false to just gloss over them.

This is one of the key findings in any sort of merger or alliance during the last decade. In growing together, cooperating depends on more than just a new and fancy organizational chart. The new management must keep and develop the identity of its company while, at the same time, strengthen the self-confidence of its management.

One example of this that our Western management team has found since joining MMC is the attitude of many employees toward the use of languages – particularly English. Foreign businesspeople in Japan are often told that it is difficult for Japanese to interact globally because they are poor in English. On a personal basis I point out that I am basically in the same boat as my Japanese friends; I have to speak in a language that is not my mother tongue, and that instead of complaining about it, we all should get on with improving our abilities. Many of my foreign colleagues still speak very little Japanese. I think this is a pity and I encourage them to improve their language skills by offering language courses. However, we are often accompanied by interpreters who make communication easy as long as all participants are willing to speak their true minds and not hide behind polite formality. Even so, we tell all our employees that English is without a doubt the lingua franca, or global tongue. But if employees have true professional abilities, we will support them despite a lack of English, while encouraging them to improve their language skills because such skills will enable us all to better interlock and thus understand the rest of the world.

Up until the '70s and '80s, Japan's mission was to catch up with the West — specifically, with America. Now that Japan has achieved that, particularly on economic terms, some commentators seem to be sensing a lack of orientation as to where the journey should lead. This has been worsened by a decade of recession after the burst of the so-called bubble economy in the late '80s and early '90s. It seems strange that I, as a German, have to encourage my Japanese colleagues and friends by telling them that, despite those years of recession, they are still the world's second-largest economy and the world's leading creditor nation — to name but two of many "No. 1 positions" for Japan — something of which they should be extremely proud. But I see a lack of confidence. A poll by the Japanese government, released in August 2003, showed that a record high proportion of seven in ten Japanese are worried about their livelihoods; two-thirds of those polled said they "worry about their everyday lives," the highest since the early '80s.

This sort of feeling might be linked to the consensus society which our multinational team is changing at MMC, and which is also changing throughout society as a whole. While everything is going well, consensus is fine, because no-one really suffers; but when things turn more difficult, as they have with the Japanese economy over the past 10 years or so, people begin to think of their own individual safety and comfort, and consensus diminishes.

One thing that I have learned is that for the Japanese, the path (*do*, as in judo, kendo, etc.) can be seen as more important than the destination. So management must accompany the employees along this path. During this process a strong management can reinforce the clear responsibilities of the individual as opposed to the traditional form of group responsibility. That is to say, a good manager in Japan must make the processes open, transparent and achievable, with practical solutions taking precedence over perfection.

My time in Japan has proved to me that Germany and Japan have things to learn from each other as both countries are faced with a pressing need for drastic reforms. Both "Japan, Inc." and "Germany AG" have empty coffers and both are under strong international, as well as domestic, pressure to reform. In fact, Peer Steinbrueck, Prime Minister of Northrhein-Westfalia, the largest German Federal state, drew a very good (if somewhat simplified) analogy when he referred to the resistance to reforms in German as a sumo wrestling match, saying, "We must finally grab hold of the fat guy."

So what do we have to offer each other? A few examples:

- My home town Berlin is proud of its transportation system, but Tokyo represents the real role model in punctuality, security and comfort of public transport.
- In fuel-cell development, Germany is striving for the perfect solution, whereas Japan is already producing fuel-cell hybrid vehicles as an interim step.

- In biotechnology, Germany is a leader, while Japan's Prime Minister Koizumi has declared it an area for further development.
- And Germany can be seen as a gateway to Eastern Europe for Japan and Japan as a gateway to China for Germany.

And what does the Alliance offer both MMC and DC?

Even in today's economic climate, Asia represents a truly titanic market and one that is growing faster than anywhere else. This is why the global partnership of Mitsubishi Motors and DaimlerChrysler is so vital. There is little doubt that the number of auto-makers throughout the world will continue to decrease. We are now witnessing a sort of endgame in the consolidation process of the automotive industry. In 1960, there were 62 independent car manufacturers; in 1980, 36. Today we have 11. The six largest account for 78% of the world market. And the process is continuing.

The future will, without doubt, be won by the multinational alliances that have the products which national markets need and the flexibility to meet those needs; that share parts and components, even platforms; that do R&D together, thus aligning new ideas in design, production and technology. Only those types of cooperation and alliances will allow for strong scale effects which in turn lead to further cost advantages. To do this, we must understand the world as a single, global market, while taking advantage of the national talents we can all bring to the whole.

It is important for our Alliance to argue against any sort of simplified comparisons between Japan and Germany, between the way in which both cultures do business and "talk car." But by learning from one another and sharing with each other, we at MMC and DC believe that our two companies can take on the world – and win – with an open heart and an open mind.

21

A MODEL FOR ASIA

Frank-Jürgen Richter & Pamela C.M. Mar

In 1992, one year prior to releasing this book, we published *Recreating Asia: Visions for a New Century*[1], in which we envisioned a renaissance of ideas in five principle areas of public life. We betted on an Asia that:

- is an equal-opportunity territory
- has clear-sighted leaders with vision and focus
- has transparent governance frameworks and solid governing institutions
- is tightly integrated economically and globally at ease
- remains respectful of national traditions and cultural distinctions

Since then, we have seen much of the promise of these ideas dissipated or lost, albeit, in most instances, not because of a particular party or person's failing, but due to a general coincidence of unfortunate circumstances. Many global and regional disappointments can be linked to the SARS epidemic, to recession, to the war in Iraq, to the rocky roads to trade liberalization, to the crisis in North Korea. We have become painfully aware that seemingly unrelated events can reverberate on distant shores and in different sectors.

Where the downfalls have been traceable, we find that, in almost all cases, ethics — or rather the lack thereof — has been involved. Asia's ethical void has echoed loudly in the past year, and the many instances we

[1] Frank-Jürgen Richter and Pamela C.M. Mar, R*ecreating Asia: Visions for a New Century*, John Wiley & Sons, Singapore, 2002.

cited in the Introduction to this book are only the start of what could be a very long list. This is no coincidence. In fact, contemporary Asia's ethical void spoke first through the Asian financial crisis, and remains an open issue.

Thus, if the first book was generally about recreating Asia, this second is a more specific and modeled attempt to propose recreating Asia through ethics. TOTAL ETHICAL MANAGEMENT (TEM) proposes both a re-grounding in the fundamental values which have supported Asia's development thus far, as well as an orientation for the way forward. We hold that while Asia's fundamental values were once sufficient for a simpler time of the past, they alone are insufficient for the intensely globalized and interconnected world that we all face. What is needed, and what we have tried to provide, is a roadmap for undertaking the transformation that will embed ethics into everyday life across Asia.

The corporate sector receives special attention, not because it is more corrupt but only because it has become integral to so many aspects of society and public life. Two centuries ago, companies adopted much more the "silo" approach: independent operations, and direct, uni-planar contacts with clients and partners. That has moved through an age of alliances and reaching out to selected groups (starting with government), and has now entered the age of multi-layered and cross-national social contacts. Thus, areas that were almost devoid of business presence would today, have to deal with business on a regular basis. Even when dealing in social organizations or governments, the "best practices" which have been honed in the business world — such as accountability, institutional governance and project management — have become part of the operating language. We witness today the increasing integration and collaboration of business, government and other actors in society, to jointly address challenges in the contemporary landscape. A new ethical grounding — in which all actors play a part — will have benefits across society and make such collaborations successful. This is the wave of the present and future.

Observers will rightly note the similarities, at least in form, between Total Ethical Management and Total Quality Management (TQM).[2] TEM goes beyond TQM, which is a mere expression of re-aligning processes along the maxim of quality. The principles of TQM, for instance, involve people, examine their work flow and develop ways to improve their output, thus eliminating waste. All corporate activity, especially in large organizations, is geared towards quality, enabling managers and employees to focus on achieving excellence in operations, with positive results for customer and client satisfaction. Unfortunately, in some instances, intense focus had the effect of creating a narrow bandwidth approach. Thus, instead of enabling a corporate meter to roam over the broad band of fulfilling focus, strategy and quality control, the company would veer too heavily to the last of these. Enron was certainly a company which was very quality- and customer-oriented. However, with no backing in ethics, the company tended towards the lowest ethical standards, which precipitated its very public break-up.

That enthusiasm for TQM has faded over the years, as with many business trends, is therefore not surprising. High quality standards can only guarantee corporate success on a very basic and immediate level. Despite a sincere interest in providing quality products and services, many organizations never got off the ground floor. For others, a considerable amount of time, energy and money was invested in developing and supporting a TQM program that would improve management, increase efficiency and foster team spirit. Yet, in time, programs lost momentum and the current status and success of TQM is questionable for many corporate organizations.

TEM is a dramatic, three-part initiative for change which, ideally, should be undertaken simultaneously and immediately after its adoption:

- **Ethical X-Ray:** All parts, activities and management functions should undergo a thorough "ethical x-ray" to identify the decisive nodes for ethical conduct. This includes not only core drivers of the business, but also support and administrative functions.
- **Ethical Immersion:** The whole organization should undergo an ethical immersion to apply high standards to all parts, processes, operations and management functions along high ethical lines. This could even change the company's core business drivers and success factors and thereby realign the entire organization. Throughout the process, success lies in applying the ethical value

---

2   Total Quality Management (TQM) is the concept of systematically improving the quality of products and processes through the ongoing participation of all employees in problem-solving efforts across functional and hierarchical boundaries. TQM is said to have originated with the work of W. Edwards Deming, who formulated many of his ideas during World War II when he taught American industries how to use statistical methods to improve the quality of military products. He later guided the Japanese industry's recovery after World War II by urging Japanese corporations to improve their product designs and production processes until the overall quality was unsurpassed. Deming proposed to shift the focus from a purely profit orientation to the management of quality. See Deming, W. Edward, *Out of Crisis*, Cambridge, Massachusetts Institute of Technology, 1986.

chain holistically and not in fragmented bits. It needs to be made relevant to the organization, from leadership to the grassroots and throughout the corporate culture. TEM is highly participatory; the best immersion results from drawing input and ideas from all parts and not just from the top.

- **Outreach:** Corporations that practice TEM should ensure that their ethical culture also informs their public citizenship in a broader sense. This touches not only marketing in a generic sense, but also actively reaching out to other organizations, companies, regions and individuals to share best practices, deepen their ethical makeup and solidify the presence of ethics throughout society.

Today, it is common to talk of the relations between "business and society," as in corporate social responsibility and especially in society's drive to force corporations to be accountable at all levels. Through TEM, we envision business becoming an integral part of society and, indeed, becoming an agent and leader of sustainable social development. TEM is a broad set of principles which provide a basis for corporations, and it will be refined as it is implemented.

So why Asia?

We have chosen to focus on Asia in this study for two reasons. One is the region's intense need for TEM at the present. Indeed, without a fundamental ethical reorientation, we believe that lasting growth and development will be harder to ignite and sustain. The second reason derives from Asia's deep philosophical, religious and cultural heritage, which has endowed it with potentially strong roots for building an ethical program that is suited to contemporary life. Ethics in Asia is therefore an interactive and iterative process. As Asia is changed by TEM, some of Asia's unique cultural and philosophical roots will also change the field of global ethics. This process will ensure true diversity in global ethics, and make it more robust for applications across more domains and in more regions.

This book is a start, and we are looking forward to seeing the concept applied all over the world. Some of the contributors to the book may be role models for TEM and may help us to spread the word. Through the application of TEM and the engagement of individual and collective capabilities across corporations, governments and civil society, we can begin to imagine the world as a better place.

Index

A

Accession, China to WTO   284
Accountability   16, 89, 111, 131, 162, 171, 172, 182, 190, 192, 200, 205, 207, 211, 212, 218, 231, 232, 249, 259, 270–274, 278, 279, 281, 282, 284–286, 290–292, 310–312, 321, 324, 327
Accounting   7, 23, 33, 34, 55, 80, 93, 129, 132, 138, 141, 142, 164, 172, 214, 216, 242, 250, 263, 272, 275, 278, 280, 281, 284, 288, 289, 293, 310, 311, 315, 320
Agricultural Bank   177
aid   67, 151, 246, 253, 254, 266, 307
Aids   234, 261
Air pollution   238
Al-Qaeda   35, 87
Anti-globalization movement   159, 233, 234, 237, 239
Aristotle   19, 21, 22
Asean   45, 111, 139, 140, 143
Asian crisis   5, 11, 48, 128, 131, 134, 139, 144, 262, 271
Asian Development Bank   264
Asian Free Trade Area   244
Asian value   3, 10, 127, 144, 271
Association of Chartered Certified Accountants (ACCA)   243
Auditing   214, 217, 288
Australia   255
Autonomy   9, 68, 69, 265, 279, 280, 302
Ayala Group   167, 169

B

Bangladesh   45, 102, 213, 218, 246, 255
Bank of Shanghai   216, 217
bankruptcy   251, 294, 314
batsu   175, 330, 331
belief   3, 6, 7, 10, 14, 32, 43–48, 65, 76, 83, 88, 133, 140, 149, 164, 192, 196, 223, 225, 249, 309

Barnard, Chester I.   146
board of director   214, 216, 279, 282, 287, 292, 299, 303–305, 311, 312
Bollywood   83
Branding   190, 191
brands   5, 84, 96, 97, 101, 162, 177, 190–200, 222, 229, 244, 284, 330
bribery   5, 90, 317
bubble economy   124, 174, 221, 228, 331
Buddha   19, 44, 63–66, 68–77, 81
Buddhism   10, 20, 38, 43, 44, 47, 63, 64, 66, 67, 69–74, 76, 81, 82, 88, 93, 206, 229

C

Caijing   123, 181–189
Cambodia   213, 246
Capacity Building   95, 264, 266
Capital market   184, 272, 273, 277, 278, 284, 286, 288, 289, 292, 293, 309, 316, 321
Capital, intellectual   241, 289
Capitalism   6, 26, 30, 35, 46, 55, 60, 63, 77, 89, 100, 114, 116, 117, 122, 145, 146, 147, 153, 159, 165, 180, 237, 281
Central bank   272
Chaebol   306–315, 320, 321
Chief executive officer (CEOs)   63, 190, 293, 297, 304, 325
China Securities Regulatory Commission   263, 281
China, People's Republic of   61
Christianity   45, 88
Civil society   4, 7, 13, 14, 94, 95, 167, 204, 207, 209, 210, 234, 239, 240, 260, 335
Clash of civilizations   38, 124
Coca-Cola   96, 198
Cold War   28, 35, 37, 111, 233
Collectivism   40, 49

Communication 11, 22, 27, 89, 123, 155, 166, 175, 195, 196, 199, 236, 244, 245, 261, 283, 285, 287, 290, 291, 293, 303, 327, 329, 331
Communism 35, 38, 47, 55
Competition 53, 54, 62, 105, 134, 135, 138, 139, 143, 159, 162, 184, 185, 281, 288, 308, 315
Confucius 18, 21, 44, 51–53, 58, 60–62, 89, 223, 225
Conglomerate 138, 275, 307, 310, 313
Corporate Citizenship 10, 160–166, 170–173, 199, 204–206, 248, 249, 251, 257–262, 265–269, 279
Corporate culture 31, 39, 104, 207, 319–321, 335
Corporate governance 8, 145, 177, 179, 180, 205–207, 210–212, 214, 216, 218–220, 249, 262–264, 270, 271, 273–278, 281, 282, 285, 289, 292–294, 296–299, 301, 302, 304, 310, 315, 320
Corporate social responsibility 13, 160, 165, 191, 192, 210, 211, 213, 218, 220, 241, 242, 249, 335
Corruption 6, 8, 9, 11, 12, 17, 20, 26, 29, 30, 38, 39, 61, 84, 88, 90, 110, 131, 135, 184, 210, 211, 213, 218, 220, 239, 242, 250, 252, 255, 270, 271, 274, 281, 282
Creativity 10
Culture 9, 21, 22, 23, 30, 31, 33, 35–39, 46, 48, 80, 87, 91, 94, 96, 97, 104, 122, 141, 161, 168, 174, 175, 178–180, 193, 194, 207, 248, 252, 265, 268, 271, 272, 285, 290, 291, 319–321, 327, 330, 333, 335
Currency speculation 111

D

DaimlerChrysler 325, 333
Deregulation 309
Developing nations 40, 128, 242
Development, economic 38, 54, 100, 101, 105, 128, 150, 157, 204, 206, 236, 238, 241, 281, 283, 307, 308
Development, rural 170, 193

Development, social 4, 75, 166–168, 170, 203, 204, 207, 209, 248, 249, 261, 269, 335
Dhamma 63, 64, 67–71, 73, 77
DHL 248, 249, 251–262, 265–269
Digital Divide 198, 260, 261
discontinuity 328
Disparity 148, 162
Diversity 16, 179, 248, 269, 335
Drugs 8, 25, 31
dukkha 64, 74

E

Economic growth 9, 90, 128, 130, 134, 143, 192, 203, 205, 227, 235, 238, 239, 285, 306–308
Economics 16, 78, 81, 86, 91, 94, 96, 98, 99, 102, 116, 117, 129, 163, 234
Edo 224, 225
Education 10, 20, 21, 23–25, 31–34, 37, 69, 71, 91, 102, 130, 135, 136, 149, 154, 155, 157, 163, 168, 179, 195, 196, 198, 227–232, 240, 251, 252, 261, 267, 268, 273, 318, 320
End of History 305
Enlightenment 19, 34–37, 62, 64, 68, 70
Enron 20, 33, 55, 92, 132, 145, 184, 223, 232, 250, 255, 272, 293, 294, 324
Entrepreneurship 10, 54, 205, 261
Equal opportunities 40
Estrada, Joseph 9
Ethics 3–7, 9, 11, 13, 14, 16–19, 21–24, 27, 31, 33, 34, 37–40, 44–46, 48, 49, 52–55, 57–59, 61, 63, 67–74, 76, 77, 81, 88–92, 121–123, 127–132, 134, 135, 137–140, 142–145, 173, 175, 178–180, 184, 189, 191, 193, 198, 199, 203, 206, 210, 220–224, 228–231, 233, 240, 243, 264, 316, 317, 319–321, 321, 335
Ethics Management 316, 317, 320, 321
Europe 13, 17, 31, 34, 37, 40, 60, 106, 111, 130, 132, 146, 148, 156, 160, 164, 171, 172, 207, 235, 236, 256, 257, 278, 285, 329, 330, 331, 333

F

Fair Trade Law   311
Family-owned firms   132, 219, 271, 275, 277
Federation of Korean Industries (KFI)   264, 316
feng shui   47
Feudalism   26, 94
Financial contagion   30
Financial crisis   3, 4, 9, 20, 55, 110, 113, 124, 164, 206, 238, 239, 250, 262, 272, 274, 306, 310, 324
Financial Times   186, 243, 244
Foreign capital   270, 307
Foreign Direct Investment (FDI)   105, 137, 144, 235
Foreign exchange   84
Foreign investor   109, 111, 280, 290
Freedom   32, 35, 59, 69–71, 73, 81, 90, 93, 109, 189, 259, 280, 293
Furukawa, Motohisa   4, 221

G

Globally Generally Accepted Accounting Principles, GAAP   280, 288, 289
gaijin   327
GDP   83, 91, 105, 106, 111, 148, 176, 178, 209, 233, 235, 241
Gandhi, Indira   84
Gandhi, Mahatma   249
Global citizenship   204, 205, 207, 248
Global Competitiveness Report   8
Global health initiative   260, 261
Global institutions   84
Global standards   171, 271, 281, 286
Globalization   11, 25, 27, 31, 34, 35, 38, 49, 62, 78, 79, 84, 85, 89, 97, 106, 116, 129, 138, 142, 145–150, 157, 159, 161, 162, 172, 176, 179, 192, 233–237, 239, 240, 280, 286, 289, 290

H

High-tech   62, 308
Hinduism   10, 43, 45, 47, 83, 88, 93, 206
Hippocrates   17

Hobbes, Thomas   35, 204
Hong Kong   7, 13, 39, 43, 47, 57, 61, 147, 187, 192, 217, 233, 243, 245, 256, 263, 271, 276–278, 284, 285, 292, 294, 295
Hong Kong Shanghai Banking Corporation   13, 217
Hu Jintao   7
Human rights   60, 162, 171, 205, 210, 234, 237, 244, 251, 253, 258, 259, 267

I

I Ching   16, 17
International Finance Corporation (IFC)   216, 217
ILO   142, 144, 252, 259
International Monetary Fund (IMF)   111, 139, 212, 215, 234
India   18, 25, 26, 29, 44, 45, 67, 71, 83–94, 100, 134, 170, 193, 197, 218, 239–242, 246, 249–254, 256, 258, 263
Indifference   68, 160
Individualism   329, 331
Indonesia   8, 9, 12, 20, 43, 45, 101, 105, 107, 121, 124, 127–132, 134–139, 141–143, 210, 213, 214, 218, 219, 237, 238, 249, 254, 255, 258, 264, 270, 294
Indonesia Bank Restructuring Agency (IBRA)   215
Industrial Renewal   205, 207, 306
Information technology   168, 169, 174, 178, 179, 289
Infrastructure   105, 158, 192, 193, 226, 246, 251, 254, 267, 271, 278, 317, 320, 321
Innovation   54, 62, 133, 205, 258, 330
Instability, financial   247
Intellectual capital   241, 289
Intellectual property rights   26
Interest rate   307, 308
Internet   25, 89, 109, 169, 175, 179, 195, 236
International Accounting Standards (IAS)   272, 275, 281, 284, 289
International Institutions   209
International Labour Organization (ILO)   252

Islam   20, 32, 35, 38, 39, 43, 45, 47, 88, 89, 96, 98–107, 109–117, 206, 255
Iwasaki, Yataro   330

J

Japan   4, 5, 35, 39, 44–47, 56, 58, 60–62, 105, 106, 109, 111, 124, 125, 130, 147, 148, 161, 164–166, 174–180, 219, 221–225, 227–232, 235, 236, 239, 242, 256, 258, 264, 271, 278–280, 285, 325–334
jen   44, 206
Jung, Carl   16, 17, 38

K

Kant, Immanuel   26
Karma   10, 45, 49, 69, 71, 76
Knowledge   23, 27, 31, 32, 51, 52, 60, 65, 66, 70, 75, 79, 88, 102, 117, 177, 229, 269, 319
Koizumi, Junichiro   337
Koran   45
Korea, North   5, 6, 31, 179, 323
Korea, South   5, 14, 84, 105, 106, 107, 255, 256, 264, 270, 294
Kuala Lumpur Stock Exchange (KLSE)   111, 263, 272, 273

L

Labour   252
Lao Tzu   18, 36
Leadership   3, 7, 21–23, 39, 52, 92, 109, 122–124, 150, 160, 166, 169, 170, 238, 260, 265, 267, 296, 321, 335
li   44
Lifetime employment   4, 10, 124, 228, 326

M

Mahathir   31, 99–101, 103, 107
Malaysia   43, 45, 98–109, 111, 113, 114, 116, 124, 196, 198, 237, 238, 255, 263, 270–273, 294

Management   4, 14, 21, 23, 31, 44, 62, 83, 103, 107, 110–113, 121–123, 132, 133, 144, 146, 147, 152, 161, 171, 172, 174, 182, 183, 187, 194, 198, 203–207, 215–217, 219, 226, 241–245, 248, 251, 252, 257, 258, 262, 268–271, 275, 279, 282, 286, 289, 291–321, 324, 326–332, 334, 336
Manchester-capitalism   122
Mao Zedong   57
Materialism   44
Matsushita, Konosuke   147, 226, 231
McDonalds   34, 245
McKinsey   210, 330
Mecca-Cola   96–98, 117
Media   4, 7, 14, 23, 25, 38, 52, 76, 79, 83, 85, 89, 92, 94, 102, 107–109, 111–113, 116, 117, 121, 123, 124, 153, 169, 175, 181–189, 192, 194, 245, 252, 256, 261, 262, 279, 293, 297, 314, 321, 334
Mencius   44, 53
Metaphysics   18, 26, 36, 38, 45, 60
military   32, 35, 334
Mill, John Stuart   25, 30, 35
Ministry of Foreign Trade and Economic Cooperation (MOFTEC)   285
Minority shareholder   219, 274, 275, 277, 279, 281, 294–296, 298, 299, 301, 310, 312
Mitsubishi Motors   325, 333
mochiai   279, 280
Mongolia   214, 215
Monks   64, 68, 69, 74, 77
Monopoly   26, 53, 135
Multimedia   108, 109
Multimedia Supercorridor (MSC)   108, 109
Multinational Corporations (MNCs)   213, 233, 234, 242

N

National Public Service Ethics Law   231
National Trades Union Congress (NTUC)   145, 150, 154, 155, 158
Nationalism   56

Nature   7, 10, 25, 48, 60, 64, 67, 76, 77, 81, 91, 104, 122, 134, 230, 263, 294, 295, 302
Nepotism   8, 60, 110, 131
NGO   197, 255
Nietzsche, Friedrich   36
Nike   36, 121
Nippon Keidandren   333
Non-governmental organizations (NGOs)   145, 197, 204, 233, 255, 320
Non-performing loan   93, 229, 315

O

OECD   89, 148, 212, 255, 259, 260, 267
Olympics   84, 87
Open Society   30, 32
Opening up   6, 179
Organization structure   152

P

Panchtantra   85
Paradigm   32, 38, 162, 163, 241, 310, 320, 321
PAS   99, 101–104, 107, 109, 112–114
Pax Americana   36, 37
People's Action Party (PAP)   150
Philippines   8, 9, 14, 43, 45, 107, 165–169, 172, 213, 214, 219, 238, 246, 251, 253, 254, 256, 258, 264, 270, 294
Philosophy   3, 10, 16–22, 24, 27, 37–40, 46, 47, 55, 56, 58, 63, 73, 78, 79, 91, 101, 102, 131, 164, 213, 224–227, 320, 329
Plato   19, 23, 24
Politics   3–5, 12, 22, 23, 27, 61, 62, 94, 108, 114, 116, 123, 290, 332
Poverty   6, 83, 86, 87, 108, 160, 162, 165, 167, 169, 192, 209, 211, 218, 220, 250, 252, 261, 262
Practicability   70
PricewaterhouseCoopers (PWC)   270, 273, 281, 282, 286
Private sector   6, 12, 14, 127–132, 135, 136, 138, 140, 160–162, 165, 170, 209–212, 220, 261, 273, 282, 283

Privatization   161, 215
Prophet Mohammed   45
Prostitution   252
Protestantism   47
Proton   106
Public Accountability   205, 207, 270
Public Relations   123, 163, 190
Public Sector   6, 211, 214, 231

R

Recession   105, 106, 132, 155, 174, 308, 323, 331, 332
Reebook   244
Reform   6, 12, 20, 28, 54, 83, 87, 94, 95, 99, 110, 115, 128, 167, 182, 189, 210–213, 215, 216, 218–220, 239, 244, 250, 263, 273, 274, 278, 280–283, 286, 297, 306, 309–311, 313–315, 319–321, 332
Regional integration   46
Regional relations   4, 124, 127
Regionalism   139
Religion   3, 10, 21, 28, 29, 38, 43–49, 55, 60, 62, 63, 67, 69, 71–74, 88, 104, 115, 132, 203
Research and development (R&D)   80, 105, 137, 138, 141, 199, 333
Resource allocation   176
rinri   221, 223–232
Roh Moo-hyun   5
Rome   32, 34, 35, 37, 38, 147, 162, 181, 186
ROSC/FSAP initiative   212
Russell, Bertrand   21

S

Sanskrit   88
Sarbanes-Oxley Act   297
SARS   7, 147, 181, 186–189, 192, 323
Schooling   250, 252
Science   22, 24, 25, 27, 28, 37, 39, 51, 54, 56, 70, 90, 102, 115, 117, 166, 171, 225, 241
Security   8, 76, 83, 136, 148, 185, 228, 252, 254, 256, 332

September 11   35, 234, 256

Shanghai   6, 26, 183, 216, 217

Shareholder   13, 80, 114, 122, 131, 133, 141, 145, 146, 159, 160, 169, 173, 176, 177, 195, 203, 205, 212, 216, 217, 219, 226, 243, 247, 249, 250, 253, 264, 265, 269, 274–277, 279–281, 291–304, 309–312, 314, 315, 317, 318

Shibusawa, Eiichi   225

Shinsegae Co., Ltd   317, 318

Shintoism   45, 46, 47

Siam Cement Group   132, 133, 143

Sikhism   45, 88

Singapore   7, 8, 13, 28, 31, 39, 46–48, 51, 55, 66, 99, 145, 147–159, 219, 238, 250, 256, 263, 264, 266, 270, 271, 274–276, 285, 295, 296, 301, 323

Smith, Adam   293, 297

Snow Brand Milk   5, 177

Social contract   12, 94, 191, 192

Socialism   55, 57, 281

Societal governance   204, 207, 233

Sony   109, 176

soto   124, 224

stability   37, 128, 133, 140, 212, 247, 248, 269, 282

Stakeholders   23, 80, 124, 125, 146, 162, 163, 172, 176, 191, 193, 194, 196, 197, 199, 200, 204, 205, 233, 240, 245, 249, 260, 265, 268, 273, 287, 290, 291

State-owned enterprise (SOE)   6, 216, 277, 282

stock market   9, 111, 125, 174, 182, 183, 264, 292, 299

strategy   79, 121, 131, 163, 188, 196, 206, 210, 213, 217, 241, 244, 251, 253, 261, 269, 289, 315, 316, 321, 325

Sustainability   8, 84, 86–88, 121, 162, 172, 203, 206, 219, 240, 242, 243, 249, 271, 279, 286

Sweatshops   121, 234

T

Taiwan   47, 57, 61, 69, 106, 179, 243

Tang Dynasty   54

Taoism   18, 21, 45, 47, 60

Tata Group   134, 139, 197

tatemae   331

Technical assistance   212

Technology, information (IT)   94, 168, 169, 174, 178, 179, 195, 289, 308

Technology   11, 24, 28, 37, 39, 54, 78, 94, 105, 121, 141, 147, 167–169, 174, 175, 178, 179, 219, 241, 256, 261, 284, 289, 333, 334

telecommunications   283, 285

Terrorism   33, 35, 37, 87, 256

Thailand   9, 14, 43, 44, 63, 78, 105, 107, 132, 213, 214, 219, 246, 254–256, 258, 270, 294

The East India Company   29

The Four Noble Truth   64, 66

The Middle Path   19, 66, 67, 79, 81

Tokyo Electric Power   5, 175

Tolerance   49, 89, 132, 234

Total Ethical Management (TEM)   4, 14, 15, 121, 122, 123, 203, 204, 205, 207, 324– 336

Total Quality Management (TQM)   324, 325

Trade   11, 26, 29, 54, 55, 58, 66, 86, 89, 106, 112, 127, 129, 130, 132, 141, 142, 144, 147, 148, 150, 155, 156, 198, 199, 234–237, 243, 244, 249, 265, 284, 285, 293, 308, 310, 311, 317, 318, 323

trade, free   244

trade unions   150, 155, 156, 244

Transparency   7, 55, 89, 111, 131, 140, 177, 178, 182, 184, 192, 211, 212, 218, 219, 231, 232, 239, 249, 263, 264, 271–274, 276–279, 281, 282, 284, 286, 288–292, 306, 310, 311, 315, 316, 320, 327

Transparency International (TI)   39, 90, 255, 270, 285

Trust   3–5, 9, 11, 12, 20, 32–34, 51, 54, 58–60, 62, 76, 81, 113, 122–124, 127, 131, 134, 136, 145, 150, 164, 169, 191, 204, 207, 221–226, 228, 231, 232, 250, 251, 286, 312, 316

Tyco   250

U

uchi   124, 125, 224
UMNO   99, 100, 102, 103, 107, 108, 110, 112–114
Uncertainty   4, 7, 11, 55
Union Carbide   30, 241, 242, 256
United Nations (UN)   37, 83, 198, 237, 253, 258, 261
UN Global Compact   258
UN Commission on Human Rights   60, 101, 162, 171, 205, 210, 234, 237, 244, 251, 253, 258, 259, 267
United States   55, 57, 97, 106, 132, 148–150, 152, 156, 164, 175, 176, 227, 286, 287, 293, 294, 297–299, 301, 303
Universality   70, 89
Urbanization   227, 234, 245, 246
USAID   215, 216

V

Values   3, 7, 10, 21, 22, 29, 40, 46, 51, 52, 55–59, 61–63, 73, 77, 81, 83, 84, 88–94, 97, 101, 104, 111, 115–117, 122, 123, 144–146, 149, 150, 161, 164, 168, 172, 173, 176, 179, 191, 204, 210, 221, 223, 228, 231, 248, 249, 269, 271, 290, 292, 309, 315, 316, 318, 321, 324, 330
Venture capital   177
vinaya   64, 67
Virtue   16, 19, 21, 28, 38, 39, 54, 60, 64, 67, 68, 74, 82, 223, 284, 301

W

Wages   24, 147, 148, 150, 155–157, 245, 252
Wealth, distribution   141
Weber, Max   30, 46, 54, 60, 115
Women   60, 77, 158
Woori Bank   306, 314, 315, 319
World Bank   89, 130, 209, 211–213, 215, 216, 219, 220, 234, 262, 294
World Economic Forum   3, 5, 8, 37, 240, 260, 265, 267, 268
World Health Organization   187, 261
World Trade Centre   86
World Trade Organization   141, 142, 234, 236, 264, 284, 285, 308
WorldCom   145, 250, 293, 294

Y

Yangtze River   238
Yuhan-Kimberly   318

Z

zaibatsu   175
Zen   45
Zhu Rongji   39